Critical essays on
Tennessee Williams

DATE DUE

Critical Essays on
TENNESSEE WILLIAMS

CRITICAL ESSAYS
ON
AMERICAN LITERATURE

James Nagel, General Editor
University of Georgia, Athens

Critical Essays on

TENNESSEE WILLIAMS

edited by

ROBERT A. MARTIN

G. K. Hall & Co.

New York

G. K. Hall & Co.

1633 Broadway
New York, NY 10019

Library of Congress Cataloging-in-Publication Data

Critical essays on Tennessee Williams/edited by Robert A. Martin.
    p.   cm. — (Critical essays on American literature)
    Includes bibliographical references (p.) and index.
    ISBN 0-7838-0042-8 (alk. paper)
    1. Williams, Tennessee, 1911–1983—Criticism and interpretation.
  2. Southern States—In literature.   I. Martin, Robert A.
II Series.
PS3545.I5365Z615   1997
812'.54—dc21   97-21446
                                                  CIP

The paper used in this publication meets the minimum requirements of American National Standard for Information Sciences—Permanence of Paper for Printed Library Materials. ANSI Z39.48-1984. ∞™

10 9 8 7 6 5 4 3

Printed in the United States of America

Once again for John, Doug, Carole, and Christy with love;
and for Linda with love and thanks

TENNESSEE WILLIAMS IN HIS KEY WEST STUDIO.

Contents

General Editor's Note

◆

This series seeks to anthologize the most important criticism on a wide variety of topics and writers in American literature. Our readers will find in various volumes not only a generous selection of reprinted articles and reviews but original essays, bibliographies, manuscript selections, and other materials brought to public attention for the first time. This volume, *Critical Essays on Tennessee Williams,* is the most comprehensive collection of essays ever published on one of the most important modern dramatists in the United States. It contains both a sizable gathering of early reviews and a broad selection of more modern scholarship. Among the authors of reprinted articles and reviews are Walter Kerr, Mary Ann Corrigan, John Gassner, Ruby Cohn, Jordan Y. Miller, and Kimball King. In addition to a substantial introduction by Robert A. Martin, there are also six original essays commissioned specifically for publication in this volume, new studies by Brenda Murphy on the revision of *Camino Real,* R. B. Parker on *The Glass Menagerie* and *The Two Character Play,* Thomas P. Adler on *Sweet Bird of Youth,* Esther M. Jackson on the concept of "plastic form," Walter J. Meserve on survivors and dreamers in Williams's plays, and Nancy M. Tischler on death as a metaphor. We are confident that this book will make a permanent and significant contribution to the study of American literature.

JAMES NAGEL
University of Georgia

Publisher's Note

◆

Producing a volume that contains both newly commissioned and reprinted material presents the publisher with the challenge of balancing the desire to achieve stylistic consistency with the need to preserve the integrity of works first published elsewhere. In the Critical Essays series, essays commissioned especially for a particular volume are edited to be consistent with G. K. Hall's house style; reprinted essays appear in the style in which they were first published, with only typographical errors corrected. Consequently, shifts in style from one essay to another are the result of our efforts to be faithful to each text as it was originally published.

Acknowledgments

I would like to extend my thanks and gratitude to the many prominent scholars for their generosity in allowing me permission to use their essays. For original essays I thank Thomas P. Adler, Dianne Cafagna, Esther M. Jackson, Walter Meserve, Brenda Murphy, Nancy Tischler, and Gerald Weales. For permissions to reprint previously published essays, I thank the authors whose names appear in the Views and Overviews listings in the Table of Contents. For any omissions, I bear the primary responsibility. For exceptional generosity and assistance in checking bibliographical entries, I owe a huge debt of gratitude to Professor James J. Martine, gentleman, friend, and scholar. For his invaluable information and advice I thank Professor James Nagel, general editor of this series.

ROBERT A. MARTIN

Plays and Short-Story Collections

PLAYS

1940   *Battle of Angels* (Boston)
1945   *The Glass Menagerie* (New York)
1947   *A Streetcar Named Desire* (New York)
1948   *Summer and Smoke* (New York)
1951   *The Rose Tattoo* (New York)
1953   *Camino Real* (New York)
1955   *Cat on a Hot Tin Roof* (New York)
1956   *Sweet Bird of Youth* (Miami)
1957   *Orpheus Descending* (revision of *Battle of Angels*) (New York)
1958   *Garden District* (*Something Unspoken* and *Suddenly Last Summer*); (Off-Broadway). *Period of Adjustment* (Miami)
1959   *Sweet Bird of Youth* (New York)
1960   *Period of Adjustment* (New York)
1961   *The Night of the Iguana* (New York)
1963   *The Milk Train Doesn't Stop Here Anymore* (New York)
1964   First version of *The Eccentricities of a Nightingale* (summer stock production)
1966   *Slapstick Tragedy:* (*The Mutilated* and *The Gnädiges Fräulein*) (New York)
1967   First version of *The Two-Character Play* (London)
1968   *Kingdom of Earth* (*The Seven Descents of Myrtle*) (New York)
1969   *In the Bar of a Tokyo Hotel* (Off-Broadway)
1971   Second version of The *Two Character Play*, retitled *Out Cry*, produced in Chicago
1972   *Small Craft Warnings* (Off-Off-Broadway)
1973   Third version of *The Two Character Play* (*Out Cry*) (New York)

1975   First version of *The Red Devil Battery Sign* (Boston); Fourth version of *The Two Character Play* produced Off-Off-Broadway

1976   Second version of *The Red Devil Battery Sign* produced in Vienna. *This Is (An Entertainment)* produced in San Francisco. Second version of *The Eccentricities of a Nightingale* produced in Buffalo and in New York

1977   *Vieux Carré* (New York)

1978   *Tiger Tale* (Atlanta); *Crêve Coeur* (Charleston)

1980   *Clothes for a Summer Hotel* (New York)

1981   *A House Not Meant To Stand* (Chicago); *Something Cloudy, Something Clear* (Off-Off-Broadway)

ONE-ACT AND SHORT PLAYS

Moony's Kid Don't Cry, At Liberty, The Long Goodbye, The Purification, The Dark Room, The Case of the Crushed Petunias, The Long Stay Cut Short, or The Unsatisfactory Supper, Ten Blocks on the Camino Real, 27 Wagons Full of Cotton, The Strangest Kind of Romance, Auto-Da-Fé, Portrait of a Madonna, I Rise in Flame, Cried the Phoenix, Hello from Bertha, The Lady of Larkspur Lotion, This Property Is Condemned, The Frosted Glass Coffin, The Last of My Solid Gold Watches, Lord Byron's Love Letter, A Perfect Analysis Given by a Parrot, Talk to Me Like the Rain and Let Me Listen, Three Players of a Summer Game, I Can't Imagine Tomorrow, Confessional, Demolition Downtown, Kirche, Kutchen, und Kinder, Some Problems for the Moose Lodge, Steps Must Be Gentle, Lifeboat Drill, Now the Cat with Jewelled Claws, This is the Peaceable Kingdom, or Good Luck God

SHORT-STORY COLLECTIONS

27 Wagons Full of Cotton (New York: New Directions, 1945, 1953).
One Arm and Other Stories (New York: New Directions, 1945, 1954).
Hard Candy and Other Stories (New York: New Directions, 1954).
The Knightly Quest and Other Stories (New York: New Directions, 1966).
Eight Mortal Ladies Possessed: A Book of Stories (New York: New Directions, 1974).
Collected Stories, with an introduction by Gore Vidal (New York: New Directions, 1985).

Introduction

ROBERT A. MARTIN

Following the death of Tennessee Williams on 24 February 1983, popular and scholarly writing on Williams has virtually exploded. Williams has, at last, found the readership and audience that evaded him the last few years of his life. Though Williams is now recognized as an authentic voice and experimenter in American drama, many critics had written him off following *Night of the Iguana* (1961) and his subsequent decline into drugs and drink. Such issues are dealt with reasonably and randomly in the vast scholarship surrounding Williams and his plays as well as in several of the essays in this collection. Williams's reputation as a highly original playwright was built on his portrayal of Southern life and conflict in his major plays: *The Glass Menagerie* (1945), *A Streetcar Named Desire* (1947), *The Rose Tattoo* (1951), *Summer and Smoke* (1948), *Cat on a Hot Tin Roof* (1955), *Sweet Bird of Youth* (1959), and *Night of the Iguana* (1961). Along with Arthur Miller, Williams was the most admired playwright in America during the 1940s and 1950s. Both he and Miller were generally considered the theater's best artists since Eugene O'Neill changed the direction of American theater in the 1920s and 1930s. Such a judgment is, for the most part, still accurate, with Edward Albee close behind.

Williams led a somewhat irregular life as a young man and was in the habit of moving about constantly. His lifelong fear of his father (symbolized as "Big Daddy" in *Cat on a Hot Tin Roof*), his love for his sister Rose (represented as Laura in *The Glass Menagerie*), and his resentment of his mother (subtly portrayed as Amanda in *The Glass Menagerie*) gave Williams a firm basis on which he could build variations of family relationships and work out several preoccupations that plagued him his entire life. He revised constantly, often rewriting a produced play several times, much to the despair of scholars attempting to trace a chronological path of his writings. In 1975 Williams published *Memoirs,* an account of his homosexuality and various experiences in and out of the theater.[1] *Memoirs* may have hurt Williams's public image (he later thought his homosexual revelations were a mistake).

In spite of Williams's restless moves between New York, New Orleans, Key West, and the major cities of Europe, his plays—written about the loners, the outcasts, and the fragile people whose dramatic situations involve lost dreams and last chances—managed to garner quite a few prizes. Nearly all of his plays through *Night of the Iguana* met with critical acclaim from New York theater critics. *Menagerie* won the New York Drama Critics' Circle, Donaldson, and Sidney Howard awards; the film of *Streetcar* won the New York Film Critics' Circle Award; *Cat on a Hot Tin Roof* won the Pulitzer Prize, the Drama Critics Award, and the Donaldson Award. *Night of the Iguana* won the New York Critics' Circle Award, and in 1969 Williams was awarded the Gold Medal for Drama by the American Academy of Arts and Letters (this and subsequent awards were given for his overall achievement, not for a specific play). In 1972 he was awarded the National Theatre Conference Award, and in 1974 he was given the Entertainment Hall of Fame Award as well as the Medal of Honor for Literature from the National Arts Club. For most playwrights these honors collectively would have signified a lifetime of success in the theater, but Williams's last few years were filled with disappointments and an inability to repeat his earlier success. But he never gave up trying and seemed to prize the daily task of writing. In his *Memoirs* Williams asked rhetorically:

> Why did the critics turn on me so violently in the fifties and the early sixties? I suspect it was a cabal to cut me down to what they thought was my size. And what is my size? It is, I trust, the size of an artist who has consistently given all that he has to give to his work, with a most peculiar passion. . . . Truth is the bird we hope to catch in "this thing," and it can be better approached through my life story than an account of my career. Jesus, career, it's never been that to me, it has just been "doing my thing" with a fury to do it the best that I am able. (*Memoirs,* 173)

I BIOGRAPHIES AND MEMOIRS

Of primary interest and importance to Williams scholars is the publication of *Tom: The Unknown Tennessee Williams* by Lyle Leverich.[2] This is the best biography of Williams to date and follows his life, objectively and dispassionately, up to the production of *The Glass Menagerie* (1945) and to Williams "writing a play he would title *A Streetcar Named Desire.* Awaiting him was what he called 'the catastrophe of success' " (*Tom,* 592). Leverich also includes family photographs and a genealogy of the Williams family. This volume (along with others to follow) will certainly become the definitive work on Williams's life. Leverich is a man of the theater, primarily; he met Williams in 1976 while Leverich was producing *The Glass Menagerie* and *The Two-Character Play.* In 1979 Williams appointed Leverich as his official biographer. Arthur Miller has said of the work, "I think it will be a great service to Williams's reputation."[3] In addition to providing a chronology of Williams's life, *Tom* is an alive and compelling portrait. The only other biography published since Williams's death is *The Kindness of Strangers: The Life of Tennessee Williams* by Donald Spoto, which is, unfortunately, flawed in its facts and research.[4] Spoto takes a psychological approach to Williams and his plays that does not result in clarification or illumination.

Memoirs written by those who claim to have known the man behind the plays abound. Some are revealing, most are disappointing. One questions the motivation for their writing. *Remember Me to Tom,* written by Williams's mother, Edwina Dakin Williams, with Lucy Freeman,[5] reveals much about Edwina's husband, Cornelius (he's bad), and digresses on her Southern girlhood. While interesting as a basis for mention in Williams's plays, the digressions are uninteresting in themselves. She includes excerpts from Williams's early work journals, correspondence, and some totally irrelevant speculation on Williams and his plays. One thing this book makes clear is that Mrs. Williams never understood her son, nor was she able to see that she was the model for Amanda. A sort of companion volume is *Tennessee Williams: An Intimate Biography* by Williams's brother, Dakin Williams, and Shepherd Mead.[6] Although Dakin writes more clearly than his mother, it appears that he never quite approved of his brother; he once had him committed to a mental hospital, supposedly for his own protection. Dakin's book presents another view of the material found in Williams's own *Memoirs* and in *Remember Me to Tom* and attempts to trace Williams's life in the theater.

Bruce Smith, a journalist and public relations professional, wrote *Costly Performances, Tennessee Williams: The Last Stage.*[7] He knew Williams from 1979 to 1981 and claims Williams told him to write "a rather black sequel to my *Memoirs.*" (4) This might well have been an offhand remark made casually to flatter a new friend, but given Williams's later misgivings about having included his sexual activities in *Memoirs,* the remark seems of questionable veracity. Smith relates mostly gossip enlivened by frequent mention of celebrities. His observations and conversational tidbits are unsubstantiated and undocumented. Harry Rasky, a noted filmmaker who produced the documentary *Tennessee Williams' South,* wrote, *Tennessee Williams: A Portrait in Laughter and Lamentation.*[8] Rasky is considerably better than Smith at evoking Williams in all his eccentric habits. Based on taped conversations made during the shooting of the film and as part of the film itself, Rasky's book provides a view of Williams from the perspective of a filmmaker more comfortable with a camera than with notes and scholarship. Dotson Rader in *Tennessee: Cry of the Heart* notes that when with Williams he "kept, with his [Williams's] knowledge, notes, letters, journals . . . other papers . . . and conversations that we taped" (author's note, n.p.).[9] Rader clearly liked Williams but was often exasperated with him. The book contains some interesting anecdotes (its subtitle is "An Intimate Memoir of Tennessee Williams") but, like Bruce Smith's "memoir," does little else, especially for the serious student of Williams. Rader's book is explicit about Williams's sexual life and the young men whom he paid to share it. In all these books one wishes the authors had quoted more that was verified—written, taped, or quoted in correspondence. Instead, the reader must accept the validity of the memoirs on faith, with considerable skepticism thrown in for good measure.

II   WILLIAMS'S LETTERS, INTERVIEWS, AND ESSAYS

Tennessee Williams' Letters to Donald Windham, 1940–1965 nicely illuminates Williams's work on *The Glass Menagerie* during its development before it went to Broadway and contains details of revision and concept.[10] *Five O'Clock Angel: Letters of Tennessee Williams to Maria St. Just, 1948–1982,* with a brief preface by Elia Kazan, is interesting in spite of St. Just's inserted commentary.[11] Mostly devoted to news of Williams's travel, theater productions, and personal relationships, his letters nevertheless reveal that he believed his career in the U.S. theater was over and that he was "totally washed up" (286) by 1973. In a bizarre turn of events, St. Just seized control of Williams's estate and tried to cancel previous commitments to writers and producers as coexecutor. Her death in 1994 opened up publication opportunities for many Williams scholars.

Conversations with Tennessee Williams, edited by Albert Devlin, is a useful and well-chosen set of interviews selected from the many hundreds Williams agreed to over five decades.[12] The editor's acumen in selecting the 35 interviews offers insight into and acquaintance with the subject. *A Look at Tennessee Williams,* edited by Mike Steen, is an informal, lively collection of interviews that offers a look at Williams's plays from the perspective of actors, friends, and others.[13] Thomas R. Atkins in "The Astonishing Mystery of Life: The Playwright Talks about His Work" in *Tennessee Williams Literary Journal* reports an interview with Williams in Orlando, Florida, in 1981.[14] Cecil Brown in "Interview with Tennessee Williams" for *The Partisan Review* provides an in-depth view of Williams at one of his low points,[15] while David Frost in "Will God Talk Back to a Playwright?" reports a television interview in *The Americans* and manages to draw out Williams on his life and work, however superficially.[16] Robert C. Jennings in "Playboy Interview: Tennessee Williams" does well in getting Williams to loosen up somewhat and talk seriously.[17] This is a surprisingly well done interview, considering its source.

Dotson Rader conducts a long interview with Williams published in *The Paris Review* as "The Art of Theatre V: Tennessee Williams,"[18] while Jere Real reports on an interesting interview with the playwright in "An Interview with Tennessee Williams" in *Southern Quarterly.*[19] Finally, in *Folio,* an anonymous interviewer questions Williams on general but nevertheless fundamental topics of writing and the theater.[20] During his years in the theater Williams gave hundreds of interviews—far too many for a complete listing here. The reader interested in the complete range of interviews would do well to examine those listed in the bibliography by Drewey Wayne Gunn, *Tennessee Williams: A Bibliography,* second edition,[21] or the year-by-year accumulation published in *Modern Drama* annually in the June issue, or in the annual *Modern Language Association (MLA) International Bibliography.* Also of value for references through 1981 is John S. McCann's *The Critical Reputation of Tennessee Williams: A Reference Guide,* which lists publications year by year.[22]

Williams's writings have been collected in several ways. The most obvious are his plays, in many editions and combinations. Also worth mentioning here is *Tennessee Williams: Collected Stories,* edited by Gore Vidal.[23] This collection includes 50 short stories, including some previously published in *One Arm & Other Stories, Hard Candy, The Knightly Quest,* and *Eight Mortal Ladies Possessed,* plus his uncollected or unpublished stories. Many of these stories were written as outlines or tryouts for plays, such as "Portrait of a Girl in Glass," which became *The Glass Menagerie,* and "Players in a Summer Game," the antecedent of *Cat on a Hot Tin Roof.* Readers not familiar with Williams's short stories will find this collection reveals another side of Williams's immense talent. Williams's plays are collected in *The Theatre of Tennessee Williams,* Volumes 1–8.[24] Readers of those volumes will want to have *Where I Live: Selected Essays* for Williams's firsthand comments on the context of his play openings and personal thoughts on the theater.[25] Many of these essays were published in newspapers, magazines, and collections at or near the times his play premiered. Comments on *Streetcar, The Rose Tattoo, Camino Real,* and *Sweet Bird,* plus reflections on his world and friends, make for a delightful adjunct to the plays. In addition to the numerous interviews (all previously noted), *Where I Live* along with the memoirs and letters are all of interest to the Williams scholar.

III   NEWSLETTERS, REVIEWS, AND LITERARY JOURNALS

Considering that Williams has occupied a major place in American drama since the 1940s and 1950s, it is amazing that so few publications devoted exclusively to his life and work have appeared. The first, *The Tennessee Williams Newsletter,* edited by Stephen S. Stanton at the University of Michigan, attracted a considerable interest and following but was unable to continue because of a lack of financial support.[26] From 1979 to 1981, the *Newsletter* published five issues containing reviews of plays and books, articles, production notes, interviews, and Williams news. It then became *The Tennessee Williams Review* and the editorship shifted to Northeastern University in Boston, where it died a quick death due to editorial and financial problems.[27]

The *Review* at Northeastern supposedly published volumes 3 and 4 (Fall 1981–Spring 1983), although many subscribers never received a single copy. With no Williams journal in operation between 1983 and 1989, Williams scholars and theatergoers were considerably encouraged by the appearance of the *Tennessee Williams Literary Journal* (premier issue, Spring 1989), which has continued under the able editorship of W. Kenneth Holditch backed by a distinguished editorial board (as of 1996): Jacob H. Adler, Milly S. Barranger, Allean Hale, Richard F. Leavitt, Lyle Leverich, Gene Phillips, Nancy Tischler, and Dennis Vannatta.[28] The *Journal* offers a full range of Williams news, reviews, and articles plus a useful calendar of events.

IV BIBLIOGRAPHIES

Most of the bibliographies listed here have been examined for accuracy and information; all are useful in different ways. No bibliographical list is complete due to the changing nature of the subject. One of the earliest bibliographies is Nadine Dony's "Tennessee Williams: A Selected Bibliography" in *Modern Drama* 1 (1958),[29] expanded by Charles A. Carpenter Jr. and Elizabeth Cook's addenda in *Modern Drama* 2 (1959).[30] Drewey Wayne Gunn on "The Various Texts of Tennessee Williams' Plays," *Educational Theatre Journal,* is an early version of Gunn's full-length work, *Tennessee Williams: A Bibliography.*[31] Delma E. Presley added valuable material to the scholarship in "Tennessee Williams: Twenty-five Years of Criticism," *Bulletin of Bibliography.*[32] Catherine M. Arnott in *Tennessee Williams on File* provides a selective, brief bibliography,[33] while Thomas P. Adler, Judith Hersch Clark, and Lyle Taylor fill in some blanks with "Tennessee Williams in the Seventies: A Checklist" in *The Tennessee Williams Newsletter.*[34] Charles A. Carpenter in "Studies of Tennessee Williams' Drama: A Selective International Bibliography: 1966–1978" in *The Tennessee Williams Newsletter* covers the international scene on Williams's drama published since 1966 in every Roman alphabet language.[35] He adds a note of alarm that most bibliographies up to 1978 "do not give a full picture of Williams scholarship even to 1970." Alan M. Cohn seems to confirm Carpenter by publishing "More Tennessee Williams in the Seventies: Additions to the Checklist and the Gunn Bibliography" in *The Tennessee Williams Review.*[36] Drewey Wayne Gunn in *Tennessee Williams: A Bibliography* published a work that gives full details of primary sources, interviews, essays, academic studies, and production information.[37] All of these resources have been largely superseded by Drewey Wayne Gunn's *Tennessee Williams: A Bibliography,* second edition (1991), in which many of the omissions and errors of the 1980 work have been corrected.[38] But Gunn's 1991 bibliography is already dated, and the scholar seeking information on works published in the 1990s would do well to check the annual bibliographies in *Modern Drama*

(June issues), in the *Modern Language International Bibliography* annual, and the annual "Checklist of Scholarship on Southern Literature" in the *Mississippi Quarterly*. Also of use is the annual *American Literary Scholarship* published by Duke University Press, which evaluates individual and selective publications. This source generally is two years behind, because all publications for a given year must be collected and evaluated by academic readers. *The Tennessee Williams Literary Journal* keeps readers informed of new publications through its "Calendar" and "New Releases" sections but is published only twice a year. In the *Journal's* Spring 1989 issue, Pearl Amelia McHaney provides "A Checklist of Tennessee Williams Scholarship: 1980–87," which lists "bibliographies, interviews, critical books, biographies, collections of essays, and scholarly articles."[39] McHaney does a fine job here and says she hopes to provide "annotations of articles and brief descriptions of book-length volumes" in future checklists.

A very complete bibliography of Williams's work, *Tennessee Williams: A Bibliography,* University of Pittsburgh Series in Bibliography, edited by George W. Crandall, is a comprehensive volume priced too high for most individual scholars to own but is a valuable addition to a library that can afford the $125 cost.[40] Illustrated with pictures of dust jackets and many other items of interest, this work is essential for Williams scholars and should be in every major library. In addition to drama bibliographies attached to general as well as specific works on Williams and drama, Williams scholars will want to consult John S. McCann's *The Critical Reputation of Tennessee Williams,* which lists items published in "all popular and scholarly press criticism" between 1939 and 1981 (previously noted).[41] This work also provides a welcome brief summary of each item listed, an introduction reviewing the mass of material published up to 1981, and a reliable chronology. For those interested in foreign criticism and news of Williams's reputation abroad, Zhu Lian Qun published "A Bibliography of Tennessee Williams in China, 1975–1992" in *Studies in American Drama: 1945–Present.*[42] Williams's plays were not permitted in China during his peak years, and this is the first bibliography of Chinese criticism of his work.

V CRITICAL STUDIES: BOOKS

This section, as with the following section on articles, does not pretend to cover all publications on Williams, nor does it in any way pretend to select one work over another. The items listed here are intended to give an indication of the more serious and substantial scholarship that has issued from (usually) academic sources, presses, and journals. Three books of serious and noteworthy criticism appeared in 1961. The first, Nancy M. Tischler's *Tennessee Williams: Rebellious Puritan,* finds that Williams follows the "pattern of the romantic nonconformist" in plays, stories, and poems.[43] This is an early evocative and insightful work that still has its rewards for the first-time reader. Published in 1961, it established a high standard of scholarship. In 1961 Signi Falk's *Tennessee Williams* appeared; it was revised and updated in 1978.[44] Falk covers a wide range of topics—personal, psychological, and sexual imagery, among others—and has been often quoted and praised. The third study, *Tennessee Williams: The Man and His Work* by Benjamin Nelson, discusses themes, techniques, and basic beliefs along with early biographical details.[45] It is somewhat ironic that these three studies, while vastly different, were published concurrently at the beginning of Williams's decline, starting the trend toward serious critical examination of his work. Williams's often-quoted remark to Gore Vidal, "I slept through the sixties," to which Vidal replied, "You didn't miss a thing" (quoted in the introduction to *Tennessee Williams: Collected Stories,* xxv), is perhaps symbolic.[46] Nineteen sixty-one was the last year in which Williams had a major play on Broadway (*Iguana*) that was an unqualified hit with the critics.

Off to an impressive start and while Williams slept, Tischler et al. were followed a few years later by Francis Donahue's *The Dramatic World of Tennessee Williams*[47] and by Esther Merle Jackson's *The Broken World of Tennessee Williams.*[48] Jackson's important book is the fourth distinctive early study of influences and criticism. In a brief study (46 pp.), Gerald Weales in *Tennessee Williams* and in *American Drama Since World War II* perceptively draws out the "fugitive" motif from Williams's biographical background.[49] John Styan in *The Dark Comedy* surveys the plays with penetrating effect and analysis.[50] In 1969 Thomas E. Porter published *Myth and Modern American Drama,* firmly establishing the mythical relationship that bound Williams to the South and to the past.[51] Ruby Cohn's fine work *Dialogue in American Drama* produced much of value in the essay "The Garrulous Grotesques of Tennessee Williams."[52] Almost nothing of note appeared in book-length studies until 1977 when Maurice Yacowar's *Tennessee Williams and Film* began to call attention to the role and growing importance of film in Williams's work.[53] The first picture biography of Williams appeared in Richard F. Leavitt, editor, *The World of Tennessee Williams,* which reproduced photos from stage and film productions.[54] Foster A. Hirsch produced a reliable survey in *A Portrait of the Artist: The Plays of Tennessee Williams,*[55] and Gene D. Phillips advanced the importance of film to Williams's work in *The Films of Tennessee Williams,* adding to Yacowar's study of 1977 and focusing on the films and their directors.[56] Felicia Hardison Londré brought out *Tennessee Williams,* covering 41 plays up to the *Two-Character Play.*[57]

Other than collections of essays, scholarly investigations of Williams and his work dwindled to almost nothing in the early 1980s. Although Williams died in 1983 and critical studies increased rapidly afterward, it is sad that for most of his career as a playwright Williams and his plays received very little scholarly attention; he was at the mercy of theater critics and reviewers in the popular press who attacked him regularly during the 1970s and 1980s.

Tennessee Williams, a book published as a tribute, appeared in Gale's DLB Documentary Series.[58] Although not a scholarly work, it is a well-illustrated biography full of interesting documents. C. W. E. Bigsby's *A Critical Introduction to Twentieth Century American Drama,* volume 2, *Tennessee Williams, Arthur Miller, Edward Albee* is a carefully written and well-thought-out study from the perspective of a British academic.[59] Also of note is the publication of reliable factual data in *Tennessee Williams on File* (Methuen, 1985), by Catherine M. Arnott.[60] Although essays continued to appear in 1985, no scholarly books of criticism appeared in 1985 or 1986. In 1987 several books appeared, a few already mentioned here in other sections. Roger Boxill's *Tennessee Williams* attempts a "comprehensive study," but only in the sense that it mentions every play Williams ever wrote.[61] His main analysis is directed toward *Menagerie, Streetcar, Summer and Smoke,* and *Cat on a Hot Tin Roof.* Irene Shaland's *Tennessee Williams on the Soviet Stage* surveys the plays produced in the Soviet Union after 1960.[62] She also provides a succinct history of the theater in the Soviet Union since 1939. In addition to Judith Thompson's study, *Tennessee Williams' Plays: Memory, Myth, and Symbol,*[63] which the reviewer in the 1988 *American Literary Scholarship* termed "derivative," there also appeared Dennis Vannatta's *Tennessee Williams: A Study of the Short Fiction.*[64] As most scholars know, Williams's fiction is a much-neglected part of his work and deserves further study. Nineteen eighty-nine saw the inaugural issue of the *Journal of American Drama and Theatre,*[62] published by the Center for Advanced Study of Theatre at CUNY–Graduate School. This publication promises to be an important source of Williams articles. Aside from Rasky's book,[65] no new book-length studies appeared in 1986, but of note was the first issue of the *Tennessee Williams Literary Journal* (Spring 1989).

In 1990, two books were published on Williams's work, both by seasoned Williams scholars: *The Glass Menagerie: An American Memory* by Delma E. Presley[67] and *A Streetcar Named Desire: The Moth and the Lantern*[64] by Thomas P. Adler.[68] Both part of Twayne's Masterwork Series, they offer astute readings, and analysis of each play and a summary of critical thought, including brief chronologies and bibliographies. Nineteen ninety-one brought no new scholarly works except Drewey Wayne Gunn's updated and corrected second edition of his 1980 *Tennessee Williams: A Bibliography.*[69] [previously noted.] In 1992 many more articles on Williams appeared, but no new books of interest to scholars. Nineteen ninety-three brought a new book on Williams: *Tennessee Williams: Everyone Else Is an Audience,* which focuses on Williams's fears of failure and death, and his relationships with women.[70] Ronald Hayman draws heavily on previously published sources and summarizes rather than analyzes the plays. David Savran in *Communists, Cowboys, and Queers: The Politics of Masculinity in the Work of Arthur Miller and Tennessee Williams* hardly seems to have any point in assessing Williams's plays.[71] Savran attempts to polarize Miller and Williams in terms of their sexual preferences. Such efforts may satisfy some politically but do little to explain the plays. The promise of the book's title is unfulfilled. A more scholarly assessment of Williams is found in Brenda Murphy's *Tennessee Williams and Elia Kazan: A Collaboration in the Theatre*.[72] Murphy is a careful scholar with facts and deals splendidly with the collaboration in *Streetcar, Camino Real, Cat on a Hot Tin Roof,* and *Sweet Bird of Youth*. Nicholas Pagan in *Rethinking Literary Biography: A Postmodern Approach to Tennessee Williams* offers what the title says: a compelling postmodernist view that examines old material in a new way.[73] Nineteen ninety-five saw Alice Griffin's *Understanding Tennessee Williams*, a carefully considered view of the man and his work.[74] Worth mentioning again is Lyle Leverich's biography *Tom: The Unknown Tennessee Williams*, which for Williams scholars is the major publishing event of the 1990s.[75]

VI   MANUSCRIPTS AND ESSAYS

Williams's primary manuscripts, letters, photos, and assorted papers are at the University of Texas (Austin) in the Harry Ransom Humanities Research Center. Various materials are located at Harvard University; Columbia University's Rare Books and Manuscript Library (contents of Key West House); the University of California, Los Angeles; the University of Delaware; and the New York Public Library's Theatre Collection. The bulk of the Williams material, and the most important items, are in the University of Texas collection.

Essays and articles on Williams's life and plays have grown to massive proportions. To attempt to list all the significant articles would take more space than is devoted to this entire book. Instead of attempting such an impossible task, I would urge interested readers to refer to Gunn's bibliography for works through 1991; to the annual (June) bibliographies in *Modern Drama;* to the annual *MLA Bibliography;* and to the annual *American Literary Scholarship*.[76] Most of the essays of interest to scholars have been gathered over the years in collections.

Jordan Y. Miller, editor, gathered one of the earliest collections on *A Streetcar Named Desire* in Prentice-Hall's Twentieth Century Interpretations series.[77] Miller reprints reviews from the commercial theater and essays by Signi Falk, Durant da Ponte, and Christopher Bigsby, among others, with the usual brief bibliography in Prentice-Hall's format. A giant step forward in Williams criticism is taken by Jac Tharpe, editor, in *Tennessee Williams: A Tribute*.[78] Thorpe gathered 53 original essays by such well-known Williams scholars as Jacob H. Adler, Esther M. Jackson, Philip C. Kolin, Jerrold A. Phillips, Mary Ann Corrigan, Nancy M. Tischler, Robert Emmet Jones, Delma Eugene Presley, and Judith J. Thompson. This is the largest collection of original essays published to date. (In 1980, Tharpe selected 13 of the original 53 essays for publication by the University Press of Mississippi as *Tennessee*

Williams: 13 Essays in paperback.) Stephen S. Stanton published a Twentieth Century Views volume entitled *Tennessee Williams: A Collection of Critical Essays,* which drew from portions of books and reprinted journal essays by Robert Bechtold Heilman, Ruby Cohn, Gerald Weales, Thomas P. Adler, Esther Merle Jackson, Arthur Ganz, Nancy Tischler, and Judith Hersh Clark, among other contributors familiar to readers.[79] Twentieth Century Interpretations published *The Glass Menagerie: A Collection of Critical Essays,* a volume with a fine introduction by the editor, R. B. Parker, and with reviews and essays by Gilbert Debusscher, Lester A. Beaurline, R. B. Parker, Benjamin Nelson, Tom Scanlan, and Roger B. Stein, among others.[80]

In 1987 Harold Bloom edited *Tennessee Williams,* and in 1988 he published similar volumes on *A Streetcar Named Desire* and *The Glass Menagerie.*[81] While the essays chosen for these volumes are fine in themselves—all are reprints from standard drama journals—Professor Bloom appears to know little about modern drama and next to nothing about Tennessee Williams as a dramatist. His introductions might be a disservice to the beginning student. Reportedly, Bloom is editing more than 200 volumes of essays on different periods and different authors; that is probably the problem.

Also in 1987, Dorothy Parker edited *Essays on Modern American Drama,* a volume of essays selected from *Modern Drama* journal articles on Tennessee Williams, Arthur Miller, Edward Albee, and Sam Shepard.[82] Selections on Williams by Nancy Baker Traubitz, Brian Parker, Mary Ann Corrigan, and Leland Starnes nicely delve into the complexity of Williams's work. Of interest to Williams scholars from another point of view is an article edited by Philip C. Kolin (one of the most active Williams scholars), *"A Streetcar Named Desire:* A Playwright's Forum" in *Michigan Quarterly Review.*[83] Kolin provides the reflections on *Streetcar* of 35 playwrights including Robert Anderson, Horton Foote, Jerome Lawrence, Terrence McNally, Megan Terry, and Wendy Wasserstein. Kolin has also edited a collection of 15 original essays, entitled *Confronting Tennessee Williams's "A Streetcar Named Desire": Essays in Critical Pluralism.*[84] Essays by advocates of Critical Theory, Marxism, feminism, reader response, deconstructionism, formalism, mythology, and gender theory, among others, make for a lively and interesting collection. As editors of *Studies in American Drama, 1945–Present,* Philip C. Kolin and Colby H. Kullman brought out a special issue of the journal, devoted primarily to the plays of Williams.[85] Essays were expanded studies from a 1993 Williams conference. "Each of these essays," the editors note, "charts new—and startling even for Tennessee Williams studies—territory" (113).

Readers of Williams's life and plays will find interesting—and unusual—John Lahr's "The Lady and Tennessee" in the *New Yorker* of 19 December 1994, which describes Williams's friendship with Maria St. Just and its rather ominous implications for Williams papers and letters at the time.[86] Among the details, Lahr covers the sad results of St. Just's guardianship of the estate: scholars were refused permission to quote, letters remained uncollected and unedited, and Williams's journals remained unpublished.[87] In addition, no plans were under way to publish Williams's unpublished works, even though doing so would provide Williams scholars with a generation of work. Guest editor Philip C. Kolin edited a special issue (Fall 1995) of the *Mississippi Quarterly* with contributions by Willie Morris, Patricia Grierson, (interviews), Allean Hale, Kimball King, Thomas P. Adler, Colby H. Kullman, Philip C. Kolin, and Robert Bray (interview with Dakin Williams).[88] In his introduction, Kolin defines Williams as "the South's greatest playwright and arguably America's most distinguished." Williams scholars will want to obtain this special issue. In addition, Kolin published seven articles on Williams in 1995 and eight in 1994—an impressive record and a boon to Williams studies.

VII   CONCLUSION

Looking back down the line, one finds that serious studies of Williams have increased erratically but impressively in the years since his death. Williams believed that critics had turned against him and that scholars had little or no interest. At one time he considered moving to another country to escape the hostility he felt American critics directed at him. He was, in fact, correct. To see just how much the New York critics turned against him one has only to read the denigrating comments that followed his plays after *Night of the Iguana.* Arthur Miller *and* Tennessee Williams were systematically made the object of derision and contempt for not writing plays that were up to the "standards" of the reviewers. Miller, like Williams, has recently had his plays produced in England, a country that still seems to have a theater and a culture that values playwrights' insights into the human condition. But time has come round for Williams, and the essays in this collection are an attempt to overcome the previous lack of understanding and appreciation Williams has experienced. My intention was to select essays that represent the best critical thought and insight on Williams's plays (the play is always the thing). In addition, these essays and the space devoted to them are intended to be somewhat representative of the full range of Williams criticism, though I have avoided the most vitriolic reviews.

William's plays in the fifties and sixties were fresh, poignant, imaginative, and vivid portrayals of Southern life and culture, often subtly disguised through images and characters of a sexual nature. To post–World War II audiences, they were news from an alien world filled with lonely, dispossessed outsiders attempting to enter the materialistic world. Everyone, from Blanche in *Streetcar* to the Reverend Shannon in *Iguana,* reflected some part of the audience's feeling of being dislocated in a new world, of being forced by exhaustion, circumstances, or just bad luck to seek a new start. For Tennessee Williams it *was* life, and he made us see it clearly.

ROBERT A. MARTIN
Michigan State University

Notes

1. Tennessee Williams, *Memoirs* (New York: Doubleday, 1975).
2. Lyle Leverich, *Tom: The Unknown Tennessee Williams* (New York: Crown, 1995).
3. Arthur Miller, publisher's excerpt on dust jacket of *Tom.*
4. Donald Spoto, *The Kindness of Strangers: The Life of Tennessee Williams* (New York: Little, Brown, 1985).
5. Edwina Dakin Williams with Lucy Freeman, *Remember Me to Tom* (New York: Putnam's, 1963).
6. Dakin Williams and Shepard Mead, *Tennessee Williams: An Intimate Biography* (New York: Arbor House, 1983).
7. Bruce Smith, *Costly Performances, Tennessee Williams: The Last Stage* (New York: Paragon, 1990).
8. Harry Rasky, *Tennessee Williams: A Portrait in Laughter and Lamentation* (New York: Dodd, Mead, 1986).
9. Dotson Rader, *Tennessee: Cry of the Heart* (New York: New American Library, 1985).
10. Donald Windham, *Tennessee Williams' Letters to Donald Windham, 1940–1965* (New York: Holt, 1976).
11. Maria St. Just, *Five O'Clock Angel: Letters of Tennessee Williams to Maria St. Just, 1948–1982* (New York: Knopf, 1990).
12. Albert Devlin, ed., *Conversations with Tennessee Williams* (Jackson: Univ. Press of Mississippi, 1986).
13. Mike Steen, ed., *A Look at Tennessee Williams* (New York: Hawthorn, 1969).
14. Thomas P. Atkins, "The Astonishing Mystery of Life: The Playwright Talks about His Work," *Tennessee Williams Literary Journal* 1, no. 2 (Winter 1989–1990): 35–40.
15. Cecil Brown, "An Interview with Tennessee Williams," *The Partisan Review,* 45 (1978): 276–305.
16. David Frost, "Will God Talk Back to a Playwright?" *The Americans* (New York: Stein, 1970), 33–40.
17. Robert C. Jennings, "Playboy Interview: Tennessee Williams," *Playboy,* April 1973, 69–84.
18. Dotson Rader, "The Art of Theatre V: Tennessee Williams," *The Paris Review* 81 (Fall 1981): 144–85. Rpt. in *Writers at Work: The Paris Review Interviews,* 6th series, ed. George Plimpton (Viking, 1984): 75–121.
19. Jere Real, "An Interview with Tennessee Williams," *Southern Quarterly* 26, no. 3 (1988): 40–49.
20. "Interview with Tennessee Williams," *Folio* 3 (Spring 1958): 6–9.
21. Drewey Wayne Gunn, *Tennessee Williams: A Bibliography,* 2d. ed. (Metuchen, N.J.: Scarecrow, 1991), 301–31.
22. John S. McCann, *The Critical Reputation of Tennessee Williams: A Reference Guide* (Boston: G. K. Hall, 1983). [Annotates each article by description or evaluation.]
23. Gore Vidal, ed., *Tennessee Williams: Collected Stories* (New York: New Directions, 1985).

24. Tennessee Williams, *The Theatre of Tennessee Williams,* 8 vols. (New York: New Directions, 1971–94). [Will eventually include all of Williams's plays.]

25. Tennessee Williams, *Where I Live: Selected Essays,* ed. Christine Day and Bob Woods, by Tennessee Williams (New York: New Directions, 1978).

26. *The Tennessee Williams Newsletter,* ed. Steven Stanton. Published at Ann Arbor, Mich., vol. 1, no. 1 (spring 1979) to Vol. 3, no. 1 (Fall 1981). Five issues.

27. *The Tennessee Williams Review,* published at Northeastern Univ., Boston, vol. 3, no. 2 (fall 1981) to vol. 4, no. 2 (Spring 1983).

28. *The Tennessee Williams Literary Journal,* ed. Kenneth Holditch (New Orleans), (Spring 1989–present).

29. Nadine Dony, "Tennessee Williams: A Selected Bibliography," *Modern Drama* 1 (1958): 181–91.

30. Charles A. Carpenter and Elizabeth Cook, "Addenda" [to Dony's bibliography], *Modern Drama* 2 (1959): 220–23.

31. Drewey Wayne Gunn, "The Various Texts of Tennessee Williams' Plays," *Educational Theatre Journal* 30 (October 1978): 368–75.

32. Delma E. Presley, "Tennessee Williams: Twenty-five Years of Criticism," *Bulletin of Bibliography* 30 (Jan.–Mar. 1973): 21–29.

33. Catherine M. Arnott, *Tennessee Williams on File* (London: Methuen, 1985), 77–80.

34. Thomas P. Adler, Judith Hersch Clark, and Lyle Taylor, "Tennessee Williams in the Seventies: A Checklist," *The Tennessee Williams Newsletter* 2, no. 1 (1980): 24–29.

35. Charles A. Carpenter, "Studies of Tennessee Williams' Drama: A Selective International Bibliography: 1966–1978," *The Tennessee Williams Newsletter* 2, no. 1 (1980): 11–23.

36. Alan M. Cohn, "More Tennessee Williams in the Seventies: Additions to the Checklist and the Gunn Bibliography," *The Tennessee Williams Review* 3, no. 2 (1982): 46–50.

37. Drewey Wayne Gunn, *Tennessee Williams: A Bibliography* (Metuchen, N.J.: Scarecrow, 1980). [Gunn's first version.]

38. Drewey Wayne Gunn, *Tennessee Williams: A Biography,* 2d ed. (Metuchen, N.J.: Scarecrow, 1991).

39. Pearl Amelia McHaney, "A Checklist of Tennessee Williams Scholarship: 1980–87," *The Tennessee Williams Literary Journal* 1, no. 1 (1989): 65–76.

40. George W. Crandall, ed., *Tennessee Williams: A Bibliography* (Pittsburgh: Pittsburgh Univ. Press, 1994).

41. See note 22.

42. Zhu Lian Qun, "A Bibliography of Tennessee Williams in China, 1975–1992," *Studies in American Drama: 1945–Present* 8, no. 2 (1993): 214–16.

43. Nancy M. Tischler, *Tennessee Williams: Rebellious Puritan* (New York: Citadel, 1961).

44. Signi Falk, *Tennessee Williams* (Boston: Twayne, 1961).

45. Benjamin Nelson, *Tennessee Williams: The Man and His Work* (New York: Obolensky, 1961).

46. See note 23.

47. Francis Donahue, *The Dramatic World of Tennessee Williams* (New York: Ungar, 1984).

48. Esther Merle Jackson, *The Broken World of Tennessee Williams* (Madison: Univ. of Wisconsin Press, 1965).

49. Gerald Weales, *Tennessee Williams* (Minneapolis: Univ. of Minnesota Press, 1965); and "Tennessee Williams' Fugitive Kind," in *American Drama Since World War II* (New York: Harcourt, 1962), 18–39.

50. John Styan, *The Dark Comedy* (Cambridge: Cambridge Univ. Press, 1968), 208–17.

51. Thomas E. Porter, *Myth and Modern American Drama* (Detroit: Wayne State Univ. Press, 1969), 153–56.

52. Ruby Cohn, *Dialogue in American Drama* (Bloomington: Univ. of Indiana Press, 1971), 97–129.

53. Maurice Yacowar, *Tennessee Williams and Film* (New York: Ungar, 1977).

54. Richard F. Leavitt, ed., *The World of Tennessee Williams* (New York: Putnam, 1978).

55. Foster A. Hirsch, *A Portrait of the Artist: The Plays of Tennessee Williams* (Port Washington, N.Y.: Kennikat, 1979).

56. Gene D. Phillips, *The Films of Tennessee Williams* (Philadelphia: Art Alliance Press, 1979).

57. Felicia Hardison Londré, *Tennessee Williams* (New York: Ungar, 1979).

58. Margaret A. Van Antwerp and Sally Johns, eds., *Tennessee Williams,* DLB Documentary Series, vol. 4 (Detroit: Gale, 1984).

59. C. W. E. Bigsby, *Tennessee Williams, Arthur Miller, Edward Albee, A Critical Introduction to Twentieth Century American Drama,* vol. 2, (Cambridge: Cambridge Univ. Press, 1984), 15–134.

60. See note 33.

61. Roger Boxill, *Tennessee Williams* (London: Macmillan, 1987).

62. Irene Shaland, *Tennessee Williams on the Soviet Stage* (Lanham, Md.: United Press of America, 1987).

63. Judith Thompson, *Tennessee Williams' Plays: Memory, Myth, and Symbol* (New York: Peter Lang, 1988).

64. Dennis Vannatta, *Tennessee Williams: A Study of the Short Fiction,* Short Fiction Series, no. 4 (New York: Twayne, 1988).

65. See note 8.

66. *Journal of American Drama and Theatre* (New York: Center for Advanced Study of Theatre at CUNY–Graduate School, 1989–present).

67. Delma E. Presley, *The Glass Menagerie: An American Memory* (New York: Twayne, 1990).

68. Thomas P. Adler, *A Streetcar Named Desire: The Moth and the Lantern* (New York: Twain, 1990).

69. See note 21.

70. Ronald Hayman, *Tennessee Williams: Everyone Else Is an Audience* (New Haven: Yale Univ. Press, 1993).

71. David Savran, *Communists, Cowboys, and Queers: The Politics of Masculinity in the Work of Arthur Miller and Tennessee Williams* (Minneapolis: Univ. of Minnesota Press, 1992).

72. Brenda Murphy, *Tennessee Williams and Elia Kazan: A Collaboration in the Theatre* (Cambridge: Cambridge Univ. Press, 1993).

73. Nicholas Pagan, *Rethinking Literary Biography: A Postmodern Approach to Tennessee Williams* (Rutherford, N.J.: Fairleigh Dickinson Univ. Press, 1993).

74. Alice Griffin, *Understanding Tennessee Williams* (Columbia: Univ. of South Carolina Press, 1995).

75. See note 2.

76. *American Literary Scholarship* (Durham, N.C.: Duke Univ. Press, published annually).

77. Jordan Y. Miller, ed., *A Streetcar Named Desire* (Englewood Cliffs, N.J.: Prentice-Hall, 1971).

78. Jac Thorpe, ed., *Tennessee Williams: A Tribute* (Jackson: Univ. Press of Mississippi, 1977). Reprinted with 13 of the original essays as *Tennessee Williams: 13 Essays* (Jackson: Univ. Press of Mississippi, 1980).

79. Stephen S. Stanton, ed., *Tennessee Williams: A Collection of Critical Essays* (Englewood Cliffs, N.J.: Prentice-Hall, 1977).

80. R. B. Parker, ed., *The Glass Menagerie: A Collection of Critical Essays* (Englewood Cliffs, N.J.: Prentice-Hall, 1983).

81.   Harold Bloom, ed., *Tennessee Williams* (New York: Chelsea House, 1987). Bloom also put together similar volumes on *The Glass Menagerie* and *A Streetcar Named Desire,* also published by Chelsea House in 1988.

82.   Dorothy Parker, ed., *Essays on Modern American Drama* (Toronto: Univ. of Toronto Press, 1987).

83.   Philip C. Kolin, "*A Streetcar Named Desire:* A Playwright's Forum," *Michigan Quarterly Review* 29, no. 2 (Spring 1990): 173–203.

84.   Philip C. Kolin, ed., *Confronting Tennessee Williams's A Streetcar Named Desire: Essays in Critical Pluralism* (Westport, Conn.: Greenwood, 1992).

85.   Philip C. Kolin and Colby H. Kullman, eds., *Studies in American Drama: 1945–Present* 8, no. 2 (1993): 113–74, 214–16. [A special issue devoted primarily to Tennessee Williams and his plays.]

86.   John Lahr, "The Lady and Tennessee," *New Yorker,* 19 December 1994, 76–97.

87.   As of fall 1996, Nancy M. Tischler and Albert Devlin were editing the collected letters of Williams for publication by New Directions Press in 1999 or sooner.

88.   Philip C. Kolin, guest editor, *Mississippi Quarterly* 48, no. 4 (Fall 1995): 575–805. [A special issue devoted to Williams's plays.]

REVIEWS

◆

[THE GLASS MENAGERIE]

{From the *New York Journal-American*}

ROBERT GARLAND

Make no mistake about it, a very fine play and a truly great performance came night-before-last to the Playhouse. The very fine play is Tennessee Williams' "The Glass Menagerie." The truly great performance is that of Laurette Taylor as The Mother, its most important character. In all her distinguished on-stage days, Miss Taylor has reached no greater histrionic heights than this.

Eddie Dowling, in association with a newcomer in the theatre whose name is Louis Singer, has given "The Glass Menagerie" a fresh and remarkably effective production.

Supporting Laurette Taylor are Mr. Dowling himself, the lovely Julie Haydon, the gifted Anthony Ross. Complementary music has been composed by Paul Bowles. The direction is Mr. Dowling's, with the assistance of Margo Jones. Jo Mielziner has gone out of the way to supply a setting which, with the use of scrim, lights and imagination, is as fluid as a motion picture background.

With all these things in mind, especially the deeply touching performance of the Peg-O' My Heart of yesteryear, the Mrs. Midget of yesterday, and The Mother of today—

Well, small wonder there were applause and cheers and bravas night-before-last in 48th st., where applause and cheers and bravas have not been heard too frequently of late. I wouldn't be surprised if "The Glass Menagerie" were the outstanding production of the waning season of 1944–45, running off with the Pulitzer and the Drama Critics' prizes . . .

Here and now, I cast my votes for Tennessee Williams, playwright, and Laurette Taylor, player.

There's little doubt that Tennessee Williams is a playwright to be reckoned with in the current theatre. Not only where night-before-last's "The Glass Menagerie" is concerned, but also when his locally unproduced "You

Reprinted from the *New York Journal-American*, 2 April 1945, 6.

Touched Me" is taken into consideration. He writes deftly and well. And, which is more important, he has something definite to say and knows how to say it definitely.

Basically, "The Glass Menagerie" tells the simplest of stories. There are The Mother, an erstwhile Southern belle; Her Daughter, an unhappy moon-like cripple, and Her Son, a dreamer.

The Mother might well be known as Fallen Grandeur. She lives in her glamorous past. And Anthony Ross is right as a trivet as The Gentleman Caller. Having seen him, I'd never have him otherwise. It's a play-going privilege to see these four fine players cooperating at the Playhouse.

The craftsmanship—the playwriting, which is memorable; the playacting, which is flawless; and the production, which is inimitable—makes of "The Glass Menagerie" a masterpiece of make-believe.

[THE GLASS MENAGERIE]

{From the New York *Sun*}

WARD MOREHOUSE

There was great acting on the stage of the Playhouse Saturday night. Laurette Taylor, her talent undimmed by long months of inactivity, dug deep into the reservoir of her art and contributed to the play called "The Glass Menagerie," a performance of such sustained skill and expressive force that it must be put down as the very finest that the Broadway theater has offered during the entire season.

"The Glass Menagerie," written by Tennessee Williams, and his first play to reach New York, is fragile and poignant. It is a vivid, eerie and curiously enchanting play and it is made an eventful one by the appearance of Miss Taylor as a faded and bedraggled Southern belle from a past long receded. "The Glass Menagerie," as it is acted and presented at the drama-hungry Playhouse, is something to see, to cheer about, and to see again.

There were many in Saturday night's audience who have been watching Miss Taylor across the years. Some of those at the Playhouse premiere saw her as Peg, others have cherished memories of her as Luana and Rose Trelawny and 'Aunted Annie from "Out There." And now she returns to fascinate us all, and to bring into play the unused resources of the past few years, in the role of a nagging mother who prattles forever of her feted delta girlhood and who is trying to provide a gentleman caller, plus security, for her shy and crippled daughter.

Miss Taylor captures a Southern accent magically, and with her mumblings and pauses, her detached, half-completed sentences, she brings Amanda Wingfield to life—Amanda who could have been the bride of a planter's son but who married a telephone man instead; Amanda uprooted and living drably in a St. Louis alley tenement. Her daughter is the psychopathic Laura, who lives in a dream world and collects glass animals; her son, Tom, works in a warehouse, but he has poetic yearnings—and the wanderlust.

Reprinted from the New York *Sun*, 2 April 1945, 10.

Amanda whines and scolds and coaxes and pretends. She is bitter, pitiful and ridiculous. She nags her son about going to the movies, about the way he sits at the breakfast table, and finally prods him into bringing home a friend from the warehouse to meet his sister Laura. Amanda puts on her deep-South airs and her chiffon out of the long ago and the dressed-up Laura captures a strange and evanescent beauty as Mr. O'Connor comes for supper. And as Amanda and Tom are doing the dishes Mr. O'Connor discovers Laura to be the girl he used to call Blue Roses during their high school days. He gives her a wonderful build-up talk to cure her of her sense of inferiority, and he kisses her, but he won't be calling again. No, he's already engaged to a girl he met on a moonlight steamer.

So ends Laura's hope for romance—and the play. Tom is off to his wanderings, to the moon and lesser distances, walking out as his carefree and hard drinking father did before him, and Amanda is holding Laura close in her protecting arms, frustrated but still not conceding defeat.

[THE GLASS MENAGERIE]

{From the *New York World-Telegram*}

BURTON RASCOE

Eddie Dowling and Louis J. Singer brought to the Playhouse Saturday night the much-heralded play, "The Glass Menagerie," by Tennessee Williams, which not only caused the critics, when the drama was first produced in Chicago, to employ their most superlative of superlatives but also caused editorial writers to devote commendatory space to it.

They were right. I never hope to see again, in the theater, anything as perfect as Laurette Taylor's portrayal of The Mother in "The Glass Menagerie." Nor do I hope, many times, to see anything as wonderful as Anthony Ross' performance as The Gentleman Caller in this beautiful play. Here is make-believe so real it tears your heart out.

The play hurts you . . . hurts you all through. It arouses in you pity and terror. That, according to Aristotle, is what tragedy is for; it is supposed to drain you of these emotions, so you can go on living. "The Glass Menagerie" certainly does that.

Mr. Williams has put some laughs in "The Glass Menagerie," but they are laughs growing out of a situation. They are not Broadway wisecracks. When you laugh the characters would be, in real life, surprised that what they said struck you as funny. They are not trying to be funny; they are creatures caught in the most ordinary but the most terrible of tragedies—that of trying to live when they have no sensible reason for their living.

I can't say anything adequate to Miss Taylor's creation of The Mother in "The Glass Menagerie." You can't describe a sunset.

She was there—a simple, sanely insane, horrible Mother, pathetic and terribly human and terribly real. She succeeded in destroying every vestige of hope and beauty and joy in the lives of the two people who loved her—her son and her daughter.

She had no love for anyone except herself. She was married once to a handsome young Irishman, who was charming and beguiling—but he drank.

Reprinted from the *New York World-Telegram,* 2 April 1945, 8.

She didn't drink. Therefore she had one up on him. Apparently she told him so many times that he was a drunkard that he drank himself to death just to get shut of her telling him that. . . . But she kept a smiling picture of him in the death-house she created for her son and daughter; and she kept tucked away a faded tulle evening gown in which she had once danced with him. She liked to remind her miserable son and her even more miserable daughter that she had once been a pretty, gay-hearted bride of a gay blade of a drinking Irishman.

She is a fluttery hen with her two soul-misshapen brood. He (Eddie Dowling) smokes too much, she tells him constantly, and he spends too much money going to motion pictures. He doesn't take care of himself, she says; the way he spends money on cigarets and movies she doesn't know what is to become of them.

She, of course, is always sick. She is always worn out telling her son he shouldn't smoke, and telling her crippled daughter (Julie Haydon) that she should forget she is a cripple. She arranges a dinner party, where she expects to marry her daughter off; but she can't help prepare the food—she is so tired out and so busy seeing there won't be any smoking or drinking.

The daughter has been in love with The Gentleman Caller (Anthony Ross) ever since they were in high school, but now she had rather not meet him and let him see she is not physically perfect.

The story is this. A widow has used up her deceased husband's life insurance. She has kept her son under her thumb and tied him to her apron strings. But there is no Clytemnestra-complex here. She doesn't even love her son, she merely keeps him under a sense of obligation and thus succeeds in destroying his will to live.

The money is running out. Mother wants to marry off the crippled daughter. She makes her son invite his best friend—a fellow war plant worker—to dinner in order to throw her daughter at the chap. But this Army reject, who is struggling to keep faith in himself and therefore boasts too much about how good he is, has already obligated himself to marry someone else. He loves the crippled girl, but there is nothing he can do about it. His moral scruples are such that he can't even kiss her the way she wants to be kissed.

There is frustration everywhere in this stark tragedy; so you are glad that, for a brief time, Miss Haydon (until they were broken by her brother's sudden senseless outbreak) had her glass animals to play with . . . they were something she could love and regard as her own.

This play is an event of the first importance.

[A STREETCAR NAMED DESIRE]

{From the New York *Sun*}

WARD MOREHOUSE

Tennessee Williams has written a gaudy, violent and fascinating study of the disintegration of a Southern belle in "A Streetcar Named Desire," put on last evening at the Barrymore. It is played with uncommon skill and it has been carefully and expertly staged by Elia Kazan.

Williams is again writing of a locale that he knows. He has put some earthy characters, jolting humor and pungent writing—and along with writing that is occasionally high-flown—into his absorbing story of crumbled grandeur in the delta country. His title is taken from the name of a streetcar that careened unconcernedly through the New Orleans quarter in which he lived.

This new play by the author of "The Glass Menagerie" presents a tale of two sisters, well born, whose plantation was lost in debt. The younger sister, Stella, has achieved a certain security in marriage to a simple, hard-working, brute of a boy, an ex-G.I. of Polish parentage, and she loves him. The other and older girl, Blanche, neurotic and desperate, comes a-calling.

Her own marriage ended in a revolting tragedy. She lost her job as schoolteacher and was driven out of the town of Laurel after having become the town trollop. She takes refuge in Stella's cramped, dingy, curtained-off quarters as the play begins and it depicts her downhill course and her last, pitiful efforts to save something out of the wreck of her life.

"A Streetcar Named Desire" is not a play for the squeamish. It is often coarse and harrowing and it is frequently somewhat jerky in its blacked-out sequences, but it is a playwriting job of enormous gusto and vitality and poignance and Irene M. Selznick has given it the advantages of Kazan's extraordinarily knowing direction, Lucinda Ballard's costumes and Jo Mielziner's scenery. Mielziner's fine setting reveals the interior of the squalid flat in which the Kowalskis have their brawling and blissful moments, and the device of a scrim curtain provides frequent glimpses of the street outside.

Reprinted from the New York *Sun,* 4 December 1947, 44.

There is some superb acting upon the Barrymore's stage. There is quite a good deal of Amanda, out of "The Glass Menagerie," in the character of Blanche, the faded, shattered daughter of the South, who is played by Jessica Tandy. It's one of the longest roles ever assigned to an actress and Miss Tandy comes through with a compelling performance. Her final crack-up is beautifully done.

Marlon Brando turns in his finest work to date in his characterization of the slow-witted, virile, uncomprehending young husband. Kim Hunter, making her first New York appearance, is human and direct, a first-rate young actress, and she makes Stella a genuine person. Karl Malden is tremendously effective as the gawky, naive suitor who is agonized by the revelation of Blanche's past. Ann Dere and Richard Garrick are silent and menacing as the grim couple from the asylum who come at the younger sister's bidding to take Blanche away.

"A Streetcar Named Desire" is an intense play, packed with genuine theater. It is a full evening's worth, and it is sometimes as much of a show as it is a play. It will be at the Barrymore when the sidewalks of 47th street are sizzling under next summer's heat.

[A STREETCAR NAMED DESIRE]

{From the *New York World-Telegram*}

WILLIAM HAWKINS

"A Streetcar Named Desire" is a terrific adventure in theater. Tennessee Williams models out of the rawest materials and his finished art is harsh realism.

It is lost souls that preoccupy him, the people whose sensitivity condemns them to total disappointment. The rude bluffness of living which destroys them is the same harshness that hurts or toughens everybody.

Blanche Du Bois is the sort of woman whose imagination would have let her make a great deal of a little. In destitution she creates a facade of pathetic glory out of baths and scents, and shabby finery and paste jewelry.

She springs from the same source as the Mother in "The Glass Menagerie," but Mr. Williams has written a much stronger, surer play about her.

After her marriage's sordid ending she has struggled to keep up the remnants of an ancestral Southern estate. Her existence meant constant association with old age and death. Her school teaching job is gone and she makes an ostensible visit to her married sister.

Stella, philosophical and earthy, is entirely happy in a simple lusty existence with Stanley, a Polish mechanic, whom Blanche considers an ape. Their life is elemental with violent outbreaks and ecstatic reconciliations.

The play is basically an enthralling account of the conflict between Blanche and Stanley. They have no sympathy or understanding and a deep contempt for each other. The only rare agreement by either of them is for the sake of Stella.

The one thing they know in common is physical desire. Stanley is an honest animal who needs no motivation for anything he does other than he wants to do it at that particular moment.

Blanche, out of loneliness and desperation, rationalizes everything she does until she can assure herself of a motive that involves charity or nobility in an expression of her dainty exquisite self. Her life has become loose in the

Reprinted from the *New York World-Telegram*, 4 December 1947, 36.

most degraded sense, but she clings to an elegance to which she insists her taste and sensitiveness entitle her.

The nervous rasp of their mutual irritation is depicted in terms of rare theatrical tension and excitement. There are scenes of violence and raw emotion that leave you pop-eyed and gasping. And there are quiet, gentle scenes that in their way are just as absorbing.

Where Laurette Taylor brought magnetic quickness to "Glass Menagerie," Elia Kazan has done the same here with his brilliant direction.

Jessica Tandy, in the monumental role of Blanche, infallibly projects the two essential planes of the character. One is the immediate unrelenting hopelessness of the woman, and the other her desperate falseness. She makes her pathos repellent rather than sympathetic, giving the play credibility and a tumultuous effect on the emotions.

As the story progresses one wishes that Blanche would only slip over into recognizable derangement, but the scarring truth is that she never quite does.

Marlon Brando plays the blunt and passionate Stanley with an astonishing authenticity. His stilted speech and swift rages are ingeniously spontaneous, while his deep-rooted simplicity is sustained every second.

Kim Hunter is mellow and philosophical as the devoted Stella who tries to synchronize two impossible loyalties, and Karl Malden is eloquently unrelaxed as the hesitant suitor who almost saves Blanche.

[A STREETCAR NAMED DESIRE]

{From New York *PM*}

LOUIS KRONENBERGER

A Streetcar Named Desire is by all odds the most creative new play of the season—the one that reveals the most talent, the one that attempts the most truth. It carries us into the only part of the theater that really counts—not the most obviously successful part, but the part where, though people frequently blunder they seldom compromise; where imagination is seated higher than photography; and where the playwright seems to have a certain genuine interest in pleasing himself.

That is the most important thing about *A Streetcar Named Desire;* a more important thing, it seems to me, than that *A Streetcar* is by no means always a good play. It falls down in places; it goes wrong in places. But what is right about it is also, in today's theater, rare. There is something really investigative, something often impassioned, about Mr. Williams' feeling for his material. There is something—in the play's best scenes—that reveals deeper intimations, as well as sharper talent, than most of Mr. Williams fellow-playwrights can boast. And there is a willingness to be adventurous in the pursuit of truth.

The problem of truth isn't made any simpler because Mr. Williams' heroine happens to be the most demoniacally driven kind of liar—the one who lies to the world because she must lie to herself. His Blanche Du Bois, whose gradual disintegration is the subject of his drama, is Southern-genteel and empty of purse; highly sexed and husbandless; full of fine-lady airs, and the town's most notorious tramp. When she comes to New Orleans to visit her sister and brother-in-law in their shabby quarters, she drags her whole paste-diamond dream world—her airs and pretenses, her nymphomania posing as straitlacedness—with her. But her brother-in-law, a warmhearted but violent and no-nonsense roughneck, sees through her at once and proves her nemesis. When he finds her trying to turn his wife against him, and then trying to nab his best friend in marriage, the brother-in-law gets the goods on

Reprinted from New York *PM*, 5 December 1947, 2.

Blanche and brutally shows her up. She loses her guy; while her sister is in the hospital, her brother-in-law takes her to bed; and when she blabs, her brother-in-law argues that she is crazy, and has her committed to an asylum where she would all too soon be due in any case.

In Blanche, Mr. Williams hasn't quite contrived a real, progressive study in disintegration; except toward the end, his method is too static, with Blanche often a kind of fascinating exhibit—but an exhibit none the less. What both she and the play need is less repetition and more variety; there were times, toward the middle of the play, when I found myself fairly bored. In the last and best third, however, there is a genuine release of emotional excitement; and the conflict between Blanche and her brother-in-law—which may not be Mr. Williams' theme, but is certainly his story—is always good theater, and quite often good drama. And just because it doesn't much induce us to take sides, it comes to move us, in the end, as part of the malignity and messiness of life itself. It brings a certain dry pity, along with a certain new power, into Mr. Williams' work; *A Streetcar* is an enormous advance over that minor-key and too wet-eyed work, *The Glass Menagerie*.

It has had, moreover, a very good production. Mr. Kazan has capitalized on all its vividness and innate sense of theater without ever letting it topple over into mere theatricalism.

[SUMMER AND SMOKE]

{From the *New York Journal-American*}

ROBERT GARLAND

Intentionally or unintentionally, as the case may be, Tennessee Williams has written an illuminating and unnecessary foreword to his "A Streetcar Named Desire." Under the title of "Summer and Smoke," Margo Jones of Dallas proudly presented it last evening at the Music Box. There, promptly on the stroke of eight, the season's best-dressed, best-behaved and best-intentioned first-night congregation was seated to receive it.

When I say that, in "Summer and Smoke," Mr. Williams has written a foreword to his "A Streetcar Named Desire," a foreword is exactly what I mean. Although the Blanche Du Bois at the Ethel Barrymore is known as Alma Winemiller at the Music Box, they are one and the same. Maybe Miss Winemiller of Glorious Hill turned herself into Miss Du Bois of Belle Reve when she went to stay with her married sister 'way down south in New Orleans.

At any rate, I am here to tell you that the Tennessee Williams–hungry playgoer could, at any weekend matinee, leave the Music Box at teatime and take up where he left off that evening at dinner at the Ethel Barrymore. For, in "Summer and Smoke," the author of "A Streetcar Named Desire" goes to great pains to explain at length how Blanche Du Bois got the way she is when she shows up nymphomaniacally in the Vieux Carre.

And I wish I were here to tell you that the Tennessee Williams–hungry playgoer would be sure to have as good a playgoing time at "Summer and Smoke" as he is sure to have at "A Streetcar Named Desire." But he will not! Just as Lillian Hellman's "Another Part of the Forest" was an illuminating and unnecessary foreword to her "Little Foxes," which had come before, Mr. Williams' new play is also inferior to the old. And talkier!

Yet all the stock Tennessee Williams figures are up on the stage. Especially the females of the deep Deep Southern species. The Alma Winemiller played by Margaret Phillips is, as I have written, the Blanche Du Bois played

Reprinted from the *New York Journal-American*, 7 October 1948, 21.

by Jessica Tandy. And Blanche Du Bois is the Laura Wingfield played by Julie Haydon. So, I beg you, do not let Mr. Williams' apologetic pieces in the Sunday papers persuade you otherwise.

In "Summer and Smoke," Alma Winemiller, a clergyman's frustrated daughter, has an overpowering yen for John Buchanan, a physician's unfrustrated son. And, as was the case with Blanche and Stanley in "A Streetcar Named Desire," and Laura and Jim in "The Glass Menagerie," the female's frustration is more deadly than the male's lack of it. Nowadays, at the Music Box, Alma's frustration talks her right into the arms of a certain Mr. Kramer.

For no good reason, Mr. Kramer is a traveling salesman right out of a smoking-room story. And, as the final curtain falls at the Music Box, Alma Winemiller wanders away with him. Out into 45th Street she goes, I fancy. Then up to 47th where, as Blanche Du Bois, she continues her career as a windy Dixie introvert who, I am sure, is done exactly right by. Only, at the Music Box, the bad little good girl is no Jessica Tandy.

Not that Margaret Phillips, pinch-hitting, fails to do justice to Tennessee Williams' last example of acute Southern discomfiture. But Tennessee Williams' last example of acute Southern discomfiture does not do justice to Margaret Phillips. As for Tod Andrews as Jim O'Connor-into-Stanley Kowalski-into-John Buchanan, he is as impolitely picaresque as the occasion calls for. The others, under Margo Jones' direction, are all there.

[SUMMER AND SMOKE]

{From the New York *Sun*}

WARD MOREHOUSE

"Summer and Smoke," in which Tennessee Williams combines metaphysics with realism and symbolism, is a rueful and disturbing play that makes its way, gropingly, through two acts and numerous scenes. It brings forth beautiful performances from Margaret Phillips and Tod Andrews, but the total effect is one sharp disappointment. The first performance was given last evening at the Music Box.

Yes, let it be recorded at the outset, "Summer and Smoke" does bear a resemblance to "The Glass Menagerie" and to "A Streetcar Named Desire." But it is not up to the standard of either. It has a certain gallantry and dignity of its own, but it comes through as a blurry and indefinite play, and frequently a quite tedious one.

Tennessee Williams puts his locale in his native Mississippi. He is writing of an idealistic and oversensitive girl, a minister's daughter, who loves a small-town doctor's son living next door. She is shy and virtuous and she has a mirthless, nervous little laugh. Alma is a neurotic, given to affectations and self-exaltation, and she wants to keep her relationship with the boy—Dr. Johnny they call him—spiritual. But Johnny is realistic and ruffianly and there comes the night at the Casino by the lake when she rejects his proposals and goes home alone.

Things happen in the town of Glorious Hill. Johnny's father is killed. Johnny takes hold of himself and takes on responsibility and respectability. By this time Alma has dropped to a lower plane, coming around to his former ways of thinking—and Johnny is engaged to one of her vocal pupils. Alma is facing a bleak and shadowy future as she goes off with a shoe salesman to the Casino beside the lake.

"Summer and Smoke," told to the incidental music of Paul Bowles and played within another of Jo Mielziner's imaginative settings, is an ironic play, one with some scenes of tenderness and beauty, but also one that never takes

Reprinted from the New York *Sun*, 7 October 1948, 28.

on any dramatic progression. There are some windy and listless interludes and a certain monotony overtakes the character of Alma Winemiller in her visionary phases and after her descent from her spiritual level.

Margaret Phillips is fascinating in her playing as the confused, tremulous and introspective Alma. There is a captivating performance from Tod Andrews as the unrepressed Johnny, who becomes suddenly high-minded. Marga Ann Deighton makes a pitiful and believable figure as Alma's demented and babbling mother, who eats ice cream cones walking along the street.

Raymond Van Sickle is excellent as the dull clergyman. There are good performances from Anne Jackson, Betty Greene Little and Earl Montgomery, and a tremendously engaging one from Ray Walston, playing the role of the salesman Alma meets in the little park. Margo Jones has given the play intelligent, professional direction.

"Summer and Smoke" is minus the magic of "The Glass Menagerie" and without the drive of "A Streetcar Named Desire." It has many affecting moments, but it is definitely one of Tennessee Williams's lesser achievements.

[THE ROSE TATTOO]

{From the New York *Daily Mirror*}

ROBERT COLEMAN

We know of no modern playwright who can create moods like Tennessee Williams. But, unfortunately, Williams is prone to create his moods on a level of frustration and neuroticism. Even when he tries to be affirmative, he is usually negative. And we believe that the world today needs moral affirmation and not negation.

This is apropos of Williams' latest play, "The Rose Tattoo," which Cheryl Crawford brought to the Martin Beck Theatre last evening. The new arrival is a study of sex-mad Sicilians living along the Gulf Coast between New Orleans and Mobile. It is particularly concerned with Serafina Delle Rose, whose husband has been destroyed by the authorities while transporting dope concealed beneath loads of bananas on his mighty ten-ton truck.

Serafina remembers her husband as a descendant of Sicilian nobility and the acme of everything that a volatile woman should crave in a man. After his tragic death, she places his ashes in an urn beside a statue of the Virgin. Later, she is terribly disillusioned to discover that her paragon-husband had feet of clay.

So, in a Williams mood of distraction, she gives herself to an itinerant truck-driver, who has the body of her deceased husband and the head of a clown. Shocked by her mother's faithlessness, Serafina's 15-year-old daughter, who had been graduated from high school that day, rushes off to emulate the affair with an unwilling and protesting young sailor.

"The Rose Tattoo" takes its title from the fact that Serafina's husband, rival and shiftless suitor all have roses tattooed on their chests. And the springboard for the tragedy is: ". . . the streams are in their beds like the cries of women and this world has more beauty than a ram's skin painted red," from T. S. Eliot's translation of "Anabasis."

William Rose Benet, in his "The Reader's Encyclopedia," says: "Anabasis means a journey upward." We can only say that Williams, in paraphrasing

Reprinted from the New York *Daily Mirror*, 5 February 1951, A-1.

Eliot and Xenophon, has taken a journey downward to the very depths of human degradation. He has penned a play that has moments of compassion, beauty and sheer nastiness.

In the last act of "The Rose Tattoo," for instance, a lecher drops an unmentionable article on the stage. And there are episodes that can be construed as sacrilegious. Personally, we were revolted. We do not think these dubious elements add anything to a confused play. Rather, we believe they are going to antagonize decent playgoers.

Maureen Stapleton gives a dynamic performance as Serafina. Phyllis Love, Eli Wallach and Don Murray are outstanding in other roles. Only lack of space prevents our paying tribute to at least a dozen other excellent contributions.

Daniel Mann, an up and coming young director, has done an exceptional job with a difficult script. And Boris Aronson has designed a superlative setting.

"The Rose Tattoo" is a provocative play. You will either like it or dislike it immensely. Count us among the dissenters.

[THE ROSE TATTOO]

From the *New York Journal-American*

JOHN MCCLAIN

The chief operatives in "The Rose Tattoo"—Maureen Stapleton, Phyllis Love, Eli Wallach and Don Murray—deserve a better fate than that which befell them Saturday night in the new Tennessee Williams play which opened at the Martin Beck Theatre.

Miss Stapleton, in particular delivered one of the most arduous and exacting performances of the year but regrettably the theme is thin, frequently offensive and never sufficiently provocative.

Many persons, among them Mr. Shakespeare, have devised a drama around the single idea of a seduction but the more successful have done it with greater taste and ingenuity. Never before, to my knowledge, has a rather simple biological situation involved so many extraneous characters and so many words—or been so pretentiously elevated.

The story Mr. Williams tells is that of a Sicilian immigrant's young widow, living with her teen age daughter in a small house and worshipping at the shrine of her departed husband's ashes, prominently displayed on the parlor table.

The deceased had a rose tattoo emblazoned on his chest and it seems that following conception this same insignia would appear on his wife's breast.

Along comes Eli Wallach, a truck driver, and the rest of the action involves his ultimately successful effort to recreate this strange phenomenon.

To achieve this he produces a similar rose tattoo on his own chest and convinces the widow, among other things, that her late lamented had been guilty of considerable extra-marital activity beyond her ken.

The result is that she shatters the vase containing her husband's ashes and repairs to the boudoir with Mr. Wallach.

There are thousands of neighbors and children, lending movement and atmosphere to the proceedings, and there is a subordinate love story involving

Reprinted from the *New York Journal-American,* 5 February 1951, 8.

her daughter, played by Phyllis Love, and a sailor, Don Murray. There is even a goat which is chased across the stage at intervals, but none of these alter or enhance the simple basic problem.

I thought there were two compelling scenes: (1) where Miss Stapleton first meets Mr. Wallach and, (2) where Don Murray tears himself away from Miss Love in the last act.

I publicly promised that I would not use the expression "tour de force" in describing the performance of Miss Stapleton, so I can only say that it was magnificent throughout and worthy of more notable material. Mr. Wallach, last seen in a minor role in "Mr. Roberts," gave great credibility and humor to his difficult part.

The direction by Daniel Mann impressed me as being somewhat cluttered at times, although that may have been the fault of all the people who were required to appear and disappear frequently and for no good reason.

I do not happen to know what a house in a "village populated mostly by Sicilians somewhere between New Orleans and Mobile" would look like, but Mr. Boris Aronson's single set seemed suitable.

I don't think "Rose Tattoo" is a good show, but I'm looking forward to seeing these new players back on the boards in something more worthy of their abilities.

[THE ROSE TATTOO]

{From the *New York World-Telegram and The Sun*}

WILLIAM HAWKINS

Type—Comedy
Topic—Love
Virtue—Novelty
Debit—Talky
I find it—Most unusual

Tennessee Williams has hit a new stride for himself in "The Rose Tattoo." As in his other three plays, "Streetcar," "Menagerie" and "Summer and Smoke," he is again dealing with a neurotic woman. The difference is that here his mood is humorous and the ending is relaxed and happy.

The hub character is a Gulf Coast widow of Sicilian ancestry. She is an intense, mercurial extremist who wallows in all her emotions with no sense of humor. She is a fanatical Catholic, until in her childish way she decides that religion has betrayed her.

The theme of this story is her demented regard for the memory of her husband, whose ashes she keeps in an urn in her parlor.

She still sews for a livelihood, but normal living has stopped. She sees nobody, refuses to dress and tries to suppress her daughter.

The dead man had a rose tattooed on his chest. The play tells how the widow must finally face the fact that a blond dealer in a gambling house down the road has the same tattoo, for a very good reason. She takes up living again with a grand flourish, in the arms of a lonely truck driver, and relents about her daughter's pathetic little romance.

In its favor the play has atmosphere and warmth. Its theme seems fresh and engrossing, and most of the talents involved in the production are youthful.

On the other hand the humor often seems glued to the surface, and passages of the play are endlessly chatty and repetitious. This is particularly true

Reprinted from the *New York World-Telegram and The Sun,* 5 February 1951, 10.

of the second act, where the widow keeps up a clamor of every notion that comes into her head, and her new suitor responds with brashly pronounced gags.

The role of the widow must be about as long as Hamlet. She is never off stage, and every conversation in the play takes place with her. This is a tremendous assignment, particularly for so unjaded an actress as Maureen Stapleton.

Miss Stapleton gives one of the most honest performances I remember ever witnessing. She hypnotizes herself into moving and even looking like this character, whom she physically resembles not in the least.

She lacks the technique to make the impersonation powerful. What she projects is just life size.

It seems to me that she has been allowed to start in too high a gear, so is left with the capacity only of going back to the same place emotionally. Doubtless one of the toughest things in the theater is to make a humorless woman winning. If Miss Stapleton has not the resource or range to do this, she certainly does a valiant, often absorbing job.

As the new beau, Eli Wallach has a more contained portrait to paint, and it comes off most successfully. He is the little fellow for whom everything turns out wrong. The actor plays it for complete passion, and gets comic effects from the character's intensities.

Phyllis Love is dewy and dynamic as the daughter, and Don Murray is unbelievably right-looking as her sailor beau. Of the many neighbors, most impressive are Ludmilla Toretzka as a stern friend, and Augusta Merighi as an overweight busybody.

[CAMINO REAL]

{From the *New York Journal-American*}

JOHN MCCLAIN

The new Tennessee Williams play, "Camino Real," which opened at the National Theatre last night will divide any audience that sees it into two sharp categories: Those who understand it, and those who don't. I'm afraid I must identify myself with the latter.

The theatre is a medium for poetry and symbolism, for freedom of thought and expression, but it should also adhere to some reasonably orthodox method of transmission.

There is not the slightest doubt that Mr. Williams has some provocative and high-flown thoughts about love and life, and he is capable of lyrical and humorous and sometimes utterly earthy writing, but it seems to me that in this instance he knocked himself out being oblique.

One is obliged to wonder whether the utter confusion doesn't result from the fact that the original idea was in itself somewhat muddled.

However soaring and symbolic, I cannot think of one great play, from Shakespeare to Christopher Fry, whose premise could not be reduced to a simple sentence—and I will defy Mr. Williams to explain "Camino Real" in less than a page of small print.

Or, if his message was reasonably understandable, why he chose this abstruse means of telling it.

As I interpreted it—and I may be quite wrong—the Camino Real is Life. On one side of the street is a plush hotel and on the other side, a flophouse. There is a door, center stage rear, through which various characters enter, and there is a pawnshop and a fountain, and the square in which the action takes place.

Into this setting are projected hordes of strange people: A gentleman of fortune, a blind lady mendicant, a baron, a tired courtesan, a titled Englishman and his avaricious wife, Lord Byron, a gypsy, her daughter, the crew of an airliner, Don Quixote, and an American youth named Kilroy, to name a few.

Reprinted from the *New York Journal-American*, 20 March 1953, 20.

What happens to them is, I guess, the author's conception of what happens to most people—and it ain't good. The gentleman of fortune (just call me Casanova) cannot experience true love when the opportunity is presented; the courtesan is reduced to squandering her last farthing for the affection of a younger man; Kilroy pays the supreme price for leaving his ever-loving wife merely because he has an enlarged heart.

Lord Byron speaks at some length about the agony of seeing Shelley's remains burning, all this somehow suggesting his own personal tragedy of having wandered from the muse to the fleshpots.

Interspersed throughout this, and more, is a ribald fiesta; the departure of a plane, "The Fugitivo" (symbol for escape catch?); an exceedingly humorous and uncomplicated seduction scene between Kilroy, the fortune teller and her daughter, and a tortuous finale in which Kilroy walks around juggling his own enlarged heart (solid gold, yet).

In all honesty it must be recorded that Eli Wallach, Joseph Anthony, Frank Silvera, Jo Van Fleet, Jennie Goldstein, Hurd Hatfield and Barbara Baxley exert all their abundant talents toward making the proceedings plausible.

And Elia Kazan, who supervised and directed, succeeds in making the entire cast behave as if they knew what they were saying.

But in the words of Mr. Silvera, early in the first act, "What is this all about?"

[CAMINO REAL]

{From the *New York World-Telegram and The Sun*}

WILLIAM HAWKINS

"Camino Real" is a brilliant and riotous adventure. It succeeds in making tangible for all your senses the delirious pains and ecstasy of a wild dream.

The first thing evident about this brave and stimulating new play of Tennessee Williams is that explanations of it that suit you may not suit anybody else. The playwright has composed his work in terms of pure emotions. They are abstract, without excuse or motivation. What you see and hear is the effect on the heart, of human nature when it is greedy or hilarious or sorry for itself.

In none of Williams' most distinctive work is he optimistic. He best understands pathos. The tragic littleness of his characters lies in the fact that their happiness never exists in the present, but only in past memories and future hopes. Right now they are searching, but disconsolate.

It will depend on you just what positive assertions "Camino Real" contains. I believe the play says in the end that there is a special kind of endlessness for romantics who live with gallantry or who have the capacity to simply dream far beyond their material wherewithal, or their evident spiritual capacity.

The play bounds literally into the audience several times. It has no limits of time or space. The set is a walled community, from which the characters ceaselessly try to escape, without success. Only Don Quixote, who calls himself "an unashamed victim of romantic folly," has access to the outside, and finally Kilroy goes with him.

Kilroy is a central figure, an ex-boxer, always the Patsy, the fall guy, who asks so little and always gets short-changed. But he never quits hoping, and dies slugging away. His last vitality goes in a breeze of passion for the innocently wanton daughter of the gypsy.

Reprinted from the *New York World-Telegram and The Sun,* 20 March 1953, 28.

The other principal story is a romance between the aging, hunting Camille, and the fading Casanova, who yearns now only for tenderness and faithfulness.

Lord Byron goes off to seek his early true romantic self, after describing Shelley's boiling brain, and the salvage of his heart. In the end, though the street cleaners come for his body, Kilroy recovers his own golden heart, but trades it for some dusty finery to give the gypsy's daughter, a romantic to the end.

The play has subdued sequences of tenderness and pathos. It also has scenes of cataclysmic violence. The near escape of Kilroy, the battle to ride the escape plane are hair-raising, as is the wild fiesta to crown the "tired old peacock," Casanova.

There is no space to do faint justice to the many thrilling aspects of this production. Its conception is so inspired, and its execution so exciting, that there is no question of not liking it, but only of just how you, personally, will happen to enjoy and find yourself stirred by it.

The acting is intelligent and penetrating, with highly authoritative performances in even brief roles. Eli Wallach is urgent and vibrant as Kilroy. Jo Van Fleet has breathtaking range as Camille. Barbara Baxley is both sly and touching as the wanton girl and Jennie Goldstein is rambunctious and raucously earthy as the Gypsy.

Joseph Anthony is handsome and passionately tragic as Casanova, Frank Silvera is sleek and superior as an interlocutor, and Hurd Hatfield is authoritative and striking in the contrasted roles of Byron and Quixote.

Kazan has directed the play with courageous sweep and a great palette of emotional colors. Lemuel Ayers' setting is a challenging combination of the concrete and the mystic.

[CAT ON A HOT TIN ROOF]

{From the New York *Daily Mirror*}

ROBERT COLEMAN

In "Cat on a Hot Tin Roof," which the Playwrights' Company brought to the Morosco Theatre Thursday evening, Tennessee Williams has penned a bitter play about mean people. The language is the strongest heard hereabouts in quite a spell. Williams doesn't call a spade a spade, but rather a steam shovel.

We came away with the impression that Tennessee is disturbed about death and the shoddiness of women. The cat in question is a restless, ambitious girl married to a sensitive husband who wants no part of her. For she had accused him of an unnatural relationship with a college mate and fellow football player.

The action takes place in the bedroom of a manor house on the biggest plantation in the Mississippi Delta. The boy's father, and the lord of the manor, is a "turkey neck" who has worked himself up from nothing to millions and wonders if it was all worth it. He too, hasn't much use for his addle-pated spouse.

In the end, with the head of the family dying of cancer, the boy and the insatiable cat determine to have an heir, because his loathing for a shifty brother and sister-in-law is worse than that for his own unscrupulous wife. It's a cynical finish to a hard-boiled drama.

Much of the language is right from the barnyard and such as would never be heard in a decent aristocratic home. But these people are anything but aristocrats, and much less than decent. They are neurotic, frustrated, and fascinated by bawdy speech.

Even though the Williams characters are repulsive to those accustomed to the niceties, the amenities, of life, they generate a lot of emotional tension and excitement. Under Elia Kazan's direction, they perform their pieces with the virtuosity of opera singers blending arias with choruses.

Barbara Bel Geddes has almost a monologue in the first act, as the cat, and brings it off triumphantly. Burl Ives contributes an unforgettable

Reprinted from the New York *Daily Mirror*, 25 March 1955, 21.

characterization as the doomed land owner who wonders if money and power have compensated for a rather empty existence. Ben Gazzara, who was outstanding as the bully in "End as a Man," plays the disillusioned son and husband with restraint and admirable effect.

Mildred Dunnock is excellent as a shrill, well-meaning mother. Madeleine Sherwood and Pat Hingle are devastatingly realistic as two schemers, "sometimes called Sister Woman and Brother Man." The heads of the brood are known as Big Papa and Big Mama. Ugh!

"Cat on a Hot Tin Roof" is not a play we would want to see again. Once is enough. But we think it will prove a sensational hit. Hopeful customers were already in line at the box-office before the rise of the curtain on the first Manhattan performance. We trust their stomachs are stronger than ours.

After all, Williams is a craftsman, and has a big following. In this instance, as in "Camino Real," he is absorbed with disturbed and disturbing people, tired of living and scared of dying. People of little integrity, willing to make enormous compromises for the easiest way out.

[CAT ON A HOT TIN ROOF]

{From the *New York Journal-American*}

JOHN MCCLAIN

Tennessee Williams is a playwright who can sock you and shock you and he has never exhibited these abilities to better advantage than he did last night in "Cat on a Hot Tin Roof," which opened at the Morosco Theatre. It is a powerful and provocative evening; you are torn between fascination and revulsion, but you are held.

On the bright side of the agenda it seemed to me that Williams has fashioned his most compelling characters and brought them into clearer focus than in any of his previous efforts. These are people closer to our ken and their problems are at least comprehensible to most of us.

But again the entire proceedings have a strange and somehow unsavory flavor; there is an absence of warmth and tenderness. And there is the implication, at least, that the most motivation in the play derives from an unnatural relationship. This may be life, to be sure, but how stark and unremitting can you get?

The favorite son of a rich Southern plantation owner has taken to drink and finds himself unable to rid himself of an infatuation for his college roommate.

The roommate has since died, but the young heir lives with the memory of their relationship and is hence incapable of either normal relationship with his wife or any protracted periods of sobriety.

His elder brother, a dreary and orthodox married man, has been busy producing heirs and now with the father teetering at death's door, it is a question of who will come into the family fortune.

The play rather clearly divides itself into three stanzas: the unrequited relationship between the boy and his wife, the hassle over the inheritance, and the final resolution involving the whole family.

Along the way it seemed to me there was unnecessary vulgarity and embarrassing expletive. We know a spade is a spade, but it doesn't have to be

Reprinted from the *New York Journal-American*, 25 March 1955, 20.

a dirty, fetid, miserable, filthy garden implement. Mr. Williams shouldn't have to resort to that.

Here, of course, the author owes a great debt to Barbara Bel Geddes, Burl Ives, Ben Gazzara and Mildred Dunnock, who are entrusted with the words, and Elia Kazan, who has achieved a masterful job of direction.

This is a particular triumph for Mr. Ives, in his first serious non-musical role, as the patriarch.

Miss Bel Geddes is appealing and authoritative as the wife of Mr. Gazzara, who fulfills his promise of last season in the difficult part of the mixed-up young husband. Mildred Dunnock, as the mother, Pat Hingle and Madaleine Sherwood, as the other son and his wife, heighten the dramatic impact.

You may not go all the way with "Cat"—you may be baffled and assaulted at times—but you won't be bored.

[CAT ON A HOT TIN ROOF]

{From the *New York World-Telegram and The Sun*}

WILLIAM HAWKINS

Tennessee Williams offers at the Morosco Theater a turbulent opera about avarice and mendacity in the modern South in "Cat on a Hot Tin Roof."

The play functions like a snake charmer. It holds one's hypnotized and breathless attention, while it writhes and yowls and bares the souls of its participants with a shameless tongue.

The major figure is that of a dying millionaire planter, self-made and with a Titanic patience. The cancer that is destroying him stimulates his two daughters-in-law to clawful efforts to cut in on his fortune.

One of the girls has made her bid for popularity through indomitable fertility. She has produced a brood of what must stand as the South's most horrifying children, and promises more.

The lady of the title is in more serious personal trouble. Ambitious and poor, she has caught the magnetic younger son, an ex-athlete who has forsaken TV sports announcing for the bottle.

As the play progresses it develops that the Cat is denied conjugal attentions because she has, through jealousy, caused the collapse and death of her husband's devoted lifelong friend. Only in the end is the truth of the two men's puzzling relationship clarified.

What the author chiefly says is that even the best intentions do not avoid the inherent mendaciousness of modern living. All these people are lying to themselves and each other. It takes a white hot climax of emotion to drag the actual truth into the open.

This stylization is immensely effective. Elia Kazan gives it flourish, innovation and freedom.

Reprinted from the *New York World-Telegram and The Sun*, 25 March 1955, 28.

Barbara Bel Geddes is magnificent as the ambitious frustrated young wife. She rarely stops talking in the first act, but captures the volatile intonation of Southern speech like a native.

Co-starred with her is Burl Ives as the dying father. He cuts a magnificent figure, like a rock mountain, as he relates his earthy jokes and whips his family into line.

The most astonishing performance of the evening is that of Mildred Dunnock as the mother. She manages to be tasteless, rowdy and featherbrained in a horrifying manner, which is yet always genuine.

Ben Gazzara plays the disturbed and alcoholic husband, in a rare physical performance. With one foot in a cast throughout, he must hop and fall and drag himself about painfully, and does so with great grace.

[SWEET BIRD OF YOUTH]

{From the *New York World-Telegram and The Sun*}

FRANK ASTON

A magnificently theatrical storm of passion, bigotry and tolerance swept through the Martin Beck last evening. It was "Sweet Bird of Youth," by Tennessee Williams, exquisitely directed by Elia Kazan and mounted by Jo Mielziner with the inventiveness and richness that have made him famous.

The eye of the storm is Geraldine Page, and tossed about with her is Paul Newman. With the flashing assistance of Sidney Blackmer and a notable cast, they act out a cruel probing of two lost souls—a washed-up movie queen and an unstable fellow of 29 who laments, "I couldn't go past my youth, but I have gone past it."

They are introduced Easter morning in the fancy bedroom of a Florida town where the boy grew up and betrayed the 15-year-old daughter of the local political boss. He has returned as the current kept man of the ex-star, who is a mixture of neuroses, delusions and comical flashes of common sense. He is racing toward something he can never gain, while she is fleeing the ruins of something she never had.

Unaware of the suffering he has caused his hometown sweetheart, the man refuses to heed warnings of a few old friends that, on the boss' orders, the girl's brother and several bull-necked associates are about to castrate him. In an electrically bitter climax, the star is convinced she is about to renew a career of glory, "for out of my tortured and tormented past I have created something that is true."

Rejecting her pleas to accompany her, the man awaits his fate, remarking that the on-coming knives cannot deprive him of what he already has taken from himself.

The handsomely lithe Miss Page makes a memorable thing of the film queen, sweeping from moans to rages to posturing to inner terrors to

Reprinted from the *New York World-Telegram and The Sun,* 11 March 1959, 30.

vainglorious and laughable self-admiration. Her speech, mannerisms and perceptiveness must have seemed a gold mine to Mr. Kazan.

Mr. Newman is superb in a role that requires him to be almost constantly repugnant. As the vulgarian and racist, Mr. Blackmer is just right.

Among their brilliant aids are Diana Hyland, Madeleine Sherwood, Charles Tyner, Rip Torn, Martine Bartlett and Logan Ramsey. Offstage music is provided by Paul Bowles. Anna Hill Johnstone designed fine clothes, especially those for Miss Page.

And someone deserves a bow for using an upstage drop as a giant TV screen to show a rabble-rouser at work.

[SWEET BIRD OF YOUTH]

{From the New York *Daily Mirror*}

ROBERT COLEMAN

Tennessee Williams has no peer at depicting the weirdies of the world, and he has a genius for reducing people to the lowest common denominator. Which probably explains why the human inmates of his dramatic zoos fascinate nice and normal people. He writes about degeneracy with a touch of the poet and knows how to shock the customers.

In "Sweet Bird of Youth" Williams is again dealing with the abnormal and frustrated. He is concerned with a fading movie star who faces the future with hashish and vodka. An ambitious young punk attempts to blackmail her into furthering his career and helping him carry off the daughter of a Southern political boss with whom he is in love.

Ironically, it is the resourceful old-timer who makes a comeback, while the would-be actor is destroyed. In other words, the veteran luminary has more monster and moxie in her makeup than her ineffectual adversary. At the final curtain's fall, the broken egotist asks not for pity or even understanding but for a recognition of the evil that's in us.

Geraldine Page, who won stardom through the delicacy, the reticence, of her acting, is giving a compelling, bravura performance as the temperamental screen heroine who is rejuvenated by word of good notices on what she thought was a flop. Once soft-spoken, Miss Page can now be heard beyond the confines of the Martin Beck.

Paul Newman etches a frightening portrait of a small-town hotshot who hasn't the stuff to be a bigshot. His disintegration, when he finally faces up to reality, has genuine emotional impact. Newman, as well as the audience, was moved by the concluding passages of the play. There were tears in his eyes as well as in those of many out front.

Sidney Blackmer couldn't be improved upon as a silver-tongued demagogue. He's slick and ruthless. Diana Hyland has effective moments as his daughter, who has had to have an operation to cut out a disease she caught

Reprinted from the New York *Daily Mirror*, 11 March 1959, A-1.

from the young climber. Rip Torn is as mean as a Texas steer as her vengeful brother. And Madeline Sherwood stands out as the Boss's outspoken fancy woman.

Elia Kazan has directed "Sweet Bird of Youth" with semistylized technique. His method is just right, for Williams uses Elizabethan asides in the revelation of character. Jo Mielziner has designed settings that emphasize the moods and movement. Anna Hill Johnstone has created some real eye-fillers for Miss Page to wear.

Williams has put just about everything but the proverbial kitchen sink into "Sweet Bird of Youth," and he's mixed his ingredients with skill. The sordidness of his saga is relieved on occasion by sardonic humor, and, for a change, he even has one of his tortured, bewildered souls climb out of the gutter.

Make no mistake about it, "Sweet Bird of Youth" is hypnotic theatre, and Cheryl Crawford has given it an exciting production. It spells box-office dynamite. It should make the Beck's turnstiles run hot-boxes for months to come. It may make your Aunt Nellie shudder, but we suspect she'll be describing its sensations at the next meeting of her bridge club.

[THE NIGHT OF THE IGUANA]

{From the *New York Journal-American*}

JOHN McCLAIN

The silence of reverence is a first night phenomenon that heralds a hit in symbols louder than a banner headline, and last night at the premiere of Tennessee Williams' "The Night of the Iguana," at the Royale Theatre, the audience rose above coughs, sniffles and postnasal drip to pay the performers the ultimate compliment of soundless respect.

There were those, no doubt, who left the theatre with loud objections, others who emerged with a sense of confusion or bewilderment; but none, believe me, who had not been caught and fascinated by what they'd seen.

For this is in many respects the most fruitful and versatile exercise by our best living playwright. Within the broken-down environs of a cheap Mexican resort hotel he has created a mood of pervading loneliness and despair as intrusive as the Equinoxial storm that stirs sudden lightning flashes and gushes through the tattered roof.

The desolation, the emptiness, are in his people: the tough, sex-starved widow who runs the hotel; the neurotic, defrocked minister, and the gentle maiden lady from New England.

Thrown together in this squalid setting their human needs become explicit, and from their conflicts comes the realization that life must be endured, and that the spirit will somehow survive even beyond the limits of anguish.

Mr. Williams veers off in many philosophic directions in this searing pastorale, but he is chiefly concerned with the relationship of The Reverend T. Lawrence Shannon and Miss Hannah Jelkes, the sad, fortyish lady who travels the world with her grandfather ("the oldest practicing poet in the world"), painting quick portraits, for a fee, while the nonagenarian recites poetry to hotel guests.

Rev. Shannon, having been relieved of his cloth for sexual irregularities, has landed at the Costa Verde hotel, near Acapulco, on the verge of one of his

Reprinted from the *New York Journal-American,* 29 December 1961, 9.

periodic mental breakdowns. The proprietress, an old friend, is prepared to offer him a bed and will, in fact, share it with him if he wishes.

But then Miss Jelkes and her grandpa arrive, penniless but prepared to offer their services to the guests in return for lodging. There is a strange and immediate rapport between the discredited cleric and the lonely artist.

The play's most poignant moments—scenes of enormous compassion—grow out of the understanding of these two people, their mutual need for companionship and roots, their final moments of nobility in small gestures of unselfishness to aid one another.

The Iguana? Mr. Williams is miserable without a symbol, and I guess this one represents people. This Iguana has been chained under the verandah, waiting to be eaten by the natives, until the New England lady gets the preacher to set him free. People, in other words, are pretty ugly beasts, but they have a right to be free.

And speaking of people, free or otherwise, there is an impressive list of gifted ones in this play:

Bette Davis, displaying an unbuttoned shirt, a shock of flame-colored hair and the most raucously derisive laugh this side of a fish wharf, is marvelously brash and beguiling as the owner of the Costa Verde; Margaret Leighton reaches new levels in her distinguished career as the forlorn and fading artist from Nantucket; Patrick O'Neal, in his Broadway debut, gives a powerful performance as the sick and desperately disturbed ex-minister; and Alan Webb is exceptionally convincing as the senile poet.

There are also two strenuously effective contributions by Patricia Roe, as an embittered Texas lady, and Lane Bradbury, as a juvenile victim of one of the parson's sexual misadventures.

Oliver Smith has designed a shoddy tropical trap that would do credit to "Rain"; and Frank Corsaro has directed with apparent reliance and perception.

"The Night of the Iguana" may not be everybody's cup of tequilla, but don't dally on the way to the box office. I think it'll be ALMOST everybody's.

{THE NIGHT OF THE IGUANA}

{From the *New York World-Telegram* and *The Sun*}

NORMAN NADEL

Under the splintering porch, the iguana, a giant lizard left over from an earlier eon, struggles in almost noiseless panic against the rope tied around his horny neck. He does not know that in the morning the Mexican children will poke out his eyes with sticks, burn his tail, and similarly amuse themselves until it is time for the creature to be cooked and eaten for its tender white meat.

The iguana does know that he is captive, and that he cannot reach the dark security of the rain forest only yards away. He is desperate, and without resource, and he struggles.

This is the symbol. Tennessee Williams, a man of ominous symbols, is the playwright. "The Night of the Iguana," which opened last night at the Royale Theater, is the play.

It is an awesome and powerful new drama, vividly laced with strident comedy, merciless in its candor, and shockingly explicit in its probing of human loneliness.

On the porch of a filthy resort hotel on the west coast of Mexico simmers as strange an assortment of human derelicts as ever came out of Tennessee Williams (which is very strange indeed).

Bette Davis is Maxine, the proprietress—freshly widowed but not exactly shattered by grief. In tight dungarees and an unbuttoned shirt that shows the flaccid flesh down to her waist, she casually courts seduction for pleasure or patronage.

Patrick O'Neil is The Reverend T. Lawrence Shannon, who has just abandoned the party of female Baptist seminary teachers he is supposed to be escorting around Mexico, who faces a statutory rape charge for having seduced a 16-year-old girl with them, who had been locked out of his church

Reprinted from the *New York World-Telegram and The Sun,* 29 December 1961, 10.

long before on charges of fornication and heresy (both in the same week), and whose sanity is threadbare.

Margaret Leighton is Hannah Jelkes, itinerant charcoal sketcher and water color artist, and faithful companion of her 97-year-old grandfather (Alan Webb), "the oldest living and practicing poet in the world."

One of the traveling teachers (Patricia Roe) sweats frustration and shrills vengeance at their obscene and fraudulent tour escort. Her teen-age charge (Lane Bradbury) snivels and yammers an infantile anguish of love and betrayal at her seducer. Two noisome Nazi couples (Bruce Glover, Laryssa Lauret, Heinz Hohenwald, Lucy Landau) represent the moral decay elsewhere in the world, this year of 1940.

There is wry humor in these people, but out of it emerges the strangely poignant, sometimes repellent point of the play. As the night of the iguana writhes on, and as the ancient poet struggles to complete his final song, Hannah and Shannon tear the thin skin off their loneliness, and needle-probe deep and painfully into the flesh beneath.

Williams, who already has spelled out the nature of much normal and abnormal sex in his plays, eventually comes to more unspeakable aberrations in this. The unspeakable is spoken, and it is justified because it might logically have been spoken under such strange conditions and by a man so twisted as Shannon.

Still, there is a tortured beauty to this play. Most of it is incorporated in the genteel self-sufficiency and virginal vulnerability of Hannah, in the exquisite portrayal by Miss Leighton. Director Frank Corsaro has kept the play both deep and translucent. Oliver Smith's setting of the Costa Verde Hotel is eloquent of heat and decay.

Not even Williams has ever evolved a more complete autopsy of loneliness than this. "The Night of the Iguana" stands far apart from most of this season's plays, but it stands high.

[CLOTHES FOR A SUMMER HOTEL]

{From the *New York Times*}

WALTER KERR

The most dismaying thing about Tennessee Williams's pursuit of the poor, sad ghosts of Scott and Zelda Fitzgerald, "Clothes for a Summer Hotel," is the fact that Mr. Williams's personal voice is nowhere to be heard in it. It is as though the playwright's decision to deal with actual people—not only the Fitzgeralds but Ernest Hemingway and the Gerald Murphys as well—had momentarily robbed him of his own imaginative powers.

At first glance, as we settle at the Cort, it would seem that at least four imaginations are to be extensively employed: the author's, director José Quintero's, scenic designer Oliver Smith's, and costumer Theoni V. Aldredge's. As the obligatory ground-smoke rolls away—why must so many plays open with rolling swirls of groundsmoke, and where does it comes from?—we get a glimpse of the barred doors and windows within which the broken Zelda is caged.

The facade of the asylum itself is suggestively shattered, abruptly ending in a jagged, unsettling line that will leave room for the low hills and dour clouds beyond it, for the blazing flamebush that symbolically decorates the grounds. Miss Aldredge has aided and abetted Mr. Smith's vision of the last waystop at the edge of the world by using snatches of clothing as though they were malleable as dreams. When a ragged, tousled inmate (not Zelda) who imagines she has invented the marcel-wave of the 20's (and who can say she hasn't?) must be hurried back to her room, the feat is accomplished by two nuns in dangerously spiked wimples who swiftly cover their deranged quarry with vast black cloaks that resemble bats' wings.

The picture is provocative, and Mr. Quintero steps in to create others. As his author continues to fantasize freely, skipping about in time and place in search of a dramatic heartbeat, the director is ready with easy and graceful dissolves. He swiftly transforms the earnest and sober latter-day Scott into a

Reprinted from the *New York Times*, 27 March 1980, C 15. Copyright © 1980 by the New York Times Company. Reprinted by permission.

quivering ruin on his remembered 40th birthday; he puts together a stony frieze of rigid onlookers as an overage Zelda clumsily struggles to prove she can dance.

No one has let down the production physically or visually. An ominous red flash regularly lights up the third-story windows by way of intimating Zelda's coming fiery death. A sound that is somewhere between a knell and a siren's wail quickly aborts any conversation that mentions death at all. Meantime a wonderfully simple and quite pretty party-tent made of little more than bright streamers and toy lanterns seems to defy—in its jazz-age overeagerness— all the failures that lie in wait.

But no one is able to do a single thing to bring the performances to plausible, troubled, passionate life. We meet Scott Fitzgerald first, in the person of Kenneth Haigh, pacing the garden as he awaits his wife at the asylum gates, gripping the back of a wooden bench for support, compulsively fingering his tie as though he could at least get *that* straight. All too soon, though, we notice that these gestures are random, repeated, without cumulative significance. We're scarcely surprised that when Geraldine Page appears as Zelda, she asks him if he is thinking of taking up ballet, too.

When Miss Page does come on, flanked by guardian German nuns, she comes on in appalling, possibly half-calculated disarray. In contrast to the white ducks and sports jacket of Scott's Hollywood life (hence the play's title), she looks like a gypsy moth that's been put through a shredder, leaving only her pink ballet dancing slippers more or less intact.

Her auburn hair has been mercilessly clawed; her mysterious leggings are rigid with wrinkles; the oversize cloak in which she smothers him as she leaps forward for a mocking kiss seems made of ancient rat-fur. Scott has been told that her mind is relatively clear, that she is in a state of remission. Yet it is at once evident that there will be no going back for this rudderless woman, ever.

Now, that *should* explain why we feel no personal contact between this Scott, this Zelda. Both are nearing the end of their lives; the past is irretrievable. But, almost at once, something else is bothering us. The performers who are *playing* Scott and Zelda seem to be making no contact, either. Miss Page flounces, postures, shrieks obscenely, subsides into small fidgets. Mr. Haigh never changes expression, never responds—not even with surprise—to the flighty shifts of mood. Estrangement, remoteness seem total.

Even so, we bide our time, knowing that in this variant on the memory-play we'll be dipping back into earlier, somewhat saner years, years when communication must have been possible. We do dip back, only to discover that nothing has changed. Miss Page, astonishingly, continues to play on one note, a vigorous but unstable whine. Mr. Haigh, who all but disappears from the play for a time, remains the abstracted, evasive fellow who flew in—so late in the day—from California.

It's not that the two do not find arresting moments for themselves. Miss Page makes a strikingly giddy bit of business out of leaving a lover's bed with the spread trailing after her as though it were a ballgown. Mr. Haigh's tongue sharpens up noticeably in an acrid exchange with an exceedingly irritating Ernest Hemingway. But there's no growth, no change, no flow of life anywhere for us to piece together.

For which the playwright must bear his share of responsibility. It would seem that, out of all his interest and research, Mr. Williams hasn't arrived at a defined attitude toward either of his unhappy artists. There is no fresh, idiosyncratic insight into what made two miserable people click. We are simply being told what we already know. We *don't* know why we are bothering to retrace the terrain now.

The play is structurally wasteful: three whole scenes are devoted to Zelda's affair with a French aviator, an affair apparently meant to provoke Scott's jealousy; but Scott shows few signs of caring. And the play's borrowings are easy and obvious ones: Mrs. Pat Campbell is on hand to repeat a single anecdote, Ernest Hemingway (rather well played by Robert Black) for the now-familiar business of baiting Scott sexually.

Strangest of all, though, is the absence of the author's inimitable flair for language. The stiffness of routine biographical drama intrudes: "Ladies and gentlemen, Mrs. Patrick Campbell!" Platitudes are offered ever so solemnly: "The solitude of a lunatic is never broken." Though there are occasional echoes of the real thing (after World War I, the music of Vincent Youmans "floated over the city like a deep violet wash"), the finest playwright of our time has spent his evening trying hard, much too hard, to sound like other people. People out of books.

"Clothes for a Summer Hotel" is Tennessee Williams holding his tongue.

VIEWS

◆

The Circle Closed:
A Psychological Reading of
The Glass Menagerie and
The Two Character Play

R. B. PARKER

"He thought he could create his own circle of light."

In the Bar of a Tokyo Hotel

I

On February 25, 1983, I was correcting galley proofs of a Twentieth Century Interpretations volume on *The Glass Menagerie* when it was announced over the radio that Tennessee Williams had died in a New York hotel, bizarrely choking on a plastic bottle-top while under the influence of barbiturates.[1] A spate of eulogies followed. Walter Kerr called him "the greatest American playwright. Period."; and Marlon Brando affirmed more personally that Tennessee Williams "was a very brave man . . . he never lied or flunked. He told the truth as best he perceived it, and never turned away from things that beset or frightened him."[2] I sadly added a last item to the chronology at the back of my anthology.

I had been asked to edit that collection of essays because, in casual chat with the general editor, I said it seemed to me perverse to reduce the heavy theatricalism of *The Glass Menagerie,* as most productions do, and particularly wrong to dismiss its film projections as awkward, pretentious, and jejune—

Reprinted with permission of the author and the publisher from *Modern Drama* 28, (December 1985): 517–34.

as even sympathetic critics like Lester A. Beaurline and Gerald Debusscher had recently maintained.[3]

There are two distinct versions of *The Glass Menagerie* in print. The Dramatists Play Service's "acting edition" is based on the version actually staged by Eddie Dowling in 1945 (and still preferred for most productions). This has no projections or mimed action, and the text shows considerable rewording, especially in the Amanda speeches and in Tom's "framework" speeches (that is, those speeches in which Tom-remembering introduces and comments on the play directly to the audience). The other version, known as the "reading edition," published originally by Random House and currently by New Directions, is the one that Williams, having bowed to Dowling's pressure for changes in the performance text, nevertheless insisted be printed and has enshrined in his *Collected Theatre*. This does have the projections; much of the play's early business must be mimed (for example, in scene one, the family is directed to mime eating with non-existent knives, forks and food); and the wording is much more complex and ironically ambivalent than in the acting text. In particular, there is a certain self-conscious, overelaborate "poeticizing" quality in Tom's framework speeches, particularly at the end, which produces what is perhaps one of Williams's most characteristic effects as a theatre artist, the effect of self-conscious symbolism (let us call it) which can be seen at its fullest development in *Camino Real*, and which is also integral to the peculiar "Memory Play" effect he was pioneering in *The Glass Menagerie*, a point that will be returned to later.

To research background for the anthology, I visited the University of Texas at Austin in order to examine the big Williams archive that had recently been deposited in the Humanities Research Center there, only to be appalled at the sheer amount of material that confronted me. Williams was a compulsive writer: he spent four or five hours at his typewriter every morning, no matter where he was, partly as therapy but also as the one consistency in his otherwise anarchic life; and he was a compulsive rewriter, who explained to one of his interviewers:

> Finishing a play, you know, is like completing a marriage or a love affair. . . . You feel very forsaken by that, that's why I love revising and revising, because it delays the moment when there is this separation between you and the work.[4]

He was apt to put the same material through many different forms: poem, short story, one-act play, full-length play (rewritten several times), novel, and film or television script; and he claimed that no work could be considered fixed until he had stopped working on it. Three years ago, the Texas material was only roughly sorted out by title; and, to compound confusion, in revising Williams had the habit of mixing altered pages with pages from earlier drafts that needed no change. There is thus a huge problem for some dedicated scholar in the future, sorting out the sequence of these textual alterations—

especially when one remembers that the Texas archive will have to be collated with other Williams material at the Barrett Library of the University of Virginia and the mass of papers the playwright willed at his death to Harvard University.

From the pile of "Gentleman Caller" revisions (the original title of *Menagerie*) and related drafts of the short-story version, "A Portrait of a Girl in Glass," it became clear that the genesis of the play—and, more importantly, Williams's own emotional relationship to his material—were infinitely more complex than had hitherto been understood. Four impressions in particular stood out.[5] In the first place, many of the discarded drafts were much more like what we have come to think of as typical Williams writing: that is, they were more sexually charged, more violent, and more blackly humorous (especially at Amanda's expense) than the final play. And the eventual omission of these elements perhaps explains Williams's own curious lack of enthusiasm for this, his most widely produced and best-loved play, the one that established his reputation. He scrawled on the cover of his final typescript: "The Glass Menagerie, a rather dull little play by Tennessee Williams"[6]; and we find him writing to his friend Donald Windham in 1943: " 'The Gentleman Caller' remains my chief work, but it goes slowly, I feel no overwhelming interest in it. It lacks the violence that excites me, . . ."[7] Even after its phenomenal success, he warned *Time* magazine that in it: ". . . I said all the nice things I have to say about people. The future things will be harsher."[8]

In the second place, the drafts reveal two new aspects of the symbiotic relationship between the brother and sister (Tom and Laura). This relationship not only is more central to the play's action than might have been assumed from the critics' concentration on the mother (Amanda), but also is treated with a startling range of moods: in particular, with a considerable variety of attitudes to the Laura character, ranging all the way from quiet, stoic heroism at one extreme to sheer neurasthenic bitchiness at the other.

In the third place, Williams clearly had great difficulty in devising a suitable end. There are numerous drafts of both happy and sad conclusions, which seem to show that what he wanted intuitively was a complex *mixed* reaction to the end—mingling relief and guilt, bravado and regret, ruthlessness and gentle pity—for which he found it very difficult to create an adequate dramatic form. (He seems to have worked intuitively, trying to get the right "feel.") And finally, related to this problem, we find him experimenting in the drafts with various sorts of "frameworks" to contain the remembered incident of the gentleman caller, including one which I think is especially worth recalling in which Tom argues directly and a little abrasively with the audience about the truth of the memory he is presenting—an element more discretely retained in the final play in such distancing devices as Tom's celebrated opening speech: "Yes, I have tricks in my pocket, I have things up my sleeve. . . . I give you truth in the pleasant guise of illusion."

Williams's solution was, of course, his virtual invention of the "Memory Play" form, which, as Paul T. Nolan has pointed out,[9] differs from either a confessional format or the involuntary recall of stream-of-consciousness expressionism because in the Memory Play we not only see exclusively what the narrator consciously wants us to see, but also see it only in *the way* he chooses that we should. It is precisely here that the main interpretative problem of *The Glass Menagerie* lies. It is a problem both of "mood"—that is, the complex attitude that Tom-remembering has to the events he recalls—and of "tone"—that is, the slightly mocking, not wholly ingenuous stance that Tom seems to take to the audience, a stance that is much more subtle and ambiguous than the sentimental, poetic sincerity (lightened with a few wry laughs) that has determined the way of acting Tom-the-narrator since Eddie Dowling first created the role.

The key to both these problems lies in the ambiguity of Tom's attitude to Laura. This attitude is, of course, basically one of loving regret for having abandoned her; but we should remember that in the short story "A Portrait of a Girl in Glass," which is one of the alternative presentations of the same incident, there is a distinct, if guarded, hint of incestuous attraction between brother and sister.[10] In the reading version of *The Glass Menagerie,* moreover, we have to cope with several film projections which seem to *mock* Laura's terror at Jim's advent and her hopelessness when he leaves; and we must also recognize the ruthlessly self-damaging implications of Tom's final command, when he bids Laura blow out her candles to plunge not only herself but also Tom-remembering into the final stage black-out.

There are hints of complexity in the brother's remembrance of his relation to his sister, then, that seem directly linked to the very innovative "plastic theatre" devices of the staging (to use Williams's own terminology in the Production Notes to the play). I wish to argue, therefore, that implicit in the very structure of *The Glass Menagerie* is a connection between sex and art whose common denominator is a recognition and fear of solipsism—of consciousness turned in on itself, "inordinately possessed of the past" (as Williams has described his work in general), where theatre is not simply an emotional escape but also a form of introversion. Williams's Memory Play uses the box-within-box structure perfected by Pirandello as a comment on the self-referentiality of theatre; and its final effect is rather like that famous mime of Marcel Marceau in which a man trapped in a small box worms his way out of it only to find himself trapped in a bigger box outside. The *angst* of such introversion for the dramatist comes out at the end of Williams's essay "The Timeless World of a Play" (published originally with *The Rose Tattoo*), where he worries that:

> unless [the playwright] contrives in some way to relate the dimensions of his tragedy to the dimensions of a world in which time is *included*—he will be left among his magnificent debris on a dark stage, muttering to himself.[11]

This image of abandoned solipsism prefigures a play written at the end of Williams's career to which *The Glass Menagerie* is most intimately related, the play known variously as *The Two Character Play* and, more vividly, as *Out Cry*. Talking to Mike Wallace about things he had learned from psycho-analysis in the 1950s, Williams explained:

> . . . a term I've come across lately is "infantile omnipotence." . . . That is what we all have as babies. . . . All [the infant] has to do is cry out and it will be comforted, it will be attended to. All right. We grow up a little and we discover that the outcry doesn't meet this tender response always. . . . [the infant] meets a world which is less permissive, less tender and comforting, and it misses the maternal arms—the maternal comfort—and therefore, then, it becomes outraged, it becomes angry.[12]

It is the contradictoriness of this emotion—its tenderness, need, revulsion, and anger—that must be the focus of our concern.

II

Solipsism that exists in sibling love and solipsism that can result when drama is used therapeutically come together very illuminatingly in a play that Tennessee Williams first issued in 1967 with the title *The Two Character Play*, then rewrote in 1971 and again in 1973 as *Out Cry*, only to revise it yet once more in 1975 under its original title—which also happens to be the title of its play-within-the-play.

Though its implications were not probed, the relation of the play to *The Glass Menagerie* was immediately recognized. Claudia Cassidy, the reviewer whose praise had prevented Williams's backers from closing *Menagerie* during its Chicago try-out, noted that: "[Williams] said in *The Glass Menagerie*, 'This is a memory play.' Well, in a sense so is *Out Cry*"; and another critic, Peggy Prenshawe, saw the play as "in some ways like a sequel to *The Glass Menagerie*."[13] Williams himself regarded it as the masterpiece of the second half of his career. "I think it is my most beautiful play since *Streetcar*," he is reported as saying on the cover of the New Directions edition, "and I've never stopped working on it. . . . It is a *cri de coeur*, but then all creative work, all life, in a sense is a *cri de coeur*." And in his startlingly frank *Memoirs*, on which he was working while he revised *Out Cry*, he calls this play "the big one," the one "close to the marrow of my being," in which he was "very deeply emotionally involved." "I considered *Out Cry* a major work," he insists, "and its misadventure on Broadway has not altered that personal estimate of it.[14] Moreover, he was not alone in this estimate; the play was also highly regarded by his agent, Audrey Wood, and by several important theatre people, including Michael Redgrave and Hume Cronyn. Of particular interest for us is the latter's enthusiastic comment that, "in a fashion, there was more revelation of Tennessee in that play than in anything of his that I have ever read."[15]

The action of the play is stripped down almost to allegory. An actor-playwright, Felice Devoto, and his actress sister, Clare, find themselves abandoned by their theatre company (who claim they are insane) in an underground theatre in some unknown, icy northern state, with a performance due before an animally antagonistic audience. There is a clear indication of incestuous feeling between the two. Felice turns a ring on Clare's finger, we are told, as "a sort of love making"; and after a crisis towards the end of the play, they compulsively "embrace—like two lovers meeting after a long separation." Though Clare is unwilling to go on with the performance, Felice insists that they put on a play called *The Two Character Play,* that he is still in process of writing, arguing that they can ad lib when his text runs out.[16] This play-within is also about a brother and sister, also called Felice and Clare, who live in the southern USA and are afraid to leave the family house where their astrologer father killed their mother for wanting to send him to the state asylum, then shot himself.[17] The play-within has the brother and sister reminiscing about their childhood and recollecting their parents' murder-suicide: Clare is looking for the murder weapon, a revolver that Felice (who has also been in the state asylum) has hidden; and they make several abortive attempts to contact the outside world or leave the house, which they recognize as having become their "prison." Felice introduces improvisational material into the play which seems designed to make the brother and sister re-enact their parents' tragic relationship, and Clare desperately keeps evading the implications of this, to a point, just before the end, of completely breaking out of the play-within illusion. The siblings then discover, however, that their audience have left the auditorium; there is no longer anyone backstage; the doors are locked; and the theatre, now also described as a "prison," is getting darker and colder. The only escape left to them is returning into the southern warmth of the play-within-the-play and completing its fatal action—which involves Clare finding the revolver, distracting Felice with soap-bubbles, then shooting him. When the moment comes, however, she finds she cannot go through with it; and Williams comments:

> In both the total play and the play within it, two desperately gallant but hopelessly deviant beings, find themselves, in the end, with no escape but self-destruction, which fails them too.[18]

In the final version of the play (printed in volume 5 of Williams's *Collected Theatre*), Clare tries to shoot Felice and cannot; then Felice tries to shoot Clare and finds it equally impossible; then, the stage direction tells us: "As they slowly embrace, there is total darkness in which THE CURTAIN FALLS." In his notes to the director for this version, Williams says:

There may be no apparent sexuality in *The Two Character Play,* and yet it is actually the *Liebestod* of the two characters from whom the title derives. This fact should be recognized by the director and players, but then it should be forgotten.[19]

Another interesting difference between the final version and the earlier ones is that the sister in the framework (or envelope) play is now made much less attractive than Clare in the play-within: instead of being just fatigued, she is "stoned"; she is coarse and violent in language; and she scratches her brother's face.

That there should be several versions of the play is typical of Williams's method of composition, as was noted earlier; but in this case there seems also an obsessional element involved. Clare says of her brother's script: "as for *The Two Character Play,* when he read it aloud I said to myself, 'This is his last one, there is nothing more after this!' "; and Williams himself told Tom Buckley: "If I live, it'll be my best play. . . . In any case, it'll be my last long play."[20] And though, in fact, he lived to write several plays subsequently, it is nonetheless true that in *The Two Character Play* Williams, who was at the end of his tether, was trying to grapple directly with the two central and inter-locked experiences of his life: his ambiguous, near-incestuous love for his schizophrenic sister, Rose; and his compulsive need for theatre as personal escape and therapy.

We may turn at this point, then, to consider the relation of *The Two Character Play* to Williams's life and other work, circling back through these to a reconsideration of neglected aspects of *The Glass Menagerie.*

III

First, it is necessary to understand the circumstances in which Williams wrote the later play. It was a product of the late 1960s and early 1970s, when he was struggling through a period of almost total psychic collapse brought on by his lover's death, drugs, and theatrical failure. (He later called the 1960s his "stoned age.") In the later 1950s he had undergone a year of intense psycho-analysis with Dr. Lawrence Kubie, who tried to get him to abandon writing and to change his sexual orientation. Not surprisingly, this treatment merely led him even deeper into depression, so another of his doctors, Dr. Max Jacobson, introduced him to "speed" (amphetamines injected into the vein) to get him writing again and to counteract the sleeping-pill and alcohol habits Williams had already contracted. "I took sedation every night," says Williams, "and every morning I took something related to speed, so that I could still write."[21] Inevitably the result was a catastrophic breakdown.

Physically, this took the form of disorientation and frequent falls (as Clare falls down in the final version of the play); mentally, Williams was haunted by a constant unspecific terror ("The fierce little man with a drum within the rib cage," Felice calls it), resulting in bizarre late-night dashes to the nearest airport and paranoid letters to the newspapers about attempts to kidnap or murder him. Finally, in 1969 his younger brother Dakin committed him to three months' severe "cold-turkey" treatment at a psychiatric clinic in St. Louis, a traumatic experience reflected in *The Two Character Play* by references to "State Farm" and "that forbidden word . . . confinement." "Confinement has always been the greatest dread of my life," he says in *Memoirs* (p. 233); "that can be seen in my play *Out Cry*."

The other factor crucial to the play, besides this state of breakdown, is Williams's complex relation to his sister Rose, and his guilt about her institutionalizing and frontal lobotomy. The epigraph for *The Two Character Play* comes from the *Song of Solomon* 4, 12: "A garden enclosed is my sister . . . a spring shut up, a fountain sealed"; and here, of course, is the play's most obvious overlap with *The Glass Menagerie*'s Laura, whose glass unicorn—the symbol of virginity—has its horn snapped off.

The biographical circumstances which lie behind *Menagerie* are so well known that the barest summary of them should suffice. The Williams parents were badly mismatched: a rowdy shoe salesman and the prim daughter of an Episcopalian minister; and Tom and Rose, two years his elder, were raised by Mrs. Williams in their grandfather's various southern rectories while C. C. Williams was on the road. Tom was apparently a normal, aggressive little boy until he fell victim to a severe bout of diphtheria at the age of four, which led to introversion and almost complete reliance on the companionship of Rose, at that time a lively, imaginative little girl. In *Memoirs* (p. 119), Williams says:

> I may have inadvertently omitted a great deal of material about the unusually close relations between Rose and me. Some perceptive critic of the theatre made the observation that the true theme of my work is "incest." My sister and I had a close relationship, quite unsullied by any carnal knowledge. As a matter of fact, we were rather shy of each other, physically. . . . And yet, our love was, and is, the deepest in our lives and was, perhaps, very pertinent to our withdrawal from extrafamilial attachments.

This imaginative symbiosis was intensified by the family's move to St. Louis, where the father's firm had given him a desk job. Both children were horrified by the ugliness and violence of the big Midwestern city, by the relative poverty in which they now had to live—compared to the gentility of their grandfather's rectories—and by their father's noisy, overbearing presence; and Williams (on whom his father was particularly hard) more and more took refuge in his sister's white-painted bedroom with its window-shade drawn down against the ugliness of the alley outside (according to

"Portrait of a Girl in Glass," a savage chow here used to corner and kill cats), where Rose's collection of fragile glass animals represented for her brother "all the small and tender things that relieve the austere pattern of life and make it endurable to the sensitive."[22] However, as Williams recounts in an early short story, "The Resemblance Between a Violin Case and a Coffin" (*Hard Candy* [1954]), this close relationship was disrupted by Rose's arrival at puberty, when—the story suggests—Williams may also have transferred his sexual feelings for his sister to the handsome boy with whom she took her music lessons. Interestingly, an article in *New York,* 25 July 1983, records that at the time of his death Williams was working on a screen-play called *Ladies' Choice,* based on this short story and on another, entitled *Completed,* about the very same event.[23] In part three of one of his poems, "Recuerdo," he movingly records:

> At fifteen my sister
>   no longer waited for me,
> impatiently at the White Star Pharmacy corner
>   but plunged headlong
>   into the discovery, Love!
> Then vanished completely—
> for love's explosion, defined as early madness
> consumingly shone in her transparent heart for a season
> and burned it out, a tissue-paper lantern!
>   . . . My sister was quicker at everything than I.[24]

According to *Memoirs,* Rose was a normal, if highly sexed girl who was driven into schizophrenic withdrawal by the combination of her mother's prudery and her father's appalling social blunders; but Williams also bitterly blamed himself. "It's not very pleasant to look back on that year [1937]," he writes, "and to know that Rose knew she was going mad and to know, also, that I was not too kind to my sister." He tells of her tattling on a wild party he gave during their parents' absence, in resentment of which he hissed at her on the stairs, "I hate the sight of your ugly old face!", leaving her stricken and wordless, crouched against the wall. "This is the cruelest thing I have done in my life, I suspect," he comments, "and one for which I can never properly atone."[25] Later that year Rose was institutionalized, when, according to her brother Dakin, she became "like a wild animal," till their mother authorized one of the first frontal lobotomy operations in America, rendering Rose "a mental vegetable."[26]

As soon as he became successful, Williams took the greatest possible care of his sister: he kept a black-hung shrine to her in his bedroom[27]; he moved her in 1982 to a house next to his own in Key West, under the care of an elderly cousin; and besides the *Ladies' Choice* script he was working on at the time of his death, one of his very last plays, called *Kirche, Kuchen and*

Kinder, is a two-hander about "Miss Rose" and "the Man"—Tennessee Williams himself. Ironically, the connection has continued even after death: Williams was not buried at sea near the spot where Hart Crane jumped to his death in the Caribbean, as he had requested, but rests finally in a cemetery in St. Louis with a vacant plot next to his own waiting for the body of Rose.

It was surely this relationship that helped to establish Williams's homosexuality, with its strong sado-masochistic quality reflecting his belief that love the "Comforter" is also always and inevitably a "Betrayer."[28] Brother-sister incest themes run throughout his work.[29] Besides the four titles already noted, it appears in an early one-act verse play, *The Purification,* where a wife is murdered by her husband for incest with her brother, then both men kill themselves. *You Touched Me!,* a full-length play written in collaboration with Donald Windham, changes its D. H. Lawrence source to show an adopted son (who may, in fact, be the real son) marrying his "sister" after a shy and curiously childlike courtship where he talks of her broken dolls, of little silver bells, and of how gentle his hands are going to be. In the one-act *The Last Goodbye,* it is the introverted brother who cannot leave the family house after he has driven away his desperate, promiscuous sister with the lament: "What happens to kids when they grow up?"[30] And most obviously, in *Suddenly Last Summer* (written in 1958, after Williams's year in psycho-analysis), a young woman is threatened with lobotomy for revealing her male "cousin's" homosexuality to his possessive mother.

Closely related to incest are two other recurrent themes: an obsession with pubescent girls and a delight in androgynous young men. Among the former, one may cite the screen-play *Baby Doll;* Heavenly, the fifteen-year-old whose memory Chance Wayne pursues so despairingly in *Sweet Bird of Youth* (leading to her sterilization and his emasculating); Kilroy's passion for the ever-renewed virginity of Esmeralda in *Camino Real;* and Shannon's self-destructive pursuit of nymphets in *The Night of the Iguana.* Williams's last book of poems was called *Androgyne, mon Amour,* and in an interview with *Playboy* (April 1973), he explained that what attracted him to young men was always an androgynous quality about them. In *The Two Character Play,* the names Felice and Clare seem to have been chosen partly because they are androgynous, and Clare describes Felice himself as having shoulder-length hair like a woman.

Such themes and such a sensibility relate Williams to the late Romantic and Symbolist writers, and it seems appropriate, therefore, that Laura's odd nickname, "Blue Roses" (a play upon "pleurosis"), has been traced to "L'Idéal," a poem from Baudelaire's *Fleurs du Mal.*[31] The destructive incest of brother and sister is explored in many later romantic works,[32] most notably perhaps in Poe's *The Fall of the House of Usher* and Villiers de L'Isle D'Adam's *Axel* (where Axel and Sara are described as two halves of one androgynous whole); and androgyny is a striking aspect of much turn-of-the-century art. But, even beyond this, Williams also shares the "decadent" sensibility's idea of art as a complementary stasis to sexual involution, a related way of resist-ing the devouring rush of time (as in his essay "The Timeless World of a Play"). One of the shrewder comments made about *Out Cry,* in fact, was Clive Barnes's prophecy that the play "will one day be regarded as one of the most remarkable symbolist plays of the late twentieth-century."[33]

IV

This prophecy leads to the next point, however, because we should not jump at too simple a Freudian sexual "solution" to the experience at the root of Williams's art before we consider as well his attitude to writing and, specifi-cally, to theatre. He began to write at the age of eleven, when Rose ceased to be his "other self," and art had always been a form of personal therapy for him. "It was a great act of providence," he says, "that I was able to turn my borderline psychosis into creativity."[34] Writing became the main constant in his life, basic to his sense of identity: "if we're not artists, we're nothing," says Felice, "magic is the habit of our existence"; and Williams claimed that this literally saved his life at the time of his first breakdown in 1935—when, inci-dentally, Rose showed the earliest sign of her own insanity by coming to his room to say: "Let's die together."

The danger of living so intensely by imagination, however, is solipsism; and Williams was always aware of and acutely alarmed by this tendency in himself. Dakin tells a revealing anecdote of his brother aged seventeen, on his first trip to Europe, when Williams had a "waking nightmare" which left him shaking and drenched with sweat, "terrified by the thought of thought, by the concept of the process of human thinking, as a mystery in human life, and it made him think he was going mad."[35]

Besides reflecting the closeness of his link to Rose, therefore, the Clare-Felice relationship in *The Two Character Play* can also be seen in terms of a split in Williams's own existentialist self-consciousness. In psychological terms, it is not just Freudian "incest" that is involved, but also the Jungian problem of "psychic individuation," the self-consciousness's struggle to rec-oncile its sense of separate selves. In Williams, this struggle habitually took the form of a sexual split within himself. "I am Blanche du Bois," he claimed about his most famous heroine; "I think that more often I have used a woman rather than a man to articulate my feelings." Discussing his youthful tendency to blush, he said: "Somewhere deep in my nerves was imprisoned a young girl"—a comment he elaborated in an interview with the *New York Times* in 1975, in which he said he believed there was no person living who "doesn't contain both sexes. Mine could have been either one. Truly, I have two sides to my nature."[36] And a recurrent pattern in Williams's last plays is an unhappily symbiotic couple used as a symbol for the prison of introverted imagination, the ego unable to escape the twin circles of self and family: Miriam and Mark in *In the Bar of a Tokyo Hotel,* for instance; Leono and her brother in *Small Craft Warnings;* or the institutionalized Zelda in *Clothes for a Summer Hotel,* accusing Scott Fitzgerald of having drained away her life to create his art.

This pattern is especially interesting in relation to some of the most recent psychological thinking about incest. Whereas for classical Freudians incest is wholly a sexual issue, for more recent theorists it is a taboo necessary for psychic individuation—the individual's need to separate himself from an overriding attachment to what the jargon calls his primary "love object" (usually the mother, or mother-substitute), with psychosis arising when the boundaries between self and "love object" are not maintained (as Felice and Clare finish each other's sentences and constantly employ "chiasmus"— a grammatical mirror effect—in their sentence structures). The theory is that, at the time when a young child is trying to separate his consciousness of self from his identification with his mother, he becomes prey to a double anxiety: anxiety at losing his sense of identity if he loses his "love object" (hence his constant, obsessive returns to her), yet equally his fear of not attaining full individuation if he does not have the necessary aggression to break away— what the New York psycho-analyst Margaret S. Mahler calls "man's eternal struggle against both fusion and isolation."[37] This anxiety happens at the toddler age, but can recur again and again at later stages; and we remember that at the time of Williams's childhood illness and later in his isolation in St. Louis, Rose was the only person in the world who accepted him without reservation, who shared a secret imaginative world with him, who loved him, and whom he could love with all the emotional intensity of a deeply sensitive and beleaguered child; and this love was Williams's main form of self-assertion against the world before he began to write. Moreover, according to Otto Rank, the *"Geschwester-Komplex"* in later life is particularly a revolt against existential isolation and awareness of death;[38] the idealized sister then becomes a necessary symbol of immortality, the sole guarantee against death of the body and the impermanence of desire which threaten life with meaninglessness.

When it is put into this perspective, one can see that *The Two Character Play* has a Freudian play-within-the-play about imaginative incest, in which the family is the "prison," and a Jungian framework play of solipsism in art, an obsessive recollection and restructuring of the past, in which the theatre is the "prison." In *The Two Character Play,* Felice and Clare share both solipsisms, but in *The Glass Menagerie* earlier, the sister is left to destroy herself in the prison of the home, while the brother, I suggest, is caught just as surely in the prison of memory, his own imaginative inability not to relive the past.

This situation throws doubt on the way Tom Wingfield remembers, however, that arbitrariness of the Memory Play form on which Nolan remarked. As Prenshawe says about the problem of Williams's own use of art as therapy:

> . . . viewing art as an extension of the artist, either for what he is or what he needs, leads solipsistically back to the mortal and flawed being that the artist seeks to transcend. . . . Tom Wingfield casts a magical web over experience, transforming the ordinary and ugly and even painful, into a thing of beauty. But undermining . . . [his] transformations of life into art is [his] . . . (and [his] creator's) lurking doubt that the vision is wholly truthful.[39]

V

Let us return, therefore, for a last, brief look at *The Glass Menagerie,* to see how what we can now recognize as a recurrent Williams pattern was already adumbrated in the situation and technique of his first successful play, so many years before.

To start with, the pattern throws light on the purpose behind Tom's Memory Play. This Memory Play is often spoken of as an exorcism of the past, but, if so, it is no more than an *attempt* to exorcise. It is better understood as an obsessive reliving of the experience in an attempt to come to terms with it, which recurs to Tom against his will, as is clear from the end of his last speech: "Oh, Laura, Laura, I tried to leave you behind me, but I am more faithful than I intended to be." This is the pattern of Yeats's *Purgatory* or Sartre's *Huis clos* (for which Williams expresses admiration in *Memoirs,* p. 149): the pattern of guilty re-enactment.

Similarly, understanding of the pattern throws light on the element of overelaborateness, of slightly false posturing, poeticizing and self-conscious symbol making in some of Tom's framework speeches, especially towards the end. This element is admitted by Williams himself in *Memoirs* (p. 84):

> I agree with Brooks Atkinson that the narrations are not up to the play. . . . Thank God, in the 1973 television version of it, they cut the narrations down. There was too much of them.

Yet as Thomas L. King demonstrates, in the "reading edition" Tom's soliloquies:

> . . . alternate between sentiment and irony, between mockery and nostalgic regret, and they all end with an ironic tag, which, in most cases, is potentially humorous. They show us the artist manipulating his audience, seeming to be manipulated himself to draw them in, but in the end resuming once more his detached stance.[40]

The very sense of "forcing" in the style makes us question the integrity of the speaker, alerting us to ambivalences in his attitude: his wish to justify himself as well as to grieve, his surrender to emotion but at the same time his ironic, self-defensive distancing from it.

And this sense of ambivalence, of wishing to withdraw and deny *at the same time* as to relive and accept, is particularly important for the much maligned projection device. Like the theatricalism of having the characters mime eating or Tom playing the first scene "as though reading from a script," projections such as the sailing vessel with the Jolly Roger which accompanies Tom's dreams of adventure (and links them, incidentally, to Jim's high-school swaggering in *The Pirates of Penzance*) serve to maintain an ironic distance between the early Tom-within-the-play and the later Tom-remembering, through whose presentation the audience must *willy-nilly* experience the play.

Moreover, this device achieves more than reducing the sentimental "nostalgia" which Williams admits in his Production Notes is the "first condition" of *The Glass Menagerie;* its black, occasionally jarring, not-so-funny humour (that in *Out Cry* Williams calls the "jokes of the condemned") also throws light on Tom's mocking, self-protective attitude to the pain he is involuntarily reliving. The exaggeration of projections such as "Annunciation," when the gentleman caller is announced, or "The Sky Falls," when Amanda hears that he is already engaged, is like the obtrusive playing of the Ave Maria by *"the fiddle in the wings,"* in that it both mocks Amanda's self-dramatizing and *also* shows us Tom trying to distance himself from the pain of his feelings of guilt about her.

Moreover, the theatricalism has a further effect. It creates a gap between the commentary of Tom-remembering and the audience's own emotional reactions to events, like that Texas draft in which Tom is made to argue about the play directly with the audience. And this appears most disturbingly in relation to Laura, who is otherwise a wholly sympathetic character without the dimension of absurdity that is clear in Amanda, Jim, and Tom himself. She is given such a parodic dimension, however, by projections like "NOT Jim!" or "Terror," "Ah" followed by "Ha," or "Gentleman caller waving good-bye—gaily," prompting Gilbert Debusscher to protest in his *York Notes* (1982) on the play:

> ... the legends would appear [to be] unintentionally ludicrous and would introduce a dismaying note of parody into the most poignant scenes. ... Fortunately, Eddie Dowling ... sensed how damaging the projections might prove in a play as delicate as *The Glass Menagerie,* and ordered them out. (pp. 64–65)

But suppose this effect was not "unintentional," that the parody was deliberate! Does this not, in fact, reflect very accurately the self-lacerating aggression necessary for the individual who is trying to free himself from too close an emotional dependence on his central "love object"? And is this not what the whole play is about? In his Production Notes, Williams says:

> When a play employs unconventional techniques, it is not, or certainly shouldn't be, trying to escape its responsibility of dealing with reality, or interpreting experience, but is actually or should be attempting to find a closer approach, a more penetrating and vivid expression of *things as they are.* (italics added)

This consideration brings us finally to a reassessment of the end of the play: Tom's command, "Blow out your candles, Laura—and so goodbye," that plunges both of them into the dark. We have seen a similar effect at the end of *The Two Character Play* described by Williams as a *Liebestod* (but one that must not be blatant); and we must associate it with the "holy candles" said to glisten in Laura's eyes, with the fact that the candlesticks came from a church that was struck by lightning, and with the way that the final blackout re-enacts Tom's previous betrayal of the family to darkness when he misappropriated the electricity money—just as his deliberate smashing of his glass at the end, in exasperation at his mother, recapitulates his earlier, accidental smashing of Laura's glass animals and Jim's disfigurement of the unicorn (both light and glass being symbols for Laura herself, who is described as resembling "transparent glass touched with light"). If we take into account, furthermore, the fact that Tom bids Laura put out her own candles, surely what we are faced with at the end is not *only* a regretful, tender and pathetic mood (though, of course, we do have that, very powerfully), but also a ruthless re-enactment of Tom's original violation of his sister's trust, a loving, necessary murder like Othello's "Put out the light," in which the Comforter has turned Betrayer but in doing so has had to kill part of himself. Williams comments on similar ambivalences in the ruthless love of Maggie the Cat by quoting August Strindberg: "They call it love-hate, and it hails from the pit."

There is a shadow round the delicate *Glass Menagerie,* then, that the charm and pathos of the play should not obscure for us. Recognition that it is there makes for a more complex psychological study and also "places" the play more solidly and centrally within Williams's characteristic view of human nature and particularly of love. Appreciating the work of Harold Pinter, Williams commented:

> The thing that I've always pushed in my writing—that needed to be said over and over—[is] that human relations are terrifyingly ambiguous. If you write a character that isn't ambiguous, you are writing a false character, not a true one.[41]

This ambiguity extends to the Tom-Laura relationship, which, far more than the cruder, more obvious relation to Amanda, determines the play's tone and mood; and its main key lies in the expressionistic dramaturgy of *The Glass Menagerie*—the various devices that ironize, distance, and complicate emotional response—which is so often ignored or unjustly dismissed. That dramaturgy anticipates from the first the obsessions and techniques with which Tennessee Williams's career concluded.[42]

Notes

1. Dakin Williams claims that his brother may have been murdered, since the bottle from which the cap came was not found in his hotel room, and it is unlikely that anyone would try to open such a bottle with his teeth: see "Interview with Dakin Williams," eds. Margaret Van Antwerp and Sally Johns, *Tennessee Williams, An Illustrated Chronicle: Dictionary of Literary Biography,* Documentary Series, IV (Detroit, 1984), 404.

2. Cited by John J. Goldman, *Los Angeles Times,* 26 February 1983, and Don Singleton, "Drama Great Tennessee Williams Dead," *New York Daily News,* 26 February 1983, respectively.

3. See Lester A. Beaurline, "The Director, the Script, and the Author's Revisions: A Critical Problem," in *Papers on Dramatic Theory and Criticism,* ed. David M. Knauf (Iowa City, 1969), p. 89; Gilbert Debusscher, *York Notes on "The Glass Menagerie"* (London, 1982), p. 65.

4. Joanne Stang, "Williams: 20 Years After 'Glass Menagerie,' " *New York Times,* 28 March 1965, II:3.

5. I discuss these drafts more fully in "The Composition of *The Glass Menagerie:* An Argument for Complexity," *Modern Drama,* 25 (September 1982), 409–422.

6. See Stang, loc. cit.

7. *Tennessee Williams' Letters to Donald Windham, 1940–1965,* ed. Donald Windham (New York, 1977), p. 94.

8. "The Theater: the Winner," *Time* (23 April 1945), p. 88.

9. Paul T. Nolan, "Two Memory Plays: *The Glass Menagerie* and *After the Fall,*" *The McNeese Review,* 17 (1966), 27–38, rpt. in *Twentieth Century Interpretations of "The Glass Menagerie,"* ed. R.B. Parker (Englewood Cliffs, N.J., 1983), pp. 144–153.

10. There is a similar implication in some of the earlier drafts of Tom's last speech in the play. "A Portrait of a Girl in Glass" also hints at a homosexual attraction between Tom and Jim.

11. See Tennessee Williams, *Where I Live{:} Selected Essays,* eds. Christine R. Day and Bob Woods (New York, 1978), p. 54.

12. Mike Wallace, "Tennessee Williams," in *Mike Wallace Asks: Highlights From Controversial Interviews,* ed. Charles Preston and Edward Hamilton (New York, 1958), p. 20; rpt. in *Tennessee Williams, An Illustrated Chronicle,* pp. 192–193.

13. Claudia Cassidy is quoted in Dakin Williams and Shepherd Mead, *Tennessee Williams: An Intimate Biography* (New York, 1983), p. 308; Peggy Prenshawe, "The Paradoxical Southern World of Tennessee Williams," in *Tennessee Williams: A Tribute,* ed. Jac Tharpe (Jackson, Miss., 1977), p. 17.

14. Tennessee Williams, *Memoirs* (Garden City, N.Y., 1975), pp. 129, 179, 228, 233.

15. Quoted by Dakin Williams and Shepherd Mead, p. 271.

16. Formally, the play is much influenced by such typical off-off-Broadway techniques as "transformations" and the "transflip."

17. There is a similar situation at the end of Williams's novel *Moise and the World of Reason* (1975), where the narrator and the woman artist Moise (who barricades herself from the

"world of reason" by retreating to "a circle of Magic") crouch like Felice and Clare behind closed doors.

18. Quoted from Williams, "Notes for *The Two Character Play*," *Tennessee Williams Review*, 3 (Spring–Fall 1982), 3–5, in *Tennessee Williams, An Illustrated Chronicle*, p. 247.

19. Quoted by Thomas P. Adler, "The Dialogue of Incompletion: Language in Tennessee Williams's Later Plays," *Quarterly Journal of Speech*, 61 (1975), 57, n. 27.

20. Quoted from Thomas Buckley, "Tennessee Williams Survives," *Atlantic*, 266 (November 1970), in *Tennessee Williams, An Illustrated Chronicle*, p. 279.

21. Quoted in Dakin Williams and Shepherd Mead, p. 289.

22. Quoted in Lincoln Barnett, "Tennessee Williams," *Life*, 16 February 1948, p. 118.

23. See Peter Hoffman, "The Last Days of Tennessee Williams," *New York*, 25 July 1983, pp. 42, 44–45.

24. *In the Winter of Cities{:} Poems by Tennessee Williams* (Norfolk, Conn., 1956), p. 80.

25. *Memoirs*, pp. 121–122.

26. Dakin Williams and Shepherd Mead, pp. 63–64.

27. There is a picture of this shrine (dedicated to St. Jude, the patron saint of hopeless cases) in *Tennessee Williams, An Illustrated Chronicle*, p. 355.

28. "The Comforter and Betrayer," in *The Winter of Cities*, p. 44.

29. See John Strother Clayton, "The Sister Figure in the Plays of Tennessee Williams," *Carolina Quarterly*, 12 (Summer 1960), 47–60, rpt. in *Twentieth Century Interpretations of "The Glass Menagerie*," pp. 109–119. A more extreme position is argued by Daniel A. Dervin, "The Spook in the Rain Forest: The Incestuous Structure of Tennessee Williams' Plays," *Psychocultural Review*, 3 (1979), 153–183.

30. A similar transposition of the brother-sister roles is experimented with in one of the Texas drafts of *The Gentleman Caller*.

31. See Cora Robey, "Chloroses–Pâles Roses and Pleurosis–Blue Roses," *Romance Notes*, 13 (1971), 250–251.

32. For views of incest in Romantic and post-Romantic literature, see Eino Railo, *The Haunted Castle* (London, 1927); Mario Praz, *The Romantic Agony* (London, 1954); and Russell M. Goldfarb, *Sexual Repression and Victorian Literature* (Lewisburg, 1970); also J. Hillis Miller, *The Disappearance of God* (Cambridge, Mass., 1973). Bizarre support is lent to such a connection by the fact that in his flat in New Orleans, "there was a large bust of Lord Byron . . . whose lips he sometimes kissed before retiring into a four-poster brass bed." (See Lyle Leverich, "Tennessee Williams' Vieux Carré," *Tennessee Williams Review*, 4 [Spring 1983], 29.) Byron is, of course, a major character in *Camino Real*.

33. Clive Barnes, "Tennessee: a National Treasure," *Stagebill* (Washington, D.C.), February, 1975, p. 27.

34. Quoted by Gene Ruffine, Larry Nathanson, Doug Feiden, "Torment of Tennessee Williams," *New York Post*, 26 February 1983, p. 1.

35. Dakin Williams and Shepherd Mead, p. 25.

36. See *Memoirs*, p. 17; Mel Gussow, "Tennessee Williams on Art and Sex," *New York Times* (3 November 1975), p. 49.

37. See Margaret S. Mahler, *On Human Symbiosis and the Vicissitudes of Individuation* (New York, 1968), and "On the first three subphases of the Separation-Individuation Process," *International Journal of Psychoanalysis*, 53 (1972), 333–338. For a Jungian approach, see Rexford Stamper, "*The Two-Character Play*: Psychic Individuation," in Tharpe, pp. 354–361.

38. See Otto Rank, *Das Inzest-Motiv in Dichtung und Sage* (Leipzig, 1912), pp. 656 ff.

39. Prenshawe, p. 24.

40. See Thomas L. King, "Irony and Distance in *The Glass Menagerie*," *Educational Theatre Journal*, 25 (1973), 214, rpt. in *Twentieth Century Interpretations of "The Glass Menagerie*," p. 85. King drew his insights from having several times acted the role of Tom.

41.   Quoted in Lewis Funke and John E. Booth, "Williams on Williams," *Theater Arts,* 46 (January 1962), 18.

42.   Versions of this paper were presented to the Psychology and Literature Seminar, Toronto, in November 1983, and the Graduate Department of English, University of British Columbia, in February 1984. It is to appear in a new anthology, *Critical Essays on Tennessee Williams,* edited by Robert A. Martin, to be published by G. K. Hall in 1997.

Realism and Theatricalism in
A Streetcar Named Desire

MARY ANN CORRIGAN

On the morning after the premiere of *A Streetcar Named Desire* in 1947, Joseph Wood Krutch commented: "This may be the great American play." From the perspective of more than a quarter of a century later *A Streetcar Named Desire* appears to be *one* of the great American plays. Its greatness lies in Tennessee Williams' matching of form to content. In order to gain sympathy for a character who is in the process of an emotional breakdown, Williams depicts the character from without and within; both the objectivity and the subjectivity of Blanche are present to the audience. In *A Streetcar Named Desire* Williams synthesizes depth characterization, typical of drama that strives to be an illusion of reality, with symbolic theatrics, which imply an acceptance of the stage as artifice. In short, realism and theatricalism, often viewed as stage rivals, complement each other in this play. Throughout the 1940s Williams attempted to combine elements of theatricalist staging with verisimilitudinous plots and characters. His experiments either failed utterly, as in *Battle of Angels* in which neither literal nor symbolic action is convincing, or succeeded with modifications, for instance by the removal of the screen device in *The Glass Menagerie.* In *A Streetcar Named Desire* Williams is in control of his symbolic devices. They enable the audience not only to understand the emotional penumbra surrounding the events and characters, but also to view the world from the limited and distorted perspective of Blanche. The play's meaning is apparent only after Williams exposes through stage resources what transpires in the mind of Blanche.

When the audience meets Blanche, she is at the same stage as Laura of *The Glass Menagerie:* one more of life's frustrating disappointments is enough to insure final retreat from the world. Blanche does not retreat without a struggle; the progress of her struggle determines the forward movement of the play's action. To communicate Blanche's subjective state at each stage of

Reprinted with permission from *Modern Drama* 19 (December 1976): 385–96.

the action, Williams asks in his stage directions for aural and visual effects, some of which distort the surface verisimilitude of the play. Elia Kazan was careful to preserve these elements of stylization when he directed the original Broadway production. He explains: "One reason a 'style,' a stylized production is necessary is that a subjective factor—Blanche's memories, inner life, emotions, are a real factor. We cannot really understand her behavior unless we see the effect of her past on her present behavior."[1] The setting, lighting, props, costumes, sound effects and music, along with the play's dominant symbols, the bath and the light bulb, provide direct access to the private lives of the characters.

Williams' setting is emotionally charged and, as usual, described in great detail in the stage directions. Both the inside and the outside of the Kowalski house appear on stage. The house is in a slum in the old section of New Orleans. The backdrop designed by Jo Mielziner for the original production featured angled telephone poles, lurid neon lights and ornately decorated facades on crumbling structures. Despite its dilapidation, Williams insists that the section "has a raffish charm," especially in the blue light of the sky "which invests the scene with a kind of lyricism and gracefully attenuates the atmosphere of decay." Stanley is at home in this neighborhood and Stella has learned to like it, but its charm eludes Blanche, who says of it: "Only Poe! Only Mr. Edgar Allan Poe!—could do it justice!" Blanche finds the Kowalski environment cramped, foul and ugly, so unlike her childhood home, Belle Reve, "a great big place with white columns." In coming to New Orleans, Blanche is brought face to face with an ugly reality which contrasts with her "beautiful dream." To show the relation between the decadent New Orleans street life and the events inside the Kowalski flat Williams asks that the back wall of the apartment be made of gauze to permit, under proper lighting, a view of the city alley. This wall becomes transparent in the rape scene.

Williams uses costuming, props, and lighting to convey the emotional strength of his characters and to reinforce the dichotomy between Blanche and Stanley. The overwrought, emotionally drained Blanche always wears pastels in half-lights; Stanley, the "richly feathered male bird," appears in vivid primary colors under strong, garish light. Blanche's clothes establish her uniqueness even in her first appearance on stage. Williams writes in the stage directions:

> *Her appearance is incongruous in this setting. She is daintily dressed in a white suit with a fluffy bodice, necklace, and earrings of pearl, white gloves and hat, looking as if she were arriving at a summer tea or cocktail party in the garden district. . . . There is something about her uncertain manner, as well as her clothes, that suggests a moth.*
> (Scene I)

Gerald Weales points out that Blanche's clothes are a characterizing device and a way of separating her from her surroundings: "Blanche is going to be destroyed by the end of the play and Williams wants her first appearance . . . to imply that end. Costume here becomes a way of foreshadowing the events to come."[2] By the time Blanche appears the audience has already met the bellowing Stanley, dressed in work clothes, who hurled a blood-stained package of raw meat at his wife. Stella, despite her surprise, deftly caught the bundle; she has learned to function in this society.

The Poker Night scene also exploits the capacity of light and color to create mood. As he so often does, Williams cites an example from the visual arts as a model for the effect he wishes to create:

> *There is a picture of Van Gogh's of a billiard-parlor at night. The kitchen now suggests that sort of lurid nocturnal brilliance, the raw colors of childhood's spectrum. Over the yellow linoleum of the kitchen table hangs an electric bulb with a vivid green glass shade. The poker players—Stanley, Steve, Mitch and Pablo—wear colored shirts, solid blues, a purple, a red-and-white check, a light green, and they are men at the peak of their physical manhood, as coarse and direct and powerful as the primary colors. There are vivid slices of watermelon on the table; whiskey bottles and glasses.* (Scene III)

Williams' description seems to emphasize the vibrancy of this scene, but Van Gogh's *Night Café*, obviously his model, is harrowing in its luridness, its color contrasts and tilted perspective suggesting moral degeneracy. Surely Williams intends the poker players to be frightening in their physical strength. Primitive tastes and pleasures are the norm in the Kowalski set, and those who fail to conform to this norm have no chance of survival.

Music and other sounds also communicate a sense of the ineluctable primitive forces that operate in the Vieux Carré. From the Four Deuces, a nearby night spot, come the sounds that express New Orleans life: blues, jazz, honky-tonk. Elia Kazan comments on the function of the "blue piano" music which is in the background of much of the action:

> The Blues is an expression of the loneliness and rejection, the exclusion and isolation of the Negro and their longing for love and connection. Blanche, too, is looking for a home, abandoned and friendless. . . . Thus the Blue piano catches the soul of Blanche, the miserable unusual human side of the girl which is beneath her frenetic duplicity, her trickery, lies, etc.[3]

The Blues plays as Blanche arrives in the Vieux Carré and is particularly dominant when she recounts the deaths at Belle Reve (Scene I) and when she kisses the newsboy (Scene V). As Blanche is being led away to the asylum and Stella cries uncontrollably, the music of the blue piano swells (Scene XI). At one point this music catches the soul of Stanley too: when Stella leaves him, and he sobs, "I want my baby," the " '*blue piano*' plays for a brief interval" (Scene III). But normally, the uncomplicated obtrusive rhythms of the honky-tonk express Stanley's personality. This music dominates the rape scene.

There is subjective as well as objective music in the play. Only Blanche and the audience hear the Varsouviana polka, which was played as Blanche's husband shot himself. The music, through its association in her memory with impending death, becomes a symbol of imminent disaster. Blanche hears it, for instance, when Stanley hands her a Greyhound bus ticket for a trip back to Laurel (Scene VIII). The music of the Varsouviana weaves in and out of the scene in which Mitch confronts Blanche with his knowledge of her background. Williams writes in the stage directions: *"The rapid, feverish polka tune, the 'Varsouviana,' is heard. The music is in her mind; she is drinking to escape it and the sense of disaster closing in on her, and she seems to whisper the words of the song"* (Scene IX). In the same scene the polka tune fades in as the Mexican street vendor, harbinger of death, arrives, chanting "Flores para los muertos." Reality in all its harshness and ugliness is epitomized for Blanche in these aural and visual reminders of death. She hears this music too in the last scene, when Stanley and the asylum matron corner her. Williams uses the symbolism attaching to Blanche's frequent bathing in order to further lay bare her inner nature. As an aspect of the visiting in-law joke, Blanche's "hogging" of the bathroom is amusing, and the earthy Stanley's references to his bursting kidneys add to the humor. But the serious symbolism is nevertheless obvious: "Blanche's obsessive bathing is a nominal gesture of guilt and wished-for redemption."[4] Like her drinking, her bathing is an escape mechanism. The ritual cleansing which takes place in the tub restores Blanche to a state of former innocence. Once again she is young and pure in a beautiful world.

The bath is a particularly functional symbol in Scene VII, in which it is used to reveal the dual world of Blanche's existence and the tension between Blanche and Stanley. Stella is setting the table for Blanche's birthday party, to which Mitch, the one person who offers Blanche a genuine possibility for redemption, has been invited. As the scene progresses, it becomes apparent that this birthday will be anything but happy. The festive occasion that falls flat is a staple of drama. Shakespeare, Chekhov, Pinter and Williams use it to intensify the ironic discrepancy between appearance and reality. As Blanche bathes in preparation for the party, Stanley reveals to Stella the particulars of her sister's sordid life. The stage directions read: *"Blanche is singing in the bathroom a saccharine popular ballad which is used contrapuntally with Stanley's speech."* The louder Stanley gets in his insistence upon the undeniable facts about Blanche, the louder Blanche sings in the bathroom. Her song asserts the capacity of the imagination to transform mere facts:

> Say, it's only a paper moon, Sailing over a cardboard sea—
> But it wouldn't be make-believe If you believed in me!
> . . . .
> It's a Barnum and Bailey world, Just as phony as it can be—
> But it wouldn't be make-believe If you believed in me!

When Stanley's recital reaches its climax with the most damning charge of Blanche's seduction of a student, *"in the bathroom the water goes on loud; little breathless cries and peals of laughter are heard as if a child were frolicking in the tub."* Thus the two Blanches are counterpoised. In emerging from the bathroom, Blanche immediately senses the threat that Stanley's world of facts poses to her world of illusions. Her usual contented sigh after the bath gives way to uneasiness: "A hot bath and long, cold drink always give me a brand new outlook on life! . . . Something has happened!—What is it?" Background music reflects her fear: *"The distant piano goes into a hectic breakdown."*

Blanche is as obsessed with lights as she is with baths. Her first request when she comes to the Kowalski home is that the overhead light be turned off; subsequently she buys a paper lantern to cover it. On one level, of course, Blanche's dislike of bright lights is a matter of vanity: dimness hides the signs of aging. But it is clear that the light bulb has a further significance, perhaps unconscious, for Blanche, who says to Mitch: "I can't stand a naked light bulb, any more than I can a rude remark on or a vulgar action" (Scene III). Just as the naked light must be toned down by an artificial lantern, so every sordid reality must be cloaked in illusion. Stanley, on the other hand, likes as much light as possible; the clear cold light of day and the naked bulb reveal to him what is *real* and, therefore, what is *true*. And the *facts* of Blanche's former life, which Stanley assiduously "brings to light" for all to see are necessarily abhorrent to Blanche, who has different standards of truth. Mitch, having been "enlightened" by Stanley, tears the paper lantern from the bulb and demands to take a good look at Blanche.

> BLANCHE. Of course, you don't really mean to be insulting!
>
> MITCH. No. just realistic.
>
> BLANCHE. I don't want realism. I want magic! Yes, yes, magic! I try to give that to people. I misrepresent things to them. I don't tell the truth, I tell what *ought* to be truth. And if that is sinful, then let me be damned for it!—*Don't turn the light on!* (Scene IX)

Being forced to face the kind of reality that she refuses to recognize as significant is the cause of Blanche's breakdown. In the last scene, as Blanche is led away, Stanley tears the paper lantern off the light bulb—he has no use for it—and extends it to her: *"She cries out as if the lantern was herself."* Blanche is as delicate and pathetic as a paper lantern; she cannot deflect the hard light of Stanley's vision of reality.

The scene in which Stanley imposes his vision of reality on Blanche, the rape scene, is comprehended and accepted by the audience largely because of the visual and aural details through which psychological intangibles are made objective. At the beginning of Scene X the audience is aware of Blanche's tenuous emotional state. Her appearance indicates that she is beginning to retreat into her world of illusions:

> . . . she has decked herself out in a somewhat soiled and crumpled white satin evening gown and pair of scuffed silver slippers with brilliants set in their heels.
> Now she is placing the rhinestone tiara on her head before the mirror of the dressing-table and murmuring excitedly as if to a group of special admirers.

Blanche, although revelling in her fantasies, is still capable of distinguishing them from actual events. In the middle of her feigned discussion with her admirers she catches sight of her face in a hand mirror, recognizes it as real, and breaks the mirror. At this point Stanley appears in his "*vivid green silk bowling shirt,*" to the tune of honky-tonk music, which continues to be heard throughout the scene. When Stanley confronts Blanche with his knowledge of her background, the abominable reality that Blanche detests begins to impinge upon her: "*Lurid reflections appear on the walls around Blanche. The shadows are of a grotesque and menacing form. She catches her breath, crosses to the phone and jiggles the hook.*" For Blanche the telephone is an avenue to a better world. When she sought what she called a "way out" for herself and Stella in Scene III, the telephone and telegraph were the means to effect her plan. Again she attempts to escape into a different world by calling her Texas millionaire. But when she can't give a number or an address, the operator cuts her off. Reality again! The stage directions indicate the result on Blanche of this thwarting of her plans: "*She sets the phone down and crosses warily into the kitchen. The night is filled with inhuman voices like cries in a jungle.*" Blanche has been sensitive to sound throughout the play. In the first act she jumped at the screech of a cat; later, when Stanley slammed a drawer closed, she winced in pain. Now "the cacophony that we hear is inside Blanche's head—imaginary sounds and real sounds turned grotesque and horrible by her fear."[5] To make Blanche's mounting fears tangible Williams uses the scrim:

> Through the back wall of the rooms, which have become transparent, can be seen the side-walk. A prostitute has rolled a drunkard. He pursues her along the walk, overtakes her and there is a struggle. A policeman's whistle breaks it up. The figures disappear. Some moments later the Negro woman appears around the corner with a sequined bag which the prostitute had dropped on the walk. She is rooting excitedly through it.

The New Orleans street figures are analogues of all that reality means to Blanche: violence, theft, immorality, bestiality. No wonder she tries to escape it. She returns to the telephone: "Western Union? Yes! I—want to—Take down this message! 'In desperate, desperate circumstances! Help me! Caught in a trap. Caught in—' Oh!" There is no escaping reality now, for its arch crusader, Stanley, is back:

> The bathroom door is thrown open and Stanley comes out in the brilliant silk pajamas. He grins at her as he knots the tassled sash about his waist. . . . The barely audible 'blue

*piano' begins to drum up louder. The sound of it turns into the roar of an approaching
locomotive. . . .*

Blanche reads the meaning of the sounds perfectly: she will be forced to
become part of this world of hot music and lust. Her tormentor teases her
with the spectre of her fears:

> You think I'll interfere with you? Ha-ha!
> *(The 'blue piano' goes softly. She turns confusedly and makes a faint gesture. The inhu-
> man jungle voices rise up. He takes a step toward her, biting his tongue which protrudes
> between his lips.)*

Blanche's gesture of threatening Stanley with a broken bottle is the last and
the easiest of the challenges she poses for him. Springing like an animal at
prey, he catches her wrist: *"The bottle top falls. She sinks to her knees. He picks up
her inert figure and carries her to the bed. The hot trumpet and drums from the Four
Deuces sound loudly."* Blanche's involuntary journey to the depths of sordidness
results in her losing contact completely with any kind of reality. The theatrical devices, aural and visual, which represent not objective occurrence, but
inner action, enable the audience to understand Blanche's ordeal and her
retreat into insanity.

Williams depicts the total defeat of a woman whose existence depends
on her maintaining illusions about herself and the world. Blanche is both a
representative and a victim of a tradition that taught her that attractiveness,
virtue, and gentility led automatically to happiness. But reality proved
intractable to the myth. Blanche's lot was Belle Reve, with its debts and
deaths, and a homosexual husband who killed himself because, for once, her
sensitivity failed her. Blanche's "amatory adventures . . . are the unwholesome
means she uses to maintain her connection with life, to fight the sense of
death which her whole background has created in her."[6] Since "the tradition"
allows no place for the physical and sensual, she rejects this aspect of her personality, calling it "brutal desire." Kazan writes: "She thinks she sins when she
gives into it . . . yet she does give into it, out of loneliness . . . but by calling it
'brutal desire,' she is able to separate it from her 'real self,' her 'cultured,'
refined self."[7]

If Blanche is the last remnant of a moribund culture, Stanley is in the
vanguard of a vital and different society. Even Blanche recognizes his strength
when she says, "He's just not the type that goes for jasmine perfume, but
maybe he's what we need to mix with our blood now that we've lost Belle
Reve" (Scene II). If Blanche's philosophy cannot make room for "brutal
desire," Stanley's comprehends little else. Williams describes him:

> *Since earliest manhood the center of his life has been pleasure with women. . . . He sizes
> women up at a glance, with sexual classifications, crude images flashing into his mind
> and determining the way he smiles at them.* (Scene I)

It is only fitting that Stanley destroy Blanche with sex. As Benjamin Nelson writes, sex "has been her Achilles heel. It has always been his sword and shield."[8]

The conflict between Blanche and Stanley is an externalization of the conflict that goes on within Blanche between illusion and reality. The illusion sustaining her is her image of herself as a Southern belle, a fine, cultured, young lady. The reality is a lonely woman, desperately seeking human contact, indulging "brutal desire" as an affirmation of life. Blanche's "schizoid personality is a drama of man's irreconcilable split between animal reality and moral appearance."[9] This drama is played out not only in Blanche's mind, but between Stanley and Blanche as well. Stanley strips away Blanche's illusions and forces her to face animal reality. In doing so, he demonstrates that reality is as brutal as she feared. She has no choice but to retreat totally into illusion. Thus, the external events of the play, while actually occurring, serve as a metaphor for Blanche's internal conflict.

In pitting Blanche and Stanley against one another, Williams returns to his oft-told tale of the defeat of the weak by the strong. But, for a change, both figures represent complex and morally ambiguous positions. Blanche is far from perfect. She is a liar, an alcoholic, and she would break up the Kowalski marriage if she could. Despite his rough exterior, Stanley genuinely loves and needs his wife, and he cannot be blamed for protecting his marriage against the force that would destroy it. The ambiguity of Blanche and Stanley makes them more realistic than many of Williams' characters, who are often either demons (philistines with power, wealth and influence) or angels (helpless, sensitive, downtrodden artists or women). Although Williams depicts both positive and negative personality traits in Blanche and Stanley, his attitude toward the two characters changes in the course of the play. In the beginning Williams clearly favors Stanley by emphasizing his wholesome natural traits, while dwelling on Blanche's artificiality. But such, we learn, are the deceptive appearances. The more Williams delves into Blanche's inner life and presents it on stage, the more sympathetic she becomes. Stanley's true nature also becomes apparent, in its negative effect upon her psyche, and, in the end, she is the undisputed moral victor.

Kazan's production deliberately emphasized Stanley's positive traits. In his notes on directing the play Kazan specifies that Blanche be presented as the "heavy" at the beginning of the play. Simultaneously, of course, Stanley is to evoke the audience's sympathy. Harold Clurman reports on this aspect of the original production: "Because the author does not preach about him but draws him without hate or ideological animus, the audience takes him at his face value. . . . For almost more than two-thirds of the play, therefore, the audience identifies itself with Stanley Kowalski. His low jeering is seconded by the audience's laughter, which seems to mock the feeble and hysterical decorativeness of the girl's behavior"[10] Clurman, in going on to condemn the attempt to ingratiate Stanley with the audience, overlooks the dramatic value of making Stanley appealing initially. Stanley is, after all, not a monster. He bears remarkable resemblance to the kind of hero that Americans love, the hero of the westerns or the tough detective stories: the gruff masculine pragmatist who commands the adulation of women even as he scorns them for his male companions. That he is not as harmless, as "right" as he seems is precisely Williams' point. The play forces the members of the audience, as well as Blanche, to face "harsh reality," for they learn that what they instinctively admire and view as healthy is really a base egotistical force, destructive of what it cannot comprehend. The audience too moves from illusion to reality. The initial tendency is to resent Blanche and her airs, to applaud Stanley every time he "takes her down a peg." But slowly, as the veil of illusion lifts, both Stanley and Blanche are seen more clearly. Marlon Brando, who played Stanley in the Kazan production and in the movie, was an excellent choice for an appealing Stanley. Irwin Shaw commented on Brando's Broadway performance:

> *He is so appealing in a direct, almost childlike way in the beginning and we have been so conditioned by the modern doctrine that what is natural is good, that we admire him and sympathize with him. Then, bit by bit, with a full account of what his good points really are, we come dimly to see that he is . . . brutish, destructive in his healthy egotism, dangerous, immoral, surviving.*[11]

It is the rape scene that finally reveals the true horror of Stanley. As Blanche is made to face unpleasant reality in this scene, so is the audience.[12]

Williams remains as much as possible within the conventions of verisimilitude in using theatrical devices to reveal Blanche's distorted vision of reality. The audience is, however, aware that baths and light bulbs have a meaning for Blanche apart from their functional existence. The further Blanche retreats from reality, the more Williams distorts the surface realism of the play. The purpose of the transparent wall in Scene I is not to reveal what is actually occurring in the alley, but to provide the necessary milieu for the defeat of illusion and to offer objective correlatives for Blanche's fears. Similarly, the subjective sounds enable the audience to share Blanche's past experiences and her present terrors.

In theme and technique *A Streetcar Named Desire* is, in the words of Henry Taylor, the play "toward which . . . all Williams' work has been heading."[13] The characters of his early one-act plays, of *The Glass Menagerie* and of *A Streetcar Named Desire* who doggedly cling to an imaginative vision of what life ought to be, while resolutely ignoring what life is, are invested with a dignity denied those who accommodate themselves to imperfect existence. The theme of the necessity of illusions lends itself to theatricalist treatment, since the non-objective world, which is far more important to Williams' characters than the objective one, must somehow be made tangible on stage. Williams' use of theatrical devices to objectify thoughts and feelings is much more sophisticated in *A Streetcar Named Desire* than in his hitherto most successful play, *The Glass Menagerie.* In the earlier play Williams thought he needed a screen to depict exact and obvious equivalents for his characters' thoughts. In *A Streetcar Named Desire* he relies more upon the suggestive qualities of costuming and staging to communicate psychological tendencies more subliminal than thought. *The Glass Menagerie*'s musical themes, particularly the sentimental fiddling and the jolly roger tune, reflect not so much the characters' inner lives, as the author's ironic perspective on them. On the other hand, in *A Streetcar Named Desire,* the nightclub music and the Varsouviana convey the emotional states of the characters at each stage of the action.

The realism of *A Streetcar Named Desire* distinguishes it from *Summer and Smoke* (written before, but produced after *Streetcar*), with which it is superficially related. In *Summer and Smoke* the conflict is between two abstractions; in *A Streetcar Named Desire,* it is between two people. The angel, anatomy chart, and divided stage of *Summer and Smoke* simplify Alma and John so that they represent abstract qualities. John, who represents first Body and later Soul, lacks the ambiguity that makes Stanley a good dramatic character and a worthy opponent for Blanche. Stanley is as much a bundle of contradictions as his antagonist. His strength, brutality, and virility are balanced by his vulnerability to Blanche's attacks, his awkward attempts at tenderness, and his need for his wife's approval. The unexpected character changes of *Summer and Smoke,* the "turnabouts" necessary to demonstrate the proposition that Body and Soul are irreconcilable, have no parallel in *A Streetcar Named Desire.* The only event of any significance in *Summer and Smoke,* Alma's transformation, is not depicted on stage; it occurs between the acts. By contrast, Blanche's gradual emotional collapse is presented stage by stage. When Williams can no longer convey the disintegration of her mind by depicting only objective reality, he resorts to distortion of verisimilitude in order to present subjective reality. Blanche does not mechanically move from one extreme to the other; she suffers and undergoes—on stage. The difference between *A Streetcar Named Desire* and *Summer and Smoke* is not, as an occasional critic has suggested, between a melodramatic and a "subtle" presentation of the same action, but between a play that finds adequate expression for the conflicts between and within individuals and one that sidesteps such conflicts completely.

Williams achieves his most successful revelation of human nature in its totality in this play in which he distorts the realistic surface as little as possible and only when necessary. The audience accepts as believable the direct depiction of Blanche's fantasies because the necessary touchstone in recognizable reality is consistently maintained. John Gassner writes: "The solution of the esthetic crisis in the theatre depends on our knowing when and how to combine the resources of realistic and theatricalist artistry."[14] *A Streetcar Named Desire* reveals an unerring sense of when and how to combine realism and theatricalism.

Notes

1. Elia Kazan, "Notebook for *A Streetcar Named Desire,*" in *Directors on Directing,* ed. by Toby Cole and Helen Chinoy (Indianapolis, 1963), p. 364.

2. Gerald Weales, *A Play and Its Parts* (New York, 1964), p. 118.

3. Kazan, p. 371.

4. Joseph N. Riddel, *"A Streetcar Named Desire:* Nietzsche Descending," *Modern Drama,* 5 (Spring, 1963), 426.

5. Weales, p. 106.

6. Harold Clurman, *The Divine Pastime* (New York, 1974), p. 12.

7. Kazan, p. 368.

8. Benjamin Nelson, *Tennessee Williams: The Man and His Work* (New York, 1961), p. 146.

9. Riddel, 425.

10. Clurman, p. 16.

11. Irwin Shaw, "Masterpiece," *The New Republic,* 22 December 1947, 35.

12. The sympathetic bond between the audience and Stanley is not merely the result of Brando's interpretation of the character. Stanley has been played differently, notably by Anthony Quinn, who emphasized the brutality of the character. But even Eric Bentley, who preferred Quinn's performance to Brando's, remarks on the inconsistency that occasionally arose between the text and the interpretation by Quinn (e.g., "When Anthony Quinn portrays Kowalski as an illiterate we are surprised at some of the big words he uses"). He also concedes: "In all fairness, I should admit that when I directed the play myself I could not stop the audience's laughing *with* Kowalski *against* Blanche." *In Search of Theater* (New York, 1947), p. 88.

13. Henry Taylor, "The Dilemma of Tennessee Williams," *Masses and Mainstream,* 1 (April, 1948), p. 54.

14. John Gassner, *Directions in Modern Theatre and Drama* (New York, 1956), p. 138.

The Grotesque Children of *The Rose Tattoo*

LELAND STARNES

That realism should be the convention fundamental to the work of Tennessee Williams is altogether logical. Until his late adolescence, Williams had little opportunity to see any form of theater other than the American cinema, and this form, of course, is firmly grounded in the realistic approach. Even the external shape of Williams's theater shows especially clear evidence of this cinematic influence:[1] a succession of episodes, "fade-outs" and "fade-ins," background music, gauze scrims, and expressive lights focussed to simulate "close-ups"—all devices immediately recognizable as film technique, itself a more poetic kind of realism.

Often clearly aspiring to the conditions of poetry, Williams creates for himself an advantage which is not always available to other dramatists who start from the realistic or naturalistic base: like Synge and O'Casey, he puts his words into the mouths of an essentially imaginative people who speak in the rhythms and colorful imagery of a region favorable to poetry. Even more to the point for our present subject, by staging his dramas in a realm just so much apart from "average" American life as the deep South and by having his characters speak in the distinctive language of that realm apart, Williams succeeds in distancing his plays from the purely realistic mode to a degree sufficient to justify and disguise a certain characteristic exaggeration and distortion of reality which permeates his entire canon. Under the speech of most of his characters there runs the faint but unmistakable thorough bass of grotesque folk comedy. The tone provided by this suggestion of the comic folk tale varies according to Williams's intention, and, accordingly, the success of its effect depends upon the amount of distance he would have us put between the characters and ourselves.

Williams's opening scene in *Orpheus Descending*, for example, is an excellent study of his use of regional elements for these ends; we have only to examine the craftsmanship in this Prologue to an imperfect play to perceive how ingeniously (and how meticulously) this restless perfectionist has always

Reprinted with permission from *Modern Drama* 12 (February 1970): 357–69.

gone about the business of constructing the artistic reality he thought indispensable to the coming to life of his vividly theatrical people.

> The set represents in nonrealistic fashion a general drygoods store and part of a connecting 'confectionery' in a small Southern town. . . . Merchandise is represented very sparsely and it is not realistic. . . . But the confectionery, which is seen partly through a wide arched door, is shadowy and poetic as some inner dimension of the play.[2]

Then immediately, before this nonrealistic background, we hear language of such color that we realize the realm in which our action will take place is indeed very much apart.

DOLLY. Pee Wee!
BEULAH. Dawg!
DOLLY. Cannonball is comin' into th' depot!
BEULAH. You all git down to th' depot an' meet that train! (p. 4)

Pee Wee and Dog, "heavy, red-faced men," verify the initial comic impression with a gag line as they "slouch through . . . in clothes that are too tight for them . . . and mud-stained boots."

PEE WEE. I fed that one-armed bandit a hunnerd nickels an' it coughed up five.
DOG. Must have hed indigestion. (p. 4)

As Pee Wee and Dog go out the door, Beulah begins the play's exposition:

> I wint to see Dr. Johnny about Dawg's condition. Dawg's got sugar in his urine again, an as I was leavin' I ast him what was the facks about Jabe Torrance's operation in Mimphis. (p. 4)

When a few lines later Beulah begins her monologue, which "should be treated frankly as exposition," Williams says, "spoken to audience . . . she comes straight out to the proscenium, like a pitchman. This monologue should set the nonrealistic key for the whole production." (p. 6) The exposition is thus delivered in the idiom of folk comedy and takes advantage of the comedic possibilities in its theatricalist style. Beulah first describes with grim relish the circumstances of Papa Romano's death; as she expounds at some length upon her convictions concerning the faithlessness of most marriages, her manner is that of back-fence gossip. But as she thus prepares a mordantly ironic background for our first view of Lady and Jabe Torrance, the tone of the scene modulates from what at first appeared to be cracker-barrel comedy to the extreme grotesque.

BEULAH.   Then one of them—gits—*cincer* or has a—stroke or somethin'?—The other one—

DOLLY.   —Hauls in the loot? (p. 10)

The comic grotesquery of these women is obviously essential to Williams's initial exposition of both characters and situation. As a kind of comic chorus, they provide not only environmental context in terms of which we are to interpret events, but, in their comic hypocrisy, an objective view of both the appearance and the reality of the principal characters and their predicament as well. When Jabe Torrance, mortally ill with cancer, returns from the hospital they greet him with mendacity the ironic significance of which the audience immediately perceives.

BEULAH.   I don't think he's been sick. I think he's been to Miami. Look at that wonderful color in his face.

DOLLY.   I never seen him look better in my life!

BEULAH.   Who does he think he's foolin'? Ha ha ha!—not *me!* (p. 23)

There are two groups of women, and two women in each group. Williams even arranges their lines so as to verify the comic effect he intends us to see in this visual repetition by having them echo each other's words in almost music-hall style.

BEULAH.   Lady, I don't suppose you feel much like talking about it right now but Dog and me are so worried.

DOLLY.   Pee Wee and me are worried sick about it.

LADY.   About what?

BEULAH.   Jabe's operation in Memphis. Was it successful?

DOLLY.   Wasn't it successful? . . .

SISTER.   Was it too late for surgical interference?

EVA.   Wasn't it successful?

BEULAH.   Somebody told us it had gone past the knife.

DOLLY.   We do hope it ain't hopeless.

EVA.   We hope and pray it ain't hopeless. (*All their faces wear faint, unconscious smiles.*) (pp. 25–26)

We are reminded of T. S. Eliot's similar handling of verbal repetition in *The Cocktail Party* when Julia tells the story of Lady Klootz and her son who could hear the cry of bats. But Williams's use of the device here, of course, is probably intended as comic suggestion of repetition as it is usually heard in the classic chorus.

It is obvious that Williams is nowadays more concerned than ever with this matter of distance between his characters and his audience. The recent unfortunate production of *Slapstick Tragedy* and Williams's own remarks about his intentions in that work indicate that he is in the process of experimentation and is therefore, we should hopefully say, in transition. Some critics have gone so far as to argue that *Slapstick Tragedy* should not have been given professional production. The two short plays are indeed more clearly akin to thumbnail sketches than to finished canvases, and each has been written with baffling incompatibilities of content and style. But whatever the aesthetic shortcomings of this latest effort, we are forced to observe in *Slapstick Tragedy* that Williams again instinctively seeks the freedom from the strictures of photographic realism that grotesque comedy allows him, and his natural antic gifts have always been such that we should be encouraged to believe that it is within the realms of such comedy that he may eventually find the new mode he seeks. *The Rose Tattoo,* which was first produced in 1951, endures as a model of Williams's stylistic integrity, and it is appropriate that such a play should have been chosen for successful revival in the 1966–67 season at New York's City Center. In this surprisingly profound play, Williams of course again resorted to the creation of his own realm and to the writing of the language of that world, both of which provided aesthetic distance for the characters inhabiting that realm and explained or justified their exaggerated behavior. His context was the South again—the Gulf Coast between New Orleans and Mobile—and it was, moreover, an Italian community within that area. We were thus twice removed from "normal" reality, and Williams worked with extraordinary effectiveness within the self-imposed limitations of that reality.

In production, it would be unwise if not impossible to attempt to minimize the distancing effect that the national or regional characteristics of Williams's central characters should have upon an audience. This ethnic identity is manifestly Williams's keystone for the structure of his characters, and in *The Rose Tattoo* he stresses it repeatedly and purposefully in every scene of the play:

> JACK. Mrs. Delle Rose, I guess that Sicilians are emotional people . . .[3]
>
> BESSIE. I'm a-scared of these Wops. (p. 42)
>
> THE STREGA. . . . They ain't civilized, these Sicilians. In the old country they live in caves in the hills and the country's run by bandits. (p. 24)

Williams wants us to see clearly that he is writing about a special people with a special set of given circumstances: "they ain't civilized"; they are "wild," "emotional," "childlike," and they do everything "with all the heart." So it is, then, that our introduction to Serafina Delle Rose takes place in "an interior that is as colorful as a booth at a carnival." Indeed, we cannot avoid noticing the extreme and vivid uses of color; such Van Gogh audacities are apropos for the broader statement that Williams wants to make. Moreover, the set in which Serafina sits is scarcely more colorful than the lady herself. As vivid as a circus poster, she

> looks like a plump little Italian opera singer in the role of Madame Butterfly. Her black hair is done in a high pompadour that glitters like wet coal. A rose is held in place by glittering jet hairpins. Her voluptuous figure is sheathed in pale rose silk. On her feet are dainty slippers with glittering buckles and French heels. . . . She sits very erect, . . . her ankles daintily crossed and her plump little hands holding a yellow paper fan on which is painted a rose. Jewels gleam on her fingers, her wrists and her ears and about her throat. (p. 2)

This, it scarcely need be said, is exaggeration. It is enthusiastic—and not actually terribly extreme—intensification of an already intense person for the purposes of vivid theatrical examination of her being. Quite obviously, the actress entrusted with the performance of such a role should have at least a working knowledge of the bigger, more "operatic" styles of acting and should not, as was unfortunately the case with Maureen Stapleton in both New York productions, be circumscribed by an earthbound naturalism which allows few if any glimpses of the theatrical size ultimately attainable in this characterization. While the Serafina Williams describes has not actually left the realm of naturalism, those characteristics which mark her individuality are stressed to just such a degree that they verge upon or actually become both theatricalist and comically grotesque; and by this preliminary visual presentation of the character and the realm she inhabits, we are alerted to expect the comic incongruity which ensues in her subsequent actions.

And so it is that our introduction to Alvaro Mangiacavallo, Serafina's thematic antagonist, is accomplished in a scene which borders upon farce and which makes heavy use of national characteristic for comedic effect. Alvaro, sobbing in pain and frustration because he has been kicked in the groin during a fight with an irate salesman, flees into the house to hide his shame, and Serafina, weeping in sympathy, offers to repair his torn jacket. The scene is audacious in its comedy—comedy which is, moreover, ingenious as expositional device—as the two characters continue a conversation which would probably be unexceptional if it were not for the fact that each of them is shaking with sobs. "Stop crying so I can stop crying," Serafina says. "I am a sissy," says Alvaro. "Excuse me. I am ashame." (p. 81) At some point in our laughter, however, it might occur to us to ask if perhaps the exaggeration of national or folk characteristic had not been carried to too great an extreme and whether we might have passed altogether into the realm of the stage Italian and from thence into mindless farce. The question, surely, is not as primly academic as might at first appear, as upon its answer depend our interpretation of this play and our evaluation of the spiritual worth of these persons.

Critical reaction to the play at its first appearance in 1951 was such as to provide reason to conclude—at that time, at any rate—that Williams's work here was at least uneven or uncertain. For example, Margaret Marshall, reviewing the play in *The Nation,* said that "in the second act the serious mood quickly evaporates; and the proceedings descend into cheap farce which must be seen to be believed. The absurd and the vulgar contend for place. . . ."[4] Kenneth Tynan, always a great admirer of Williams, found "the play's complex structure—short scenes linked by evocative snatches of music—too poetic for its theme,"[5] and George Jean Nathan simply said that the play was "sensational sex melodrama, pasted up with comedy relief. . . ."[6] Such critics at that time, then, asked whether Williams had not indeed drawn his ironies and exaggerations with too bold a stroke in this play. They apparently assumed that to push the protagonist so far into comic or grotesque incongruity as to make this incongruity his or her dominant dramatic value was to risk making the character so childlike or of such an inferior level of sensibility as to become a target for the destructive laughter of superiority. A playwright of Williams's genre is limited by his protagonist's perception, they believed, and so, then, is the force of his play. *The Rose Tattoo* was thought by many at that time to be a less significant play—"just a comedy"—because Williams had resorted to farcical exaggeration which all but destroyed any serious thematic intent. Some writers went so far as to deny the probability of any really new or valuable insights into the condition of human suffering in the "vulgar farce" of "child-minded Sicilians," and others questioned the likelihood that "the psychological aberrations of the universe can be quickly settled on one big bed."[7] We can enjoy Serafina, they implied, and we can even sympathize with her on occasion, but we cannot see her as representative of anything significant in reality after having laughed at her shenanigans for three acts.

It is interesting and even a little amusing to compare such reactions with those of the writers who received the play with surprised enthusiasm when it was revived at City Center last season. Laughter which had in 1951 been deplored as destructive or emblematic of cheap farce was now seen to be either a mark of the play's timelessness or the work of a skillful director who had managed through perceptive reinterpretation to bring the play up to date. Walter Kerr decided that the play had "outwitted time. Outwitted 16 years, anyway, and likely to improve the score further."[8] Henry Hewes, writing for the *Saturday Review,* perhaps best exemplified this new vision of the play when he said that it "probably was not Mr. Williams's intention to write *The Rose Tattoo* as a grotesque comedy, but that is what this new presentation seems, and that is why it appears not the least bit dated." Hewes said, moreover, that to emphasize the grotesquery, the director, Milton Katselas, concentrated on creating the "wild and irrational" surroundings for Williams's fable, and, as a result, "everything that happens is ironic—so that we laugh at the ridiculousness of the events at the same time that we recognize the characters' agonizedly sincere involvement in them."[9] And yet, in 1951, as Williams waited for his play to open at the Martin Beck Theatre, he had said, "I always thought of [*The Rose Tattoo*] as funny in a grotesque sort of way";[10] and in his famed Preface to the play[11] he had specified grotesquery or "a certain foolery" as the probable stylistic solution for the playwright who would satisfy the peculiar conditions laid down for him by his modern, skeptical audiences.

What Hewes and a surprising number of critics both in 1951 and in 1966 have failed to realize is that comedy is and always has been an essential part of the typical Williams drama. A certain amount of laughter may, or indeed *must,* be at the expense of the Williams protagonist, as it is clear that Williams has always meant us to see that even the noblest human being is often guilty of ridiculous incongruity and is thereby laughable. Most of the modern writers—certainly those of the so-called Absurdist genre—find that they have to reduce the protagonist (when there is one) to imperception in order to make the point they want to make. The concomitant feeling of superiority toward the protagonist in such case is, we recognize, a necessary part of Absurdist technique: we must be kept aloof and at a distance from the characters, because their actions and not the characters themselves are the important things, and our involvement with them as people would serve to establish the existence of values or of a coherence that the play was written to deny. But Williams does not typically concern himself with the faceless protagonist of Absurdist or surrealist farce.[12] In *The Rose Tattoo,* he clearly wanted to acknowledge and accept the limitations imposed upon him by characters of "instinctive"—rather than rational—sensibility, and to see this condition as altogether fundamental to his design. "Our purpose," he said, "is to show these gaudy, childlike mysteries with sentiment and humor in equal measure. . . ." (p. xiv) In any but the most superficial reading of *The Rose Tattoo,* one cannot help but be struck with the frequency of references concerning the childlike qualities of these characters, and most particularly of Serafina and Alvaro. "Their fumbling communication," Williams says, "has a curious intimacy and sweetness, like the meeting of two lonely children for the first time." (p. 88) Serafina, having climbed upon a chair to reach a bottle of wine, "finds it impossible to descend . . . Clasping the bottle to her breast, she crouches there, helplessly whimpering like a child." (p. 83) The acceptance of the childlike characteristics of Williams's characters is not only fundamental to their proper interpretation and performance, but leads as well—almost syllogistically—to comprehension of the symbolism of the play, and from thence, as in any poetic work of integrity, back again to even deeper understanding of the characters. Having once conceded that most of Williams's Romantic symbolism is appropriately akin to association psychology one finds the logic of this statement somewhat nearer to hand.

Thus, by way of penetrating Williams's almost Wordsworthian concept of the importance of the childlike element in Serafina and Alvaro, it is, strangely enough, most pertinent to consider first the significance that he would have us see in the Strega's black goat. Normally an easy "symbol" of sexual desire, the goat makes a significant appearance to objectify Serafina's emotional situation at several pivotal points in the action—once, for example, when Rosario's mistress, Estelle Hohengarten, appears to order the silk shirt; again after Alvaro and Serafina have discovered their attraction for each other in Act II; and as an offstage bleat when Serafina makes her desperate assignation with Alvaro in Act III. The device as staged is grotesquely comic, and each time the goat escapes to run wild in Serafina's backyard the incident begins in farcical pandemonium and evolves finally into a ludicrous parody of a Bacchic procession, with a "little boy . . . clapping together a pair of tin pan lids . . . wild cries of children . . . the goat's bleating . . . and farther back follows the Strega . . . her grey hair hanging into her face and her black skirts caught up in one hand, revealing bare feet and hairy legs." (pp. 98–99)

Having once established an aural connection between the goat and the "wild cries of children," Williams goes on to introduce these child sounds almost as choric amplification at subsequent points when something happens to stir Serafina's wild passion for Rosario. Alvaro unwraps the rose silk shirt, and the cries are heard again; Serafina suffers the desperate urge to smash the urn containing her husband's ashes as a little boy's cries parallel her excitement outside the window. And at the end of Act II when Serafina lifts her eyes to the sky and begs the dead Rosario's forgiveness for believing the "lie" about his infidelity, "a little boy races into the yard holding triumphantly aloft a great golden bunch of bananas. A little girl pursues him with shrill cries. He eludes her. . . . The curtain falls." (p. 101)

Obviously then, the connection between children and goat is more than merely aural. For Williams, their significance is reciprocal and complementary; they are altogether thematic, and as lyrical devices they symbolize or objectify in tangible form both "lyric and Bacchantic impulses" which Williams sees embodied in their purest crystalline state in his Sicilians. *The Rose Tattoo,* he said,

> is the Dionysian element in human life, its mystery, its beauty, its significance. . . . Although the goat is one of its most immemorial symbols, it must not be confused with mere sexuality. The element is higher and more distilled than that. Its purest form is probably manifested by children and birds in their rhapsodic moments of flight and play . . . it is the limitless world of the dream. It is the fruit of the vine that takes earth, sun, and air and distills them into juices that deprive men not of reason but of a different thing called prudence.[13]

Serafina and Alvaro are Italian, and, for Williams, "the Italians [reveal] a different side of human nature than any I [have] ever known. I think Italians are like our Southerners without their inhibitions. They're poetic, but they don't have any Protestant repressions. Or if they do have any, their vitality is so strong, it crashes through them. They live from the heat."[14]

It follows, then, that Williams's portraits of these Sicilians—and particularly that of Serafina—will reveal them as vivid embodiments of these impulses. These are Serafina's special set of given circumstances; she is at the outset, like Williams's Southerner, a more intense person than most, a creature from a realm apart. And, again like Williams's Southerner, being thus unique, she excites Williams with motivation and material for the creation of another intensely theatrical person. As almost pure distillation of those elements of human character most meaningful to Williams she will necessitate from him a bolder stroke of the brush, a more daring use of color, a stronger contrast of light and shade—or, to vary J. L. Styan's metaphor, a wider swing of the pendulum of dramatic balance on both sides of the neutral reality.[15] And as crystallization of those grotesque human characteristics more typically instinctive than rational, more visceral than cerebral, and more childlike than mature, she will inevitably commit certain of the comic incongruities usually attributed to children and will be "criticized" accordingly by the corrective laughter of her "civilized" audiences. Our laughter at Serafina, then, is as Williams would have it: in our very act of laughing we are to verify her freedom from "prudence," "empiric evidence," and "civilization." In the first few pages of the play, this Dionysian freedom is acknowledged immediately as we sense her gusty vitality and her intensely sexual devotion to her husband; we perceive that she is aware of life, that she reaffirms life and rejoices in it, and in so doing she prepares us for laughter that is free and full. Then, as we, the audience, realize that we see a reality above and beyond her limited or childish conception of it, we naturally react to her at first in much the same way that we respond to persons we recognize as being of inferior sensibility; as we realize that she in effect inhabits a world that is out of step or incongruous with "the everyday man's" reality, we criticize her with the laughter of superiority and consider her as by definition comic. Henri Bergson would probably have described her behavior as "mechanical" as she ignores or is unable to recognize fact as it appears before her but rather chooses to continue to act upon the conventions and maxims peculiar to her world, even as they are disproved or denied:

> JACK. It is a hard thing to say. But I am—also a—virgin. . . .
> SERAFINA. *What? No.* I do not believe it.
> JACK. Well, it's true though. . . .
> SERAFINA. You? A sailor? (p. 57)

> SERAFINA. What are you? Catholic?
> JACK. Me? Yes, ma'am, Catholic.
> SERAFINA. You don't look Catholic to me! (pp. 58–59)

And, of course, Serafina's vehement condemnation of her daughter's passion for the young sailor is in ironic—and laughable—contrast to her own concern with sexuality. We soon realize, of course, that this comes about because of the fact that in her own world of intense sexuality she is led to see the same exaggeration in her daughter's world, and she in effect flails out at chimeras which are largely of her own making. Moreover, the incongruous contrast between the enormity of the effort she expends and the size of the problem with which she is dealing—what Freud would term the "quantitative contrast"—causes her to be seen as a grotesquely comic character. Thus, in her eyes, no sailor, regardless of how young, can be innocent; tight trousers must inevitably signify sexual license; a spring dance at a high school is manifestly given for purposes of sensual indulgence; and a school picnic chaperoned by teachers becomes a maenadic orgy: "The man-crazy old-maid teachers!—They all run wild on the island!" (p. 71) So Serafina forces the young man to pledge chastity while kneeling before the shrine to the Virgin—a shrine which she herself has dedicated to sexual love.

The scene at the beginning of Act III in which we see Serafina struggling frantically, "with much grunting," to get the girdle from around her knees before Alvaro arrives is almost pure vaudeville; by Joseph Wood Krutch's definition, our protagonist is here reduced to the status of a clown. Speaking of the typical farcical character, Krutch says that "the climax of our amusement coincides with the climax of his discomfort, or worse. The chief personages in farce usually are—or are put in a situation where they seem to be—clowns. And a clown is a butt, or victim. In high comedy we usually are laughing at ourselves; in farce, at somebody else."[16] But more to the point of our present discussion—in allowing us this glimpse of Serafina, Williams achieves another of his bold critical strokes whereby we are made to scrutinize the protagonist from the objective viewpoint that such grotesque comedy provides.

But to make endless catalogue of Serafina's comic incongruities would profit us but little; most of them could be analyzed, if analysis were needed, by reference to the "quantitative contrast" idea, or some version thereof, and to the Freudian "release of inhibitive energy." In any event, the resulting laughter is gratifying to Williams, as it is in all senses Dionysian. However, the essential fact concerning this laughter has yet to be said. It is simply that having criticized Serafina to such an extent and from such a superior vantage point, we end by retaining a clear image of her dignity and worth: she remains, when all is said and done, a person of some stature and significance. Of course, it must be said that it is altogether indicative of Williams's success in this play that we are able to say of Serafina, after having laughed long and loudly at her, that we recognize her genuine and sizable capacity for love, and that it is in very point of fact this same extraordinary characteristic which is the significant element in her downfall. It is, in a sense, her *hamartia,* her tragic flaw.

In recognizing Serafina's special stature in this respect, we perceive in her being a universal in which we all share, and we sympathize. Even as we are led to laughter by Serafina's extremities of behavior in her loss of control after Rosario's death—

> [Rosa] crouches and covers her face in shame as Serafina heedlessly plunges out into the front yard in her shocking déshabille, making wild gestures. . . . As Serafina paces about, she swings her hips in the exaggeratedly belligerent style of a parading matador. (pp. 28–29)

—we recognize an extremity which is as peculiar to tragedy as it is to comedy. Even as we are made to laugh by the incongruity of her actions—or, as by them we see our own standards of "normal," adult reality reaffirmed—we see the intensity of the grief which alone could cause such behavior; in our very act of laughing we seem almost heartlessly—but how effectively—to verify the extent of this visceral being's feeling. Hers is a love and a grief so great they threaten her destruction; by this fact alone she suggests a greatness, and in that tragic flaw is centered the principal tension of *The Rose Tattoo*.

With Rosario's death, Serafina's predictable reaction was to attempt to continue her worship in as close an approximation to its former pattern as possible. In so doing, of course, she chose to continue in blind devotion to her dead husband and became a prisoner of her own self-deception. Instead of association with living beings, she chose the motionless dummies of the dressmaker; instead of love bestowed on the living, she chose adoration before the ashes of the dead; and instead of actuality and engagement in the present, she chose memory and nostalgia for the past. It is interesting, then, to note that in speaking thus of Serafina, we find her to be another of Williams's variations of the "weak, beautiful people who give up with such grace," and around whom he structures his every play. In terms of Williams's typical character deployment, Serafina is actually a direct descendent of Laura Wingfield in *The Glass Menagerie* and of Alma Winemiller in *Summer and Smoke*. But, on the other hand, like Blanche DuBois, she is an active protagonist rather than a passive, and to her in turn will come thematic antagonists—like Alvaro—who will contest her view of herself and who will thereby provide the means for a gradual, cumulative view of her character.

In our admission that Serafina's remarkable capacity for love triumphs over her more comedic aspects—or, rather, by having us concede that those very childlike characteristics which make her comic also give Serafina stature—Williams succeeds in having us reaffirm for him that fact about human relationships which is woven somehow into most of the work of this avowed Romanticist and which, however phrased, expresses what remains for him man's closest approximation to a dependable absolute: the human being transcends his own pathetic insignificance only when he puts himself aside to love another person. In loving another, Williams would have us see in *The Rose Tattoo,* man most nearly succeeds in conquering the ultimate enemy of all significance, time. Before Rosario's death, Serafina says of her life with him:

> Time doesn't pass. . . . My clock is my heart and my heart don't say tick-tock, it says love-love! (p. 8)

At the end of Act I, however, after Rosario has been killed, Serafina winds her daughter's watch before her shrine, and glaring fiercely at the watch she pounds her chest three times and says:

> Tick-tick-tick! . . . Speak to me, Lady!
> Oh, Lady give me a sign! (p. 64)

With love gone from her life, time's passing and the transience of all meaning are now all she can see.

Then, at the end of the play, when Serafina has re-entered life through the discovery of new love with Alvaro,

> she holds the watch to her ear again. She shakes it a little, then utters a faint, startled laugh. (p. 140)

Time has been arrested for her again, and Williams, the supreme Romanticist, would have us see the stopping of her daughter's watch as significant of Serafina's spiritual rebirth.

> Love is itself unmoving,
> Only the cause and end of movement,
> Timeless. . . .[17]

Notes

1.   See Esther Merle Jackson's excellent study of Williams's form in *The Broken World of Tennessee Williams* (Madison, 1965), pp. 37–42.

2.   *Orpheus Descending* (New York: New Directions, 1958), p. 3. Subsequent quotations from this play will refer to this edition, and pagination will be given in the text.

3.   *The Rose Tattoo* (New York: New Directions, 1951), p. 60. Subsequent references to *The Rose Tattoo* will pertain to this edition, and pagination will be indicated in the text.

4.   "Drama," *The Nation,* CLXII (February 17, 1951), 161–162.

5.   *Curtains* (New York, 1961), p. 264.

6.   *Theatre Book of the Year, 1950–51* (New York, 1951), p. 211.

7.   Walter Kerr, "Theatre," *The Commonweal,* LIII (February 23, 1951), 493.

8.   "A 'Rose' Flowers Anew," New York *Times,* November 20, 1966, Sec. 2, p. 31.

9.   "Theater—Off the Leash," *Saturday Review* (November 26, 1966), 60.

10.   Quoted in Vernon Rice, "Tennessee Williams Writes a Comedy," New York *Post* (February 1, 1951), 36.

11.   "The Timeless World of a Play," pp. vi-xi, esp. p. x.

12.   It is true, of course, that character was not uppermost in Williams's methodology in *Camino Real,* but even in this extraordinary play he depended upon it for some of his most startling scenes. In the "Gnädiges Fräulein" of *Slapstick Tragedy,* his title character vacillates confusingly between surrealism and naturalism and at last founders in ineffectuality for lack of definition; we have the frustrating impression, therefore, of a potentially exciting concept that might have worked but which was either carried too far or not far enough. The explanation in this case, I suggest again, lies in Williams's present and hopefully transient uncertainty concerning point of view and subject matter in his work.

13.   "Tennessee Williams Explains His . . . Comedy, 'The Rose Tattoo,' " *Vogue* (March 15, 1951), 96.

14.   Williams, quoted in Rice.

15.   *The Dark Comedy* (Cambridge, England, 1962), p. 85.

16.   "The Fundamentals of Farce," *Theatre Arts,* XL (July 1956), 92.

17.   T. S. Eliot, "Burnt Norton," *Collected Poems* (New York, 1936), p. 220.

Williams and the Broadway Audience:
The Revision of *Camino Real*

BRENDA MURPHY

Working with the texts of Tennessee Williams's plays is always complicated. Not only did he publish different versions of most of his scripts for reading and acting, he often revised the scripts substantially for new productions between editions. *Sweet Bird of Youth,* for example, appears in one form in *Esquire* in April 1959, in a significantly different form in the "reading version" published by New Directions after the Broadway production in 1959, and in yet another form in the Dramatists Play Service "acting version" that is based on the script as Williams revised it for a Los Angeles production in 1961. Williams even rewrote plays completely several years after they were first produced or published and gave them new names, as in the case of *Battle of Angels* and *Orpheus Descending, Summer and Smoke* and *Eccentricities of a Nightingale,* and *Out Cry* and *The Two-Character Play.*

This notion of the script as a protean thing, changing shape and substance as a play develops, in collaboration with director, designer, actors, producer, and audience, was central to Williams's working method. Because he called attention to it in the published script, Williams's revision of *Cat on a Hot Tin Roof* at the suggestion of director Elia Kazan has become undeservedly notorious. Although he was particularly responsive to Kazan's suggestions, Williams also rewrote his plays at the suggestion of producers, designers, actors, and even critics. In his mind, a script was not finished until it described a production that had taken satisfying shape on the stage and had been apprehended successfully by its intended audience.

At first glance, *Camino Real's* textual history seems uncharacteristically simple. Even its reading and acting versions are virtually identical. As the editor's note in the published versions of the play explains, however, the script that is now read or performed "is considerably revised over the one presented on Broadway . . . three characters, a prologue and several scenes that were

This essay was written specifically for this volume and appears in print here for the first time by permission of the author.

not in the Broadway production have been added, or reinstated from earlier, pre-production versions, while other scenes have been deleted" (9).[1]

A comparison of the published text with the rehearsal scripts at the University of Texas shows that Williams made minor revisions throughout the play before delivering it to New Directions and Dramatists Play Service for publication. He also made several major changes, such as the addition of the prologue and a new block one, providing a new frame for the play through the character of Don Quixote. The audience that saw the play on stage in 1953 was plunged immediately into the "survivor scene" that makes up block two of the published text and, like Kilroy, was left to figure out the world of the Camino Real as best it could. Readers of the play, and subsequent audiences, are provided with a series of clues to the play's world and its meaning that make the experience of confronting *Camino Real* much more comfortable than it was for its original audience.

The 1953 audience heard Gutman's announcement of "Block One on the Camino Real," followed by a hoarse cry. It viewed a dark and rather ponderous set composed of a plaza surrounded by a high wall at the rear and two sides of the street, on one a luxurious hotel and on the other a skid row flophouse, bar, and pawnshop. Several mannequins were seated at tables in front of the luxury hotel, while the plaza was filled with groups of street people whose costumes and makeup were inspired by the paintings of the surrealistic artist Jose Guadalupe Posada. One of the hotel guests stood talking to the mannequins as a figure in rags stumbled onto the stage muttering, "A donde la fuente?" He fell against an old prostitute on the street, who pushed him toward the fountain. Falling flat on his belly, he thrust his hands into the dry fountain and staggered to his feet with a long, desperate cry, "La fuente esta seca!" (21). A dry gourd rattled while the prostitute laughed, the other street people moaned, and the hotel guests watched from the security of the hotel windows, sipping champagne.

As the young man was shot by a policeman and died remembering his lost pony, the hotel proprietor came out on the terrace and talked to the audience, explaining that his hotel guests constantly asked each other, " 'What is this place? Where are we? What is the meaning of—*Shhhh!*' " (22). Jacques Casanova then approached the proprietor, Gutman, and their dialogue made clear that Jacques was short of funds and was waiting for "Mlle. Gautier" to guarantee his tab. Gutman explained that a number of "young explorers" had tried to get out of the Camino Real on foot and failed. As two stylized figures called the Dreamer and La Madrecita appeared, Gutman got on the telephone to a "Generalissimo" to explain that the "forbidden word" was about to be spoken. The Dreamer spoke the word "hermano," brother, to the Survivor, who then died. Then Gutman and a loud, brassy character called the Gypsy began to prepare a fiesta to distract the people from a possible uprising against the martial government.

When Kilroy arrived in the next "block," the Broadway audience of 1953, used to realistic, representational theater, was already as bewildered as Kilroy was by the Camino Real. Like the hotel guests, the audience wanted to know where it was and how to get out of there. The play was clearly not realistic. A symbolic realm was suggested by the name "Camino Real"; by the presence of the archetypal figures La Madrecita and the Dreamer and the legendary figures Casanova and Marguerite Gautier, better known as "Camille"; by the empty fountain and the significance of the word "brother." The first scene appeared to make a political statement, but this was dissipated by the introduction in later blocks of Proust's Baron de Charlus, Lord Byron, and Don Quixote as characters and the allusions to the films *Casablanca, Camille,* and *The Hunchback of Notre Dame* in story lines involving Kilroy's conflict with Gutman, Marguerite's relationship with Jacques, and Esmeralda's exploitation by the Gypsy. The caged bird that Lord Byron carried with him as he ventured off alone into "Terra Incognita" was clearly symbolic, as was Kilroy's golden heart, "the size of the head of a baby," and Lord Byron's allusion to Trelawney's snatching Shelley's heart from his burning corpse.

The system of signification in which Williams's symbolism functioned was far from obvious, however, a problem that had been anticipated from the beginning of the production process by Williams, director Kazan, designer Lemuel Ayers, producer Cheryl Crawford, and everyone else involved in the play's production. As soon as Crawford found it almost impossible to raise the money for this new play by Broadway's most successful playwright-director team, the production team realized that it would have a difficult time reaching the Broadway audience with Williams's symbolic fantasy. Even after several readings and lengthy explanations, the financial people who backed Broadway plays remained confused by *Camino Real* and were very skeptical about its potential to be a hit with the theatergoing public. Later, to measure the play's success at reaching its intended audience, Kazan had assistant Hope Abelson take notes on comments overheard at the New Haven opening and report major areas of confusion. The audience's major questions, predictably, centered on an expectation of realism from the play, or, failing that, an easily definable relationship between the people and events on stage and the symbolic realm they signified. Abelson reported four "big questions" among the crowd at intermission: where is this, when is this, how did the characters get there, and where do they want to go if they don't even know where they are?[2] The reaction of the fairly sophisticated New Haven audience confirmed Kazan's fear that American audiences were going to have trouble with the play's structure, based as it was on thematic development rather than on a "through-line" or single action involving a clear protagonist.

The audience's confusion became a given as the production developed. On 5 March Abelson put her finger on the central problem the production team faced in creating a successful Broadway play. Audience members who walked out, she suggested, seemed to be elderly ladies and businessmen and their wives who resented being confused. She was of course describing the core of the Broadway audience. If these people walked out on the play, it would be impossible to salvage. Trying to head off the confusion problem Williams and Kazan engaged in some carefully placed preproduction education of their anticipated New York audience.

The first effort was a joint interview they gave to Henry Hewes for the *Saturday Review* during the Philadelphia tryout. In his article, Hewes commented that many members of the Philadelphia audience, bewildered by the play, had borne down on the playwright "with questions about the play's meaning that he accepts with a mixture of amusement and amazement. 'You give me another $4.80 and I'll give you a lecture,' he jokes to earnest-minded patrons."[3] In the interview, Williams had given Hewes a lecture on *Camino Real* for free, explaining modestly:

> "I haven't worked these things all out consciously and I never realized they might be confusing until I started reading the play to prospective backers. . . . The theme," says the playwright affably, . . . "is, I guess you could say, a prayer for the wild of heart kept in cages. *Camino Real* doesn't say anything that hasn't been said before, but is merely a picture of the state of the romantic nonconformist in modern society. It stresses honor and man's own sense of inner dignity which the Bohemian must reachieve after each period of degradation he is bound to run into. The romantic should have the spirit of anarchy and not let the world drag him down to its level. Don Quixote, who appears at the end of the play, is the supreme example of the obstinate knight, gallant in meeting ultimate degradation and unashamed at being the victim of his own romantic follies." (32)

Williams also downplayed his use of symbolism in the interview, explaining, "To me, using a symbol is just a way of saying a thing more vividly and dramatically than I could otherwise. . . . However, I don't believe in using symbols *unless* they clarify" (32).

Kazan tried to prepare for avant-garde staging that was unfamiliar to a Broadway audience in 1953. " '*Camino Real* is the most direct subjective play of our time,' " he said. " 'It's Tennessee speaking personally and lyrically right to you. That's one reason we've pulled the audience inside the fourth wall by having the actors frequently speak directly to the spectator and by having some of the exits and entrances made through the aisles of the theatre" (33).

While the play continued to confuse and alienate Philadelphia audiences, Williams and Kazan decided that a direct assault on the New York theatergoing public would be necessary if the play was to have a chance on Broadway. Both Williams and Kazan wrote articles for the New York Sunday papers that appeared on 15 March, four days before *Camino Real*'s New York opening. In his piece for the *New York Times,* subsequently reprinted as the foreword to the play, Williams indicated that he accepted the alienation of some of the audience as inevitable, while he professed not to understand it:

> There have been plenty of indications already that this play will exasperate and confuse a certain number of people which we hope is not so large as the number it is likely to please. At each performance a number of people have stamped out of the auditorium, with little regard for those whom they have had to crawl over, almost as if the building had caught on fire, and there have been sibilant noises on the way out and demands for money back if the cashier was foolish enough to remain in his box. . . . I am at a loss to explain this phenomenon, and if I am being facetious about one thing, I am being quite serious about another when I say that I had never for one minute supposed that the play would seem obscure and confusing to anyone who was willing to meet it even less than halfway.[4]

Williams used the Sunday *Times* article to prepare his New York audiences for the play by explaining some of its more controversial elements as well as hinting to New Yorkers that they wouldn't want to be as provincial as the Philadelphians had been in rejecting his avant-garde work. He explained that the play was "the construction of another world, a separate existence," its people archetypes of "certain basic attitudes and qualities with those mutations that would occur if they had continued along the road to this hypothetical terminal point in it" (5). He stated clearly that "a convention of the play is existence outside of time in a place of no specific locality," but demystified the notion that it was an "elaborate allegory" by comparing it to *Peter Pan*. He wrote that he considered *Camino Real's* appeal to be its unusual degree of freedom, and that his desire was "to give these audiences [his] own sense of something wild and unrestricted that ran like water in the mountains, or clouds changing shape in a gale, or the continually dissolving and transforming images of a dream" (5).

Anticipating the charge that the play was unnecessarily obscure and image-laden, Williams remarked, "We all have in our conscious and unconscious minds a great vocabulary of images, and I think all human communication is based on these images as are our dreams; and a symbol in a play has only one legitimate purpose which is to say a thing more directly and simply and beautifully than it could be said in words" (6–7). Finally, he had a word for "those patrons who departed before the final scene." "These theatregoers may be a little domesticated in their theatrical tastes," he suggested (7).

In this article Williams enlarged on many of the points he had made when Henry Hewes interviewed him and Kazan in Philadelphia two weeks before. He continued his efforts to educate the audience right up until the day before the opening, when he gave an interview to a reporter from the more plebeian *New York Post* that was a vernacular rendering of the *Times* article. After noting that although "an article appearing Sunday in one of the morning newspapers revealed the Williams with fingers on the typewriter keys as vague and high-flown, the talking Williams . . . is simple and direct," the reporter quoted Williams as saying that *Camino Real* "is quite pure and simple in its meanings. . . . There's nothing you can't find in the Gospel. All the people in the play are faced with a terminal situation in their lives, some ultimate crisis. It is a study of people facing a final crisis."[5] It was the man on the street's *Camino Real*.

Kazan's article appeared in the Sunday *Herald Tribune*. Besides defending the presentational device of direct address to the audience, Kazan tried to demystify the complex visual code of the production by explaining in straightforward language the combination of realism and fantasy that was making *Camino Real* difficult for audiences to apprehend:

> Is it a fantasy? It seems not to me. It speaks of the reality underneath 'real' life. . . . I don't know what the scholars will say. I only know that the effort of the play is to make the fantastic events of one man's living today not more remote, not more special, but to somehow illuminate them and make them felt. If life sometimes seems fantastic, the function of poetry is to make it seem 'real' and 'close.'[6]

Having anticipated the charge of obscurity with his notion of realistic fantasy, Kazan went on to counter the charge of pessimism that he assumed was bound to come:

> I feel that this play, being a plea for the size and importance of the individual 'soul,' is finally a step forward into an affirmation. Its beauty is its compassion. Its wisdom is in the tolerance of its morality. Its worth is in this fact: that the author is not anxious to hide something about himself, is trying to say the complex thing and say it just as he feels it.[7]

Unfortunately this careful preparation had little effect on the New York audience. The New York critics were much less open-minded about the play than their provincial colleagues had been. They complained about its obscurity, its intellectual pretension, its symbolism, and its pessimism. Richard Watts of the New York *Post* said *Camino Real* proved that "a talented and ambitious playwright, with an authentic lyric gift, can, by taking great pains and growing studiously pretentious, pick up his own drama and hurl it into oblivion."[8] Another reviewer said that Williams had "knocked himself out being oblique."[9] Walter Kerr complained that Williams was "hopelessly mired in his new love, symbolism."[10] Pervading these complaints was a clear note of anti-intellectualism, stated most overtly by the critic from the *Daily News:* " 'Camino Real' may, indeed, become the darling of self-conscious intellectuals. . . . But don't count on any help from me, because I am not the brainy type."[11]

Some of the negative reaction came not from what the critics didn't understand but from what they thought they did. While none of them saw the play as Williams and Kazan had meant to present it, as a celebration of the romantic bohemian's enduring spirit in a hostile environment, many rejected Williams's vision of life on the Camino Real. The usually sympathetic Brooks Atkinson understood the play's method but not its meaning. Calling it a "cosmic fantasy," he said it contained Williams's "version of truth about human destiny": "Although it is horrifying, it is also pathetic. For it is a world surrounded with death and inhumanity, and decked with the flowers of evil. Even the people who respect Mr. Williams' courage and recognize his talent are likely to be aghast at what he has to say."[12] In his view, "the fantasies that boil through the central plaza of the play have a psychopathic bitterness in them." John Mason Brown, who as a magazine critic had a longer time to think about his response to the play than the first-night critics, concluded:

> On the evidence supplied by 'Camino Real' it would be safe to say that few writers, even in these times when many authors' sole faith is their belief in man's baseness and meanness, have held the human race in lower esteem than Mr. Williams or found the world less worthy of habitation. . . . The world through which Mr. Williams guides us is a sorry mixture of Gehenna, the Kabash seen (and inhaled) at noon, the 'Inferno' as written by Mickey Spillane, and 'Paradise Lost' in a translation by Sartre. . . . In his cosmos man is finished and unworthy of redemption.[13]

The general confusion was blamed on what was seen as Williams's highly inappropriate reliance on symbolism, both verbal and visual. Walter Kerr noted that Williams was "attempting to apply the methods of lyric poetry— the images made of illogical and unexpected combinations, the processes of free association, the emphasis on mythology—to the spoken stage." Kerr objected to the indeterminism of Williams's system of signification: "The poetic imagination must have something realistic to exercise its imagination on, some actuality to serve as a point of departure. 'Camino Real' is all departure and no point. The author is here preoccupied with techniques for getting at truth, without having any particular truth he wants to get at. The play is all method—studiously applied—and method applied to a vacuum."[14] Eric Bentley called the play's style "deliquescent-rococo."[15]

Camino Real's condemnation by the critics was nearly unanimous, and, for the most part, the theater public followed suit. This condemnation inspired a rather heated rebuttal from New York's theatrical and artistic communities, however. After the first-night reviews, which were devastating to Williams, a group of artists and writers signed a "Statement In Behalf of a Poet" which was meant for "that public which in general, does not go to Broadway plays," insisting that "when a major work of dramatic art by some miracle of production manages to appear in the bleak climate of contemporary theatre, we believe this public ought to know about it. . . . *Camino Real* is the finest play Tennessee Williams has yet written ... it is a work of the imagination—romantic, intensely poetic and modern."[16] This statement was signed by Willem de Kooning, Lotte Lenya, John Latouche, Herbert Machiz, Gore Vidal, and Jane and Paul Bowles, among others. Support came from a less likely quarter when Edith Sitwell wrote a letter to the *Herald Tribune* complaining about Walter Kerr's review: "I believe it to be a very great play, written by a man of genius—one of the most significant works of our time."[17] Of nine letters about *Camino Real* printed in the *New York Times* on 5 April, one complained that "Mr. Williams' much-vaunted 'freedom' of form and expression does not seem to include freedom from cliches and tired symbolism . . . Mr. Williams seems to have profited from a poor college course in romanticism."[18] Another called the play "a childish protest against reality." Other writers, however, pointed to an "enthusiastic ovation at the final curtain" and a "cheering and wildly appreciative audience" as evidence of the play's power and significance. The heat and depth of feeling about this play may be difficult to understand outside the context of the early fifties, when Williams's advocacy of bohemianism and his existentialist view of the times was sharply at odds with the prevailing pressures toward conformism, and any suggestion of political oppression by capitalist forces, such as that in the "survivor scene," might bring on charges that the author was a "red." One New Haven critic called *Camino Real* "one of the most controversial plays to hit this village in many seasons. . . . Reaction to this latest Tennessee Williams opus ranged from out-and-out raves for a dramatic feast, to a situation of long time friends not speaking to each other after heated discussions of the play's merits."[19]

With the controversy raging and the majority of both spectators and critics clearly not understanding what his play meant, Williams took steps to remedy the situation. He tried to explain the play to some critics, and he even approached Cheryl Crawford with the idea of making major revisions in the production while it was running on Broadway.[20] In a letter to Walter Kerr, Williams wrote that he thought Kerr's review had ignored the facts that his play was a clear and honest distillation of the world and times we live in, and that it was an earnest plea for fundamental Christian attributes of the human heart through which humanity might still survive.[21]

Kerr replied that while he had seen these two things "after an intolerable amount of post-mortem speculation," the play's meaning was "something which your audience in the theater does not grasp at all—not in any sense."[22] He told Williams about the letters he had received complaining about the play's "defeatism, decadence, despair, and so on," indicating "not that people are appalled at what is actually in the play; but that people are simply not able to get through it to your intention at all." Williams had to acknowledge, Kerr wrote, that the play was not esthetically clear if so many people were completely missing the meaning Williams meant it to convey. Kerr suggested that Williams was mistaken to work so completely within the realm of symbolism. He urged Williams to return to the representational in his art, insisting, "Of course we have to break with the monotonous and prosaic 'literal' realism of our stage; of course we have to find poetic means; of course we have to create a theater of greater insight. But poetic means are not abstract means; breaking with 'literal' realism does not mean breaking with the realistic surface altogether."

Meanwhile, Williams was in Key West, hard at work on revisions for his play. On 31 March, 12 days after *Camino Real*'s New York opening, he wrote to Cheryl Crawford that he was resurrecting a prologue about Don Quixote from an earlier version of the play. This was the source of the prologue that begins the published play, establishing it as a "dream play" and thus placing it clearly within the realm of conventional expressionism. In the new prologue, Don Quixote, dressed as an old desert rat, appears on the stage followed by Sancho Panza. Quixote speaks of "that green country he lived in which was the youth of his heart" (15), where he learned the values of nobility, truth, valor, and "devoir." Sancho explains that he knows where they are, looking at a chart and reading, "Continue until you come to the square of a walled town which is the end of the Camino Real and the beginning of the Camino Real. Halt there . . . and turn back, Traveler, for the spring of humanity has gone dry in this place" (15). The difference between the romantic's "royal road" and the "real road" that he now confronts having been clarified, Quixote takes the chart and continues reading, "There are no birds in the country except wild birds that are tamed and kept in . . . *Cages!*" (15).

In these few lines, Williams took the freely resonant symbols of the play as produced—the marginalized but still questing romantic, the Camino Real, the dry fountain, the caged bird—and gave them specific meanings within the play's system of signification. The reader or spectator need no longer wonder about the meaning of the Camino Real or its symbolic nature. Williams also set up the basic conflict between the pragmatic realist Sancho, who heads back to La Mancha after he learns where he is, and the heroic romantic Quixote, who says, "The time for retreat never comes!" (16). This conflict forms a basis for understanding the difference between characters who try to flee the Camino Real, as Marguerite at first does, and those who confront it, as Lord Byron, Jacques, and eventually Kilroy do.

With the play's fundamental symbolism determined and its thematic conflict established, Don Quixote falls asleep, establishing its theatrical idiom. For the occasional spectator who might be unaware of the conventions of expressionism, Williams has the old knight spell them out: "And my dream will be a pageant, a masque in which old meanings will be remembered and possibly new ones discovered, and when I wake from this sleep and this disturbing pageant of a dream, I'll choose one among its shadows to take along with me in the place of Sancho" (16). This speech foreshadows the ending, in which Kilroy decides to join Don Quixote in his quest, as well as determines the precise nature of the theatrical experience the audience will have in the next 16 scenes. At the end of the prologue and in the new Block One, the character Prudence appears with Jacques, to explain that Marguerite is Camille and to tell her story, which is paradigmatic for all the residents of the luxury hotel.

With this careful preparation, the reader or spectator is far better equipped than the first audience was to apprehend the significance of the events when the Survivor stumbles onto the Camino Real to die and Kilroy arrives to begin his journey of discovery. To make the play's theme clearer, Williams also revised the dialogue, notably Esmeralda's prayer in Block Fifteen, the speech that has most often been quoted to explain the play:

> God bless all con men and hustlers and pitch men who hawk their hearts on the street, all two-time losers who're likely to lose once more, the courtesan who made the mistake of love, the greatest of lovers crowned with the longest horns, the poet who wandered far from his heart's green country and possibly will and possibly won't be able to find his way back, look down with a smile tonight on the last cavaliers, the ones with the rusty armor and soiled white plumes, and visit with understanding and something that's almost tender those fading legends that come and go in this plaza like songs not clearly remembered, oh, sometime and somewhere, let there be something to mean the word *honor* again! (90–91)

In this speech, Williams summarizes the experience of each of his romantic bohemians, clarifying the thematic significance they share. Kilroy, Marguerite, Jacques, Lord Byron, and Don Quixote have all lost their way in the mundane and cruel reality of the Camino Real but have found a way to pursue the ideal of honor again. In the new ending Williams wrote for the play, Jacques and Marguerite come together in an embrace signifying their newly consecrated romantic love while Kilroy follows Don Quixote out as the old knight speaks the closing line: "*The violets in the mountains have broken the rocks!*" (93). The ending is a visual and dialogic answer to Marguerite's earlier pessimism about the power of love to overcome the hostility of the Camino Real: "But tenderness, the violets in the mountains—can't break the rocks!" (64). In revising his ending, Williams made clear to the audience that he agreed with Jacques' answer: "The violets in the mountains can break the rocks if you believe in them and allow them to grow!" (64).

Camino Real closed after sixty performances, a commercial as well as critical failure. Three years after its production, with the 1956 production of *Sweet Bird of Youth* in Coral Gables, Florida, Williams began his custom of trying out each new play in a regional theater, revising it extensively before he involved it in a Broadway production. Williams's revision of *Camino Real* in direct response to its audience's complaints proved to be the foundation for a working method that is the norm for playwrights in the 1990s. For Williams's career the experience was a useful but costly lesson. For the play,

its value is questionable. The revised *Camino Real* is certainly easier to understand than the script that went into production. Its meaning is clearer, its
symbolic system more determined. But something is also lost in giving up the
free play of its earlier signifying system and the unconventionality of its earlier theatrical idiom. "My desire," Williams wrote in the foreword to his play,
"was to give these audiences my own sense of something wild and unrestricted that ran like water in the mountains, or clouds changing shape in a
gale, or the continually dissolving and transforming images of a dream" (5).
The published *Camino Real* lost some of this wildness and freedom to the
restrictions that were necessary to convey its meaning to its intended audience. Tennessee Williams was a playwright, after all, and his art was not personal but public. Through every stage of interaction with director, designer,
producer, actors, and audience, its essence was communication, and communication meant compromise. The published texts of his plays are in a sense
the records of his compromise with the theater, a compromise that was not
always made willingly, but was almost always made, for as Tennessee
Williams well knew, his art would not have survived without it.

Notes

1. *Camino Real* was published in 1953 by New Directions and Dramatists Play Service
and reprinted in *Theatre Arts* 38, (August 1954): 34–65, and volume 2 of *The Theatre of Tennessee Williams* (New York: New Directions, 1972). Because it is the most complete record of
the production, this and following page references are to the Dramatists Play Service version
(New York, 1953).

2. Hope Abelson, "Notes on *Camino Real*" January–March 1953. Billy Rose Theatre
Collection, New York Public Library for the Performing Arts. Unpublished typescript.

3. "Tennessee Williams—Last of Our Solid Gold Bohemians," *Saturday Review* 18
(March 1953): 25–27. Reprinted in Albert J. Devlin, ed., *Conversations with Tennessee Williams*
(Jackson: Univ. Press of Mississippi, 1986), 30. Subsequent page references are to this collec-
tion and appear in the text.

4. Tennessee Williams, foreword to *Camino Real* (New York: New Directions, 1953),
viii–xi.

5. Vernon Rice, "The Talking Tennessee Williams," New York *Post,* Sec. 2, 18 March
1953, 66.

6. Elia Kazan, "Playwright's Letter to the World," New York *Herald Tribune,* Sunday,
15 March 1953, sec. 4.

7. Ibid.

8. Richard Watts, "An Enigma by Tennessee Williams," New York *Post,* 20 March
1953, 62.

9. John McClain, "Williams' Play Baffling to Some," New York *Journal-American,* 20
March 1953, 15.

10. Walter F. Kerr, "Camino Real," New York *Herald Tribune,* 20 March 1953, 12.

11. John Chapman, "Symbols Clash in 'Camino Real,' " New York *Daily News,* 20
March 1953, 63.

12. Brooks Atkinson, "Tennessee Williams Writes a Cosmic Fantasy Entitled 'Camino
Real,' " *New York Times,* 20 March 1953, 26.

13. John Mason Brown, "Seeing Things: The Living Dead," *Saturday Review* 15 (April 1953): 28–30.

14. Kerr, "Camino Real."

15. Eric Bentley, *The Dramatic Event* (New York: Horizon, 1954), 107.

16. Willem de Kooning et al., "Statement In Behalf of a Poet," 1953. Billy Rose Theatre Collection, New York Public Library for the Performing Arts, Mimeographed.

17. Edith Sitwell, letter to the editor, New York *Herald Tribune,* 3 April 1953, sec. 2.

18. "Concerning 'Camino Real,' " nine letters to the drama editor, *New York Times,* 5 April 1953, sec. 2.

19. Clippings file, *Camino Real,* 1953. Billy Rose Theatre Collection, New York Public Library for the Performing Arts. Unidentified clipping.

20. Tennessee Williams, letter to Cheryl Crawford, 31 March 1953. Billy Rose Theatre Collection, New York Public Library for the Performing Arts.

21. Tennessee Williams, draft typescript letter to Walter Kerr, Billy Rose Theatre Collection, New York Public Library for the Performing Arts.

22. Walter F. Kerr to Tennessee Williams, 13 April 1953, *Dictionary of Literary Biography: Documentary Series,* vol. 4, *Tennessee Williams,* ed. Margaret A. Van Antwerp and Sally Johns (Detroit: Gale, 1984), 139.

Blanche DuBois and Maggie the Cat:
Illusion and Reality in Tennessee Williams

DIANNE CAFAGNA

"Humankind cannot bear very much reality," T. S. Eliot once wrote.[1] From the stranglehold of another culture, the tradition of the South, Tennessee Williams in *Where I Live* put it this way: "We're all of us sentenced to solitary confinement inside our own skins."[2] Steeped in this inheritance of "manners" and "mendacity," Williams felt caught within what Hugh Holman has called "a union of opposites, a condition of instability, a paradox."[3] Williams was deeply troubled on one hand by an urge to become part of his society, and on the other by a fear of conforming to the meaningless drudgery of familial obligation. Such a paradox led Williams to dramatize his southern characters' necessary illusions in facing the grim realities of twentieth-century life.

In much of Williams's early dramatic work, this paradox of choice sits squarely on the shoulders of his female protagonists. These women seek a means of survival or escape. From birth Williams's women struggle against an emotional and social tide that prevents any lateral movement. As adults they are thrust unwittingly into the depths of the predatory caste society of the South. To survive they must struggle up like fighting fish against the surface of reality; to escape they must scuttle down the depth of illusion to rock bottom. As Jeanne McGlinn writes, "A woman is presented at a moment when frustration has led to a crisis. She has only two possible ways of acting: to face reality or to retreat into illusion."[4] In portraying the dramatic dilemmas of Blanche DuBois in *A Streetcar Named Desire* and Maggie Pollitt in *Cat on a Hot Tin Roof*, Williams achieves a delicate contrast between a woman who is fortified by illusion and one who risks all stability to "face the crisis and choose to live in the real world."[5]

According to C. W. E. Bigsby, Frank Merlo, Williams's longtime companion, said that Tennessee's personal crisis could be perceived in much the same light—"to bear and finally transfigure the world's impinging chaos."[6] Williams's personal struggle with illusion and reality is clearly illustrated in a 1943 letter to Donald Windham:

This essay was written specifically for this volume and appears in print for the first time by permission of the author.

We all bob only momently above the bubbling, boiling surface of the torrent of lies and distortions we are borne along. We are submarine creatures, for beneath that surface is the world we live in, with its names and labels and its accepted ideas. And over it only is the oxygen unadulterated which we can only breathe in spasms now and again, and the only vision which is pure at all.[7]

In both *Streetcar* and *Cat,* as Bigsby insists, "He [Williams] opted for neither truth nor illusion but for the need to resist. Maggie the Cat uses truth; Blanche illusions."[8] Williams's female protagonists cannot be reduced to formulas. The paradox lies in the very fact that they suffer. Williams understood Blanche's flights of illusion as both a form of suicide at social displacement and an attempt to regain the lost promises of her aristocratic birth. And though Maggie may settle for a place amid the New South, she will not live amid the squalor of an "Elysian Fields."

Blanche is a proud symbol of the doomed aristocratic South refusing to settle for the new industrial squalor. Her rebellion from a new world derives from the Keatsian notion of beauty, an ideal that, though continuously eluding her, keeps her from facing the horrid truth of her life. In contrast, Maggie is, ironically, "the only aristocrat," by Williams's own admission in Donald Spoto's biography,[9] although she is a woman of practical means. She uses beauty as a physical weapon; she uses her good looks to seduce adversaries who live behind illusions. She knows the danger of illusion and falsehood is isolation and helplessness, and, unlike Blanche, she wants her beauty to be tangible and available. Maggie is not interested in the idea of aristocracy and beauty—she is interested in the aristocrats themselves. Whereas Blanche, at the close of *Streetcar,* leaves Stella and Stanley's flat lost in her last beautiful illusion, Maggie hisses down the curtain of *Cat* with the spoils of truth she has extracted from Brick and Big Daddy's beautiful lies.

When Blanche is escorted out by "the kindness of strangers" (*SND,* 178)[10] to the asylum, she has retreated into a deeper state of delusion, has become again the vulnerable southern aristocrat. The irony of that famous line rang for an unforgettable moment in the ears of the late-1940s theatergoing public. No other line of dramatic dialogue is more responsible for marking Williams's place beside fellow realists like Arthur Miller and William Inge. Blanche's exit is afforded to no better than a stranger, yet she preserves her poise because she refuses to insist upon exhuming the buried ugly truths of her illusion as a sanctuary and won't play her trump card as Maggie does at the close of *Cat.*

Blanche's mothlike flight from reality plays itself out in Williams's symbolic tapestry of abstracted imagery. The opening stage directions set this beautiful comparison in motion:

> *She is daintily dressed in a white suit with a fluffy bodice, necklace and earrings of pearl, white gloves and hat. . . . Her delicate beauty must avoid a strong light. There is*

something about her uncertain manner, as well as her white clothes, that suggests a moth. (SND, 5)

Peggy Prenshaw elaborates: "Like Sandra . . . , Blanche, Alma (*Summer and Smoke* and *Eccentricities of a Nightingale*), and even Laura of *Glass Menagerie* represent the last of the southern ladies. Mothlike, sensitive, and fragile in a way that is ultimately self-destructive, they are portrayed as romantic idealists undone by a graceless and callous age."[11] Williams echoes this thought in his *Memoirs:* "Nowadays is, indeed, lit by lightning, a plague has stricken the moths, and Blanche has been 'put away.' . . ."[12] Even in the rape scene, Blanche is adorned in *"a somewhat soiled and crumpled white satin evening gown and a pair of scuffed silver slippers with brilliants set in their heels"* (SND, 151)—as Vivienne Dickson suggests, she is "a tattered moth."[13]

This mothlike vulnerability, what Thomas Adler names her "nostalgic dream of the past,"[14] stands in sharp contrast to Maggie's formidable catlike persona. Maggie will not be crushed:

> *. . . (Shouting above roar of water). . . . {her} voice is both rapid and drawling. . . . has the vocal tricks of a priest delivering a liturgical chant, the lines almost sung, always continuing a little beyond her breath so she has to gasp for another. (CHTR, 17)*

Hailing from no plantation, Maggie accepts the law of the jungle. Afraid of facing her own inner truth, she claws her way through illusions Brick and Big Daddy use to hide from the encroaching reality of mendacity, alcoholism, homosexuality, and death. If she can shed light upon what her enemies fear most, then her fight for truth becomes survival, that "oxygen unadulterated" Williams wrote of to Donald Windham.[15]

While Blanche decorates a shabby room, adorning a lightbulb to escape the reality of mirrors, Maggie gathers up Brick's liquor bottles and turns out "the rose-silk lamp" (CHTR, 173). Maggie rushes catlike at sounds, at doors, at people as if fighting for survival. She brings to light what Blanche must escape—the explosion of reality within her pretty world of deceit. Both women are visitors trying to forge a new home in social worlds that do not welcome them. Yet Blanche's tactics are worn out. She does not hold any longer Maggie's stamina, her embroidered plans wilted over years of loss. Blanche, as even her name suggests, is as Joseph Riddel describes, "the pallid, lifeless product of her illusions, of a way of life that has forfeited its vigor."[16] What lives in her past, Belle Reve, her family's plantation, slightly corrupted over time in translation, means beautiful shore in French.[17]

Following Williams's credo of desire as the opposite of death, Blanche tiptoes through the slums of Elysian Fields, fresh off the streetcar Desire, lugging in her suitcase the memory of a ruined civilization. Though she wishes entry into this primitive realm, she feels battered by exposed truths of her deviant sexuality and failed marriage, collapsing with her homosexual husband's brutal suicide. Unlike Maggie, Blanche can only glimpse these terrible recurring realities, the gunshot that always interrupts the Varsouviana polka in her tortured mind, the urge to confess that has possessed her spirit and severed her from nostalgic dreams of beauty. Although Blanche desperately anticipates the impact of reality with illusion, she, like Maggie, must face the music.

What separates them is Maggie's willingness to face this impact, her willingness to risk all by exposing Brick's tormented inner life and the truth about Big Daddy's cancer. Her animal sexuality makes her appear fearless in the opening scenes of *Cat;* it is a weapon by which she shatters the illusions of beauty Brick cannot. Though in this Maggie is Blanche's opposite, they do share certain excruciating truths. Both women are haunted by the presence of a man who died by their unkindness, each has blood upon her conscience— Blanche for her young husband, Maggie for Brick's close friend and college teammate, Skipper. Maggie, ironically, has gained a degree of control over reality and Brick by her guilty act. Blanche has turned away from reality, believing her cruelty to be a transgression of a Puritan upbringing. Maggie speaks directly of her terrible truth, not with Blanche's cloaked Victorian idiom. In act 1, Maggie teases Brick that his dying father, Big Daddy, lusts for her. Margaret: "I sometimes suspect that Big Daddy harbors a little unconscious 'lech' fo' me . . ." (*CHTR,* 23). This is a marked contrast to Blanche, who could never risk such an acknowledgment, such contemporary sexual openness, and who would never use a term like unconscious—which is far too Freudian and twentieth-century in vernacular. Maggie talks like a warrior, a desperate flirt who does not rely on the illusionary manners of a lady. She uses every inflection her body and voice have to offer. No truth about Skipper or booze or death is too dark for her. Maggie, like cancer, is the harsh reality the Pollitt family must learn to live with. In a family where reality itself is an illusion, she must win Brick back to her bed and secure Big Daddy's rich lands despite her lack of offspring.

If Maggie must trick her husband and in-laws to survive a childless marriage, then Blanche, unmarried, childless herself, must disguise a failed life. She must transform the harsh light of Stella and Stanley's dank apartment— hang her Chinese lantern and with colored paper diminish the wrinkled evidence of age. Blanche (to Mitch): "I can't stand a naked light bulb, any more than I can a rude remark or a vulgar action" (*SND,* 60). As Joseph Riddel has observed:

> Blanche lives in a world of shades, of Chinese lanterns, of romantic melodies that conjure up dream worlds, or perversions turned into illusionary romances, or alcoholic escape, of time past . . . and of Christian morality that refines away . . . the very indulgences that give Stanley's life a vital intensity.[18]

Because of the contrast between her Victorian upbringing and constant romanticizing, because she paints illusion upon the reality of her broken world, she must paradoxically escape farther into the recesses of a lonely isolation that makes it more and more impossible for her to survive, or to know kindness, the great cherished gesture of illusion.

The recurring theme of withdrawal into a world of illusion pervaded Williams's life, not just the lives of his characters. In 1947, Williams had eye surgery that resulted in his wearing, for a time, a gauze mask, giving him, as he writes in *Where I Live,* "the excuse . . . to withdraw from the world behind a . . . mask."[19] As Eugene O'Neill suggested, masks are part of the human attempt to disguise the spiritual, to bury an inner need to seek truth and reality, "starved in spirit by their soul-stifling daily struggle to exist as masks among the masks of the living."[20] Williams asks, in *Where I Live,* "Was Blanche DuBois a liar?"[21] Or is Blanche simply unequipped to make that most tenuous of transfers from the streetcar Desire to the cemetery at Elysian Fields? Jacob Adler puts it this way: "The symbols in *Streetcar* . . . grow out of the reality, not the reality out of the symbols."[22]

The sharp rise of post–Civil War industrialism prevented any true recovery for the South. Blanche in all her ruined pride and transplanted European civility is the illusion of hope Williams wished to rescue from a morally decaying society. Spoto writes that Williams based Blanche on his mother, Edwina, who as an actress played the archetypal "southern belle," erasing from her own personality any manner or figure of speech that wasn't typical of the role. After her marriage to Cornelius Williams (Tennessee's father), she began to affect a "somewhat grand, slightly imperious manner," this in light of rumors of her husband's "misconduct."[23] Edwina, writes Spoto, "knew he [like Stanley] was a . . . drinker, an open gambler . . . ."[24] Later, she would "faint" during his violent outbursts at home, much like Blanche does in the face of Stanley's attack in scene 10: Blanche *"moans . . . sinks to her knees. . . . her inert figure"* (*SND,* 162).

Conversely, Maggie attacks the Pollitts and is seldom passive. She doesn't trust the illusory world in which Blanche floats like a moth toward a candle. She also knows she cannot trust the broken relations she suffers with Brick and Big Daddy, that they will not abandon the lie their lives depend on. Any authentic human interaction, especially Maggie's vengeance for truth, scares these men. Neither can face the ugly truth intimacy might bring. Brick cannot risk uncovering the truth about his friendship with Skipper, and Big Daddy cannot risk uncovering Brick as anything less than his strong heir apparent. Williams juxtaposes Maggie's ironic interrogation into the lives of her men's self-delusion against a backdrop of the sprawling fertile plantation. And it is with a certain irony that she confesses to Brick, "Truth, truth! What's so awful about it? I like it" (*CHTR,* 57). For Maggie, money is that illusory cushion she wishes to curl up on like a cat; only money can soften the blow age will make of her physical beauty.

> You can be young without money, but you can't be old without it. You've got to be old *with* money because to be old without it is just too awful, you've got

to be one or the other, either *young* or *with money,* you can't be old and *without* it.—That's the *truth, Brick.* . . . (*CHTR,* 55)

As Blanche descends into the poverty of Elysian Fields, the ugly truth of her illusions of beauty are stripped away even as Maggie rises toward another illusion—a vision of false beauty she cannot yet afford. Maggie cannot tolerate her brother- and sister-in-law, Gooper and Mae, or their "no neck monster" (*CHTR,* 17) children that epitomize for her the lie of modern American family life. Sy Kahn has suggested that Williams's use of beauty—in Maggie's case, sex—is an act of transformation to reality:

> He [Williams] . . . dramatizes sex as having the hypnotic power to subordinate the consciousness of women and to transform them. . . . In every pound of female flesh the sleeping cell can be quickened. It is at once woman's vulnerability and power.[25]

Maggie demands truth from Brick and Big Daddy through the first two acts of *Cat* to spur herself from apathy and avoid her own painful self-recognition. She fights to transform Brick's contempt for her and expose his boiling contempt for himself. Signi Falk notes, "The marriage break came when Margaret told Brick the truth about his relations with Skipper."[26] Maggie's seduction of Brick's friend reveals her own illusions about her husband. If *Cat* is the story of her triumph over deception, it is also about her victory to rescue herself from the depths of a guilt that threatens Brick and eventually destroys Blanche. Maggie (about Skipper, to Brick):

> It was one of those beautiful, ideal things they tell about in Greek legends, it couldn't be anything else . . . that's what made it so sad. . . . life has got to be allowed to continue even after the *dream* of life is—all—over. . . ." (*CHTR,* 58)

Maggie wants Brick to give up his guilt and his dependency on illusion so that she can, too, paralleling Jamie and Edmond in O'Neill's *Long Day's Journey Into Night.* Nancy Tischler stated that "Maggie . . . is no willing participant in rituals of self-destruction . . . her lust for life takes brutal forms. . . ."[27] Or as Maggie emphatically says: "*I am alive, alive!*" (*CHTR,* 61).

Blanche is afraid of the truth of her life, of reality that encroaches upon an illusion of money and youth. Her truth is that urge for imagination, an action Wallace Stevens suggests "belittles . . . imagination . . . a failure to make use of that liberty . . . what sentimentality is to feeling."[28] Foster Hirsch concludes that Blanche uses beauty or sex to transform herself; it is the movement of desire into a death wish, into self-annihilation.

> Sex is Blanche's way of punishing herself for her betrayal of her homosexual husband. . . . Like Brick in *Cat on a Hot Tin Roof,* who betrays his friend Skipper when Skipper reveals that he is homosexual, she pays dearly for her crime.[29]

Like Brick, Blanche cloaks her sexuality behind a mask of illusion; his booze and self-contempt equal her fake furs, rhinestones, and nostalgic guilt. In this way Blanche also mirrors Maggie. Blanche, too, hisses like "a cat on a hot tin roof" (*SND*, 40) at the lie of happiness modern marriage and family life profess. Unlike Maggie, Blanche has shunted her damaged spirit into a secret place. She clutches her beautiful dreams and in her mind ritualistically replays the Varsouviana during moments of crisis and high reality that explode with her husband's gunshot. She admits the truth of her husband's suicide to Mitch in scene 6, hoping he'll redeem her terrible secret with acceptance. She's even saved the dead boy's love letters like a blanket of remembered beauty to warm the chilling agony she caused. What Blanche fears from all men she reveals to Stanley:

> These are love-letters, yellowing with antiquity . . . (*He snatches them up* . . .) . . . I hurt him the way that you would like to hurt me. . . . (*SND*, 42)

To dramatize Blanche's psychological struggle, to bury the truth her guilt brings relentlessly back to the surface, Williams creates symbols of music and light. The confrontation she will face with Mitch in scene 9 and the rape in scene 10 are both foreshadowed by the act of covering and decorating a naked lightbulb, a reality too harsh and full of glare. In the colored and filtered light, the past and future merge to distort the present to a soft delirium. Morris Wolf writes:

> Williams' patterns of lighting reinforce the suggestion of time-space drift. . . . Drifting among losses, suspended . . . Williams' dramatis personae who look so frequently upon the world as if it were a dream are themselves . . . rendered almost dreamlike by lighting effects.[30]

Driven by her desire for illusion, darkness, and beauty, Blanche is vulnerable to a random influence of mood and memory, which at any moment might visit her seclusion. This motif is most savage and uncompromising in the repetition of the Varsouviana, the music that was playing at the dance before her husband's suicide. The musical chords that play within fractured moments of truth drive her to the verge of madness, into a reality she cannot bear.

> Blanche (to Mitch): . . .—love. . . . It was like you suddenly turned a blinding light on something that has always been half in shadow. . . . But I was unlucky. . . . There was something different about the boy, a nervousness, a softness and tenderness which wasn't like a man's . . . that thing was there. . . . He came to me for help. . . . I didn't find out anything until after our marriage. . . . I'd failed him in some mysterious way. . . . He was in the quicksands and clutching at me. . . . Afterwards we pretended nothing had been discovered. . . . drove out to Moon Lake Casino. . . . (*Polka music sounds, in a minor key faint with distance*). . . . We danced the Varsouviana! . . . Suddenly in the middle

of the dance the boy . . . broke away from me and ran out of the casino. A few minutes later—a shot! (*SND*, 114–15)

The polka compels Blanche's memory to a crescendo, then suddenly dies. Too much truth. Hearing again the gunshot has purged, for a lovely moment, all the fear and ugliness of reality, the impending disaster again shoved back into a schizophrenic haze, the lie of beauty and youth restored like a promise made to herself that these circumstances will never let her keep. Like Violet Venable in *Suddenly Last Summer*, Blanche cannot accept the homosexuality of her dead husband or her own sexual urges. Conversely, Violet cannot understand the homosexuality of her son Sebastian, and, as Gilbert Debusscher writes, "Her actions in the play (*Summer*) are an attempt to hide from the outside world this . . . unacceptable truth."[31] Violet says: "I won't speak again. I'll keep still, if it kills me" (411). As a fallen but mannered aristocrat, Blanche, too, only begrudgingly reveals compromising truths.

The influence of August Strindberg's play *Miss Julie* on *Streetcar* are evident. About *Miss Julie*, Spoto comments, the "tone of sexual antagonism and class conflict, brutal action and terse dialogue . . . especially influenced *A Streetcar Named Desire*."[32] The name Blanche came from Williams's days in a college fraternity, from his housemother, Blanche Eckard. In a letter to Maria St. Just, Williams cites Strindberg on the nature of tortured relations between men and women, truth and illusion: "They call it love-hatred, and it hails from the pit. . . ."[33] Williams also quotes Luigi Pirandello, who wrote, "Truth lies at the bottom of a bottomless well."[34] Brooks Atkinson summarized Williams's effort within this literary tradition after watching *Cat:*

To say that it is the drama of people who refuse to face the truth of life . . . basic truth . . . a delicately wrought exercise in . . . truth.[35]

Maggie, as well, avoids shedding too much light on her own dark secrets by forcing Brick to relive the circumstances of Skipper's suicide. Months after her failed seduction and his confession over the phone to Brick, Skipper had jumped to his death from a hotel window. Unable to come to grips with the possibility that Skipper's suicide was her fault, Maggie is determined at least to awaken Brick from his living death of booze and the lost glory of the Dixie Stars. Brick's dilemma in *Cat* recalls Blanche's in *Streetcar:* how guilt over animal desire leads to liquor or delusion. As Hirsch observes, "The play offers a grim choice to the actual or potential homosexual: he can either kill himself or drink himself into a stupor."[36] With his cynical detachment and crutch, a symbol for his dependence on the past, Brick seems to be in what Williams once called "moral paralysis."

Brick in fact clings so deftly to his illusions and his drink that he serves as the ambiguous center of the play—so much so that in one of Elia Kazan's revised productions, Nancy Tischler writes, "As a result of the change in Brick in the third act of the Broadway version, audiences may leave the theatre suspecting that the whole truth about him has not been told."[37] According to Riddel, Brick, like Blanche, drinks "to induce illusion, to extirpate moral contradictions that stand between her [him] and the pure 'Belle Reve.' "[38] Though it is immediately clear from the first two acts that Brick, like Blanche, is just waiting for the "click in the head" and to turn[ing] the hot light off" (*CHTR*, 100), what is in question is whether he truly loves Maggie, and if he will overcome his fear of the truth about Skipper before Big Daddy dies and his marriage folds. The passionate exchange between him and Maggie helps Brick begin to face the truth:

> BRICK: One man has one great good true thing in his life . . .
>
> MARGARET: . . . I said, "SKIPPER! STOP LOVIN' MY HUSBAND OR TELL HIM HE'S GOT TO LET YOU ADMIT IT TO HIM! . . .—In this way, I destroyed him, by telling him the truth that he and his world which he was born and raised in, yours and his world, had told him could not be told? . . . . Brick, I'm not good. I don't know why people have to pretend to be good, nobody's good. The rich . . . can afford to respect moral patterns . . . but I could never afford to, yeah, but—I'm honest! (*CHTR*, 59–61)

Truth as a dangerous weapon and the effort to maintain physical beauty have long ago buried dreams of beauty in Maggie's disturbed memory and allowed her, unlike Blanche, to move forward into life, to "let it continue."

As Bigsby describes the scene, "The truth of Big Daddy's cancer is kept from him. . . . The play is full of people who lie for one reason or another . . . refuse to acknowledge the truth. The word 'mendacity' echoes throughout."[39] Big Daddy: "Lying, have they been lying?" Brick's reply: "Mendacity is a system that we live in. Liquor is one way out an' death's the other . . ." (*CHTR*, 129). Yet even as *Cat* closes, no one is sure if Brick is ready to face the truth. Perhaps, as Williams wrote in *Where I Live*, "He will go back to Maggie for sheer animal comfort,"[40] which is ironic considering Spoto's appraisal of Brick as a "psychological self-portrait of Williams as idealist."[41]

The Pollitt parents, Big Daddy and Big Mama, were also based on Williams's family. Years after playing the role, Burl Ives recalled to Donald Spoto, "Tennessee told me . . . that he had written this part after his own father."[42] According to Elia Kazan, in his preface to *Five O'Clock Angel*, the character of Maggie is based on Maria St. Just, a close friend and longtime correspondent of Williams.

> If you've read *Cat on a Hot Tin Roof*, you've read the author's portrait of Maria in Maggie—all the qualities he loved in Maria are highlighted there. . . . The truth saves. So does courage. He could count on her for both.[43]

Williams himself said of *Cat* (in a letter to Maria): "Read this. You're in it" and "I'm writing about your spirit—your tenacity to life."[44] This new biographical revelation demolishes the conjecture surrounding many of Williams's characters, but Maggie in particular—that she, like Blanche, is actually the playwright in drag. So much new documentation and biographical data is arising from Williams's letters and manuscripts that such unsupported gossip needs to be dismissed as error or falsehood.

As illusion gives way to terrible reality in scene 9 of *Streetcar,* Blanche is rejected by Mitch. Her reputation in Laurel as town seductress sets the stage for her rape and eventual exile to the madhouse. As Normand Berlin points out, Stella and Stanley's bathroom is a temporary oasis for Blanche, a calm between storms in which she finds a welcome refuge in the steaming bathwater, and an opportunity to

> . . . make clean a sordid past, and . . . perfume . . . her tainted morality. The ritual of the bath is useless . . . it provides only temporary relief. Final relief for Blanche will come only with her death, and she will die, she claims, "on the sea." The difference between the bath water in Stanley's bathroom and the "ocean as blue as my lover's eyes" is the distance between Blanche's hellish present and her image of a heavenly death.[45]

Blanche tells Mitch, "I don't want realism. I want magic! . . . I misrepresent things to them [people]. I don't tell the truth, I tell what *ought* to be truth. . . . *Don't turn the light on!*" (*SND,* 145).

Blanche's confrontation with Stanley in scene 10 adds up finally to much more than a brutal feud between in-laws. On an historical level, Williams is pitting Blanche with her broken beer bottle like the last vestiges of a lost southern gentry against a vulgar but cruelly industrious generation of Stanleys wearing silk pajamas. This confrontation with Stanley pours too much light over Blanche's dark world, animating a festering reality that will push her into an irretrievable abyss of self-delusion. As Mary Ann Corrigan has stated,

> Blanche's involuntary journey to the depths of sordidness results in her losing contact completely with any kind of reality. . . . Williams depicts the total defeat of a woman whose existence depends on her maintaining illusions about herself and the world. . . . Reality proved intractable to the myth.[46]

Ironically, Blanche, unlike Alma in *Summer and Smoke,* withdraws into the decayed parlor of the old southern aristocracy with unexpected dignity. Whereas Alma gives up her dreams of beauty to become a whore at a train station, Blanche surrenders entirely to dreams and their promised salvation at the hands of strangers. Her obliteration is thus oddly distracted. Before going to the madhouse she says, "I can smell the sea. . . . I will be buried at sea sewn up in a clean white sack and dropped overboard—at noon—in the blaze of summer—and into an ocean as blue as . . . my first lover's eyes!" (*SND,* 170).

If this moment of dignity amounts to an unexpected and graceful exit for Blanche with her illusions intact, then the closing scene of *Cat* is very nearly a thematic reversal. Just as Blanche is allowed an ironic escape to the madhouse, Williams gives Maggie, too, a kind of realistic victory. At the close of *Cat,* Maggie has exposed the fraudulent lives of each member of the Pollitt family and seems to have evaded her guilt over Skipper's death. The great irony of *Cat* and of Maggie's characterization comes with her lie of pregnancy, which, unlikely as it is, feeds Big Daddy's and Big Mama's appetites for illusion. And perhaps the 1955 theatergoing public's need for illusion also, with her triumph over the Pollitts, Big Daddy's land, and Brick's deadened passion. Maggie (to everybody): "Announcement of life beginning! A child is coming, sired by Brick and out of Maggie the Cat!" (*CHTR,* 167).

In characteristic style, Williams has the last laugh in *Cat* through Maggie's clever endgame and Brick's last-minute heroics. Thus Maggie, like Blanche, is shown mercy, a way out of an impossible situation through the grace of illusion and lies. This final touch of larceny from Williams gives *Cat* and the characterization of Maggie a sharp and authentic undertone, a deeper sense of dramatic realism. As Brick has admitted earlier, "Who can face the truth?" (*CHTR,* 127). And as the curtain falls Maggie and Brick ironically square off:

MARGARET: Oh, you weak people, you weak, beautiful people!—who give up with such grace . . .

BRICK: . . . Wouldn't it be funny if that was true? (*CHTR,* 173)

Notes

1. T. S. Eliot quoted in George Niesen, "The Artist against the Reality in the Plays of Tennessee Williams," in *Tennessee Williams: A Tribute,* ed. Jac Tharpe (Jackson: Univ. Press of Mississippi, 1977), 493.
2. Tennessee Williams, *Where I Live: Selected Essays,* ed. Christine Day and Bob Woods (New York: New Directions, 1978), 76.
3. Hugh Holman quoted in Peggy W. Prenshaw, "The Paradoxical Southern World of Tennessee Williams," in *Tennessee Williams: A Tribute,* ed. Jac Tharpe (Jackson: Univ. Press of Mississippi, 1977), 5.
4. McGlinn, Jeanne M., "Tennessee Williams' Women: Illusion and Reality, Sexuality and Love," in *Tennessee Williams: A Tribute,* ed. Jac Tharpe (Jackson: Univ. Press of Mississippi, 1977), 510–11.
5. Ibid., 511.
6. C. W. E. Bigsby, *A Critical Introduction to Twentieth Century American Drama,* vol. 2, (Cambridge: Cambridge Univ. Press, 1984), 131.
7. Donald Windham, ed., *Tennessee Williams' Letters to Donald Windham, 1940–1965* (New York: Holt, 1976), 93.
8. C. W. E. Bigsby, *A Critical Introduction to Twentieth Century American Drama,* vol. 2 (New York: Cambridge: Cambridge Univ. Press, 1984), 131.

9.   Donald Spoto, *The Kindness of Strangers: The Life of Tennessee Williams* (Boston: Little, Brown, 1985), 199.

10.   Quotations from Williams's plays are cited in the text with the abbreviations listed here. Page numbers in parentheses follow each. *SND: A Streetcar Named Desire* (New York: New Directions, 1947). *CHTR: Cat on a Hot Tin Roof* (New York: New Directions, 1955).

11.   Prenshaw, "Paradoxical Southern World," 12.

12.   Tennessee Williams, *Memoirs* (New York: Garden City, 1983), 125.

13.   Vivienne, Dickson, "*A Streetcar Named Desire:* Its Development through the Manuscripts," in *Tennessee Williams: A Tribute,* ed. Jac Tharpe (Jackson: Univ. Press of Mississippi, 1977), 157.

14.   Thomas Adler, *A Streetcar Named Desire: The Moth and the Lantern* (Boston: Twayne, 1990), 31.

15.   Windham, *Tennessee Williams' Letters,* 93.

16.   Joseph N. Riddel, "*A Streetcar Named Desire:* Nietzsche Descending," in *Modern Critical Views: Tennessee Williams,* ed. Harold Bloom (New York: Chelsea House, 1987), 16–17.

17.   Since "belle" is the feminine form of the adjective "beautiful" in French, whereas "reve"—"dream"—is a masculine noun, it seems likely that the estate was originally called Belle Rive—"beautiful shore." Felicia Hardison Londré, *Tennessee Williams* (New York: Ungar, 1979), 85.

18.   Riddel, "Nietzsche Descending," 17.

19.   Williams, *Where I Live,* 18.

20.   Eugene O'Neill, "A Dramatist's Notebook," in *American Spectator,* January 1933, 122.

21.   Williams, *Where I Live,* 72.

22.   Jacob Adler, "Tennessee Williams' South: The Culture and the Power," in *Tennessee Williams: A Tribute,* ed. Jac Tharpe (Jackson: Univ. Press of Mississippi, 1977), 40.

23.   Spoto, *Kindness of Strangers,* 9.

24.   Ibid., 13.

25.   Sy Kahn, "Baby Doll: A Comic Fable," in *Tennessee Williams: A Tribute,"* ed. Jac Tharpe (Jackson: Univ. Press of Mississippi, 1977), 301.

26.   Signi Falk, *Tennessee Williams* (Boston: Twayne, 1961), 104.

27.   Nancy M. Tischler, "A Gallery of Witches," in *Tennessee Williams: A Tribute,"* ed. Jac Tharpe (Jackson: Univ. Press of Mississippi, 1977), 507.

28.   C. W. E. Bigsby, *A Critical Introduction to Twentieth Century American Drama,* vol. 2 (New York: Cambridge Univ. Press, 1984), 22.

29.   Foster Hirsch, *A Portrait of the Artist: The Plays of Tennessee Williams* (Port Washington, N.Y.: Kennikat, 1979), 32.

30.   Morris P. Wolf, "Casanova's Portmanteau: *Camino Real* and Recurring Communication Patterns of Tennessee Williams," in *Tennessee Williams: A Tribute,"* ed. Jac Tharpe (Jackson: Univ. Press of Mississippi, 1977), 270.

31.   Gilbert Debusscher, "Minting Their Separate Wills: Tennessee Williams and Hart Crane," *Modern Drama* 26 (1983): 470.

32.   Spoto, *Kindness of Strangers,* 39.

33.   Maria St. Just, *Five O'Clock Angel: Letters of Tennessee Williams to Maria St. Just, 1948–1982* (New York: Knopf, 1990), 110.

34.   Ibid.

35.   Brooks Atkinson quoted in *Tennessee Williams on File,* ed. Catherine M. Arnott (London: Methuen, 1985), 41.

36.   Hirsch, *Portrait of the Artist,* 48.

37.   Tischler, "A Gallery of Witches," 210.

38.   Riddel, "Nietzsche Descending," 18.

39.   Bigsby, *Twentieth Century American Drama,* 82.

40. Williams, *Where I Live,* 73.

41. Spoto, *Kindness of Strangers,* 200.

42. Spoto, 198.

43. Elia Kazan, preface to *Five O'Clock Angel: Letters of Tennessee Williams To Maria St. Just, 1948–1982* (New York: Knopf, 1990), ix.

44. Ibid., 107.

45. Normand Berlin, "Complimentarity in *A Streetcar Named Desire,*" in *Tennessee Williams: A Tribute,* ed. Jac Tharpe (Jackson: Univ. Press of Mississippi, 1977), 99–100.

46. Mary Ann Corrigan, "Realism and Theatricalism in *A Streetcar Named Desire,*" in *Essays on Modern American Drama,*" ed. Dorothy Parker (Toronto: Univ. of Toronto Press, 1987), 33.

The Rebirth of *Orpheus Descending*

KIMBALL KING

A theatregoer who sees six or seven plays consecutively is tempted to con-nect these works to a powerful theme which links seemingly disparate mate-rials. For example, during the 1988 to 1989 season in London the "theme of the artist" appeared to me to be the theatre's prevailing obsession. From a stylized revival of Noel Coward's *The Vortex* and an ingenious adaptation of Stoppard's radio play *Artist Descending a Staircase* to Alan Ayckbourn's futuris-tic *Henceforward* or the Royal Shakespeare Company's latest production of *The Tempest,* the nature of art and the dilemma of the artist (his ethical and aes-thetic problems) were core issues. *Orpheus Descending,* the revival of which offi-cially opened on Wednesday, 14 December 1988, is Tennessee Williams's most powerful assessment of the artist's role in the theatre and in society and an appropriate representation of the late playwright's achievement. Now that Margaret Ramsey Ltd., agents for theatre luminaries such as Ayckbourn, Edward Bond, Howard Brenton, Caryl Churchill, Christopher Hampton, David Hare, and many other of England's most distinguished playwrights, represents Williams's estate, theatregoers will expect to see serious revivals of his dramas in any given "season."

Orpheus Descending was the first production of a new theatre group orga-nized by Peter Hall under the aegis of Triumph Theatre Productions, which are owned by an American and an English producer, Duncan Weldon and Jerome Minscoff respectively. The company will hold a three-year tenancy at the Haymarket Theatre. The second production of the group, shown in fact at the Cambridge Theatre, was a highly acclaimed version of *The Merchant of Venice,* which cast Dustin Hoffman as Shylock. Peter Hall, one of the world's most brilliant and precocious directors (he was in charge of the Royal Shake-speare Company before he reached thirty), resigned as director of the National Theatre two years ago, but his new enterprise suggests that his career is now moving into another major phase. In at least the first two pro-ductions he appeared to be combining classic theatrical materials (Williams

Reprinted with permission from *The Tennessee Williams Literary Journal,* vol. 1, no. 2 (Winter 1989–90): 18–33.

and Shakespeare) with famous actors, Hoffman as Shylock and Vanessa Redgrave in *Orpheus Descending*. The high-powered combination of famous authors and superstars insured the commercial success of the "new" Peter Hall company; but it is, of course, Hall's innovative staging and intuitive sense of effective timing that gained critical acclaim. Irving Wardle, writing of the opening night *Orpheus* in the *Times,* entitled his review "Magnificent Tennessee" and praised Hall's direction of *Orpheus* (and *Camino Real* many years ago), noting that it "reawakens the primary response to this generous, funny, death-haunted writer." When Hall was interviewed about *Orpheus* in November, he commented that "it is not a naturalistic piece—played naturalistically, it is embarrassing." He added, "Failure to understand this on the part of previous directors may account for the play's lack of success in Boston and London in the Fifties." This apparently simple insight may be the largest single factor in explaining the play's successful revival.

Appropriate, innovative staging, famous actors, the playwright's elevation to the status of classic modern artist, all contributed to audience enthusiasm for a once despised play. Director Peter Hall credits his actors with revitalizing the Williams script, noting that Jean Marc Barr as Val Xavier (the Orpheus figure) had just "the right style, accent, rhythm," and that the role of Lady Torrance (Eurydice) was "a God-given part for Vanessa. She has something of a Madonna about her but she is a frustrated Italian, too," apparently referring to, among other things, her Italian accent and her passionate, "Mediterranean" manner. Irving Wardle's enthusiastic review of opening night commented favorably on the casting of the principals as well, especially praising Redgrave. He spoke first of "the naked emotional force and sense of danger that are this actress' hallmark." Her gradual unthawing, her reversions to suspicions and anger, and her death offer the greatest acting I have seen for many a day. Wardle also praised the "erotic choreography" of the ensemble, "the sound score . . . minutely judged," which "locates the action simultaneously in the actual and the mythological world." A desired surrealistic quality was added as well by Allison Chitty's sets, which are formed from "a huge honeycomb of decaying timber."

The recent triumphant revival of *Orpheus Descending* surprised critics and vindicated the author who had been obsessed with some form or other of this play during most of his adult life. In 1936, more than half a century before the recent London production, Mummers, a little theatre group in St. Louis, had produced *The Fugitive Kind,* a play which, although it bore no relation to *Battle of Angels* or *Orpheus Descending,* introduced the title Williams would choose for the film version of *Orpheus Descending* in 1960. *Battle of Angels,* completed after Williams had received a one thousand dollar Rockefeller fellowship, was produced in Boston in 1940 by the Theatre Guild. Audience outrage, among other factors, contributed to the Guild's withdrawal of the play from its repertory and a printed apology to its subscribers for presenting it in the first place. Nevertheless, its script was the unofficial first version of the play which has so recently earned widespread critical approval. The present script has not been altered in any major way since 1957 when an extensively revised *Battle of Angels* returned as *Orpheus Descending* and the play again failed both in Boston, with cries of boredom rather than anger from indifferent audiences, and later in London.

As Leonard Quirino has noted, *Battle of Angels* and *Orpheus Descending* "read together . . . reveal a highly respectable reason for their commercial and aesthetic failure: the author's frantic ambition to make each of them a compendium of almost everything he believed about life and its artistic reflection in drama" (43). A movie version called *The Fugitive Kind* earned some critical approbation in 1960, though the venture was commercially unsuccessful. Williams lived to see *Battle of Angels* restaged by the Circle Repertory Company at the Circle Theatre in New York on 3 November 1974, where it was subscribed for thirty-two performances, but like so many artists, the majority perhaps, he never saw a favorite work accorded the worth he believed it possessed, in spite of the success of numerous theatrical and cinematic ventures which interested him less.

Historically there has been a critical evolution in the appraisals of Williams's appeal. Lyrical and symbolic drama are now often preferred to realism and naturalism, candid explanations of sexual attitudes and political controversy no longer shock experienced audiences, and a writer who reevaluates gender roles in society commands immediate respect. I believe that *Orpheus Descending* has been consistently undervalued by those who failed to notice that it contained Williams's most honest and comprehensive view of his personal aspirations as an artist and of the purposes of art. It may be the most eloquent indicator of his particular contribution to modern drama.

An unpopular play by a famous playwright is an anomaly which provokes inquiry into the author's vision of the world and his role as an artist depicting that world, especially when its revival elicits an enthusiastic response from previously skeptical critics. To understand why attitudes toward *Orpheus Descending* have changed, it is helpful to place Williams in the broader context of twentieth century American theatre. Writers before Williams had examined Southern topics and settings in their plays with a harsh realism, in particular, Paul Green's *House of Connelly* and Lilian Hellman's *The Little Foxes,* which examined class structure and race relations in a region transformed from a primarily rural to an increasingly industrial economy. Two later authors made a greater impact on the world's evaluation of the Southern experience: Margaret Mitchell and Williams. Despite its popularity as a novel, it was doubtless the movie version of Mitchell's *Gone With the Wind* which presented the most enduring and romantic vision of antebellum life. Williams's theatre audiences were drawn from too narrow a social and economic range to influence international opinion, but the movie version of *A Streetcar Named Desire* (and later *Cat on a Hot Tin Roof* and *Suddenly Last Summer*) established the gothic horror of modern Southern life in the public imagination. Even Nobel Prize winner William Faulkner, a more impressive writer than Mitchell or even Williams, did not influence the masses to as great an extent. When a version of Faulkner's *The Hamlet* was filmed under the title *The Long Hot Summer,* it was transformed by the actors and the director into the Williams genre.

Williams on the screen was clearly less surreal than Williams on stage. Part of the audience delight in his movies derived from a conviction that the author had captured the decadence and depravity of Southern life. While audiences were shocked by the supposed "realism" of his characters and settings, they failed to appreciate his classical allusions and metaphors, which were generally underplayed and unnoticed. If, as Signi Falk and others have suggested, the 1950s were arid years for Williams, it is only because audiences required psychological and sociological naturalism. In addition, ideas and techniques of the French absurdists were beginning to permeate the theatre. Traumatized by the war years, French authors, in particular, used the stage to depict a barren, meaningless universe. American authors were never entirely successful when they conveyed this message. Edward Albee, more than any other writer, had, by the end of the 1950s and through the 1960s, led a kind of American "absurdist" movement. Yet it is radically different from its French counterpart. *The Zoo Story, The American Dream,* and *The Sandbox,* all by implication offer suggestions for a better society, a more responsible citizenry. Although the themes of these plays are universal, they are rooted in time, place, and social class unlike their European counterparts.

Williams's use of myth and symbolism was never fully appreciated during his lifetime. It took, perhaps, America's loss of innocence in the Vietnam War, the women's movement with its attack on stereotypical sexual roles, and sophisticated advances in literary theory to make his work truly accessible. The playwright's personal identification with the mythical Orpheus is comparable to the use of symbolic spokesmen by other American artists. Edgar Allan Poe had seen himself as Israel, a Mohammedan angel, "who sang wildly well," and Ralph Waldo Emerson was clearly Uriel, an angel whose brilliance dazzled the "stern old war-gods" of the Harvard Divinity School. Walt Whitman appropriately saw himself as a latter-day Columbus, a genuine historical figure but one who played a "mythic" role in the creation of the New World. Williams's choice of the Orpheus legend to represent his longings is comparable to T. S. Eliot's use of the Herculean myth in *The Cocktail Party.* Williams's and Eliot's Greek heroes both have the advantage of being pagan figures whose lives paralleled Christ's in that by birth they were part god and part man, they descended into the underworld, and they were ultimately resurrected. I believe Orpheus mirrors Williams's tragic-romantic view of his own life and desires—a genius with a song to sing who loses his wife Eurydice (possibly his sister Rose), descends into Hades to retrieve her, escapes but leaves her behind, and finally, although he has avoided the clutch of Hades, is ultimately torn to shreds by the sex-starved Bacchantes, who hate him for spurning all other women: artist, hero, secret incestuous lover, a thwarted romantic victim, despised and sacrificed because of his sexual preference. Williams, not, I believe, intentionally blasphemous, conceived of his mission as an artist, like Christ's as a divinity, as intended to spread a doctrine of love and to extend a hand to society's outcasts; he anticipated both a tragic, premature death (although he lived to be seventy-one) and achieved immortality in his art.

The legend of Orpheus is also ideally suited to the writer's Manichaean vision of the ongoing struggle between the forces of light and darkness on earth. Once, according to this ancient philosophy, light was consigned to heaven, while hell was plunged in eternal darkness. Man inhabited a world where the forces of light and dark were engaged in a ceaseless battle but where the exponents of each were attracted to the qualities of the other. Following the day of judgment, the forces of light will prevail over darkness once again. In *Battle of Angels* and *Orpheus Descending,* Williams makes frequent references to noises in the sky or in rooms overhead in which fierce battles between good and bad "angels" are being waged. Val, Myra/Lady, Vee Talbot and Cassandra/Carol are all good angels but doomed to at least earthly defeat. Orpheus/Val, who nearly triumphs over Pluto's reign of darkness, is nevertheless irresistibly tempted to look upon darkness since he breaks his promise to Pluto and turns back, thereby losing his right to bring Eurydice-Lady with him. Several centuries of Christian believers were followers of the Persian theologian Mani, although eventually his philosophy was condemned as heretical. Part of Williams's cosmology descends from the American Transcendentalists, who from Emerson through Whitman were tempted to merge pagan and Christian traditions into a universal romantic philosophy. The Orpheus/Christ synthesis implied the possibility of a reunited classical and Christian universe.

In another manifestation "Orpheus Descending" is a poem which appears in Williams's 1956 volume of poetry, *In the Winter of Cities.* It attests not only to the author's absorption in the Orpheus legend but also suggests, as *Battle of Angels* and *Orpheus Descending* the play do not, that the Eurydice figure who is called Myra and Lady Torrance respectively in the stage productions may be connected in his imagination with his sister Rose. This "Eurydice" is trapped in her underworld partially because she is crippled: "How could a girl with a wounded foot move through it?" (27). Recently Thomas P. Adler in *The Southern Literary Journal* persuasively argued the importance of Williams's last Broadway play, *Clothes for a Summer Hotel.* Like his first Broadway play, *The Glass Menagerie,* and in others such as *Out Cry* (1972), Adler states, Williams "obsessively links the 'love' between himself and his sister," which was the strongest relationship for the playwright and Rose and accounts perhaps for their "withdrawal from extra familiar attachments" (6). Adler does not include *Orpheus Descending* or its predecessor in his list of plays which contain strong autobiographical elements, although most critics assert that Val Xavier is clearly a spokesman for Williams himself. Only in the "Orpheus" poem do we find a blatant allusion to sister Rose; yet I believe, as Adler does, that his art had as its source " 'something' that he could not leave 'unspoken' between his sister and himself" (18).

Both *Battle of Angels* and *Orpheus Descending* describe on the most literal level the arrival in a small Southern town of an apparent vagrant named Val Xavier, who temporarily seeks employment in a dry goods store (symbolically a wasteland of material America), which is owned by a Mrs. Torrance and her impotent, bedridden husband, Jabe, who is dying of cancer. All of the women in the community are attracted to Val, and their husbands, predisposed to dislike strangers, develop an expected loathing for this exotic sensual intruder. Eventually Val and Mrs. Torrance (named Myra in *Battle of Angels* and Lady in *Orpheus Descending;* both, as variants of Mary and "Our Lady," are Virgin Mary surrogates) become lovers. They are discovered by Jabe, who shoots Myra-Lady, blames the killing on Val, who is subsequently blowtorched to death by the Klan-like citizenry. Val, Myra/Lady, and Jabe are on one level Orpheus, Eurydice, and Pluto and on another Christ, the Virgin Mary, and Satan. When Eugene O'Neill constructed a plot with similar components in *Desire Under the Elms* (1926), he depended upon a legend, the Theseus-Phaedra-Hippolytus story, and the knowledge that those in his audience who read Freud might draw Oedipal parallels. By comparison Williams's play bombards audiences with a plethora of phantasmagorical references and allusions.

The profusion of symbolic or allegorical figures and the blending of pagan and Christian stories, which bewildered and enraged Bostonians who first saw *Battle of Angels,* were all highly personal emblems of Williams. Details of the playwright's life, first provided by gossip columnists and later by literary historians, were eventually complemented by autobiography. What seemed inchoate and misleading in *Battle of Angels* now appears to confirm the patterns of a rich but uneven literary career and a troubled personal life. Prior knowledge of the author has become the organizing principle for *Orpheus Descending.* His Manichaean view of the universe, his longing for spiritual fulfillment, his belief that sex and art are avenues of expression for the soul, his obsessive attachment to Rose, his inverted sexuality, all are *leitmotifs.* Williams, man and artist, has become the key to unlock secret places. He apparently believed freedom was desirable but unattainable; yet chaos was to be dreaded.

Williams's transformation of *Battle of Angels* into *Orpheus Descending* reflects nearly two decades of experience in the theatre, a confidence derived from the successes of *The Glass Menagerie* and *A Streetcar Named Desire* and a recognition that a greater degree of subtlety need not diminish the lyrical qualities of his best writing. Many of Williams's better passages in *Battle of*

Angels are reprinted in the revised version, and the central images and plot developments remain the same. Yet the newly added material clarifies the play and attempts to simplify it. It is a help to know that Carol Cutrere of *Orpheus Descending* was originally Cassandra Whiteside because one is alerted that her abilities to prophesy disaster will go unheeded. But Carol possesses a natural sagacity that the audience instinctively respects; thus there is no need to drag remnants of the Agamemnon story into the Orpheus legend. Cassandra/ Carol also becomes the sister of the man who originally "wronged" Lady Torrance, a change which tightens the play's structure and provides a reason for David to reenter Lady's life momentarily; he must go to Lady's store to retrieve his drunken sister. The information that David abandoned Lady after her father's wine garden had been burned down is therefore revealed more naturally, as is Lady's confession that she was pregnant with David's child at the time and later had an abortion.

The wise omission of Mrs. Regan from Waco, Texas, who follows Val to his new location with false charges of rape, places the blame for his subsequent killing more directly on Jabe Torrance, the Pluto figure who has just shot Eurydice/Lady and blamed Val for it. This eliminates unnecessary melodrama and the confusion caused by a superfluous hysterical woman who can never be developed as a character. It also magnifies the evil of Jabe, who has just boasted that he, in fact, had been the leader of the hooligans who burned the wine garden, which Lady's father died defending.

Williams's more mature grasp of dramaturgy in *Orpheus* than in *Battle* can be observed in his addition to the cast of Mr. Dubinsky, a Jewish pharmacist, who is yet another outcast in an ethnically and racially biased community, and the omission of a stage direction indicating that clouds of smoke should envelop the set. (Bostonians in 1940, sufficiently alarmed by the play's subject matter, responded in panic to the possibility that the theatre building itself might possibly be on fire.) He also added a beautiful passage in the *Orpheus* version in which Val describes to Lady "those little birds" that "don't have no legs at all and they live their whole lives on the wing, and they sleep on the wind . . . never light on the earth but one time when they die." This statement confirms both Val's and Lady's aspiration toward goodness, with Lady protesting her eagerness "never to be corrupted."

Finally, the charges of blasphemy registered by critics of *Battle of Angels* are lessened when the deaths of Val and Lady occur on the Saturday before Easter instead of Good Friday. Other clever emendations improve the later play. For example, the confectionery which Lady plans to open on Easter Sunday at one end of her dry goods store looks like the wine garden of her father's speakeasy rather than like the orchard of the earlier version. Thus it becomes a reconstruction of a part of her life which she views nostalgically and which also emphasizes the magnitude of her personal loss and her obsession with wreaking vengeance on townspeople who were responsible. Then too, she learns for the first time that Jabe led the Klan-like group who burned the casino because Lady's Italian father had served whiskey to blacks. *Orpheus Descending* consolidates the action of the play on which it was based and simplifies the allusive elements without vitiating its dramatic power.

The Glass Menagerie, first produced in 1944, established Williams as a major American dramatist. While he insisted it was a "dream" play, in which Tom Wingfield's past recollections should be viewed through the haze of a scrim curtain, Williams presented a more "ordinary" family and plot, one with clear autobiographical roots. The central event of the play is a matchmaking dinner arranged for Tom's shy, handicapped sister, Laura, and a gentleman caller, who, it turns out, is already engaged to be married. The play's language is distinctive, and Williams's satire of Tom and Laura's mother, Amanda, is as comedic as it is merciless. The success of *The Glass Menagerie* was echoed, even more triumphantly, three years later in *A Streetcar Named Desire,* which earned for Williams a Pulitzer Prize. A more shocking play because it contains a promiscuous heroine who is raped by her brother-in-law on the night her sister gives birth, it is a work somewhat contained within the boundaries of realism. Stanley Kowalski, the rapist, is a provoked, ignorant blue collar worker in the slums of New Orleans, and the collapse of the Old South before a brutal new industrial order is a concept which proved sociologically interesting and disturbing to shocked audiences.

Compared to Williams's first major successes, *Battle of Angels* had surely been a witches' brew of perverted attitudes, a gothic horror tale of an "unbelievable" Southern experience. Although violence and perversion increase in later plays, so that by 1960 Bosley Crowther in a movie review felt free to speak confidently of Williams's "sordid view of life" and his "persistently decadent plays" (34), *Battle* does appear retrospectively to have contained for many theatregoers an altogether threatening dose of racism, tormented sexuality, social corruption, and innate depravity.

Tom Wingfield is an understated autobiographical figure, a would-be poet who finds life in a dingy St. Louis apartment stultifying and who longs to escape familial responsibilities. Where Tom is believable if not ordinary, a recognizable version of the aspiring author, Val Xavier embodies unconscious grandiose dreams of the thwarted artist. Val is both a self-caricature and a romanticized projection of what Williams would try to become. By offering the public *Battle of Angels* before *The Glass Menagerie,* Williams revealed his "id" before the world had encountered his "ego." Tom Wingfield, while not an effeminate or homosexual character, has no clear sexual identity and a decidedly passive nature. Val Xavier is a self-described "stud," equipped with phallic accoutrements, a snakeskin jacket and a guitar, which all the women find thrilling. In other plays the Stud would often be brutal, devoid of poetic inspiration or sensitivity toward others. Stanley Kowalski rules his domain with sexual power, hurling a package of meat at Stella when he makes his first entrance on stage.

Two sorts of males would ultimately be counterbalanced in Williams's plays—the rapacious stud, heterosexual but boorish like Kowalski, and the sensitive misunderstood victim like homosexual Sebastian (named for a saint and martyr) in *Suddenly Last Summer.* Although this division between two sorts of males is apparent in *Menagerie,* Tom is far from a decadent character, and the gentleman caller is clumsy but not unkind. How curious that Williams's first major representation of his inner self would be Val Xavier, simultaneously a sexually dominating male and a poet-victim, who claims to have been "the entertainment," presumably a hustler in tawdry New Orleans night clubs. Perhaps life taught him that phallic dominance and *agape* were incompatible, but his unceasing obsession with the Orpheus figure indicates that he secretly cherished an integrated persona. Even the protagonist's name combines Valentine, the saint and lover, with Xavier, the missionary saint. Furthermore, the Williams family "mythology" claimed St. Xavier as an ancestor. In the manner of twentieth century artists, his hero's name is a self-referential family joke, from which the audience is excluded.

Women in the acting profession have reason to admire Williams's plays as he rewarded them with major stage roles. Certainly his leading competitor in the 1940s and 1950s, Arthur Miller, failed to create memorable parts for women. But women as complex as Amanda, Laura, Blanche, and Maggie the Cat paved the way for more distorted visions of women in the horrendous personalities of Violet Venable in *Suddenly Last Summer* or the Princess in *Sweet Bird of Youth.* These women are absurdly exaggerated—fun to watch and doubtless to play—and they are increasingly fantastic. Williams made the first statement in contemporary theatre that the rape of a promiscuous woman is nonetheless a rape, a crime of violence rather than simply a sexual act; we witness Blanche DuBois's destruction by Kowalski. Williams ridiculed macho stereotypes in works such as *Cat on a Hot Tin Roof* in which Brick, Big Daddy, and Gooper disagree on what constitutes proper male behavior.

Still it would be a mistake to feel that Williams had rid himself entirely of traditional sexual bias. His female characters lose their identity when they have no man to love, they are more often treacherous than nurturing, and they tempt men to their destruction. Lady Torrance, for example, induces Val to remain in a hostile environment after his own sense of self-preservation urges his departure. It should be noted as well that while Val appears to contain the best of what a man can offer the world—music, sexual pleasure, kindness, and patience—it takes three women in both *Battle of Angels* and *Orpheus Descending* to compose one perfect female prototype. Lady Torrance is the Earth Mother (literally, as the wife of Pluto), whose two pregnancies are ironically terminated, once indirectly and once directly by Jabe. Vee Talbot, the spiritual visionary, is comical, "but by no means ridiculous," as Williams warns in the stage directions. She alone recognizes that Val/Orpheus is the resurrected Christ. Cassandra Whiteside/Carol Cutrere is the prophetess of doom but also a social activist, since she has championed civil rights and, in particular, defended a black man who was imprisoned for having had relations with a white woman. Carol, promiscuous and alcoholic, in anticipation of Blanche DuBois, is also a mistreated sister so that she is linked sympathetically to Rose Williams.

This array of women who are admired by the author in spite of his realistic evaluation of their shortcomings (Lady's greed, Vee's repressed sexuality, Carol's aristocratic self-indulgence) are nevertheless outsiders in the community (a "wop," a religious fanatic, a "psycho"); they join Val as victims and hence, according to the Williams ethic, become our saviors. Whether Val is meant to be more of a person than his female counterparts is, of course, debatable. A talented woman like Vanessa Redgrave has evidently prevailed as the principal character in the London *Orpheus* and Benedict Nightengale, referring to Redgrave as an actress "in love with risk," implies that she overshadows her co-star, Kevin Anderson, in the New York production, which opened in September and closed in December.

Another possibility is that Williams's vision of the "fugitive kind"— sensitive loners who, like Val and Carol, deserve to wear the snakeskin jacket, which Carol purchases from the Conjure Man after Val's death—is essentially pan-sexual; that is, Val and the three outsider women may all be component parts of what is good in the world and therefore will inevitably be trapped and destroyed. The message that the world is composed of predators and victims undergirds all of Williams's written work. His sympathies lie with the victims, but a suppressed heroic aspect of his temperament motivated him to use his skills as a literary artist to offer them encouragement and bestow upon them dignity.

Williams's view of the artist is a post-modernist paradox. The artist represents the light in the Manichaean struggle between the forces of darkness and light on earth, but his confrontation with evil tends to drag him toward the abyss. He must never be complacent enough to deny the existence of the horrible, which, although he repudiates it, becomes alluring. For Williams, his mission is a personal form of Christian charity—to inspire others spiritually and aesthetically, and to contribute to a more compassionate, peaceful society as a spokesperson for those unable to defend themselves. He is at once a hero and a victim; only in the lives of Christ and the saints could Williams find prototypes for leaders, champions of the people, who were also scapegoats, ultimately sacrificed by the ungrateful populace they chose to save. Liberation from the stern rules and hypocrisies of the forces of darkness often takes the form in Williams's plays of the pursuit of sexual liberation. Yet Mani, the founder of Manichaeism, disdained the flesh, insisting that all sexual pleasures were sinful. Even Williams recognized the hopelessness of reaching the souls of others through sexual contact. In *Orpheus Descending* and *Battle of Angels,* Val confesses that the aftermath of physical intimacy brings an awareness that we are "sentenced to confinement inside our own skin."

Carol similarly speaks of the dangerous aspects of her indiscriminant sexual encounters, which she seeks "because to be not alone, even for a few minutes, is worth the pain."

The artist must use his song, as Orpheus did, to charm Hades so that escape is possible. Neither Orpheus's songs nor Williams's lyrical dialogue can dispel the forces of darkness, however, and the playwright, who selected the Zelda Fitzgerald character in *Clothes for a Summer Hotel* to say with a sigh that "words are the love acts of writers," finds that his own "love act," both in life and in art, is ultimately futile. The writer may feel omnipotent when he creates a fantasy world and determines its outcome, but his temporary dominion over his art only increases his despair at the impotence of his life. Critics who have complained that *Orpheus Descending* bewildered its audience with excessive signaling failed to recognize that the playwright was engaged in a Promethean adventure, which, despite its potential for failure, he felt compelled to undertake.

Works Cited

Adler, Thomas P. "When Ghosts Supplant Memories: Tennessee Williams's *Clothes for a Summer Hotel,*" *Southern Literary Journal* 19:2 (Spring, 1987), 5–19.

Bloom, Harold, ed. *Tennessee Williams,* New York: Chelsea House, 1987.

Crowther, Bosley. *New York Times,* 14 April 1960: 34.

Falk, Signi. *Tennessee Williams.* 2nd ed. Boston: G. K. Hall, 1978.

Quirino, Leonard. "Tennessee Williams's Persistent *Battle of Angels.*" In *Tennessee Williams,* Bloom, Harold, ed., pp. 43–54.

Wardle, Irving. *Times* (London), 18 Nov. 1988: 19.

———. *Times* (London), 4 Dec. 1988: 20.

Williams, Tennessee. *Battle of Angels.* New York: Dramatist's Play Service, 1975.

———. *In the Winter of Cities.* Norfolk, Connecticut: New Directions, 1956.

———. *Orpheus Descending.* New York: Dramatist's Play Service, 1967.

Monologues and Mirrors in *Sweet Bird of Youth*

Thomas P. Adler

"Self, self, self is all that you ever think of!"
—Amanda in *The Glass Menagerie*

Of all the major dramas by Tennessee Williams that are just a cut below the handful of his finest works, *Sweet Bird of Youth* (1959) appears to have generated the least amount of critical commentary. Except for production reviews and sections in books, only three brief scholarly articles—all dating from the mid-sixties—devote themselves solely to this play: the first, by William Roulet, focuses on Christian symbolism and Chance's redemption;[1] the second, by Bernard Dukore, adduces parallels with the story of Abelard and Heloise;[2] and the last, by Peter Hays, attends to the work's classical allusions.[3] Robert Brustein's essay on the original production (in *The Hudson Review*) and the chapter from Benjamin Nelson's *Tennessee Williams: The Man and His Work* serve as fairly representative indicators of the charges of structural diffuseness, stylistic incoherence, and questionable universality often leveled against *Sweet Bird*. Structurally, the presence of Boss Finley and, indeed, of much of act 2—which Williams added to expand the play to full length—seems to these critics an excrescence on the story of Alexandra del Lago and Chance Wayne; stylistically, the apparently random insertion of nonrealistic theatrical elements seems to sit badly with the overall realism; and finally, Chance appears too special a case to be morally representative.[4] Although none of these objections is made without some justification, the generally enthusiastic response by theater (and, later, movie) audiences would suggest that the work is far from fatally flawed.[5]

When, at the close of *Sweet Bird,* Chance asks from the audience "your recognition of me in you,"[6] he is not requesting—as several reviewers of the initial production assumed was Williams's intent—that they somehow exonerate or even condone him; rather, he is raising the issue of the audience's

This essay was written specifically for this volume and appears in print here by permission of the author.

perception. That their perception, the act of looking, seeing, and judging, constitutes a central aesthetic and ethical concern in *Sweet Bird* is borne out by the playwright's use of such scenic elements as the "mirror in the fourth wall" (13) and "the big TV screen, which is the whole back wall of the stage" (106) at the end of act 2. Nelson argues that these aspects of design, together with such devices as the occasional use of direct address to the audience or the strong beams of light that illuminate individual characters, "vulgarize" the play, turning it "into a kind of theatrical three-ring circus."[7] While it readily becomes evident that Williams is not employing his nonillusionistic techniques with anything approaching orthodox consistency, there may well be more thematic point, if not programmatic nicety, than Nelson and others would admit. As he did 15 years earlier in *Glass Menagerie* and as he would later do again in *Vieux Carré,* Williams here opts for what Roman Ingarden in *The Literary Work of Art* terms an *open* as opposed to a *closed* stage.[8] Although in practice adherence to a closed stage (that is, one bounded by an imaginary fourth wall) implicitly admits that what is considered absent is really present, playing to the presence-in-absence of the spectators, theoretically a closed stage functions *as if* there were no one watching; an open stage, on the other hand, makes no pretense of being anything other than a stage or of the audience being anything but present. Yet if *Menagerie* and *Carré,* through their systematic use of a narrator/central character, are both open in the sense of consciously acknowledging the audience as observers of a performance, *Sweet Bird* is open in what Ingarden posits as a fuller sense of actively involving the spectators, "at least to a certain extent, as *participants*" in an onstage action that, once the curtain rises, extends out over the footlights into the auditorium.[9] This shift from an audience conscious of themselves as merely watchers to an awareness of themselves as somehow players is effected through the dramatist's handling of scenic images and theatrical space: mirror, screen, forestage, auditorium.

The audience's consciousness of their own role reaches its height during a scene that stands out from anything else in the Williams canon. As Albert Kalson notes in his essay on Williams's adaptation of cinematic techniques for the theater, "Only *Sweet Bird* calls for the actual projection of film onto the stage."[10] While it is true that the theater audience see the political rally, ostensibly occurring in a ballroom just offstage in act 2, through the medium of film, what they are watching is not to be regarded as a movie but rather as a live television broadcast. The distinction carries some import, since this conceit of an actual, unrehearsed TV transmission allows for the unforeseen and spontaneous outburst by an audience representative in the person of the Heckler, whose moral indignation over Boss Finley's racist demagoguery they should share. Along with watching the TV rally projected on the cyclorama that forms the back wall of the stage, the audience observe an onstage audience (Chance, Stuff the bartender, and Finley's mistress Miss Lucy) looking at the broadcast as well; and when the Heckler as the audience's representative is forcibly ejected from the meeting, hurled back out on stage "and rather systematically beaten" against "bursts of great applause" (108–9), Chance becomes the helpless, if outraged, onstage audience.

Even before the back wall functions as an oversized TV monitor, the invisible fourth wall separating the stage from the auditorium is actually treated as if *it* were the TV screen. When Stuff "makes a gesture as if to turn [it] on," and then as he and Chance look out into "the narrow flickering beam of light [that] comes from the balcony rail" (106), what they see "on-screen" is, of course, the entire theater audience. So when the picture "suddenly appears" on the back wall, the audience at *Sweet Bird* is translated into the implied audience at the rally, which the Heckler literally moves backstage to attend. This strategy of making the Heckler and the audience one with each other actually privileges the Heckler's position within the play, giving special force to his only long speech: "I believe that the silence of God, the absolute speechlessness of Him is a long, long and awful thing that the whole world is lost because of. I think it's yet to be broken to any man, living or yet lived on earth . . ." (105)—a "conviction" that C. W. E. Bigsby judges as "central to Williams's plays. . . . If God is silent then other voices must sound in other rooms. The cruelties of life must be redeemed by other means than by reference to absolute values."[11]

Williams further establishes the Heckler's privileged status through his close visual and metaphoric association with the play's male protagonist; as Finley passes through the hotel lobby on his way to the rally, "he is facing the Heckler and Chance both. . . . For a split second he faces them, half lifts his cane to strike at them, but doesn't strike" (99). Finley's henchmen, however, do not hesitate: if Chance faces literal castration at play's end, the Heckler has earlier suffered an analogous fate when the Boss's men render him speechless by a jab to the larynx, denying him the voice that gives him purpose. So to the overarching network of imagery of castration in all its forms— Heavenly's sterility; Finley's impotence; Chance's sexual mutilation; the Princess Kosmonopolis's degradation by time, drugs, and the critics; the random Black man's castration—must be added the enforced silence of the Heckler.

The screen, of course, through the device of the close-up, can be made to exaggerate one's strength and power, as with Boss Finley. It can be (mis)used to manipulate the viewers' basest instincts, as Finley does. Or it can potentially raise experience to art, making permanent what is otherwise fleeting. In her lengthy address to the audience during the first scene of the play, Alexandra, mistakenly believing that her film comeback has been a humiliating disaster, is most cognizant of the screen's ability to make an audience notice, through magnification, what they could not otherwise see: "The screen's a very clear mirror. There's a thing called a close-up. The camera advances and you stand still and your head, your face, is caught in the frame of the picture with a light blazing on it and all your terrible history screams while you smile . . ." (34).

Because people seldom appear on screen as they do in life, that is, without makeup, the screen can be used just as easily to foster an illusion as to reveal the truth, just as a mirror can on a smaller scale. Yet for an aging actress like Alexandra, the screen functions as truthful mirror, throwing back an unflattering image of herself. The enormous screen/mirror on the back wall makes clear that reality can never be completely hidden—it seeps through just as the Heckler disturbs the carefully orchestrated political meeting.

When so much depends on physical image and public adulation, as it does for the Princess (and for Chance, the fading golden boy who still hopes someday to make it in the movies), the fear of time becomes an especially fatal disease, and gazing at screens or in mirrors often leads to desperation. Alexandra's insistence that "you can't retire with the out-crying heart of an artist still crying out in your body, in your nerves" (35) not only previews the title of one of Williams's most personal plays from the 1970s but, as Donald Spoto remarks, is prophetic, like the Princess's dependence on drugs and sex, of the playwright's fortitude and endurance in the face of ever-decreasing public approbation.[12] For the Princess and Chance, the ruler of "the country of the flesh-hungry, blood-thirsty ogre" (98)—the locale that Williams would elsewhere designate "Dragon Country"—may on one level be the castrator Boss Finley; yet for the artist, Finley is aptly symbolic of those now nay-saying audiences and critics who once conferred fame, and of time itself that diminishes imaginative power without allowing surcease from creative endeavor. The work of art might "arrest time," as Williams writes in his essay "The Timeless World of a Play,"[13] but only death can arrest the true artist.

Gazing at a close-up on a screen can become, particularly when the perceiver and the thing perceived are one and the same, as deeply obsessional as looking at oneself in a mirror. And in *Sweet Bird,* Williams underscores dramaturgically the danger of becoming totally consumed with self when he links gazing at one's own image in a mirror or on a screen with the potentially self-centered impetus behind first-person narration. When the Princess again moves out onto the forestage near the end of the play, she seems so totally oblivious to any audience but herself that her words take on the quality of an interior monologue. With the stage lighting down on everything but her, condemning Chance to "the dimmed-out background as if he'd never left the obscurity he was born in," she apotheosizes herself as artist: "I've taken the light again as a crown on my head to which I am suited by something in the cells of my blood and body from the time of my birth" (116). A few moments earlier, she had talked about herself as having "out of the passion and torment of [her] existence . . . created a thing that [she could] unveil, a sculpture, almost heroic . . ." (120). The art object, the "sculpture"—in the Princess's case her image on celluloid—is frozen and unchanging; the artist, however, is fragile and diminishing, subject to time that turns people selfish and egoistic.

Just as Williams at one point in *Sweet Bird* treats the invisible fourth wall as a TV screen, he also envisions its function as a mirror; his dramatic technique, then, confirms Alexandra's identification of mirror with screen. In almost the first bit of stage business in the play, "Chance rises, [and] pauses a moment at a mirror in the fourth wall to run a comb through his slightly thinning blond hair" (13). Late in the play, Chance and the Princess force each other to confront their respective reflections in that same "mirror." Because of the effect of the glassless two-way mirror that is the imaginary wall, the theater audience view not only each of the characters and what each of them supposedly sees, but perceive as well a reflection of themselves and of the impact of time's passage upon them, and of their desire to erase that effect through illusion. This throws the action out into the auditorium, turning it into a stage and helping break down the division between spectator and performer. As the Princess looks into the fourth-wall mirror (that is, out into the audience) to apply the mask with which she faces others, she uses the mirror to watch Chance, so that this time the mirror becomes a screen on which what the Princess calls Chance's screen test is projected. The audience, too, view the screen test, as though on the screen of the imaginary fourth-wall mirror, and watch as well the reactions of the Princess, who is now the onstage audience.

In *Sweet Bird*, Williams in fact deliberately blurs the demarcation between offstage and onstage audiences during all the monologues—except the Princess's last—by having the character who is listening interrupt or respond to lines spoken to the audience. When Chance delivers his long monologue (the guise of the screen test becoming a handy ploy to help disguise extended exposition), his position on the forestage in a shaft of light is, as Kalson notes the theatrical equivalent of a cinematic close-up.[14] And if such episodes when a dramatic character directly addresses the audience are seen as analogous to first-person narration in fiction, then Williams's practice here, with both Chance and Alexandra as narrators, is equivalent to the rotating point of view, perhaps particularly appropriate in a play with a dual protagonist. During his monologue, the Princess makes believe that Chance is auditioning the role of blackmailer—a part that links him with Boss Finley, who blackmails Heavenly into appearing at the political rally in return for not having Chance killed. Chance's attempted use of Alexandra as an entrée into a career in the movies is only one of many instances in *Sweet Bird* when people treat each other as commodities and thereby prevent the kind of symbiotic relationship that could take them out of themselves.

The necessity for establishing bonds of interconnectedness between individuals that Williams emphasizes earlier in *Cat on a Hot Tin Roof* (which shares with *Sweet Bird* a set dominated by "a great double bed" and "walls [that] are only suggested" [p. 13]) and returns to later in *Night of the Iguana* provides the focal point in this play as well. But in *Sweet Bird*, bonds more often are broken rather than solidified because people are never very far from using and abusing one another to get what they want. If, at the end of scene 1, the Princess will sign over her traveler's checks only after she has indulged in lovemaking with Chance to help forget the way time has diminished her beauty and her art, by the end of scene 2 it is Chance who simply takes advantage of her to advance the slim possibility of a film career of his own. Yet Alexandra, an actress who "despise[s] pretending," is not entirely selfish, developing real feeling, perhaps even love, for Chance, "a lost little boy that [she] really would like to help find himself" (53). As she says to him: "Believe me, not everybody wants to hurt everybody" (52). During the act 3 phone call to the Hollywood columnist, Chance thinks only of hyping his name and potential stardom, repeatedly "hissing," "Talk about me! . . . Me! Me!—You bitch!" (118). Alexandra, in turn, once she hears that her comeback was a success and not the failure she had feared, becomes just as totally self-centered, kicking Chance, comparing him to a piece of her "luggage," and demanding that he leave with her so her name will not be dragged down with his. Though momentarily they "return to the huddling together of the lost" (122), the potentially salvific bond that temporarily made each of them a person rather than simply an object to the other cannot be so easily restored. When Chance finally reaches Sally Powers on the phone, he tells Alexandra, "This is as far as I can stretch the cord, Princess, you've got to meet it halfway" (117). Reaching across the gulf of incommunication requires an active going out of self. Since the other "Gulf" in the play—the body of water on whose shore the action occurs—is associated archetypally with death, the failure to connect becomes a death-in-life situation for these two.

That the opposite possibility always exists, that of a life-giving and life-sustaining relationship, is seen in the way that Chance's little act of grace in responding to Alexandra's pleas for oxygen awoke in her heart a feeling for him that she thought she was no longer capable of experiencing. Because she could still motivate, recognize, and respond to an act of kindness, she knew she had not become totally a "monster"; Chance's act helps restore her sense of self-worth—what Maggie is able to do for Brick in *Cat,* what Mitch finally fails to do for Blanche in *Streetcar Named Desire.* When Chance in his closing monologue asks for "recognition," he pleads for a moral insight on the part of the audience so that they might see and respect him as the Princess did at his best moment, as someone in whom, despite his failures, the instinct toward good has not been totally eradicated. As Hannah in *Iguana* says of Shannon, who also has lost sight of his own dignity as a human being and whom she helps redeem from a destructive obsession with guilt: "I respect a person that has had to fight and howl for his decency and his . . . bit of goodness."[15]

Sweet Bird of Youth ends, significantly, not on Easter morning—which is the moment of complete belief and hope—but on Easter evening, biblically a moment of absolute doubt and challenge to faith that can be allayed only by dependence on experiential proof of a resurrection. Boss Finley claims to have been raised up from the flames of Good Friday when he was burned in effigy, yet his rhetoric and actions prove him a perverted savior of the South. Of all his victims, only the random Black castrated as a warning to others—a mutilation Finley justifies to his supporters as a protection of Southern white purity—can be considered Christic, a wholly innocent sufferer. Chance, though he may only unintentionally have infected Heavenly, is still responsible. If his judgment that Boss Finley "was just called down from the hills to preach hate" (101) is unimpeachable, his assertion that he brings love, while it contains some truth, must be qualified as an oversimplification at best: love, if thoughtless, can harm; it has consequences that are as dire for Heavenly as anything her openly hateful father does to his victims. Even the Heckler is not totally innocent: to draw attention to Finley's evil, he must hurt the innocent Heavenly, implicating her in her father's mission by publicly taunting her over and again with the fact of her sterility. Though totally unselfish acts of caring, the only antidote to the Boss Finleys of the world—and perhaps the reason that the Heckler, like the Apostle Thomas, finds it so difficult to discern God's presence in the absence of compelling human proof—hardly exist in the world of St. Cloud, they do surface in unexpected places, like Miss Lucy's compassion for the Princess when she appears disheveled in public, totally exposed to the looks and criticism of others. Authenticity and abandonment of self-image prompt instinctive kindness and generosity.

Neither the Princess's Beckettian endurance ("we've got to go on" [122]) nor Chance's stoical resignation (his active passivity in staying to face castration) seems adequately grounded in the human love that could provide an alternative force to the Heckler's revelation of God's "silence," on which Williams confers something like privileged status through that character's close association dramaturgically with the audience. If Alexandra del Lago, as an artist figure forced "to go on" with practically nothing in the way of emotional support from others, might seem a precursor to the more ethereal Hannah Jelkes, who prays for rest ("Oh God, can't we stop now?" [127]) rather than movement or flight at the close of *Iguana,* there remains a major distinction in the moral nature of the two: no matter how desperate her own situation, Hannah has always given more than she has taken from her relationships, both fleeting and long-term: with the underwear fetishist, with Shannon, with Nonno.

Chance's concluding choral apologia to the audience tonally recalls Tom's confession at the end of *Glass Menagerie;* indeed, Chance's guilt over Heavenly's sterility might be seen as in some ways analogous to Tom's over Laura's absolute aloneness—perpetually virginal as the love object of the writer's imagination. (And, of course, both Laura and Heavenly have their real-life source in Tennessee's sister Rose, whose name he originally gave to Heavenly in early versions of *Sweet Bird.*[16] Heavenly, like Laura, is destined never to be a mother, and with Chance's castration never again to be sexually loved. Although love might be something "permanent in a world of change"

(50), it cannot turn back time, or compensate totally for artistic creativity, or restore lost innocence. As Aunt Nonnie tells Chance, "What you want to go back to is your clean, unashamed youth. And you can't" (83). The fall from grace has happened, and only expiation and endurance remain.

Nothing, then, serves to completely temper the bleakness of *Sweet Bird*'s close, the pervasiveness of God's "absolute speechlessness" in the face of man's inability to move out of self and achieve communion with the other. To battle time by retreating into selfishness, egoism, narcissism—which here finds its dramatic equivalent in compulsive gazing into mirrors and conversing with an audience of oneself—prevents the coming of the only god that Williams consistently admits, the one revealed through unselfish acts of human love. *Sweet Bird,* in its suggestion that the monologue may interiorize experience so completely that all objective perspective and outside ethical authority cease to exist, may even insist that the audience redefine conventional notions of first-person narration within drama. It perhaps raises the question of whether the dramatic monologue can ever be emotionally, psychologically, and spiritually therapeutic in the way that the concluding narrative passage in *Glass Menagerie,* for example, has always seemed, forcing a rethinking and reseeing of closure in that earlier play. If Chance can only expiate by embracing castration, denying himself the very means by which he would live and challenge time, then perhaps Tom, the poet who deserts Laura to pursue his own vocation, and even Tennessee, the dramatist who incessantly uses Rose again and again as the impetus for his works, could adequately atone only by eschewing their art—an emasculation even more complete than Chance's. Stage mirrors and dramatic monologues, each potentially an agent for truth-telling, in *Sweet Bird* are revealed to characters and audience alike as means of effecting the obsessive self-absorption and solipsism that have always been inimical to the breaking down of barriers between people, rendering Williams's use of them not only an aesthetic but a moral and thematic choice as well.

Notes

1. William M. Roulet, "*Sweet Bird of Youth:* Williams's Redemptive Ethic," *Cithara,* 3 (1964): 31–36.

2. Bernard F. Dukore, "American Abelard: A Footnote to *Sweet Bird of Youth,*" *College English,* 26 (1965): 630–34.

3. Peter L. Hays, "Tennessee Williams' Use of Myth in *Sweet Bird of Youth,*" *Educational Theatre Journal,* 18 (October 1966): 255–58.

4. Robert Brustein, "Williams' Nebulous Nightmare," *Hudson Review* 12 (1959): 255–60; and Benjamin Nelson, *Tennessee Williams: The Man and His Work* (New York: Ivan Obolensky, 1961), 266–74.

5. Since this article was first written, the most significant scholarly work on the play appears in chapter 5 of Brenda Murphy's *Tennessee Williams and Elia Kazan: A Collaboration in*

the Theatre (Cambridge: Cambridge University Press, 1992), entitled "Realism and Metatheatre: *Sweet Bird of Youth*"; 144–48 and 154 are particularly relevant in supporting the argument put forward in this essay.

6.   Tennessee Williams, *Sweet Bird of Youth* (New York: New Directions, 1975), 124. Subsequent page references appear within parentheses in the text.

7.   Nelson, *Man and His Work,* 268–69.

8.   Roman Ingarden, *The Literary Work of Art: An Investigation on the Borderlines of Ontology, Logic, and Theory of Literature* (Evanston, Ill.: Northwestern University Press, 1973), 383–84.

9.   Ibid.

10.   Albert E. Kalson, "Tennessee Williams at the Delta Brilliant," in *Tennessee Williams: A Tribute,* ed. Jac Tharpe (Jackson: University Press of Mississippi, 1977), 791.

11.   C. W. E. Bigsby, *A Critical Introduction to Twentieth-Century American Drama,* vol. 2, *Tennessee Williams, Arthur Miller, Edward Albee* (Cambridge: Cambridge University Press, 1984), 106.

12.   Donald Spoto, *The Kindness of Strangers: The Life of Tennessee Williams* (Boston: Little, Brown, 1985), 207, 231.

13.   Tennessee Williams, "The Timeless World of a Play," in *Where I Live: Selected Essays* (New York: New Directions, 1978), 49.

14.   Kalson, "Delta Brilliant," 791.

15.   Tennessee Williams, *The Night of the Iguana* (New York: New American Library, 1961), 102.

16.   Spoto, *Kindness of Strangers,* 206.

Period of Adjustment:
High Comedy Over a Cavern

GERALD WEALES

"You child—" says Florrie in *Saturday's Children* (1927), "it is funny. You're going through a period of adjustment and it's always funny." The romantic gamesplaying with which Maxwell Anderson's play ends is both correct, a proper conclusion to that kind of comedy, and suspect, coming from a playwright whose most celebrated works chronicle the inevitable corruption of innocence in an evil world. The possibility of a double response makes the Anderson play an appropriate lead-in to a discussion of Tennessee Williams's *Period of Adjustment*.

For Williams, if not for Florrie, the period of adjustment, whether within a marriage or between a person and his society, world or universe, is co-extensive with the life of the marriage or the man. Williams's first use of the phrase—at least, the first one that I have come across—is in "On a Streetcar Named Success" (*New York Times,* 30 November 1947), one of those combinations of publicity and confession that the Sunday *Times* used regularly to run to herald important openings. Describing the depression that he fell into after the success of *The Glass Menagerie,* Williams says, "I thought to myself, this is just a period of adjustment." Within the essay, it is, for he tells how he went on to write *A Streetcar Named Desire;* yet, the tone of the piece denies the positive thrust of the narrative and it ends with the line: "the monosyllable of the clock is Loss, Loss, Loss unless you devote your heart to its opposition." The phrase "period of adjustment" is a convenient and comforting label which breaks continuing or recurring situations into encompassable units. Williams spent his life coping with one period of adjustment after another with drink, drugs, sex, compulsive travel, psychoanalysis, hospitalization and, most of all, obsessive work as aids in the endeavor.

This view of life lies darkly behind *Period of Adjustment* although the titular phrase is used in the marriage counselor sense that Florrie borrowed from

Reprinted with permission of the author and publisher from *Journal of American Drama and Theatre,* vol. 1, no. 1 (Spring 1989): 25–38. First written as an original essay for this collection. Copyright © by Gerald Weales.

a sage on the New York *American*. Both couples are going through periods of adjustment—George and Isabel Haverstick after one unconsummated night of marriage, Ralph and Dorothea Bates after six years together. The phrase, each time spoken solemnly as though it were important news, sounds through the play like a refrain, one so insistent that when Ralph alters the words ("this adjustment period") there is a momentarily disorienting click in the ear which has nothing to do with the content of the line, one more unheeded bit of comfort and advice that comes just before Isabel leaves to walk the dog.[1] In a play in which so much of the comic effect depends on the repetition of words and phrases, an alteration becomes part of the joke (an old Williams trick: "Only Poe! Only Edgar Allen Poe!" Blanche cries). The repeated line in *Period* is finally less a refrain than a running gag. Walter Kerr, reviewing the New York opening (New York *Herald Tribune*, 11 November 1960), said "it's something of a wonder how the laughs get bigger each time the too-helpful phrase turns up."

"You child—it is funny." Before I turn to what is funny or, at least, comic in *Period of Adjustment*, something should be said about the odd and contradictory responses to the play and its uneasy place in the Williams canon. No one considers it a major Williams play. Although it has been performed occasionally in one regional theater or another, it is not a staple of either the amateur or the professional theater, and it has had no major production since its initial appearances in New York (1960) and London (1962).

It does not even seem to have been much loved by its author. There is no mention of the play in *Memoirs*, where Williams refers often to his famous successes or the failures that pained him most, but it is not this omission that is most revelatory. It is a carelessness about the text itself. Williams wrote and rewrote *Period of Adjustment*, as he did most of his plays, but the text became fixed in 1960 and Williams never returned to it—probably because there was no occasion, like the 1974 revival of *Cat on a Hot Tin Roof*, to push him to it. At the end of Act One of *Period*, Isabel locks herself in the bedroom and Ralph returns to the fireplace in the living room. "*No time lapse*," and Act Two begins with the sound of a car; Isabel "*looks wildly at* RALPH." Since this is not *Desire Under the Elms*, in which characters do look at one another through the wall of separate rooms, there is a problem which the acting edition solves, almost by accident, when it moves several pages of the second act into the first. That version does a lot of naturalistic tidying, seeing to it that Ralph asks for George's keys before he gets Isabel's zipper bag from the locked car and that she gives the telephone number to the operator so that her call to her father can be completed. That the playwright left the original unlikely bridge between acts when the play was printed in *The Theatre of Tennessee Williams* in 1972 suggests one of two things. Either he is so indifferent to the play that he ignores bothersome details, or he uses them as signals to indicate that *Period of Adjustment* is not a realistic play and should not be taken as such.

Williams's somewhat tenuous relationship with his own play can be seen in the flood of interviews that he gave in 1959 and 1960. The play was first performed in Miami at the end of 1958, but it was almost two years before it reached New York. Between the two openings, Williams talked to a great many reporters, and the published accounts, read side by side, show a wealth of contradictory statements and a variety of voices ranging from the solemn to the playful. His tone presumably changed according to the publication, the interviewer and his state of mind that day, and if he tripped over his own statements, he could always blame it on the "dreadful misquotations" which, he told Whitney Bolton (*The Morning Telegraph,* 3 October 1960), dogged his every utterance—Bolton interviews excepted. All these interviews were advertisements for the play in process, and the general sense of them is that there is a new Williams, perhaps thanks to psychoanalysis,[2] who has put aesthetic violence behind him. It is a nice, neat idea, suitable for a chapter break in a biography, but it is somewhat flawed by Williams's having worked on *Period of Adjustment* at the same time he was struggling with *Sweet Bird of Youth* and *Night of the Iguana,* the works that preceded and followed *Period* in New York, and according to Lewis Funke (*New York Times,* 6 December 1959), on plays called *The Milk Train Does Not Stop Here* and *The Poem of Two* (probably "The Mutilated").

Reactions to the new Tennessee Williams ranged from Donald I. Klepfer's assertion, in his review of the pre-Broadway try-out in Wilmington, that the playwright was "in a mellow, merry mood" (Wilmington *Morning News,* 13 October 1960), to Alan Brien's contention, in his review of the London production, that *Period* is "perhaps the most pessimistic and bitter of all the Williams plays" (London *Sunday Telegraph,* 14 June 1962). John Griffin, reviewing the New York production in *The Theatre* (December, 1960), expressed an interest in seeing the play done "from an entirely different viewpoint, as a scathing commentary on current American sexual mores," and Tennessee Williams, who had dedicated the printed play to "the director and the cast," told interviewers in *Theatre Arts* (January, 1962) that, after he saw Dane Clark play *Period* in summer stock, he realized that what he thought was "a happy play . . . was about as black as *Orpheus Descending.*" Production decisions and the personality of performers can obviously change the way one responds to a play, but the production in London, judging by the notices, was not that different from the one in New York. Reviewers on both sides of the ocean split over whether the play was a conventional commercial comedy or a harsh satire, and the perceptions seemed not to depend on whether they liked or disliked the play.[3] Most of those who went for satire—like many commentators since—assumed that middle-class behavior or American marriage is the target. Tom Mackin, reviewing a revival (Newark *Evening News,* 8 April 1971), found the "plight of the returning hero whose exploits no longer matter" among its insufficiently explored themes. More interesting is the statement of the "special correspondent" in the 23 November 1960 edition of *The*

London Times that the satirical subject is "our interest in closely analysing the personal problems of others while we refuse to concede that we have any problems ourselves," or Harold Clurman's acid suggestion (*The Nation,* 3 December 1960) that Williams is mocking his own audience, offering them "a jolly little play" in which they can condescend to the characters whom they never recognize as themselves.

Most of these satiric elements are in *Period of Adjustment.* It would be hard to miss the import of the McGillicuddys, cartoons as broad as the unctuous, bequest-hunting clergyman in *Cat on a Hot Tin Roof.* The incidental satire—on television, on American consumerism—is a standard Broadway joke, much enjoyed even by TV-watching consumers in the 1950s. The difficulty comes as one extends the object of satire. Are the two couples sympathetic comic figures or pathetic butts? Is this the new avuncular, warm-hearted Williams or the savage Williams who, like Cora and Billy in "Two on a Party," "loathed and despised . . . the squares of the world"? Both they and he fall somewhere in between, the characters being at once funny in their distress and touching in their funniness. When Williams wanted to indicate that he did not like the characters, he did so directly as in the stage direction which calls the McGillicuddys *"a pair of old bulls."* His amused sympathy for the two couples can be found in the stage directions and the epigraph. Chekhov may have had the self-irony to use his own fiction to show the limitations of Trigorin in *The Sea Gull,* but Williams is too sentimental to intend sardonically an epigraph that is a variant on the last stanza of one of his own poems.[4] The voice in the epigraph, like the four main characters, has a desperate need for tenderness and an inability to express it to others. Even though this conflict is a serious one for Williams, he has the wit to use *tenderness* as one of those words like *dignity* and the ubiquitous *sweet,* comic labels for possibly genuine responses. "There is such a tender atmosphere in this sweet little house . . ." says Isabel, in one of her attempts to persuade Ralph to stay with his wife. "I mean you can *breathe* the tender atmosphere in it!"

Williams's descriptions of Ralph are as direct and as ambiguous as the message in the epigraph. Ralph has a *"look of gentle gravity which is the heart"* of the character and *"a fine, simple sweetness and gentleness."* These lines from two different stage directions are intended to lead the reader (and presumably the director and the actor) to a sense of the character as clearly as Williams's statement that Blanche *"suggests a moth"* or that Brick has *"that cool air of detachment that people have who have given up the struggle."* These are suggestions, not complete characterizations. From the plays, we know that Blanche is as much tiger as moth and that Brick, as the confrontation with his father shows, is still struggling. The *sweetness* in Williams's stage direction may not have quite the taste that it has in Isabel's mouth, but his use of her favorite cotton-candy word might remind us that American popular culture has a tradition of gentle comic figures from Harry Langdon to Coach on *Cheers.* In his attempt to be helpful, Ralph is as funny as he is gentle, but Williams's emphasis in the stage directions indicates that the play is not intended as a demolition job on his main characters. He describes Isabel's "so lonesome" scene at the end of Act Two as *"a sentimental moment, but not 'sticky.'"* It is a ludicrous moment, as Isabel murmurs "Little Boy Jesus" to the statue of the Infant of Prague she cradles in her arms, but, if Shirley Temple taught us nothing else, she taught us that a scene could be outrageous and touching at the same time. Anyone who has sat through a screening of *A Streetcar Named Desire,* as I did a few years ago, and listened to a young audience laugh at passages that once broke my heart knows that audience perspective is central to the way characters are perceived. Williams seems to be using the playwright's tools of direct address to warn the audience that the satiric intentions of his play should not mask that his characters are human beings intended to elicit our sympathy, but that sympathy should not become so "sticky" that it obscures—*obfuscates,* Ralph would say— their central function as comic figures.

One of the generic bases touched by *Period of Adjustment* is Broadway comedy of the 1950s. Unlike the farces which were one of the theatrical strengths of American drama in the 1920s and 1930s, 1950s comedy tended to be earnest in both its search for laughs and its psychological problem solving. On neither count does Williams's play fit comfortably in that pigeonhole. The gag line, used by one character to put down another, is a staple of the genre, and some reviewers praised Williams for being comic in that way. The best example, the funniest line as line, is Isabel's response to Ralph's assertion that "they don't make them any better" than George: "If they don't make them any better than George Haverstick they ought to stop production!" In conventional usage, a gag does its work and then gets out of the way, but Isabel, startled by Ralph's hearty laugh, proceeds to explain that the joke is a serious statement; later, disoriented by the growing intimacy with Ralph and his continued praise of George, she repeats the joke and this time she *"utters a sort of wild, sad laugh which stops as abruptly as it started."* Williams could not be a gag writer if he wanted to, and he is as little in tune with the psychologizing of 1950s comedy as he is with its jokery. The genre at its best—George Axelrod's *The Seven Year Itch* (1952), for instance—could carry attractive characters through foolish contretemps to an ending that was at once a comfort and a message. *Period of Adjustment* might be seen as a cousin to a show like *Itch,* but for all the instant psychology that washes through the lines in Williams's play, it is more concerned with questions than with answers. He provides an ending for his comedy, not solutions to the problems of his characters. Nor that "message you can take home with you," the absence of which Sabina lamented in *The Skin of Our Teeth.*

Williams calls his play "A Serious Comedy," but there is some difficulty about the where and the what of the seriousness. There are many passages which could be lifted out of the text—and have been, by reviewers and academic critics alike—and displayed as the key to the whole thing. "Women are vulnerable creatures," says Ralph, and George answers, "So's a man."

Williams understood vulnerability and spent a good part of his playwriting life investigating that human weakness/virtue, and there is every reason to assume that many of the sentiments that come from the mouths of the characters belong to the dramatist as well. His work suggests that, like Isabel, he believes that the "whole world's a big hospital, a big neurological ward," but no shared allegiance keeps him from using the idea in a comic seduction speech. One might read the play as feminist on the basis of Isabel's "Women are human beings and I am not an exception to that rule" and Ralph's attack on the male's use of the penis as a weapon, but Isabel's rejection of humiliation is balanced by Dorothea's admission that she came *"crawling"* back home. Anyone who wants to see Williams as a marriage counselor can equate Ralph and the playwright and take Ralph's platitudes as his creator's, but Ralph's message can be and has been summed up in a popular song ("Try a Little Tenderness"). There are lines and scenes to prove that the play is serious about the defects of American culture (George says TV is "a goddam NATIONAL OBSESSIONAL"), the corruptive power of money and materialism, the fragility of youthful aspirations, the ruinous influence of parents on children, the precariousness of existence, but it is always a good idea in *Period of Adjustment* to see who is speaking and in what context. Consider Isabel's philosophical musings on the meaning of life, which Nancy M. Tischler seems to take straight in *Tennessee Williams: Rebellious Puritan.* They are triggered by Ralph's "That's life for you," which he must repeat because Isabel has not been listening to his unhappy account of his marriage. *"What* is life for us *all?"* she asks, as if in response to a cue, and then sighs her way into her "giant question mark" speech to which Ralph responds, "When did you say you got married?" The seriousness in *Period* does not lie in the "many random true and tender insights" an unwilling Jerry Tallmer found in it (*The Village Voice,* 24 November 1960), for as often as not they are undercut by context. It lies in the assumption that comedy begins in the recognizable and painful problems that regularly beset all of us.

"What they talk about is serious but the way they do it is comedy," Williams told some "friends," or so Francis Donahue says in one of those unidentified quotations that make the reading of *The Dramatic World of Tennessee Williams* such a chore. Authentic or not, the line does indicate the comic method in *Period of Adjustment.* Alan Pryce-Jones (*Theatre Arts,* January, 1961) complained, "The comedy is kept afloat entirely on conversation," and Bamber Gascoigne (*The Spectator,* 22 June 1962) faulted the play as an example of Williams's "retrospective play-making." Both were right, although both are wrong because the play is not about the Haversticks' disastrous wedding night in the Old Man River Motel or Ralph's having married Dorothea on the implicit promise of taking over her father's business. It—the first act, at least—is about Isabel's account of that night and Ralph's attempt to explain his own situation in the face of her self-preoccupation. "You often speak of having no plot in *Period of Adjustment,*" Cheryl Crawford, who produced the play, said in a letter to Williams (quoted in her autobiography, *One Naked Individual*). "You're wrong: People will rush back to their seats to find out what is going to happen." Crawford rather overstates the case (she was complaining of a lack of plot in *The Night of the Iguana*), for by the end of the act, anyone with any experience of comedy knows that it is the business of the plot to lead George and Isabel to consummation and Ralph and Dorothea to reconciliation. The interesting action in Act One is the coming together of Ralph and Isabel, not sexually although there are erotic overtones in their behavior, but as friends, comrades who can share a laugh.[5] The means to their mutual attraction is verbal, and the voices are comic.

The play opens with a not very successful parody of a pompous television commercial (The Mother-Mouse doggerel of the acting edition is better, but not much), but this is not satire. It is a way of emphasizing the conventionality of the setting ("*a 'cute' little Spanish-type suburban bungalow*") and the fact that Ralph is alone—a state that is intensified when he switches channels and picks up "White Christmas." (A Christmas play to follow the Easter of *Sweet Bird?*) This quiet scene is followed by the hubbub of the Haversticks' arrival and George's failure to get the car up the steep drive. It is probably appropriate that our first sense of George is that he can't get it up—given his fear of impotency—but that is a retrospective joke—if it is a joke at all—and the scene here, the first exchange between Ralph and Isabel, punctuated by shouts to and from the offstage George, provides the chaotic disconnection that will finally modulate into an uneasy companionship. George drives off, ostensibly to get a present for Ralph, actually for the same reason that Isabel walks the dog in Act Two—to give the other two characters a chance to play alone.

Exposition is action in this act. While Isabel lets us know about her brief career as a student nurse, her dependence on "PRECIOUS DADDY," how she met George, she conveys the incipient hysteria in the character, the growing conviction that she has been abandoned. Her account of their wedding night, the disaster that followed the long, sullen ride in the freezing honeymoon hearse, is almost a set piece like Maggie's opening monologue in *Cat on a Hot Tin Roof,* and Ralph's interruptions ("Aw") are sometimes as brief as Brick's. To keep this tale of woe in comic perspective she seems as desperate in her need for her "small zipper bag" as she does about her frightening marriage. She repeats the phrase in varying intensities (represented by different types— italics, small caps—in the printed text) and begins to load it with adjectives: "little blue zipper bag," "little blue zipper overnight bag." Although her concern about the bag may represent a transfer from an incomprehensible situation to a small dislocation, it is characteristic of Isabel's tendency to be distracted—by the child's Christmas presents under the tree, for instance. She never hears the contradictions in her flow of words. "I think my pride has been hurt," she says, explaining her anger at George, and in her next speech reprimands Ralph for reacting "out of hurt feelings, hurt pride." Her most endearing quality is the sense of propriety that keeps breaking through her chronicle of outrage and despair. Early in the act, building up a head of steam in her exasperation with George, she suddenly notices that the television is on and says, "Excuse me, you're watching TV!" Later, describing their drive down from St. Louis, she says, "Ever since then it's been hell! And I am—" and then, as though she were suddenly conscious that she was not being a proper guest, she breaks off and finishes with "—not exactly the spirit of Christmas, am I?" Williams does not need these abrupt jumps to let us see the Isabel who so admires this "*sweet* house." He can do it with a string of possessive pronouns as in her shyness about that zipper bag: "It had my, all my, it had my—*night* things in it."

Most of the New York reviewers, even those who hated the play, praised Barbara Baxley as Isabel; although she was a delight in the part, Williams deserves credit for creating a character so vividly verbal. By comparison, Ralph is muted. He does try to explain his marriage, his separation, his impending departure, the cavern into which the house is sinking ("If anyone wishes to pin a symbolism there—he may," Williams told Whitney Bolton in the interview quoted earlier, insisting that he was simply using a house that his mother bought and had to have shored up), but Isabel is usually not listening. Otherwise, Ralph can only offer cliches of comfort or ask leading questions. He is at his strongest when he uses gestures rather than words—offering her the flaming brandy, bringing her his wife's slippers, kissing the bride to still her sobs. Her self-absorption and his slightly pompous hovering presence are the comic heart of the first act.

The two-character encounter of Act One gives way to an uneasy threesome in the second act. Ralph cannot quite do the old-buddy routine with George, infected as he is by his sympathy for Isabel, and George's presence makes it impossible for him to sustain the mood on which the first act ends—even though Isabel starts calling him Ralph instead of Mr. Bates. He is forced much of the time to stand around with his oil can waiting for a chance to pour bromides on troubled water. Isabel, in direct contention with George, cannot be the waif of Act One. Her toughness shows through except in that preposterous telephone call—"Can't talk, can't talk, can't talk, can't talk, *can't—talk*"—that provides the farcical high point of the act. Add that both men get increasingly drunk as the act progresses, making Ralph more ponderous, George more contentious. Although Isabel and Ralph are on hand much of the time, this act belongs to George. We hear about his shakes in the first act; now we get to see them.

It is possible to be psychologically solemn about George's condition, but the way Williams plays with tremors in this play makes that difficult. The shakes are either a cause or a result of George's fear of impotency, but they reflect more than sexual self-doubt. According to Isabel, George began to shake in the car when she said he would have to start looking for a new job immediately, and Ralph trembles in his encounter with Mr. McGillicuddy.

Ralph tells Isabel that Dorothea used to shake whenever she approached a man, and Isabel's unfinished comment suggests that it may have been desire, not fear, that moved Dorothea; at the end of the play, as George and Isabel begin to come together, she says, "I didn't know until now that the shakes are catching!" Perhaps this congeries of shakes is supposed to suggest something about our general insecurity—the world as "neurological ward"—but the ludicrous metaphors (Dorothea's buck teeth sounding like "castanets at a distance," George shaking like "dice in a crap shooter's fist") undercut that possibility.

George on stage is the visual sign of all the shakes, seen and unseen, including those of the house ("We get those little tremors all the time," says Dorothea, when the house slips at the end of the play), but he is not a dark comedy figure of "affliction," however often he uses the word. He is primarily a big little boy in his noisy playfulness with Ralph, his hurt reaction to Isabel's having rejected him the night before, his petulance at both Ralph and Isabel. In his one unsuccessful attempt at reconciliation with Isabel in Act Two (a balancing scene to her similar attempt—"How are *you* feeling now, George?"—which he refuses), he apologizes for having implied that Isabel seduced him in the hospital and then *"slumps in a chair with a long, despairing sigh."* Like Isabel, he is easily sidetracked; they both forget their main quarrel long enough for a funny fight over whether the cocker spaniel should be called *animal* or *dog*. He also contradicts himself, but even more obviously than Isabel's shifts, his have a child's urgent sense of what will work right now. "Man an air record will cut you no ice on the ground," he says early in the act, feeling sorry for himself, but later, trying to persuade Ralph to join him in the Longhorn-breeding scheme. "Haven't you blazoned your name in the memory of two wars?" George is never more the boy than in his dream about the ranch, a longing to run away from the shake-giving real world. The idea of raising Longhorn cattle for television Westerns is as effective, if not as brutal, an image of the decline of the wide-open-spaces myth as catching wild horses for dog food (*v.* Arthur Miller's *The Misfits*). The cultural implications are there certainly, but the primary use of George's plan is to provide a counterpart to Isabel's nurse-doctor fantasy. Isabel may be little girl enough to imagine the *"youngish middle-aged* doctor" risking contagion to sweep her into his arms, but she is adult enough to laugh with Ralph at the movie origins of her dream, as she shows neatly when she switches from "I" to "she" within a single sentence. George's fantasy is more persistent, and he is so enthusiastic about it that he drags Ralph—fortified by drink and his own desire to escape—along with him.

The McGillicuddys arrive in the last act and their strident, bitter presences—which I could happily forego—momentarily alter the tone of the comedy. As Williams once said (*New York Times,* 1 May 1960), he has a taste for "cornpone melodrama," and the caricatured greed of the McGillicuddys may fall into a slapstick corner of that label. Dorothea's parents are probably in the play for their own sakes, but it would be nice to think that they are there for contrast, an ugly noise that gives way to the final pattern of the play in which, after the "*bulls,*" even the lovers' quarrels are quiet. Williams develops a fine comic movement at the end of Act Three in which George and Isabel in the living room, Ralph and Dorothea in the bedroom circle each other, the circles overlapping as we jump from couple to couple, an exchange, a speech, even a single line holding us for a moment before we jump again. The acting edition tries to tidy this process by shifting between couples only after exchanges have been completed, but this is a mistake, I think. These are intermeshing circles and both are turning slowly, running down to a single ending in which the two couples come together.

"That these four persons decide to remain with their spouses is a notion less comic than ghoulish," complained Tom F. Driver in a group review (*The Christian Century,* 28 December 1960) in which he clearly preferred *Under the Yum Yum Tree* to *Period of Adjustment.* Driver's distaste, which was shared by a number of other reviewers, is understandable only in an aesthetic world in which the end of a play can be read in just one way. Williams's own comments on the final curtain are instructive. He told an interviewer in *Newsweek* (23 March 1959) that "it has a happy ending." A year later (*New York Times,* 1 May 1960) that ending had become "non-tragic." Shortly before the play opened, he told Don Ross (New York *Herald Tribune,* 6 November 1960) that "it hasn't really a happy ending. It's only happy in the sense that all the characters are alive and that they are interested in going on living." Whatever Williams says, it is a happy ending so far as the genre is concerned, for commercial comedies do end with the lovers in one another's arms. Yet, anyone tempted to wring a message from the double union of these mismatched pairs should remember that in the typical Williams play the most his characters hope for or get is the momentary comfort of shared warmth. A not so happy ending, then, and there is the rumble that reminds them (us) that the "*sweet house*" is built over an abyss. The pattern of action and words leads to the happy ending, but the implications are darkly Williams.

Notes

1.   Ralph's line was dropped in the acting edition of the play, but an altered form of the titular phrase ("a little adjustment period") is used elsewhere in that version, in Ralph's telephone assurances to Isabel's Daddy. In this essay, unless I make specific reference to the version of the play in *Esquire* (December, 1960) or the acting edition (Dramatists Play Service, 1961), I will use the play as it was published by New Directions in 1960 and reprinted in Volume 4 of *The Theatre of Tennessee Williams* in 1972. In *Tennessee Williams: A Bibliography,* Drewey Wayne Gunn assumes that the New Directions version is a revision of the one in *Esquire,* but book publication came first. The subtitle in both *Esquire* and the acting edition is "High Point Is Built on a Cavern" instead of the New Directions's "High Point over a Cavern," a precise and funny sexual image that I prefer to the social/philosophical implications of the longer

subtitle. *Esquire* and the acting edition also share the epigraph and a number of lines that are not in New Directions. There is an awkward and unnecessary scene between Isabel and a sailor in *Esquire,* which one would expect to be the first thing to go in revision and which, as the sailorless cast list attests, did disappear in production. If that sailor appears in the earlier unpublished manuscript at the University of Texas, which I have not seen, I can only assume that he was in, then out, then in, then out again. The confusion about priority of edition was heightened by Arnold Gingrich, who congratulated himself ("Publisher's Page," *Esquire,* January, 1961) for having printed the play "months in advance of its appearance in book form." My conjecture about the order of publication, based on textual evidence alone, was confirmed by Peggy L. Fox of New Directions, who wrote me (8 November 1985), enclosing xeroxes of a number of 1960 letters indicating that the play was published by New Directions on 14 November. One of the letters, dated 28 November, was from Gingrich, apologizing in advance for the forthcoming note, the January issue of *Esquire* already having gone to the printer.

2.   In *Memoirs,* Williams says that the critical response to *Orpheus Descending* (1957), which he misdates 1959, sent him to Dr. Lawrence Kubie "for the mistake of strict Freudian analysis," and in the pre-opening essay for *Sweet Bird of Youth* (*New York Times,* 8 March 1959) that he had gone into analysis the year before. Whenever the analysis began, by early 1959 it was finished, although Williams was a great deal kinder toward Kubie then (*Newsweek,* 27 June 1960) than he would be in *Memoirs.* Of course, there is Ralph's "She had fallen into the hands of a psychiatrist" speech to counter the journalistic testimony. In the *Sweet Bird* piece, he says that he and the doctor never agreed on the word—not *hate,* as Kubie suggested—to describe his feeling for people and that he finally drifted from the couch to "some Caribbean beaches." In *Memoirs,* he indicates that the analysis ended because Kubie's only practical suggestion was that Williams break with Frank Merlo, his long-time lover.

3.   As a warning against taking first reactions too seriously, let me point out that I am here writing an apparently sympathetic examination of a play which I dismissed in my initial review (*Drama Survey,* Fall, 1961) as one that "might have been written by any of the Broadway regulars," a negative response that I carried unexamined into *American Drama Since World War II* (1962).

4.   Since "Shadow Wood" first appeared in the 1964 edition of *In the Winter of the Cities,* it is not certain—at least, from published sources—whether the epigraph was adapted from the poem or a poem grew out of the epigraphic quatrain.

5.   I have an active dread of articles with titles like "The Fire Symbol in Tennessee Williams" so I approached Krisna Gorowara's essay in *The Literary Half-yearly* (January and July, 1967) with trepidation. I was gratified to discover that he used the fireplace in *Period* not as a symbol but as a dramatic device that implemented the relationship between Ralph and Isabel in Act One, George and Isabel in Act Three.

Apparent Sophoclean Echoes in Tennessee Williams's *Night of the Iguana*

HELEN E. MORITZ

Tennessee Williams's *Night of the Iguana* runs nearly all of the first of its three acts before there is any hint of Sophocles. We are introduced to T. Lawrence Shannon, the defrocked priest who makes expenses by conducting teachers from a Baptist Ladies' College on a tour through Mexico; several of the disaffected ladies on his current tour, including Charlotte, a girl he has seduced—or been seduced by—and her irate self-appointed guardian Miss Fellowes, who is trying to have Shannon removed as tour guide; and we meet Maxine Faulk, friend of Shannon, the recent and merry widow who runs the Costa Verde Hotel. The hotel boasts a hilltop site in a lush rain forest, in view of the sea. It is this place to which Shannon, on the verge of another breakdown, has brought his tour in defiance of the itinerary, and from which he refuses, momentarily, to budge, despite threats from the school teacher and urgings by the bus driver. Maxine, for her part, prefers that Shannon give up the tour and step into her late husband's shoes at the Costa Verde.

The frantic tensions and conflicting demands of this opening are suddenly interrupted by the appearance of two characters who seem to derive from another world entirely from that inhabited by the others. The entrance of the nearly blind and deaf Nonno, at age ninety-seven the "world's oldest living and practicing poet" (1.280, 284–285),[1] supported and guided by his granddaughter Hannah, recalls the prototype for this scene, the entrance of another blind and aging man who relies on the support of a young woman, that of Oedipus and Antigone in Sophocles' *Oedipus at Colonus*. This equation seems amply borne out by closer scrutiny of the text. Furthermore, the pattern of entrances is programmatic for the course of the play: as the earthy and hysterical characters of the opening scenes are followed by the grotesque but somehow ethereal figures of Nonno and Hannah,[2] so the nasty imbroglio of difficulties immediately besetting Shannon is subsequently reconsidered on the abstract level, by means of an inter-identification of the minister with the two newcomers.

Reprinted with permission from *Classical and Modern Literature* 5 (Summer 1985), 305–14, where it was first published. The Greek text is that of A. C. Pearson in the Oxford Classical Text (1924).

In this article I show the parallel between the Williams characters and the Sophoclean characters; draw together the author's indications that we are to recognize in Hannah, Nonno, and Shannon a common bond of experience and a shared crisis of desperation, and, on that basis, suggest another level of interpretation for some features of the play; and finally, present some indirect corroboration for my view found in the work of critics of the play and in published interviews with Tennessee Williams himself. A prior disclaimer, however. I do not presume to offer a total assessment of *Night of the Iguana*—I will be ignoring the clearly present Christian symbolism and giving short shrift to the role of Hannah—but only to add a further dimension to an understanding of the work.[3]

Several parallels between Oedipus/Antigone and Nonno/Hannah have already been suggested. Like Oedipus (*OC* 1), Nonno is old and nearly blind; Hannah's first remark to her grandfather on stage suggests this allusively: "Nonno, you've lost your sunglasses." "No," he replies, "took them off. No sun" (1.277). The grandfather's virtual blindness is later made explicit by Hannah in response to a question about Nonno's continual mumbling: "He composes out loud. He has to commit his lines to memory because he can't see to write them or read them" (2.302).

Like Oedipus and Antigone, the pair have wandered extensively together. Hannah tells Shannon that they have been around the world, "almost as many times as the world's been around the sun" (1.286). And like Antigone, Hannah has given up the normal expectations of a home and family to care for the old man who needs her. Nonno tells Shannon: "She isn't a modern flapper, she isn't modern and she—doesn't flap, but she was brought up to be a wonderful wife and mother. But . . . I'm a selfish old man so I've kept her all to myself" (2.316). Similarly Oedipus compared his daughters favorably to his sons:

> "[of whom Antigone], from the time she left childhood behind and gained the strength of an adult, always—poor wretch—wandered with me and guided the old man, often going hungry and barefoot in the wild forest, worn out by storms and the parching heat of the sun, enduring it all: she considers life at home of secondary importance, if her father has care" (*OC* 345-352)

At one moment Williams even adds an element of uncertainty to the exact degree of relationship between the girl and old man, as though to reproduce the ambiguity of Oedipus' relationship to Antigone. Sophocles' character calls Antigone his child and sister (*OC* 534-535). Nonno observes of Hannah: "I call her my daughter, but she's my daughter's daughter. We've been in charge of each other since she lost both her parents in the very first automobile crash on the island of Nantucket" (2.316).

But it is not merely in their backgrounds that the figures are similar. The citizens of Colonus are at first reluctant to permit Oedipus to remain in their territory; Maxine is similarly unenthusiastic about taking on the old man and the girl. The reasons are not wholly unlike. Oedipus is regarded as a pariah, capable of bringing pollution on those he encounters (*OC* 220-236). No religious sensibility is offended by Nonno's presence, but his infirmity, shouting deafness, and grotesque pronouncements make him, in his own way, a pariah among the Costa Verde's other guests.[4] In one such pronouncement Nonno alludes to his sprained ankle in language which recalls the stages in the Sphinx's "riddle of man": "Hannah, tell the lady that my perambulator is temporary. I will soon be ready to crawl and then to toddle and before long I will be leaping around here like an—old—mountain—goat" (1.280).

Oedipus offers the boon of his own sacred resting place in return for sanctuary with the Athenians (*OC* 284-288).[5] Nonno tenders a bunch of wild orchids and promises: "if she'll forgive my disgraceful longevity and this . . . temporary decrepitude . . . I will present her with the last signed . . . com-pitty of my first volume of verse" (1.279, 281).[6] In time pity and reverence for the suppliant move Theseus and the citizens of Colonus to accept Oedipus.[7] Pity moves Maxine less deeply; she agrees to let Hannah and Nonno stay—for one night only (1.285). It will be enough.

For as Oedipus recognized his destiny in the grove of the Eumenides, Nonno has a similar sense about a place in Mexico near the sea. In the case of Oedipus, there was divine guidance from Apollo,

> "who, when he prophesied these many evils, spoke to me of rest after long years, when I had come to the final country, where I would receive lodging as guest of the dread goddesses. He said that there I would change course from this wretched life, and live as a benefit to those who received me and a bane to those who drove me out. He pledged that I would have omens of this—earthquake, or thunder, or the lightning-flash of Zeus. So [Furies], it can only be your sure winged signs that led me to this grove" (*OC* 87-98)

Destiny provides Nonno with similar apocalyptic guidance. Hannah tells Shannon that just lately, when she saw Nonno was fading, she "tried to persuade him to go back to Nantucket, but . . . he said, 'No, *Mexico*,'" and "insisted that we go on with the trip till we got to the sea, the . . . cradle of life as he calls it . . ." (2.314). Nonno had recently started his first new poem in twenty years (1.285), one which a stage direction says he knows will be his last (3.327). At their arrival Nonno can "feel and smell" the sea (1.278), and soon announces his conviction that he will finish his poem at Costa Verde. "I've never been surer of anything in my life," he says (2.310).

Oedipus' marvelous end, heralded by a divine summons of thunder and lightning, confers a mysterious benediction on the Athenians (*OC* 1456-1490, 1508-1555).[8] Nonno's end is comparably marvelous, a quiet close after a triumphant completion of his "loveliest poem" (3.373), a lyric surrender to the eternal cycle of life and a cry for courage. The completed poem, Nonno's final assertion of his dignity as a human being, confers its own blessing on his benefactors, on Shannon and Hannah. Williams has even provided the atmospheric fireworks—the dinner scene is interrupted by a furious thunderstorm (2.325-326).

These parallels, while interesting, do not in themselves contribute significantly to an understanding of *Night of the Iguana* because the relationship between Hannah and Nonno the grandfather, however moving, is dramatically secondary to that between Hannah and Shannon the minister, just as Nonno is not so central a figure as Shannon. The playwright has contrived, however, to portray these three characters—Hannah, Nonno, and Shannon —to some extent as aspects of the same personality, or more accurately, as possible responses to the same life situation. There is an inter-identification among the three which permits us to see something of Oedipus—both the younger Oedipus and the fiery Sophoclean aged one—in Shannon. And it is the inter-identification which prepares us to accept the end of the play, the completion of Nonno's poem and Shannon's capitulation to himself (and to Maxine) as a natural integration of the two men's lives.

Tennessee Williams himself attested to the bracketing of these three characters; in an interview with Seymour Peck of the *New York Times* he called them collectively the "world-conquered protagonists" of the play.[9] Within the play, the assonance of their names—Shannon, Hannah, Nonno—is a signal to their similarities.[10] All have endured long difficult travels, and "[not] just travels about the . . . earth's surface," as Hannah says. "I mean . . . subterranean travels, the . . . the journeys that the spooked and bedeviled people are forced to take through the . . . the *unlighted* sides of their natures" (3.353). Shannon had confessed to Maxine at his arrival that the "spook" which plagued him recurringly was at it again (1.262-263). A powerful sense of the linking of the two men's lives is produced in that scene where Nonno, being assisted along the path by Shannon, speaks of his poem: "I'm pretty sure I'm going to finish it here." Shannon replies: "I've got the same feeling, Grandpa." Nonno: "I've never been surer of anything in my life." Shannon: "I've never been surer of anything in mine, either" (2.310). Most vividly, all are united in the eponymous symbol of the iguana, which had been caught by the beach boys employed at the hotel. Shannon shows it to Hannah as it wriggles under the verandah: "See? The iguana? At the end of its rope? Trying to go on past the end of its goddam rope? Like *you!* Like *me!* Like Grandpa with his last poem!" (3.367-368).

If both Shannon and Nonno are "at the end of the rope," they appear to be very different ropes. The old man is approaching the end of life, as Hannah says: "It's like a blind man climbing a staircase that goes to nowhere, that just falls off into space, and I hate to say what it is . . ." (3.346). Shannon's crisis is his desperate inability to reconcile his image of himself as an ordained man of God with the sensuality of his nature to which he recurringly succumbs (e.g., 1.267-268). It is the symbol of Oedipus which creates a bridge between the two.

The cause of Oedipus' exile was his own curse on the late King Laius' killer and his subsequent recognition that, himself the object of the curse, he had fulfilled an old oracle that he would murder his father and marry his mother.[11] Prior to the recognition Oedipus had been led by his mother-wife Jocasta to deny the validity of oracles (*OT* 964-972).[12] Shannon's exile, his being locked out of his church, was also occasioned by an outrage against social sensibilities, also by, as he says, "Fornication and heresy . . . in the same week" (2.302). He had yielded to the seductions of a young Sunday school teacher—a kind of spiritual daughter, if you will. Jocasta had hanged herself when she realized what she had done; the Sunday school teacher merely grazed herself with her father's razor, but it made a scandal. The following Sunday, instead of delivering the penitent sermon he had prepared, Shannon shouted to the disapproving faces of the congregation, "I'm tired of conducting services in praise and worship of a senile delinquent . . ." (2.302-303).[13]

From that time Shannon had wandered, haunted by the event as though by Furies. The initial public offense was repeated endlessly with young girls on the tours he guided, and even pursues him onto the stage of *Iguana* in the form of Charlotte, his most recent conquest, and her "guardian" Miss Fellowes, who recreates the initial act of banishment by shrieking at him, "*Defrocked! But still trying to pass himself off as a minister!*" (1.275, 276; 3.337). Shannon refers to Charlotte and Miss Fellowes as "the teen-age Medea and the older Medea" (2.306), but in view of his personal history they would more accurately be described as "the teen-age Erinys and the older Erinys."[14]

Shannon bears his own resemblance to the fulminating Oedipus of *Oedipus at Colonus,* absorbing the internal characteristics of Sophocles' character while Nonno presents the external appearance. To the citizens of Colonus Oedipus admits the deeds that have become synonymous with his name, but vigorously denies any moral guilt.[15] The Greek gods ultimately demonstrate the truth of Oedipus' assertions of moral innocence by receiving him among themselves.[16] Shannon's protestations of innocence are somewhat harder to sustain, but he makes them with no less energy. When Maxine asks why he "want[s] the young ones," Shannon replies, "I don't want any, any— regardless of age" (1.267). At Shannon's insistence that he will shortly be resuming his former profession, Maxine reminds him that "Churchgoers don't go to church to hear atheistical sermons." "Goddamit," Shannon replies, "I never preached an atheistical sermon in a church in my life" (1.271). Later, before most of the company, Miss Fellowes shrieks, "You were locked out of your church!—for atheism and seducing of girls!" And Shannon thunders, "In front of God and witnesses, you are lying, lying!" (3.337).

Like Oedipus, too, Shannon has a kind of privileged communication with God. At the climax of *Oedipus at Colonus* comes a terrific peal of thunder (*OC* 1456), which Oedipus recognizes as a personal signal, and the repeated thunder and lightning are the proof he offers Theseus that his end has come

(*OC* 1513-1515). And moments later, in the sacred grove, the bystanders hear an unseen voice cry out to him: "Ho! You there, Oedipus, why do we hesitate to depart?" (*OC* 1627-1628). Shannon's communication with God is also in the vernacular of thunder and lightning. "It's going to storm tonight—a terrific electric storm. Then you will see the Reverend T. Lawrence Shannon's conception of God Almighty paying a visit to the world he created" (2.305). After dinner, as the storm bursts, Hannah reminds him, "Here is your God, Mr. Shannon." And he replies, "Yes, I see him, I hear him, I know him. And if he doesn't know that I know him, let him strike me dead with a bolt of his lightning" (2.326).[17]

Of course in the end Shannon does not resemble Oedipus in moral splendor. To Hannah he had earlier admitted the very thing—being locked out of his church for fornication and heresy—which he denies so vigorously to Miss Fellowes. The conflict in Shannon is such that he cannot publicly acknowledge facts inconsistent with his image of himself; he cannot revise the image in accordance with the record. But both plays end with recognition of truth. Whereas Oedipus' claims are ultimately vindicated before God and man, Shannon capitulates to his nature and agrees to stay on with Maxine, to keep her and the female patrons of the hotel happy (3.374).

At this point in the two plays, the resolutions, comparison of Shannon with Oedipus is in danger of becoming bathetic. But not even Sophocles' characters were all from the heroic mold of Oedipus. Jocasta's advice to her husband in the earlier play, rejected by that stronger character, becomes, mutatis mutandis, the principle of release for Shannon. Jocasta had said: "What should man fear, since fortune rules, and no one has clear foreknowledge of things to come?" (*OT* 977-978). Hannah puts it more simply: "The moral is . . . accept whatever situation you cannot improve" (3.363). In either case the immediate occasion for pronouncing such a rule for living is the need to account for sexual aberration—the prophecy that Oedipus would sleep with his mother in Jocasta's case, and the underwear fetish of a traveling salesman for Hannah.

Until the end of the play Shannon, unlike Oedipus of the *Colonus,* can never stop running from his oracle, can never acquiesce in Hannah's principle. That is why the double, Nonno, is necessary. It is Nonno who has lived long enough to reconcile himself with life, and to express in his completed poem the courage to accept the fact that the "zenith of . . . life [is] gone past forever," the "chronicle" is "no longer gold," but "a bargaining with mist and mould." The poem is simultaneous with Shannon's freeing of the captive iguana, and parallel to it (3.370-371). Shannon is released from the golden chronicle which he cannot maintain and starts a "second life" with Maxine. The end suits Shannon, and we have come, like Hannah, to give him his due as an individual who has never stopped striving. Hannah speaks of him in terms that could apply to Oedipus: "I respect a person that has had to fight and howl for his decency . . . much more than I respect the lucky ones that just had theirs handed out to them at birth and never afterward snatched away from them by . . . unbearable . . . torments" (3.346-347). The benediction here is not that of the universe-defying Oedipus, but it is a benediction nonetheless, one more suited to human capacity.

Three minor points of contact between the *Iguana* and the *Colonus* may be mentioned here. First, critics have noted the apparent irrelevance to the plot of the Nazi guests at the hotel who cavort around the edges of the action.[18] Williams himself has described them as "offering a vivid counterpoint—as world conquerors—to the world-conquered protagonists of the play."[19] They find their counterpart in Oedipus' son Polynices of the Sophoclean play, lurking on the border and threatening war on his homeland, oblivious to the deeper human needs of his father.[20]

Second, the ravages and alterations of time are the subject of Nonno's poem, and critics Robert Heilman and Ferdinand Leon have documented Williams's preoccupation with the theme of time in his other plays as well.[21] Perhaps no single subject is so thoroughly Sophoclean as this. One thinks of Ajax' great suicide speech (*Aj.* 646-692) and, in the *Colonus,* Oedipus' prophetic speech to Theseus on the coming war in Thebes (*OC* 607-621), especially: "And the spirit never remains the same, neither among friends, nor from one city to another" (*OC* 612-613). In an interview during rehearsals for *Iguana* Williams said, "I despair sometimes of love being lasting, and of people getting along together . . . as nations and as individuals . . . of their realizing how important, how necessary it is to do that. I've just despaired of it."[22]

Finally, the iguana itself, the lizard under the verandah of the Costa Verde Hotel which symbolically represents the situation of Hannah, Shannon, and Nonno, is not unlike the sacred Furies who reside beneath the soil of the grove of Colonus, repulsive in appearance but beneficial in effect—a double for the "monster" Oedipus who, decrepit, ragged, his eye sockets blind, will nonetheless join them in that grove as a blessing to Athens.[23]

The symbolism of the Sophoclean Oedipus in this play seems to have gone almost unnoticed; further, there has been only one passing and unelaborated allusion to Nonno as a "Tiresias."[24] The play has nevertheless moved critics to write of Shannon or Williams in terms which apply equally well to Oedipus or Sophocles. In his book *Common and Uncommon Masks* Richard Gilman says of Shannon at play's end, "there is now a sense of destiny continued under a placating star, that the painfulness of what we are and are driven to do is eased by being faced and by being given a counter-image, tenuous but lasting."[25] Howard Taubman, writing in the *New York Times,* described Williams in language which would do for the Sophocles who wrote the *Colonus* at the end of his life, having written *Oedipus the King* in middle years: "The man who can glimpse the anguish and fortitude of people who somehow have learned to survive the dark night of the soul has achieved a rare maturity. . . . [There has been] a watershed in [Tennessee Williams's] spiritual development. In this play he is beginning to transcend the raging pessimism that has permeated so much of his work. His vision is still somber, but the fury is being transformed into a kind of tragic wisdom."[26]

And what does Tennessee Williams say? In an interview with Seymour Peck of the *New York Times* he says: "These people are learning to reach the point of utter despair and still go past it with courage. That is the theme of the play, how to live with dignity after despair."[27] He is describing Shannon, Hannah, and Nonno, but he is describing their prototype as well—the despair of Oedipus the king as he recognizes with full horror who he is, and the dignity of Oedipus at Colonus, a man who has made his peace with his past and courageously transcended it, finally to be vindicated for his uncompromising insistence on human worth.

Notes

1. References to *The Night of the Iguana* are by act and page number to vol. 4 of *The Theatre of Tennessee Williams,* 7 vols. (New York: New Directions, 1972).

2. Cf. stage directions, (1.266): "Hannah is remarkable looking—ethereal, almost ghostly. She suggests a Gothic cathedral image of a medieval saint, but animated," and 1.277, "[Nonno] is a very old man but has a powerful voice for his age and always seems to be shouting something of importance. . . . He is immaculately dressed—a linen suit, white as his thick poet's hair."

3. On the Christian symbolism see, e.g., John MacNicholas, "Williams' Power of the Keys," 581–605, and Philip M. Armato, "Tennessee Williams' Meditations on Life and Death in *Suddenly Last Summer, The Night of the Iguana,* and *The Milk Train Doesn't Stop Here Anymore,*" 558–570, both in Jac Tharpe, ed., *Tennessee Williams: A Tribute* (Jackson: U Pr of Miss, 1977); and Esther M. Jackson, "Williams and the Moral Function," in *The Broken World of Tennessee Williams* (Madison: U of Wis Pr, 1965), 129–155.

4. Cf. Maxine, "They look like a pair of loonies" (1.278), and Nonno's embarrassing shouting at dinner in act 2, esp. 312.

5. Cf. 72, 84–93, 576–583.

6. Oedipus, too, placates the powerful local females with a bouquet when, at the Chorus' urging, he sends Ismene to offer the Eumenides olive shoots as part of his ritual atonement for trespass (*OC* 466-484).

7. *OC* 631-641, 556-562, cf. 461-464.

8. Cf. 94–95.

9. Seymour Peck, "Williams and 'The Iguana,' " *New York Times,* 24 December 1961, sec. 2, p. 5, where Williams also says, "Instead of one Blanche DuBois, I have three in 'Iguana.' "

10. Cf. Leonard Casper, "Triangles of Transaction in Tennessee Williams," in Tharpe, *Tribute,* 737 and 747.

11. *OT* 236-251, 787-793, 1182-1185. Shannon's fate, too, found its origins in a sexually conflicted interaction with his mother who, as Maxine says in reporting an overheard conversation, had confused his feelings about sex by spanking him for masturbation because "it made God mad as much as it did Mama, and she had to punish you for it so God wouldn't punish you for it harder than she would." Loving both God and Mama, Shannon had given it up, but harbored a secret resentment against both authority figures. As Maxine tells him, "And so you got back at God by preaching atheistical sermons and you got back at Mama by starting to lay young girls" (3.329).

12. Cf. 707–725, 851–858.

13.   Shannon must be prompted to relive this "subterranean journey" through the "darker side of his nature" by the sympathetic Hannah (2.301-304), much as Oedipus only reluctantly tells *his* dark story to the concerned citizens of Colonus (*OC* 510-535).

14.   Cf. Joseph K. Davis, "Landscapes of the Dislocated Mind in Williams' *The Glass Menagerie*," in Tharpe, *Tribute,* 198: "[Williams's hero] has necessarily become something of an Oresteian hero—a representative modern individual driven by self-admitted guilt and obsessive fears but who has a deep-felt longing to experience a redemptive vision and win back his peace of mind. Unlike Aeschylus' hero, Williams' hero is yet pursued by the Furies; thus far no divine intervention has occurred to save him and cleanse his tortured soul."

15.   *OC* 539, 548, 962-964.

16.   *OC* 1626-1628, 1661-1665.

17.   Henry Popkin, "The Plays of Tennessee Williams," *TDR* 4.3 (1960): 46, says of the archetypal Williams hero, "All are threatened because their superb qualities attract the lightning. . . . We may say that Williams starts with his Adonis [of Val in *Orpheus Descending*] for the same reason that Sophocles begins with his king of Thebes. Each is great enough to attract the lightning."

18.   E.g., Richard Gilman, "Williams as Phoenix," in *Common and Uncommon Masks: Writings on Theatre 1961–1970* (New York: Random, 1971), 141; Arthur Ganz, "The Desperate Morality of the Plays of Tennessee Williams," *ASch* 31 (1962): 292; John McCarten, "Lonely, Loquacious, and Doomed," *The New Yorker* 37 (13 Jan. 1962): 61.

19.   In the *New York Times* interview with Seymour Peck (above note 9).

20.   *OC* 1291-1438, cf. 374–381, 416–419, 442–444.

21.   Robert Heilman, "Tennessee Williams: Approaches to Tragedy," *SoR,* n.s. 1 (1965): 782–783, 787; and especially Ferdinand Leon, "Time, Fantasy, and Reality in *Night of the Iguana*," *MD* 11 (1968): 87–96.

22.   Lewis Funke and John E. Booth, "Williams on Williams," *Theatre Arts* 46 (Jan. 1962): 72–73.

23.   In the Peck interview (above, note 9) Williams says, "The iguana is a caught thing and not a very attractive thing"; neither is Oedipus, *OC* 141, 576-578. Williams goes on to say, "It's not a creature one would easily pity. . . . It doesn't stand for any particular character in the play, perhaps it stands for the human situation," and, one might add, in those "subterranean" levels mentioned by Hannah (3.353) and experienced by Oedipus as well as Shannon.

24.   Jackson (above, note 3) 28. There has been a great deal of discussion on the use of mythical symbols and archetypes in Williams's work in general, however; cf. Jackson herself, "The Anti-Hero," 68–87; Robert Heilman, "Approaches" (above, note 21) 770–790; Judith J. Thompson, "Symbol, Myth, and Ritual" in *The Glass Menagerie, The Rose Tattoo,* and *Orpheus Descending,* 679–711, and Nancy M. Tischler, "A Gallery of Witches," 494–509, both in Tharpe, *Tribute.*

25.   Gilman (above, note 18) 142.

26.   Howard Taubman, "Changing Course," *New York Times,* 7 January 1962, sec. 2, p. 1.

27.   Above, note 9.

Sexual Imagery in Tennessee Williams'
Kingdom of Earth

FOSTER HIRSCH

Like most of his work, Tennessee Williams' *Kingdom of Earth* (produced in New York in 1968 as *The Seven Descents of Myrtle*) is at least marginally about the South in decline. Also typical of Williams' usual method is the fact that much of the allegorical meaning and gothic atmosphere of the play are derived from the playwright's pervasive sexual imagery. *Kingdom of Earth* is a prolonged dispute between half brothers about the rightful ownership of the farmhouse they both claim. The decaying house, and the corresponding dilapidation of the characters, constitute Williams' lament for the South's blighted heritage—but it is the specifically sexual terms in which the brothers are identified with the house, the surrounding land, and the flooding river which is the true center of the play.

The half brothers, who represent opposing life forces, are closely associated with the sexual connotations of house and river. Lot, "a frail, delicately—you might say exotically—pretty youth of about twenty,"[1] is identified with his mother's gilt-encrusted downstairs parlor and with her equally "refined" upstairs bedroom. Myrtle, Lot's new wife, assures him that he is as "refined and elegant as this parlor," and Williams notes about the bedroom that "the aura of its former feminine occupant, Lot's mother, still persists in this room: a lady who liked violets and lace and mother-of-pearl and decorative fringes on things." Confined to the bedroom for most of the play, Lot retreats further and further into reveries of his genteel, mother-dominated past. With perhaps excessive Freudian neatness, Lot idealizes his mother and her house and curses his father, who lived and died "howling like a wild beast."

Chicken, who is part black, is Williams' perennial stud—domineering, assertive, buoyed up by sexual pride: Chicken embodies the power of the rising, threatening river. He inhabits the cave-like ground floor kitchen, the sparseness of which is relieved only by a calendar photo of a nude girl. The rough-hewn kitchen (significantly, it is the only warm room in the house) is separated from the chilly, delicate parlor by a narrow, dark, womb-like hall.

Reprinted with permission from *Notes on Contemporary Literature* 1 (March 1971): 10–13.

Williams emphasizes Chicken's animal-like quality—a quality which aligns him with the primitive father whom Lot deplores. When Lot brings Myrtle to the house, Chicken stays in his kitchen "like a crouched animal"; and when Myrtle goes to the kitchen door, she mistakes Chicken's heavy breathing for a dog's. His strange name also alerts us to his rough nature: "They named me Chicken because I set on the roof with the chickens one time this place was flooded . . . if I got hungry I'd bite the haid off one of the other chickens and drink its blood."

Williams surrounds Chicken with objects (most of which are conventionally Freudian) which italicize his pulsating sexuality. Chicken's guitar is "a real mansize instrument"; he often plays with his knife and, at one point, he carves a crude picture on the kitchen table with it; he pushes a cat through a trap door and Myrtle's fear that the cat will drown in the flooded cellar below represents her own fear of water and of Chicken's sexual threat.

Chicken, who works out in the fields and who survives floods, is Williams' hard, natural man; Lot, who stays in bed and who wears his mother's dresses, is a soft, artificial man. Lot has "a mouth like a flower"; Chicken's creed is that "a man and his life both got to be equally hard."

Myrtle is the pawn tossed from one brother to the other. She is Lot's mother and Chicken's whore, and her differing relationships to the two brothers indicate dual aspects of her sexuality. She is afraid of her instinctive attraction to Chicken, but, like the oncoming flood, Chicken has the strength to overwhelm her. Myrtle spends most of her time going back and forth between the play's two symbolic stations—the faded, transvestite elegance of Lot's upstairs bedroom and the earthy warmth of the kitchen. With each descent from bedroom to kitchen, Chicken's sexual dominance over the helpless, good-natured Myrtle is strengthened.

The three characters are continually threatened by "the low, insistent murmur of vast waters in flood or near it." Their responses to the encroaching flood clarify their sexual natures. Beyond reality, Lot is oblivious to the flood, and he dies before the inundation. Myrtle's fear of water and her reliance on Chicken to save her from drowning signal both her hostility and attraction to Chicken. Chicken, for whom "a river in flood" represents "a natural act of God," alone is unafraid of the coming flood, and sees it even as a challenge to test his philosophy of hardness. Since Lot dies before the flood, the approach of the orgasmic flood coincides with Chicken's inheritance of the land. The flood symbolizes the full release of "the lustful body," and Williams celebrates this release through the impure, but vital character of Chicken: "I'll tell you how I look at life in my life, or in any man's life. There's nothing in the world, in this whole kingdom of earth, that can compare with one thing, and that one thing is what's able to happen between a man and a woman, just that thing, nothing more, is perfect."

Kingdom of Earth, then, continues Williams' perennial investigation of various kinds of human sexuality. And it is as well the sexual imagery with which Williams builds up character and situation which reflects the play's subsidiary concern of dramatizing the moral and social history of the playwright's South.

Note

1. Tennessee Williams, *Kingdom of Earth* (New York: New Directions, 1968). All further quotations are from this edition.

When Ghosts Supplant Memories:
Tennessee Williams' *Clothes for a Summer Hotel*

THOMAS P. ADLER

"I tried to leave you behind me, but I am more faithful than I intended to be."
—Tom in *The Glass Menagerie*

"Words are the love acts of writers."

—Zelda in *Clothes for a Summer Hotel*

I

After *The Glass Menagerie,* which brought Tennessee Williams his first Broadway acclaim in 1945, the openly autobiographical nature of his drama abates almost entirely, not to re-emerge until *Vieux Carré* in 1978. The content of the later play clearly demarcates it, however, as a post-*Memoirs* work, since it treats openly what *Menagerie* had submerged—the fact of the playwright's homosexuality; nevertheless, its structure, which employs a narrator/central character named The Writer whom Williams designates as "myself those many years ago" (*Carré* 4), more closely approximates the earlier "memory" play than any other work in the Williams canon. *Clothes for a Summer Hotel* (1980) is, at first glance, biographical, telling part of the long story of Scott and Zelda Fitzgerald (and their friendship with Hemingway and the Murphys). Yet as is true also of Williams' two earlier forays into biographical drama, *I Rise in Flame, Cried the Phoenix* (1941)—about D.H. Lawrence—and

Reprinted with permission from *Southern Literary Journal* 19, no. 2 (1987): 5–19.

Steps Must be Gentle (1947)—about Hart Crane—, the autobiographical impulse remains uppermost in *Hotel;*[1] here, though, it evidences itself in ways other than just a continuing exploration of the eternal conflict between the male and female sensibilities within the artist. Less forthright than *Vieux Carré, Summer Hotel* is "a ghost play" (*Hotel* xi) rather than a "memory" one, substituting the Fitzgeralds as vaporous surrogates for the barely disguised "real life" portraits in *Menagerie*. If not as frankly confessional as *Menagerie, Hotel* still emerges as a play of guilt, spawned by the author's betrayal of the person closest to him. Beneath both Scott's dramatized relationship with Zelda and Tom's with Laura lay Tennessee's own with his sister Rose.[2] In his first Broadway play as in his last—and in several such as *Out Cry* (1973) in between—, Williams obsessively limns the "love" between himself and his sister that "was, and is, the deepest in [their] lives and was, perhaps, very pertinent to [their] withdrawal from extra familial attachments" (*Memoirs* 120).

Williams serves notice of the link between *Glass Menagerie* and *Summer Hotel* in two ways: first, through the plays' titles; and second, through the authorial discussions of dramaturgy that precede and/or begin each. The latter work gets its title because Scott arrives from the West Coast inappropriately dressed in lightweight clothes for an autumnal visit with Zelda at the Highland Hospital in Asheville, North Carolina. His journey has taken him from Hollywood to a mental asylum, from one world of make-believe to another place of delusions. Likewise, Laura's menagerie of little glass animals provides a retreat from reality in a protective world of fantasy. Although Williams' "Production Notes" to *Menagerie* (a manifesto for "a new plastic theatre which must take the place of the exhausted theatre of realistic conventions" that is hardly less significant as a document in theatre history than Strindberg's call for a very opposite naturalistic theatre in the "Author's Foreword" to *Miss Julie* over half a century before) serve to justify Williams' "unconventional techniques" (*Menagerie* 7), an audience-in-the-theatre would be told only what the narrator/central character Tom Wingfield engagingly provides in his opening monologue. His narrative renders theoretical statement an integral part of the drama when he contrasts the Ibsenite, illusionistic play ("illusion that has the appearance of truth") with the non-representational *Menagerie* ("truth in the pleasant disguise of illusion") (*Menagerie* 22). The "Author's Note" to *Hotel,* which Williams' intended audiences would read in their programs before the play, also rationalizes "taking extraordinary license with time and place" on the "grounds" that "truth of character" can thereby be "explore[d] in more depth" (*Hotel* xi). Yet there exists a major difference in tone: whereas Tom—like Williams himself in the stage directions that precede *Vieux Carré*—speaks in the first person, inviting the audience to enter into memory with him, the author of the "Note" before *Hotel* deliberately creates the impression of aloofness, hiding behind the editorial "our" and "us" and "we" and thus making the material seem more remote to an audience. Furthermore, Williams' insistence that "in a sense all plays are ghost plays, since players are not actually whom they play" (*Hotel* xi), possesses a certain ambiguity: calling attention to the mimetic nature of drama only to undercut it, he presses home not only that the actors are not really Scott and Zelda, but equally raises the possibility that the Scott and Zelda imitated by these actors are masks for still other characters or persons.

II

A traditional reading of *Glass Menagerie* as a confessional play centers the protagonist's guilt in Tom's desertion of his sister (and mother) to discover selfhood—eventually as a writer, with the play itself as the first fruits of that vocation, since it is Tom's play, as well as Tennessee's.[3] Though the imperative to find oneself cannot be fulfilled without violating the equally compelling need not to lose others in the process, it appears that the act of writing/narrating *Menagerie* has been therapeutic for its protagonist, and at least temporarily so for its ultimate author, the playwright himself: Laura does, after all, "Blow out [her] candles" (*Menagerie* 115), perhaps signifying her acceptance of an even lonelier existence than before now that she has tasted what she knows she can never again have; lit "inwardly with altar candles" by Jim's visit, she displays "a look of almost infinite desolation" after his announcement of his engagement to someone else "snuff[s] out . . . the holy candles in the altar of Laura's face" (*Menagerie* 97, 108). Tom, nevertheless, interprets, or perhaps only rationalizes, her action as releasing him from his guilt, as an absolution and an encouragement to go forward. (In *Vieux Carré*, Laura's action finds its parallel when the narrator's grandmother—again a character modelled from Williams' own family—appears "in the form of an elderly female saint" to offer a benediction, "an almost invisible gesture of . . . forgiveness . . . through understanding" (*Carré* 26–7) after The Writer's revelation of his homosexuality.)

The biographical and autobiographical evidence suggests, however, that Williams' own guilt almost certainly resides in something other—and deeper—than either his homosexuality or his having been absent at the time of, and thus having done nothing to prevent, his sister Rose's prefrontal lobotomy. The *Memoirs* (1975), which end significantly enough with the image of Tennessee again leaving Rose, this time back at Stoney Lodge sanitarium after a New Year's holiday in the city, relate an incident that Williams judges "the cruelest thing I have done in my life, I suspect, and one for which I can never properly atone." Rose, it seems, had tattled about a drunken party and obscene phone calls when their parents were away on vacation; forbidden to entertain his friends again, Tennessee "hissed at her: 'I hate the sight of your ugly face!' " (*Memoirs* 122). The playwright's brother reports another incident that would seem to provide an even closer analogue in its outlines to the action of *Menagerie*. Evidently counselled by her psychiatrist to " 'find [herself] a lover,' " Rose supposedly told one of her brother's young shoe salesmen friends "that she would welcome an attempt at lovemaking." Overhearing this, Tennessee apparently chided her, " 'I want you to know you disgust me' " (Williams and Mead 37).

Is the intense moral revulsion—which maybe Williams was still trying to atone for through Hannah, in *The Night of the Iguana* (1961), when she responds to the underwear fetishist's request by saying, "Nothing human disgusts me unless it's unkind, violent" (*Iguana* 117)—to be accounted for by a puritanical streak? Might its impetus not rather be sexual jealousy?[4] *Menagerie* provides a definite clue that it may have indeed been the latter. After Jim leaves, Amanda accuses Tom of having deliberately, though perhaps unconsciously, brought home for Laura a non-eligible bachelor: "It seems extremely peculiar that you wouldn't know your best friend was going to be married!" (*Menagerie* 113). Although insisting that the intense attraction between his sister and himself remained "quite unsullied by any carnal knowledge . . . no casual physical intimacy" even, Williams does openly acknowledge its very real presence: "Some perceptive critic of the theatre made the observation that the true theme of my work is 'incest' " (*Memoirs* 119–20). If *Menagerie,* "usually talked of as Tom's exorcism of memory . . . can just as accurately be seen as repetition," as Parker perceptively argues, then "there is also ruthlessness in Tom's final command [i.e., 'Blow out your candles'] . . . this is a kind of loving murder, a repetition of the original violation" ("Composition" 418). Tom demands, in short, that Laura remain virginal for him.

The incestuous impulse that appears obliquely in *Menagerie* is, as Clayton notes (144), the central motif in Williams' Lorca-like short play, *Purification* (1944). Yet both its verse form and the distance in time (over a century ago) and space (the Western ranch lands) help remove this highly symbolic tale of Rosario's passion for his sister Elena from too close an association with Tennessee and Rose. No such distancing occurs, however, when Williams returns to the motif in his intimate and anguished *Out Cry*. The play's epigraph from the Song of Solomon (" 'A garden enclosed is my sister' "), later repeated as a dialogue line (*Out Cry* 56); the "huge, dark statue upstage, a work of great power and darkly subjective meaning [suggesting] things anguished and perverse (in his [i.e., Felice's] own nature?)" (7); and certain segments of the until recently unpublished author's "Notes for *The Two Character Play*—"sexuality . . . is actually the *Liebestod* of the two characters. . . . a play . . . as vulnerable as Clare and Felice, and as deviant" ("Notes" 3, 4)—all rather explicitly announce the centrality of an incestuous relationship.[5] The Southern setting of the play-within-the-play of this Pirandellian drama even harks back, however slightly, to *Menagerie*. In it, a brother/sister acting team,

Felice and the mentally unstable Clare, are locked in an eventually empty theatre, which may, in fact, be a state asylum, performing "The Two-Character Play," the story of their own lives that so far has no ending. Left alone when their father killed their mother and then himself, they fear venturing out into the yard where a scenic projection of a "two-headed sunflower taller than a two-story house . . . seems to be shouting sensational things about [them]": It is "the poem of two and dark as. . . . [their] Abnormality!" (*Out Cry* 29–30).

More pertinent when seeing *Out Cry* as a bridge between *Glass Menagerie* and *Summer Hotel* than the obviously unnatural relationship between Felice and Clare is, however, the manner in which Williams rethinks the problem of closure and—given a second chance, so to speak—undoes the brother's desertion of the sister: contemplating leaving the house and "never com[ing] back, . . . go[ing] Away, away!," Felice discovers that he "can't leave [Clare] alone." In a conflict reminiscent of the final movement of *Menagerie,* he "feel[s] the house the way you feel a loved person standing close behind you. Yes, I'm already defeated. . . . It seems to be whispering to me: 'You can't go away. Give up. Come in and stay.' Such a gentle command! What do I do? Naturally, I obey" (*Out Cry* 55). If Laura accedes to Tom's demand that she free him to leave at the end of *Menagerie,* with the added knowledge that he will remain faithful to her, in *Out Cry* the brother finds himself unable to desert the sister, and so he re-enters "the house [that] has turned into a prison." Images such as this one of physical entrapment abound in Williams' later plays, and he frequently concretizes the notion of emotional enclosure through the recurrent character configuration in these works of incestuous attachments (e.g., Leona and her brother in *Small Craft Warnings* [1972]; Bodey and Buddy in *Creve Coeur* [1978]).[6]

III

Williams was perhaps justifiably concerned, to the point of begging the audience's indulgence, over the "extraordinary license" he took in *Clothes for a Summer Hotel,* a play considerably less neat in its narrative strategy than either *Glass Menagerie* or *Vieux Carré.* If the opening and closing frames that establish and solidify the "memory" convention in those two works were taken away, what would remain would be essentially linear, albeit episodic, dramas. The potentially confusing and even problematical organization of *Hotel* might be of a piece with its being "a ghost play"—more akin actually to a dream play than to the more consciously controlled memory plays. *Hotel*'s action seems to occur, in fact, in a kind of Yeatsian purgatory, an appropriate abode for characters existing in an "apparitional state" (*Hotel* xii). Yeats defines the purgatorial condition as one in which the remorseful dead "Re-live / Their transgressions . . . / many times; . . . know[ing] . . . / The consequence of those transgressions" and, in a sense, transgressing again and again through the very act of remembering. For "the impression upon [the] mind" of the dead soul is tantamount to re-enactment (431, 435). The past, then, is continually and torturingly alive in a concurrent present and future; as Scott says in *Hotel*'s closing line: "The past—still always present" (77).

This conception of time as a perpetual re-experiencing (perhaps analogous to abreacting in the psychoanalytical process) pervades *Hotel*. Scott, in appearance looking as he did when he died in 1940, arrives in Asheville in 1947, just before Highland Hospital will go up in flames, consuming Zelda and several other patients. Or, equally possible, this fire, like the one in Yeats's *Purgatory,* may be a thing already past, for Zelda, told by the Intern to "play" the meeting with Scott so that "it would seem to exist," somewhat ambiguously asks: "Why should this be demanded of me now after all the other demands?—I thought that obligations stopped with death!" (*Hotel* 8). In Act Two, Hemingway reveals to Scott that he will someday recount the story of their friendship, complete with all its "embarrassing aspects," and that the telling will be responsible, in part, for precipitating Hemingway's suicide—which is then spoken about not as some future event but instead as if it had already occurred: "You see, I can betray even my oldest close friend, the one most helpful in the beginning. That may have been at least partly the reason for which I executed myself not long after, first by attempting to walk into the propeller of a plane—that having failed, by blasting my exhausted brains out with an elephant gun" (*Hotel* 67). The Yeatsian purgatorial state— which allows for fluid shifting back and forth between 1947 and 1926—is itself a variation on the repetition compulsion, and so its adaptation here suggestively hints at the nature of *Hotel* as a guilt play as well.[7] If *Hotel*'s structure appears less immediately integral to the play's central theme than the quasi-Brechtian pattern is to the meaning of *Menagerie,* it does, once perceived, capture the obsession that imprisons a mind and an imagination in an endless cycle from which there can be no escape.

By recognizing that *Summer Hotel* "may be really about the tension, both creative and lacerating, between the male and female elements in Williams' own psyche," Kroll provides a context for considering the last work for Broadway in light of such others as *Out Cry* (95). (Even considerably earlier plays, *Night of the Iguana, Summer and Smoke* (1948), *A Streetcar Named Desire* (1947), could be viewed from this perspective: while Hannah and Nonno, Alma, and Blanche are feminine in sensibility, Maxine and Shannon, John, and Stanley are masculine.) Williams first explored this conflict in *I Rise in Flame, Cried the Phoenix,* which he apparently alludes back to in Zelda's Cassandra-like cry: "I WILL DIE IN FLAMES!" (*Hotel* 15). In *Phoenix,* the dying Lawrence wars against the frightened "little old maid in [him]self, the breathless little spinster who scuttles back down the hill before God can answer the doorbell," insisting that he will meet death from a position of strength (as Hemingway vows to do in *Hotel*), with the "bit of the male left in

[him]" (63–4). Although Frieda associates the female principle with life and the male with death, Lawrence sees differently, establishing the polarities between male/life/sunlight/young blond god on the one side and female/death/night-darkness/harlot on the other. A further dichotomy—and one which Williams later uses to link Zelda with Lawrence—is that between spirit and flesh: just as Frieda entertains the possibility that Lawrence's spirit can "Live without body . . . be just a flame with nothing to feed itself on" (*Phoenix* 68), Zelda, granting that her "body will . . . be consumed if caught in fire," still envisions a kind of transcendence for herself, since her "spirit exists in fire" (*Hotel* 22).

In *Summer Hotel,* Williams dramatizes the contention between the masculine and feminine sensibilities not, as might be expected, primarily through the conflict between Scott and Zelda, but rather through Scott's uneasiness about his own sexuality and, even more so, through the increasingly strained relationship between the virile Hemingway and the "delicate" Fitzgerald. Scott comes across as someone insecure about his masculinity; shying away from "being touched by men" (*Hotel* 54) and sensitive about being "called pretty," he openly baits homosexuals, hinting at his own fear of latent homosexuality. Zelda even becomes jealous over the way that Scott seems "magnetized" by Hemingway's physical prowess. According to Milford's 1970 biography—to which Williams attributes the genesis of his play—Zelda actually "accused Scott of a homosexual liaison" with his fellow writer, with the result that "For a while at least Scott had begun to believe her" (*Zelda* 153). In *A Moveable Feast,* which details more compactly than Milford's volume the complex jealousies between the Fitzgeralds (hers over his work, his over her French aviator lover), Hemingway recounts his attempt to bolster Scott's ego by taking him to view the sculpture at the Louvre, so that Scott would see how Zelda's belittling of his sexual prowess was motivated by an attempt "To put [him] out of business. . . . to destroy [him]" (188–9).[8] As drawn by Williams, Hemingway for his part falls under the spell of Scott's androgynous appeal and is noticeably disturbed by his sympathetic response to the touching vulnerability that Scott does nothing to disguise.

If the similarities between the schizophrenic Zelda and the mentally imbalanced Rose, both confined in mental institutions, are obvious, so, too, are those between Scott and Tennessee, who both eventually suffer crack-ups over the strain of always having to go one better than their previous successes. The Intern, in a line that recalls Blanche's fate in *Streetcar* and hints that Williams is drawing a partial self-portrait in Scott as he had in characterizing such other aging artist figures as the Princess Kosmonopolis in *Sweet Bird of Youth* (1959), urges Zelda to "Be kind [to Scott]. He's a gentle man and an artist [who] died for attempting to exist as both" (*Hotel* 69). Yet the masculine and feminine sides of Scott, rather than co-exist peacefully, remain at war. If, as the fictionalized Hemingway remarks (in a comment that could validly be applied to Williams' own artistry), "duality of gender can serve some writers well" in the creation of equally complex and compelling male and female characters (*Hotel* 64), Scott seems unflattered, even annoyed, at the compliment. Most tellingly, Williams has his Hemingway comment that Scott, by writing about Zelda over and over again, "would like to appropriate her identity and her—. . . gender" (*Hotel* 64). Taken together with Scott's earlier insistence to Zelda, "we are *one* side, indivisible" (*Hotel* 35), that perhaps echoes Miriam's question, "—Are we two people, Mark, or are we—. . . Two sides of! . . . One!" from the 1969 play *In the Bar of a Tokyo Hotel* (30), this suggestion makes explicit the link between the androgynous ideal and the incestuous impulse that occurs throughout Williams' canon.

The outline that Williams sketches of Scott and Zelda's marriage once more follows, in its essentials, Milford's feminist biography.[9] According to her, Zelda at first jumped at the chance to be Scott's "creation, his fictional girl," the model for his heroines, and embraced marriage to him as "the only means of altering the scope of her life" (*Zelda* 42, 52), of breaking away from a restrictive Southern gentility into the irresponsible, fun-loving, anything-goes lifestyle of the archetypal flapper. Yet rather quickly she came to resent being used and to chaff under the "burden of performance" (*Zelda* 77). Jealous of Scott's writing, Zelda turned to writing of her own, and later to dance, as avenues of self-expression and self-definition, coming to love her work (that "Loveliest of all four-letter words," she remarks in the play [*Hotel* 32]) to the point of obsession. Scott, desiring that she always remain his child, felt a proprietary "right to Zelda's life as his raw material" (*Zelda* 115) and became jealously protective of her as a person. Since he "was the professional writer and . . . supporting Zelda, . . . the entire fabric of their life was his material" (*Zelda* 273) and not Zelda's to use, as she did in her novel, *Save Me the Waltz*. He finally blamed her mental illness and her devotion to learning ballet, rather than his own drinking, for the lengthy dry spells in his creativity, claiming she "had used him financially. . . . exhaust[ed] his talents . . . [and] cheated [him] of his dream" (*Zelda* 323). Earlier, Williams had rendered a surprisingly similar, but totally fictional, account of a husband/artist and his wife in Mark and Miriam of *Bar of a Tokyo Hotel*. If Mark, Williams' failed artist, cannot—like Scott—"stand to be touched!" by another man (*Bar* 48), neither does Miriam—like Zelda—want her own self "obliterated" in her commitment to her husband. Both wives experience as well a romantic horror over time passing and death approaching, a fear of the decaying process shared by the Princess in *Sweet Bird* and Sissy Goforth in *The Milk Train Doesn't Stop Here Anymore* (1963). Zelda has tired, in short, of being merely "A flame burning nothing? Not even casting a shadow?" (*Hotel* 49).

If Williams' Zelda accuses Scott of using his work as a substitute for passion, she regards her own writing as her only avenue of salvation. Williams seems, indeed, to be expressing his own admiration for Zelda's fiction when he has Dr. Zeller praise the "sort of fire in her work" that Scott's more classic,

"desperately—well-ordered" writing lacks (*Hotel* 55); in an interview during
the Chicago tryout of *Summer Hotel,* Williams, attributing to passages of
Zelda's *Waltz* " 'a brilliancy that Fitzgerald was unequal to,' " concluded that
she possessed " 'as much talent as her husband did' " (Van Antwerp and Johns
363)—an assessment that Milford would perhaps not make as emphatically
but which she seems at least to imply throughout her biography as she traces
Scott's supposed borrowings from Zelda's letters and diaries and his appropri-
ation of some of his wife's stories under his own name. Employing imagery
"of a hawk which is a bird of nature as predatory as a husband who appropri-
ates your life as material for his writing" (*Hotel* 12),[10] Zelda accuses Scott of
being the "author of [her] life," of wanting only "to *absorb and devour!*" (9, 11).
That Zelda's question, "If he makes of me a monument with his carefully
arranged words, is that my life, my recompense for madness?" (*Hotel* 44),
could just as easily be asked by Williams' sister Rose brings sharply into focus
the intersection between the playwright's dramatized biography of Scott and
Zelda's relationship and the autobiography of Tennessee's attachment to his
sister. In this regard, the image of the writer as cannibalizing becomes particularly apt. Not only was Catherine's prescribed lobotomy in *Suddenly Last
Summer* (1958) one expression of man's devouring tendency, but in *Hotel* the
Intern, in an image which makes the eating and drinking of Christ's blood in
the sacrament of the Eucharist a cannibalistic act, speaks of Zelda's sacrifice
of herself so that Scott might write as analogous to Christ's shedding of blood
so that man might live (69).

IV

Clothes for a Summer Hotel concerns itself, finally, not so much with a predatory,
Strindbergian love/hate relationship, or even with the sexual duality of the
androgynous artist, as it does with the betrayals that any artist who writes
close to life must necessarily commit against those dearest to him. To the
extent that, as the narrator in *Vieux Carré* argues, "Writers are shameless
spies" (95), their art is likely to hurt and betray. In *Hotel,* Williams' imagined
Hemingway forewarns Scott about what the "real" Hemingway did in fact do
in penning *A Moveable Feast:* "some day, I'll certainly write about a man not
me. . . . He'll be completely you, Scott. In it, aspects, embarrassing aspects of
you, will be suggested clearly to the knowledgeable reader" (67). Hemingway
concludes his *apologia* by confessing that his suicidal impulses might have
been deliberate acts "to expiate the betrayals I've strewn behind me" (*Hotel*
67–8). If the act of creation, itself a compulsive activity, betrays the other,
then the art work that results can never be in itself a sufficient recompense for
the hurt it causes, and finally only self-destruction can assuage the guilt.
Hemingway would betray Scott, as Scott had betrayed Zelda, as Tennessee

has continually betrayed Rose in using her repeatedly, over and again—as Laura, as Blanche, as Alma, as Catherine, as Clare, as Zelda—as the deepest source for his art.[11] Zelda's final plea is that Scott no longer be the author of her life: "I am not your book! Anymore! *I can't be your book anymore! Write yourself a new book*" (*Hotel* 77).

The ending of *Summer Hotel* almost demands that the close of *Glass Menagerie* be seen from a new perspective. Though Laura might extinguish her candles and relinquish her hold on Tom, for him the fire still smoulders and the "goodbye" is tentative. Tom may desert Laura physically, but no spiritual or emotional or psychical separation is ever possible. Williams can use the non-representational form of *Menagerie* to impose a sense of neat closure that the action itself never achieves; form can protect even the playwright from the deeper resonances, by establishing the illusion of completion. But as Dervin suggestively argues, Tom's closing narrative monologue substitutes for an action that would resolve the conflict, or may even tend to disguise the irresolution of the conflict: "This long, anguished speech closes the play on a curious note, when one considers that Tom and Laura have spent very little stage time together . . . Tom's feelings for Laura—suddenly shown here so forcefully—may suggest that they could not be acted within the play but only uttered after it" (156).[12]

Closure in *Vieux Carré* is effected in a similar fashion, with a concluding monologue in which The Writer tells of his fear over leaving the known past to pursue the unknown future. Yet he does not demand that the other characters release him, nor does he actually desert them. Instead, he experiences sadness over their receding, "disappearing behind [him]," as well as over the fact that memories, the stuff of art, "remain with you only as ghosts" (*Carré* 116). The Writer's last line—"This house [i.e., the one that memory built and furnished] is empty now"—comes close to a Prospero-like breaking of the wand. There might, of course, be other houses made from memories in the future, but to people them imaginatively requires that the artist move out of his safety net.

If the ending of *Vieux Carré* is sad resignation, *Out Cry* closes with a desperate, Chekhovian wail from the heart that the apparent void can somehow be filled, that art can still be a transcending force—as Williams evidently believed it had been for Lawrence. For a while, Clare tries to wrest from her brother/artist the same control over her own end that Zelda does: although Felice believes that the unfinished play-within-the-play is his to command ("*It wasn't your play!*," he tells his sister), Clare orders him to "come out of the play! . . . you *wrote* it for me" (*Out Cry* 60). Her dominance, however, is only temporary; she ultimately acquiesces to Felice's demands that they go back into a play that will now move inevitably and unswervingly to the end that he will write for it—an end freezing them in their incestuous union by replicating the murder/suicide of their parents. Their only comfort is a retreat into art: "Magic is the habit of our existence" (*Out Cry* 72). But art in this instance is death, and though the stage directions insist on Clare and Felice's "accept[ing]" darkness "as a death somehow transcended" (*Out Cry* 72), the dramatic action justifies considerably less certainty than there had been at the end of *I Rise in Flame*. The magic that Clare and Felice embrace (in this instance, the theatre) is akin to the place of illusion that sustains other Williams characters: Laura's menagerie; Blanche's sanitarium; Zelda's hotel. Such magic is, though, never far from madness, and is perhaps even symptomatic of it. In *Summer Hotel,* Zelda speaks of retreat into madness or into acts of artistic creation as possible alternatives to abject submission to the human condition: "Between the first wail of an infant and the last gasp of the dying—it's all an arranged pattern of—submission to what's been prescribed for us unless we escape into madness or into acts of creation" (71). Perhaps, then, it is not too fanciful to see the homonymic pun "clothes/close" as intended by Williams to suggest the closing down of a summer hotel, or place of illusion and art. Maybe, even, a Beckettian "close of play," for Tennessee, cut off from Rose, would appear to be as desolate as Scott cut off from Zelda.

In her refusal to any longer be betrayed by Scott through his art, Zelda effectively severs him from what had been the very source of that art—her life. Williams himself, faced with the necessary betrayal of his love for Rose if he is to continue as an artist—and aware of the openness of that betrayal in a play such as *Out Cry*—in *Summer Hotel* dresses fact in the guise of someone else's life other than his own, employing seemingly innocuous ghosts as transferences for vivid, personal memories. The work becomes, then, another of Williams' own *apologias*. Yet if the act of writing *Glass Menagerie* was, at the time, evidently expiation enough, after the forthright revelation of *Out Cry* and the more guarded confessional of *Clothes for a Summer Hotel,* death (and it came to Williams a few years later) would seem to be the only adequate expiatory act. Anything less would mean the need to abjure his art, whose great source, from his first Broadway play to his last, was "something" that he could not leave "unspoken" between his sister and himself. Without Williams' love for his sister Rose, there apparently could never have been a Tennessee.

Notes

1.   Cohn takes a position opposite to the one argued here when she claims that Williams' works which "dramatize other writers" are the only ones to "escape [the] charge . . . [of being] about himself ("Tributes" 12).

2.   Spoto, who comments that "Fitzgerald was clearly modelled . . . on Williams' experience" and that "his sister [Rose] is the real character behind Zelda," quotes Williams as saying: " '[The Fitzgeralds] embody concerns of my own, the tortures of the creative artist in a materialist society. . . . They were so close to the edge. I understood the schizophrenia and the thwarted ambition" (345).

3.   See, for example, King, who emphasizes that the memory framework clearly marks *Glass Menagerie* as Tom's play, and that at the close "Tom . . . relieved of his burden . . . escapes with his artist's detachment having exorcised the pain with the creation of the play" (85).

4.   In his analysis of the short story "The Resemblance Between a Violin Case and a Coffin" (1950), which he dubs "the clinical [sic] detailed, sensitively written case history of [Williams'] childhood," Clayton explores this jealousy motif. In "Resemblance," the first person narrator is "erotically stimulated" as he watches his sister and Richard Miles rehearse a duet together, but rather than admit to wanting to "*be* Richard" whom the sister loves and therefore "wish[ing] to *love* his sister," he transfers his love to Richard, leading to "homosexual daydreams" (111–12). Yet, as Clayton concludes, "the sister figure" in Williams is consistently portrayed "as a child desired by the brother. She is a delicate and shy creature, and the brother figure experiences a great deal of guilt because of his desire for her" (118).

5.   *Out Cry* exists not only, like many of Williams' plays, in various printed versions, but also under two different titles; in its earlier forms (1967, 1971), as well as in the revision in the collected plays (1975), it is called *The Two Character Play*—which is the same as the name of its play-within-the-play—, though in the details discussed here the later revision is substantially the same as the 1973 version entitled *Out Cry* that New York audiences originally saw. That first Broadway version, furthermore, significantly takes its title from a line in *Sweet Bird of Youth* that turned out to be not only personally revealing but even prophetic for Williams in the post-*Iguana* years of his career: "You can't retire with the out-crying heart of an artist still crying out, in your body, in your nerves, in your what? Heart?" (39). Parker, in an essay which approaches *Two Character Play* in a way very similar to the one being taken here about *Summer Hotel,* sees Williams "as trying to grapple directly with the two central and interlocked experiences of his life: his ambiguous near-incestuous love for his schizophrenic sister, Rose; and his compulsive need for theatre as personal escape and therapy" ("Circle" 523). Linking introversion in sex with solipsism in art, Parker proposes that *Glass Menagerie* "is about . . . the self-lacerating aggression necessary for the individual who is trying to free himself from too close an emotional dependence on his central 'love object' " ("Circle" 530).

6.   Stanton, apparently following the lead of Adler ("Images"), discusses Williams' early play about Hart Crane as "one of the first works to present two characters of the opposite sex who are emotionally enclosed in an unconsciously incestuous or oedipal relationship and who appear as androgynous counterparts of one individual" (52).

7.   Parker suggests a connection between Tom's guilty memories in *Menagerie* and the Yeatsian purgatory ("Composition" 418).

8.   For an account of the relationship between Hemingway and the Fitzgeralds that follows the contours of *Moveable Feast* (and *Summer Hotel*) but in much greater detail, see Bruccoli.

9.   Epstein, who like Williams interprets Zelda as someone "Reduced to a character in her husband's fiction [with] little control over her entrance into cultural discourse" (346), chooses Milford's book as representative of that "type of the new feminist biography: a tragedy of isolation, suppression, and madness in which the feminine artistic consciousness breaks down when it confronts the patriarchal culture" (339).

10.   Williams perhaps discovered the "hawk" imagery that he employs in *Summer Hotel* in *Moveable Feast,* though Hemingway applies the image to Zelda rather than to Scott (178, 184).

11.   Although Cohn concludes that *Summer Hotel* is about "human betrayal" as "the price of artistic creation" ("Late" 343), she does not connect the multiple betrayals by Scott, Zelda, and Hemingway to Williams' betrayal of Rose.

12.   Despite having published his essay late in the 1970s, Dervin was evidently unaware of *Out Cry,* since at one point he comments that "no other plays [than *Menagerie* and *Purification*] remain entirely within the family" and so it would seem, strictly speaking, that "the subject of incest should . . . be ruled out" (158).

Works Cited

Adler, Thomas P. "Images of Entrapment in Tennessee Williams's Later Plays." *Notes on Modern Literature* 5(1981):item 11.

Bruccoli, Matthew. *Scott and Ernest: the Authority of Failure and the Authority of Success.* Carbondale: Southern Illinois Univ. Press, 1978.

Clayton, John Strother. "The Sister Figure in the Plays of Tennessee Williams." Rpt. in *Twentieth Century Interpretations of "The Glass Menagerie."* Ed. R.B. Parker. Englewood Cliffs, N.J.: Prentice-Hall, 1983, 109–19.

Cohn, Ruby. "Late Tennessee Williams." *Modern Drama* 27(1984):336–44.

———. "Tributes to Wives." *The Tennessee Williams Review* 4(1983):12–17.

Dervin, Daniel A. "The Spook in the Rainforest: The Incestuous Structure of Tennessee Williams's Plays." *Psychocultural Review* 3(1979):153–83.

Epstein, William H. "Milford's *Zelda* and the Poetic of the New Feminist Biography." *The Georgia Review* 36(1982):335–50.

Hemingway, Ernest. *A Moveable Feast.* New York: Bantam, 1965.

King, Thomas L. "Irony and Distance in *The Glass Menagerie.*" Rpt. in *Twentieth Century Interpretations of "The Glass Menagerie."* Ed. R.B. Parker. Englewood Cliffs, N.J.: Prentice-Hall, 1983, 75–86.

Kroll, Jack. "Slender is the Night," *Newsweek,* 7 April 1980, 95.

Milford, Nancy. *Zelda.* New York: Harper & Row, 1970.

Parker, R.B[rian]. "The Circle Closed: A Psychological Reading of *The Glass Menagerie* and *The Two Character Play.*" *Modern Drama* 28(1985): 517–34.

———. "The Composition of *The Glass Menagerie:* An Argument for Complexity." *Modern Drama* 25(1982):409–22.

Spoto, Donald. *The Kindness of Strangers: The Life of Tennessee Williams.* Boston: Little Brown, 1985.

Stanton, Stephen S. "Some Thoughts About *Steps Must Be Gentle.*" *The Tennessee Williams Review* 4(1983):48–53.

Williams, Dakin and Shepherd Mead. *Tennessee Williams: An Intimate Biography.* New York: Arbor House, 1983.

Williams, Tennessee. *Clothes for a Summer Hotel.* New York: New Directions, 1983.

———. *The Glass Menagerie,* New York: New Directions, 1966.

———. *I Rise in Flame, Cried the Phoenix.* In his *Dragon Country.* New York: New Directions, 1969, 55–75.

———. *In the Bar of a Tokyo Hotel.* In his *Dragon Country.* New York: New Directions, 1969, 1–53.

———. *Memoirs.* New York: Doubleday, 1975.

———. *The Night of the Iguana.* New York: Signet, 1961.

———. "Notes for *The Two Character Play,*" *The Tennessee Williams Review* 3(1982):3–5.

———. *Out Cry.* New York: New Directions, 1973.

———. *Sweet Bird of Youth.* New York: Signet, 1962.

Van Antwerp, Margaret A. and Sally Johns, ed. *Dictionary of Literary Biography, Documentary Series* (Vol. 4/Tennessee Williams). Detroit: Gale Research, 1984.

Yeats, W.B. *Purgatory.* In his *Collected Plays.* New York: Macmillan, 1953, 429–36.

OVERVIEWS

Tennessee Williams:
The Idea of a "Plastic Form"

ESTHER M. JACKSON

I

On 31 March 1945, a new period in the history of American drama, and indeed in that of world theater, had its formal beginning at the Playhouse Theatre in New York. That evening, Tennessee Williams's innovative drama, *The Glass Menagerie,*[1] opened to critical acclaim. Both critics and members of the widening audience who saw *The Glass Menagerie* in the years since that time came to regard this work as a new and distinctive kind of drama, a form expressive of the realities of life in the world taking shape in the final days of World War II.

The protagonist of the play, the poet-figure Tom, serves as an historian of sorts, setting the action in time and place; he is also a philosopher, commenting on the significance of the events that signal the passing of one historical epoch and the beginning of another, an epoch that would be significantly different from the ones that preceded it. Williams gave his protagonist a line in the play's closing speech that indicated something of the significance of this transition in the theater as in history itself. Tom suggests that Laura should "blow out her candles," for they can no longer suffice to illuminate the world emerging, a world more appropriately "lit by lightning."

Perhaps the most important role Tom had on that occasion was that of an artist eliciting the participation of the audience in shaping this new form of drama. In his preface to the published edition of the play, Williams echoed the commentary of his protagonist that he sought in this work to create a new kind of theater, a form capable of giving effective expression to the changing contour of human experience. He described the theatrical form given definition in this work as "plastic." He wrote of that form that everyone

> . . . should know nowadays the unimportance of the photographic in art: that truth, life, or reality is an organic thing which the poetic imagination can

This essay was written specifically for this volume and appears in print here for the first time by permission of the author.

represent or suggest, in essence, only through transformation, through changing into other forms than those which were merely present in appearance.

These remarks are not meant as a preface only to this particular play. They
have to do with a conception of a new, plastic theatre which must take the
place of the exhausted theatre of realistic conventions if the theatre is to
resume vitality as a part of our culture.

(The Glass Menagerie, production notes, 7)

Actually, the idea of form that Tennessee Williams described was not
entirely new. Eugene O'Neill, writing in the twenties, had described a form
similar to that which Williams sought to create. He called this form "super-
naturalism" and described Strindberg as an early interpreter of it.[2]

The idea of a "plastic theatre," as defined by both playwrights, corre-
sponded to notions of form shaped by European artists in the late nineteenth
and early twentieth centuries.[3] But it had an even longer—and a significantly
different—history in America. Both O'Neill and Williams differed from their
European contemporaries in an important way; that is, in their common focus
on the creation of a dramatic form expressive of social, political, intellectual,
and cultural patterns evolving in American life. To that end, both playwrights
engaged in comprehensive patterns of experimentation, designed not only to
treat new themes, but also to explore new and different techniques of theatrical exposition, techniques shaped not only in the theater itself, but also in the
related arts of poetry, fiction, music, dance, painting, sculpture, architecture,
and the developing art of film.[4]

The idea of a "plastic form"—as interpreted in The Glass Menagerie—
could be described as having evolved through the pattern of nineteenth-
and twentieth-century American arts and letters: in the visual, tactile, and
architectural forms of American painters, sculptors, and architects, as well
as in the verbal imagery of essayists such as Ralph Waldo Emerson and
Henry David Thoreau; writers of fiction such as Nathaniel Hawthorne,
Herman Melville, and Edgar Allan Poe; and poets such as Walt Whitman.
Indeed, many characteristics of this notion of theater, as Tennessee
Williams defined it, were described in the prose writings of Walt Whitman
and given expressive form in his epic poem, Leaves of Grass.[5] In his "New
World" epic, Whitman sought to "image" America; that is, to bring the
totality of its meaning—past, present, and future—within the contour of a
single plastic form.

It can be argued that Walt Whitman anticipated Tennessee Williams's
view of American life itself as the primary mode of art. In the preface to the
1855 edition of Leaves of Grass, Whitman wrote: "The United States themselves are essentially the greatest poem."[6] In this revolutionary work, the
poet interpreted America itself as a creation closely imitative of nature; that
is, as a dynamic form in which the search for individual identity is the defining motif in what is, in effect, a massive work of art.

Although he was a poet, Whitman saw drama as the medium most capable of giving expressive form to the unique character of American experience; that is, of translating the "linear" patterns of conventional historical record into "plastic forms."[7] He called for a "dramatic poetry" that could have the same expressive relationship to American life as Shakespeare had to English life. He wrote that such a dramatic poetry should not be a mere expression of surface melodies. Rather, it should aim at "the free expression of emotion, . . . it should arouse and initiate, rather than define or finish."[8] Significantly, Whitman did not conceive dramatic poetry as a mode of language "invented" by individual artists. Rather, he saw such poetry as a concretion of patterns originating in the public consciousness; that is, as a mode of expression not limited in meaning to the historical epoch in which the work is created, but one that gives assurance of its roots in the past and its promise for the future. It can be argued that Whitman's career as a poet was devoted to the preliminary codification of just such a "poetic language" as Tennessee Williams sought to develop. Whitman wrote of it,

> Language. . . . is not an abstract construction of the learn'd . . . but is something arising out of the work . . . of long generations of humanity. . . . It impermeates all . . . the Past as well as the Present. . . .[9]

It was in this New World "poetics," described in the pattern of Whitman's prose writings and given preliminary realization in his *Leaves of Grass,* that Tennessee Williams would appear to have found one source of his idea of a plastic form. For in the comprehensive pattern of experimentation that resulted in *Leaves of Grass,* the poet developed techniques of representation, organization, and interpretation that found systematic application in the works of artists of the twentieth century, in Europe and America.[10]

Central to the notion of plastic imagery exemplified in *Leaves of Grass* is the spoken word. Indeed, in *Leaves of Grass,* the "word" is the source of the creative energy generating images that assume aural, visual, tactile, and, on occasion, textural forms. Whitman invoked the assistance of the reader-hearer (spectator) in synthesizing these component images within configurations possessed of a "dimensionality" of theatrical quality. He sought to ground his poetic imagery in a spoken language that served as the point of generation for the imaginative creation of textural forms of great complexity.

Whitman's imagery—like that of the modern artists who were to follow—can be described as plastic.[11] It was composed by the synthesizing of elements of form in the consciousness of a poetic "I," the creator of a "theater of the imagination." He bequeathed this approach to American artists, particularly American playwrights of the twentieth century. The dramatic form that O'Neill and his associates in the Provincetown Theatre sought to define—and that Tennessee Williams and his artistic associates in the Playhouse Theatre undertook to create some three decades later—was conceived after the manner of Whitman's poem; that is, as the transposition of complex progressions of images into the textural language of theater.

II

A reexamination of the career of Tennessee Williams—as well as the careers of the major American playwrights who preceded him—suggests that Williams's most important contribution to the idea of a plastic theater was the creation of an American stage language capable of generating dramatic forms of poetic quality as well as popular appeal.[12] While other American playwrights—among them Eugene O'Neill, Thornton Wilder, Elmer Rice, Clifford Odets, William Saroyan, Paul Green, Lillian Hellman, and Arthur Miller—made definitive contributions to the shaping of distinctive forms of character and action and to the interpretation of social, political, and moral ideas, none would excel Tennessee Williams in shaping a spoken language capable of translating the varied patterns of life in American society into a dramatic poetry characterized by beauty as well as vitality, meaning, and a sense of universality.

From the beginning of his career as a professional playwright, Tennessee Williams undertook to adapt to the requirements of the American stage Walt Whitman's notion of a "public" language possessing the attributes of prose and poetry, a language capable of giving sensuous form to varieties of American character, setting, and action.[13] Williams did not perceive words alone to be the substance of such a theatrical language.[14] Rather, he interpreted speech as the creative factor generating a sensuous theatrical language.[15]

The preliminary shaping of a vocabulary for such a textural language was a primary objective of the one-act plays Williams wrote during the early years of his career.[16] A characteristic of Williams's technique in these early works is the augmentation of the form and meaning of words by simultaneous use of the languages of other expressive media.[17] In *The Purification,* the playwright used music to underscore the varied forms of spoken language and sound patterns and special effects to enhance the imaginative quality of speech in the short play *The Long Stay Cut Short or The Unsatisfactory Supper.* One of the most elaborate of these patterns of simultaneous exposition can be seen in the early play *Ten Blocks on the Camino Real.* Here Williams attempted to project an intricate pattern of images within a definitive structural context. In this play, he undertook to augment speech by simultaneous use of the "languages" of painting, architecture, sculpture, dance, and music. But he also added an important dimension to the spoken word itself by systematic use of patterns drawn from varieties of "slang"—the source that Walt Whitman described as the beginning point of new artistic forms, "the lawless germinal element, below all words and sentences, and behind all poetry. . . ."[18]

These early plays share with the poetry and fiction that Tennessee Williams wrote during this period a quality that he described as "personal lyricism." While the patterns of language used vary, the majority of these works represent the concretization of brief moments of poetic insight, fleeting "instants" that the playwright rendered as images of varying levels of complexity. There is, in certain of these early plays, a second "dimension." *Moony's Kid Don't Cry, The Dark Room, The Case of the Crushed Petunias,* and *The Long Stay Cut Short or The Unsatisfactory Supper, 27 Wagons Full of Cotton, The Last of My Solid Gold Watches,* and *This Property Is Condemned* appear to have a common point of beginning in the external world of action; however, these actions are reflected in "mirror" images originating in the interior world of feeling. In *Ten Blocks on the Camino Real* and *The Purification,* the playwright introduced yet a third level of exposition, one that has its point of reference in the consciousness of a choral figure symbolized in both instances by the persona of a Guitar Player—an artist through whose consciousness the vision that is the play is presumably transmitted.

Although these early plays are generally effective in their use of language— both verbal and extraverbal—they appear to have functioned for the playwright as preliminary studies; that is, as experimental works directed toward creating a "vocabulary" for a new kind of theater. While the theatrical language used in these early works was sufficient to give expression to the playwright's personal lyricism, Williams did not think it sufficient to interpret more universal levels of meaning, levels required for the creation of a genuinely plastic form. In *The Glass Menagerie,* the playwright undertook to create such a dimensional form. He sought to subject the remembered past to that intuitive mode of understanding that he styled personal lyricism, as well as to more objective analysis in the world outside of the self. To the end, he was to add to the interpretative patterns seen in his earlier plays, a level of exposition suggested, but not fully developed, in *The Purification,* a level that can be described as universal.

Williams sought in *The Glass Menagerie* to project images organized within this pattern against a background that could be described as philosophical in intent. For purposes of this theatrical inquiry, the playwright undertook to modify the structure of the family drama, extending it with elements of form adapted from the American arts of poetry, fiction, dance, and music as well as from the visual arts of painting, sculpture, and architecture. Significantly, he used as a unifying device the faculty of memory, a faculty he represented in this and other works through the aesthetic of film.

Williams's interest in filmic devices was not merely technical.[19] Throughout much of his career, the playwright used the motion picture camera as a symbol of poetic vision. In his plastic theater, poetic images were composed as by montage. But film had other uses for the playwright—uses both theoretical and practical. It offered both a logic for the fusion of elements of form drawn from a wide range of sources and a rationale for manipulations of time, place, and circumstance. In *The Glass Menagerie,* film served as a symbol of both the creative consciousness and the processes by which film transforms ordinary events taking place in life into forms of art.[20]

In this experimental work, Tennessee Williams undertook to synthesize elements of form drawn from stage and screen, as well as from the conventions of literature, within a complex theatrical imagery.[21] Significantly, in this drama he assigned the primary function of establishing reality to the language of the stage. He proposed to use the screen as the metaphor for consciousness, a consciousness both lyrical and philosophical—personal and public—in nature. But for Williams the artist, the screen served another critical function. It symbolized the process by which life is transformed into art. In *The Glass Menagerie,* it was the point of effective contact, linking the spectator to the protagonist—and both to the playwright—in the creation of the play.

III

In recent years, scholars have begun the process of charting the evolution of the distinctive form of *The Glass Menagerie* from its beginning as a work of fiction, through its development as a film script, to its realization as a new kind of drama.[22] Fortunately, Tennessee Williams himself documented the evolution of this complex idea of form in a series of notes, essays, and critical comments, a substantial number of which have been published. More recently, other materials—including drafts of *The Glass Menagerie* in various stages of its fictional, filmic, and dramatic maturity—have become available for study.[23] These materials offer important insights into the playwright's intention for this work as well as the extended creative process through which the plastic form evolved.[24]

An early notebook of major importance in this context is cited by R. B. Parker in his article "The Texas Drafts of *The Glass Menagerie.*"[25] Early drafts of Tom's speeches, written in pencil, are significant for the points at which they vary from those included in the published versions of the play. For example, in this notebook there are several versions of the opening speech of the poet-figure Tom. All differ from the acting texts in their patterns of language and more significantly, in their emphasis on the play as a form of inquiry into the human condition rather than a statement of intensely personal definition. While the emphasis of Tom's soliloquy in the acting editions of the play is essentially lyrical in tone, that of these earlier versions is essentially philosophical. The protagonist is concerned with the problem of meaning, in life as in art.

In this notebook, the playwright describes his dramatic intent in existential terms; that is, as the attempt to find such meaning in the fragments of knowable experience, through the instrumentation of art:[26]

Only in moments of passion, (of) terror,
hatred, desire; do our lives
take on a dimension that
corresponds to (the) dimensions
of life itself. War and love
create a majesty in us,
One that is (one out of hell/that the other)
demonic, the
other angelic. (The rest of the/time we contradict)
desperately deny the existence
of anything in life that
is larger than ashes dropped
from a cigarette.
This play is made of such
particles—nothing large,
nothing to correspond with
time and space but the little

Tennessee Williams, Notebook, 19

In these penciled notes, Williams offers an important insight into the vision of reality that defined the plastic form of *The Glass Menagerie:*

Infinity is the past. The
present is balanced on a
flashing needle
Someone has always just
gotten up from a table,
lighted a cigarette,
passed through a door
Someone has always
just spoken or been spoken
to. The only reality (is/the remembered one)
that has form and dimension
is the one that exists in
recollection. Now is
formless, now is almost
breathless, now is something
too little even to measure.

Tennessee Williams, Notebook, 4

The evolution of the plastic form of *The Glass Menagerie,* as documented by Lester A. Beaurline, R. Brian Parker, and Gilbert Debusscher, involved an extended process, one that saw Williams develop the ability to organize such fragments—poetic instants—within patterns both textural and structural in definition. The power of the play resided in exactly this compression of fragments—events, memories, ideas, values, and emotions—within a theatrical imagery possessed of many of the defining characteristics of *Leaves of Grass*. In addition to its dimensionality—its synthesis of social, historical, psychological, and philosophical forms and contents—this imagery possessed a quality essential to theater forms; that of dynamism, the capacity to signify action. At the same time, the imagery created for this work was capable of reflecting the qualities of beauty, tranquility, and contemplation in its characters and their inner lives.

The Glass Menagerie, as performed, is composed of seven component figures, images that surface in the memory of Tom, the poet figure. While the events themselves appear realistic, the framework in which they are set—memory—is subjective. Thus, the essentially philosophical motive of the exercise alters events of the play, transforming their identity in the course of the drama.

Williams originally planned that the visible symbol of this transformation would be a screen. He described this screen in the following terms:

> The purpose of this will probably be apparent. It is to give accent to certain values in each scene. Each scene contains a particular point (or several) which is structurally the most important. In an episodic play, such as this, the basic structure or narrative line may be obscured from the audience; the effect may seem fragmentary rather than architectural. . . . The legend or image upon the screen will strengthen the effect of what is merely allusion in the writing and allow the primary point to be made more simply and lightly than if the entire responsibility were on the spoken lines. Aside from this structural value, I think the screen will have a definite emotional appeal, less definable but just as important.[27]

In the published version of the play, the playwright observed that the screen was eliminated, because it appeared in production to be superfluous. The source of the problem lay in the difficulty of integrating elements of these two theatrical formats—stage and film—in a single expressive language. The critical problem in this, as in later instances in Williams's career, appear to be related to style. The device Williams planned to use was a component of a different filmic vocabulary, that developed by the German regisseur and teacher Irwin Piscator, an artistic collaborator of Bertolt Brecht and, in the 1940s, director of a workshop at the New School for Social Research in New York—a workshop in which Williams was for a time a student.[28] Clearly, the kind of "scenic legend" proposed for *The Glass Menagerie* would not have been congruent with the acting styles of members of this company. The screen might well have been appropriate had it made use of a filmic imagery consistent with the dominant acting style of the company and with Jo Mielziner's setting.[29]

The textural language Williams and his artistic collaborators succeeded in devising represented an integration of elements of form drawn not only from the traditions of the popular theater of the nineteenth century, but also from more formal developments in the visual arts.[30] Like O'Neill, Tennessee Williams was intensely interested in developments in painting, both in studies of American character by artists such as John Sloan and Robert Henri, and in the representations of American settings by painters such as Georgia O'Keeffe, Edward Hopper, and Ben Shahn.[31] His interest in "theatrical portraiture" is indicated in his visual characterization of Amanda in scene 2:

> She has on one of those cheap or imitation velvety-looking cloth coats with imitation fur collar. Her hat is five or six years old, one of those dreadful cloche hats that were worn in the late Twenties, and she is clutching an enormous black patent-leather pocketbook with nickel clasps and initials. This is her full-dress outfit, the one she usually wears to the D.A.R. Before entering she looks through the door. She purses her lips, opens her eyes very wide, rolls them upward and shakes her head. Then she slowly lets herself in the door. Seeing her mother's expression Laura touches her lips with a nervous gesture.
>
> *The Glass Menagerie*, scene 2 (29)

His portrait of Amanda is in sharp stylistic contrast to his characterization of Laura in scene 6:

> [Laura stands in the middle of the room with lifted arms while Amanda crouches before her, adjusting the hem of a new dress, devout and ritualistic. The dress is colored and designed by memory. The arrangement of Laura's hair is changed; it is softer and more becoming. A fragile, unearthly prettiness has come out in Laura: she is like a piece of translucent glass touched by light, given a momentary radiance, not actual, not lasting.]
>
> *The Glass Menagerie*, scene 6 (69)

These characters were placed against a setting that was itself dimensional. In Jo Mielziner's set for *The Glass Menagerie,* specific locations were defined within a flexible space. Such locations were given definition both by means of light and by an architectural pattern of receding frames—from the proscenium arch, to the partial rendition of the rear wall of the building, to a dining room separated from the living room by a wide arch. Williams commented in his notes on the "poetic truth" of this complex setting:

> The apartment faces an alley and is entered by a fire escape, a structure whose name is a touch of accidental poetic truth, for all of these huge buildings are always burning with the slow and implacable fires of human desperation. The fire escape is part of what we see—that is, the landing of it and steps descending from it.
>
> *The Glass Menagerie*, stage directions (21)

While American painters such as Georgia O'Keeffe offered precedents for Jo Mielziner's treatments of the settings against which later plays such as *Sweet*

Bird of Youth were set, others such as Edward Hopper appear to have provided models for his visualization of the urban landscape against which the action of *The Glass Menagerie* is set. It was a vision of such an urban landscape that Williams sought to invoke in his description of the setting of the play:

> The Wingfield apartment is in the rear of the building, one of those vast hive-like conglomerations of cellular living-units that flower as warty growths in overcrowded urban centers of lower middle-class population and are sympto-matic of the impulse of this largest and fundamentally enslaved section of American society to avoid fluidity and differentiation and to exist and function as one interfused mass of automatism.
>
> *The Glass Menagerie,* scene 1, stage directions (21)

The setting of *The Glass Menagerie* established a precedent that charac-terized Williams's plastic form. The setting itself was conceived as an element of his poetic language; that is, as a poetic configuration characterized by the capacity to alter its location in time, space, and sensibility, without loss of dramatic continuity. Against this poetic setting, Williams sought to project a pattern of images reconstituting the memory of the poet-figure (Tom) in the vision that is the play.

IV

If *The Glass Menagerie* established the form of Williams's plastic theater, the plays produced from 1945 to 1955 saw the playwright seeking to both refine this form and enrich it with historical, cultural, and mythic materials. Two plays of this period—*A Streetcar Named Desire* and *Summer and Smoke*—represent the height of Tennessee Williams's success in shaping a theatrical language characterized by realism, poetic beauty, and dramatic power. If *A Streetcar Named Desire* represents a development over *The Glass Menagerie* in terms of the texture of its imagery, *Summer and Smoke* can be seen as the play-wright's refinement of the theatrical language of the plastic theater. In this work, Williams achieved an exceptional level of aesthetic integration in his imagery. *Summer and Smoke* reflected Williams's ability not only to integrate verbal and visual components within his plastic form, but also to employ an integrated language to achieve specific theatrical effects of an exceedingly lyrical quality.

The Rose Tattoo was a work of significantly different vision, conforming more to the sensibility, as well as the form, of romantic melodrama. The appeal of the work resided in the romantic quality with which the playwright invested the setting and in his sympathetic characterization of the play's cen-tral figure, Serafina Delle Rose.

With *Camino Real* (1953), Williams returned to the pattern of dramatic organization given realization in *The Glass Menagerie* and further developed in *A Streetcar Named Desire* and *Summer and Smoke*. In each of these works, the playwright sought to manipulate a double exposition—one projecting images in real time, actions taking place on the stage; and another arranging these figures in patterns of meaning, poetic structures in aesthetic time. He sought to elaborate on this pattern in *Camino Real,* adding a third level of exposition. The playwright adapted the basic form established in *The Glass Menagerie* to yet another purpose, this time to the exploration of what Williams viewed as a critical plane of meaning in the world of the fifties, one that could be called "moral."[32] *Camino Real,* written in an era of international tensions, is an allegory about a world in crisis. Unlike earlier works, the drama is theological in perspective and antirealist in style.

Originally a short work for dancers, *Camino Real* assumed significantly different stylistic characteristics in this longer form. In his notes for the published version of the play, Williams commented on the "radicalization" of his idea of a plastic form. Abandoning his early commitment to the appearance of reality, he observed:

> More than any other work that I have done, this play has seemed to me like the construction of another world, a separate existence. Of course, it is nothing more nor less than my conception of the time and world that I live in, and its people are mostly archetypes of certain basic attitudes and qualities with those mutations that would occur if they had continued along the road to this hypothetical terminal point in it.
>
> Foreword to *Camino Real* (viii)

While from the perspective of dramatic literature *Camino Real* was a work of major importance, it did not in the playwright's lifetime succeed as a "theater piece." A close look at the text of this play suggests some reasons for its problem as a work for the stage.[33] Although the play's outer form seems generally similar to that of *The Glass Menagerie, A Streetcar Named Desire,* and *Summer and Smoke,* the inner form differs substantially. In contrast to earlier works, the characters in this play are allegorical; many of them have origins in works of art unknown to mainstream American audiences. But this play as a work for the stage presents an even more serious problem: the playwright appears to have substituted the sensibility of the film for that of the stage.[34] The dramatic continuity of *Camino Real* depends less on the kinds of actions that can be effectively represented on the stage than on patterns of visualization that require effective camera use.

Perhaps the most serious limitation of the work as an example of the plastic theater was the lack of genuine vitality in its spoken language. Williams was seemingly unable, in the many versions of the play he wrote, to create a spoken language possessed of the theatrical vitality or the emotional resonance of his earlier works. Instead, in performance *Camino Real* seems burdened by a spoken language unequal to its elaborate mythic structure.

The problem affecting *Camino Real*'s theatrical identity can be attributed to radical alterations in the expressive language of the plastic theater. While *Camino Real* remains the most advanced example of his experimentation with a literary form, it failed the repeated test of performance. This failure, as with the dramatist's later plays, could be considered conditional, because *Camino Real* did not yet enjoy the kind of theatrical interpretation that fulfills its stylistic requirements. A hybrid form, with emphasis on filmic modes of exposition, it seems to require an extended period of experimentation to determine the characteristics of the concrete language required to translate this text into a genuinely plastic form. Indeed, it may be the contemporary American work for which the style devised by Bertolt Brecht and Irwin Piscator would be most appropriate.

With *Cat on a Hot Tin Roof* (1955), Williams appears to have sought a corrective for such problems with expressive form. Plays produced between 1955 and 1961—works including *Something Unspoken* (1955), *Orpheus Descending* (1957), *Suddenly Last Summer* (1958), *Sweet Bird of Youth* (1959), and *Period of Adjustment,* (1960)—show evidence of a return to more realistic levels of theatrical interpretation, levels that can be described as "social." While the plays were composed as moments of poetic vision and the basic vocabulary of these works remained that of the stage, both Williams's theatrical imagery and his manner of organizing such images were altered significantly.

Whereas the images in *The Glass Menagerie* offered little objective evidence about the social environment outside of the apartment in which the play is set, these realistically oriented plays offered substantial data about the world in which the principal actions of the dramas take place and indeed about the social, political, and economic issues characterizing the periods in which these works are set. Moreover, in these "social" dramas, the playwright sought to relate the actions of the protagonists not so much to their interior lives as to the world outside of the self. Williams employed in these works a form not unlike that developed by European playwrights such as Ibsen, representing the extension of the techniques of realism to embrace secondary levels of exposition. These dramas contain two patterns of exposition, both of which converge in the plays' closing moments; one originates in the interior life of the protagonist—or protagonists—and another in the social environment of the play.

The point of transition between this third phase of the playwright's development and the final phase of his work is marked by *The Night of the Iguana* (1961). While the form of this play does not suggest a major break with the pattern of socially oriented works such as *Cat on a Hot Tin Roof,* the themes explored in *Night of the Iguana* bespeak a marked alteration in the playwright's vision. With this work, Williams seemed to turn his attention from the world of temporal experience to a search for truth in a world of eternal meaning. Concern about the relationship of temporal and eternal planes of meaning and being became a major preoccupation in the works that followed: *The Milk Train Doesn't Stop Here Anymore* (1963), *Slapstick Tragedy* (1966), *The Two Character Play* (1967), *The Seven Descents of Myrtle* (1968), *In the Bar of a Tokyo Hotel* (1969), *Small Craft Warnings* (1973), and *Out Cry* (1973) (a new version of *The Two Character Play*).[35]

The primary challenge for the playwright in this final period of his career appears to have been that of modifying the language of his plastic theater in such a way as to interpret his changing vision. His search for solutions to the problem of language involved a continuing pattern of experimentation with antirealistic methods of dramatic exposition. While plays such as *Vieux Carré* (1977) and *A Lovely Summer for Creve Coeur* (1979) returned to characters, themes, and forms of action introduced earlier in the playwright's career, other works represented major departures in form. In *This Is* (1976), *The Red Devil Battery Sign* (1977), and *Clothes for a Summer Hotel* (1980), Williams made use of techniques similar to those employed by Strindberg in his "Chamber Plays," and later by modern surrealists working in theater. While these works were conceived as extending the range of the plastic form, the theatrical languages devised for them proved inadequate for effective interpretation.[36]

Perhaps the most significant—and indeed the most successful—of the works of this late period was *Out Cry* (1975), a work published in earlier versions under the title *The Two-Character Play*. A play that like *The Glass Menagerie* emerged through an extended period of development, *Out Cry* appears to have achieved the most effective form of any work Williams wrote during the final period of his career.

In this work, Williams returned to the environment of *The Glass Menagerie;* that is, to the theater. But the theatre—the symbol of the world in the earlier work—has undergone substantial change. The playwright described this altered setting in these terms:

> At curtain rise Felice stands motionless as a hunted creature at the sound of pursuers. He is on the platform of a raked stage, a notebook hanging open from his downstage hand. There should be, at a low level, a number of mechanical sounds suggesting an inhuman quality to the (half underground) vault of a foreign theater at which he has recently arrived. He is staring from the raked platform (on which a fragmentary set has been assembled) at a huge, dark statue upstage, a work of great power and darkly subjective meaning. Something about it, its monolithic presence and its suggestion of things anguished and perverse (in his own nature?) rivet his attention, which is shocked and fearful.
>
> *Out Cry,* opening stage direction, (7)

As in *The Glass Menagerie*, in *Out Cry* Williams used elements of form drawn from stage and film. In this case, however, he used them for a more comprehensive purpose than that conceived for earlier works. The setting gives dramatic expression to not only the context of the action, but also unseen forces that appear to generate that action.[37] If *Out Cry* marked a return to the theatrical setting of *The Glass Menagerie*, the playwright appended a radically different conclusion to that earlier action.[38] Williams created a theatrically effective work of darker meaning, one in which he subjected characters, themes, and actions introduced in the earlier play to an essentially tragic interpretation.[39] In production, *Out Cry* achieves a reconciliation of formal characteristics of stage and film in a form comparable in theatrical effectiveness, if not in emotional appeal, to *The Glass Menagerie*.

V

In his idea of plastic theater, Tennessee Williams gave both theoretical and practical expression to an idea of form that had evolved through the pattern of the American arts of the nineteenth and early twentieth centuries: an idea that reflected correspondences to notions of form given realization in the pattern of European arts, but that also reflected differences related to the unique character of American experience. Williams sought in his plastic form to give expression to social, psychological, aesthetic, and moral dimensions of American life. But there was another important sense in which the idea of form Williams sought to develop could be described as plastic. That involved the close affinity of his drama to a related art—film. In his article "Tennessee Williams at the Delta Brilliant," Albert Kalson commented on the influence of the film on the playwright's vision of reality, as well as on his idea of form.[40]

Kalson, in a close analysis of Williams's techniques of dramatic exposition, documented the influence of film on both the theory and practice of the playwright's dramaturgy. He noted that Williams had had an opportunity to study film techniques in the workshop established in New York by Irwin Piscator. He concluded, however, that the influence most clearly evident in his work was one associated with another approach to film, that of Hollywood. As Kalson observes, Williams found in Hollywood an important element of his theatrical vocabulary, as well as components of his technique. Most significantly, he found a poetic vision of popular definition.

Perhaps because of this interest in the cinema—both as a spectator and later as an apprentice scriptwriter—Williams became the first American playwright of the twentieth century to earn the title "popular dramatist." The most successful of his works were those in which the attributes of stage and film were balanced to create a genuinely plastic form. Williams's plastic form reached the most advanced point of development between 1945 and 1960. During this period, the playwright had the benefit of interpretative artists capable of translating the texts of his plays into language, conventions, and styles that were both effective and appropriate for interpreting his works in a plastic theater.

One way of looking at the problems that affected Williams's work in the last period of his career is in terms of a gradual weakening of the power of his spoken language, a development that may have been due in some measure to his growing success as a writer of plays for the related medium of film. While the film had value for Williams's idea of theater in all periods of his career, it can be argued that the tension between the aesthetic of the stage and that of the screen assumed a serious tone at the height of his career; that he subsequently conceived his works in terms of the requirements not so much of the theatre, as of film. That Williams was conscious of this tension appears clear not only from notes included in his autobiographical writings, but also from his critical commentaries and the plays themselves. The foreword to *Camino Real* can be read as a measure of his preoccupation with the contrary claims of visual and verbal modes of exposition.

The plays written after *Camino Real* assumed more and more of the theatrical nature of the cinema than of the stage. Though this change in emphasis may have had some value for the treatment of character, it had negative effects for other aspects of his form. Perhaps the most negative effect of this growing preoccupation with visual imagery rather than dramatic events related to the notion of action. In *The Glass Menagerie, A Streetcar Named Desire, Summer and Smoke,* and *Cat on a Hot Tin Roof,* imagery was used to augment dramatic action; increasingly, it replaced action in the later plays. The static quality of action in the later plays—particularly in works such as *Clothes for a Summer Hotel*—reflects this preoccupation with picturization. But this essentially filmic approach to imitation had other negative effects; it altered the perspective of the later dramas—the sense of distance, scale, pattern, movement, relationship, and proportion—in terms both psychological and aesthetic. The result was a growing misalignment between word and image, a conflict that, like others, was to become in works such as *Out Cry* a thematic element in the drama itself.

Despite the problems that now appear to have limited the maturation of his plastic form during the last decade of his career, Tennessee Williams's achievement as an artist was significant. His comprehensive pattern of experimentation served both to consolidate the theatrical vocabulary of the American drama and to refine its spoken language. Over the course of his career, Tennessee Williams offered treatments of language, action, theme, and setting that are to this time unmatched for their expressive quality in the literature of the American theatre. Whereas Eugene O'Neill can be said to have established the identity of the American drama as a distinctive genre, its achievement of the status of a mature form may be attributed in significant measure to Tennessee Williams and his development of the idea of a plastic theater.

Notes

1. Tennessee Williams, *The Glass Menagerie*, New Classics Edition (New York: New Directions, 1949, 1966).

2. Eugene O'Neill, "Strindberg and Our Theatre," in *O'Neill and His Plays: Four Decades of Criticism*, ed. Oscar Cargill, N. Bryllion Fagin, and William S. Fisher (New York: New York University Press, 1961), 108.

3. See Francis Fergusson on European modernism in "*Ghosts* and *The Cherry Orchard*: The Theater of Modern Realism," chap. 5 in *The Idea of a Theater* (Princeton, N.J.: Princeton University Press, 1949), 146–77.

4. See Fergusson, "Poetry of the Theater and the Poet in the Theater," chap. 7 in *The Idea of a Theater*, 194–228. Fergusson cites Tennessee Williams as a playwright seeking to develop a "theater poetry based on realism" (224).

5. Walt Whitman, *Leaves of Grass*, Comprehensive Reader's Edition, ed. Harold W. Blodgett and Sculley Bradley (New York: New York University Press, 1965).

6. Walt Whitman, preface to *Leaves of Grass* (1855), in *Prose Works*, vol. 2, 1892, ed. Floyd Stovall (New York: New York University Press, 1963–64), 434.

7. Walt Whitman, preface to "As a Strong Bird on Pinions Free" (1872), in *Prose Works*, vol. 2, 460.

8. Walt Whitman, "Poetry To-Day—Shakespeare the Future," in *Prose Works*, 1892, 481.

9. Walt Whitman, "Slang in America," in *Prose Works*, 573.

10. See, for example, Betsy Erkkila, *Walt Whitman Among the French: Poet and Myth* (Princeton: Princeton University Press, 1980). Erkkila suggests that Walt Whitman had an important influence on the ideas of form developed by French modernists, that his experiments served as models for those of playwrights such as Paul Claudel as well as for others associated with the "new artistic spirit" that gave rise to movements such as Futurism, Cubism, and Dadaism—movements that had in common the desire to "break through the static structures of the past in order to open new vistas in man and in the world." See "Whitman and Post-Symbolism" (97–174) and "Whitman and the L'Esprit Nouveau" (175–77).

See Max Kozloff, "Walt Whitman and American Art," in *The Artistic Legacy of Walt Whitman*, ed. Edwin Haviland Miller (New York: New York University Press, 1970), 29–53. For Whitman's influence on developments in American literature, see James E. Miller, Jr., *The American Quest for a Supreme Fiction: Whitman's Legacy in the Personal Epic* (Chicago: University of Chicago Press, 1979).

11. See also Marcia Siegel, *The Shapes of Change: Images of American Dance* (Boston: Houghton Mifflin, 1979), 108. Siegel follows the evolution of form in a similar pattern of experimentation by American choreographers, including Doris Humphrey, Martha Graham, José Limon, and Alvin Ailey. She cites Whitman and his influence on painters such as Thomas Eakins and composers such as Charles Ives, an influence that encouraged a tendency to "concreteness" not evident in European arts of the period.

12. See Frank Durham, "Tennessee Williams, Theatre Poet in Prose," in *Twentieth Century Interpretations of The Glass Menagerie*, ed. R. B. Parker (Englewood Cliffs, N.J.: Prentice Hall, 1983), 121–34.

13. See Walt Whitman, "New Poetry—California, Canada, Texas," in "Notes Left Over," *Prose Works*, 519.

14.   Tennessee Williams was not the first of the modern American playwrights to be specifically concerned with the creation of a stage poetry. Such was the objective of William Vaughn Moody (1869–1910), as well as later writers such as Maxwell Anderson. Anderson's explicit statements about dramatic poetry appear in two essays. See "Poetry in the Theatre" and "The Uses of Poetry," in *Off Broadway: Essays About the Theatre* (New York: William Sloane Associates, 1947), 47–54; 87–91.

Thornton Wilder was concerned with the shaping of an American stage language, developed out of the materials of middle-class speech. See "Toward An American Language," in *American Characteristics and Other Essays,* ed. Donald Gallup (New York: Harper, 1979), 3–33.

15.   Williams wrote a considerable body of criticism, most of it devoted to stages in the progression of his idea of a plastic form. Some of the most important of these writings have been published as introductory comments to the published texts of his plays. Other important statements have been published in newspapers and periodicals. Others remain unpublished, and others may still be unknown. Some of these critical writings have been assembled in the collection *Tennessee Williams: Where I Live,* ed. Christine Day and Bob Woods (New York: New Directions, 1978).

16.   *The Dark Room, Ten Blocks on the Camino Real, The Case of the Crushed Petunias, The Unsatisfactory Supper,* and *Moony's Kid Don't Cry* appear in *American Blues* (New York: Dramatists Play Service, 1968).

17.   *27 Wagons Full of Cotton, The Purification, The Last of My Solid Gold Watches, Portrait of a Madonna,* and *This Property is Condemned* appear in *27 Wagons Full of Cotton (and Other One-Act Plays)* (New York: New Directions, 1953). Other plays in this volume include *The Lady of Larkspur Lotion, Auto-da-Fé, Lord Byron's Love Letter, The Strangest Kind of Romance, The Long Goodbye, Hello from Bertha, Talk to Me Like the Rain . . .* and *Something Unspoken.*

18.   Walt Whitman, "Slang in America," *Prose Works,* 572.

19.   See Edward Murray, *The Cinematic Imagination* (New York: Frederick Ungar, 1972), 46–67.

20.   See Gene D. Phillips on Williams and the evolution of the film of *The Glass Menagerie,* in *The Films of Tennessee Williams* (London and Toronto: Associated University Presses, 1980), 33–64.

21.   See Maurice Yacowar, "The Film Version of *The Glass Menagerie (1950),*" in *Twentieth Century Interpretations of The Glass Menagerie,* 26–30.

22.   An important body of scholarly literature is being developed on the evolution of this work. See, for example, R. B. Parker, "The Texas Drafts of *The Glass Menagerie,*" in *Twentieth Century Interpretations of The Glass Menagerie,* 53–61. See also Parker, introduction to *Twentieth Century Interpretations of The Glass Menagerie,* 1–14.

23.   See Lester A. Beaurline, "From Story to Play," in *Twentieth Century Interpretations of The Glass Menagerie,* 44–52.

24.   See also Gilbert Debusscher, "Menagerie, Glass and Wine: Tennessee Williams and Hart Crane," in *Twentieth Century Interpretations of The Glass Menagerie,* 31–43.

25.   Quoted in part by R. B. Parker in "The Texas Drafts of *The Glass Menagerie,*" in *Twentieth Century Interpretations of The Glass Menagerie,* 56.

26.   The passages quoted in this article are from notes by Tennessee Williams, written in pencil draft. The notebook is a part of the Williams Collection at the Harry Ransom Humanities Research Center at the University of Texas. Words in brackets indicate deletions.

27.   This quotation is taken from the author's production notes published in *Masters of the Modern Drama,* ed. Haskell M. Block and Robert E. Shedd (New York: Random House, 1962), 991.

28.   Maria Ley-Piscator suggests that Williams's studies with Erwin Piscator were a major factor in the shaping of his idea of a plastic form. Certainly Williams would seem to have been in some measure indebted to Piscator for the notion of fusing the forms of stage and film, as in his use of the progression of images as the basis of form and the integration of music,

dance, and the visual arts in a plastic stage language. See Marie Ley-Piscator on Tennessee Williams in *The Piscator Experiment* (New York: James H. Heineman, 1967).

29.   See Jo Mielziner's design for *The Glass Menagerie* in Jo Mielziner, *Designing for the Theatre (A Memoir and a Portfolio)* (New York: Bramhall House, 1965), 126–27. Designs for *A Streetcar Named Desire, Summer and Smoke,* and *Cat on a Hot Tin Roof* are included in this volume.

30.   The screen—with its legends—might have been a more appropriate and more effective device for *Camino Real,* a work that would appear more congenial to interpretation in the theatrical language devised by Brecht, Piscator, and their associates.

31.   See Sam Hunter and John Jacobus, *American Art of the 20th Century* (Englewood Cliffs, N.J.: Prentice Hall, 1972), chapter 3, "Insurgent Realists," chapter 4, "The New Spirit," chapter 6, "Americans at Home and Abroad," and chapter 8, "American Scenes and Symbols."

32.   For an earlier view of *Camino Real,* see Esther M. Jackson, *The Broken World of Tennessee Williams* (Madison: University of Wisconsin Press, 1965).

33.   On the problems of *Camino Real* as a work for the stage, see Mary Ann Corrigan, "Beyond Versimilitude: Echoes of Expression," in *Tennessee Williams: A Tribute,* ed. Jacque Tharpe (Jackson: University Press of Mississippi, 1977), 375–412. Corrigan suggests that the play lacks a sense of action, that it functions in effect as a spectacular parade of images and theatrical effects (403–5).

34.   A major figure in the history of this work, and indeed in that of many of Williams's plays, is Elia Kazan. Some enlightening observations about *Camino Real* appear in Thomas H. Pauly, *An American Odyssey: Elia Kazan and American Culture* (Philadelphia: Temple University Press, 1983), 165–69.

35.   The problem of an appropriate production language for these late plays remained a critical one. See, for example, the author's note to *The Milk Train Doesn't Stop Here Anymore,* where he suggests elements of style borrowed from the Kabuki theatre of Japan (New York: New Directions, 1964).

36.   See William J. Free on *Out Cry* in "Williams in the Seventies: Directions," in *Tennessee Williams: A Tribute,* 815–28.

37.   See Betty Jean Jones, "Tennessee Williams' *Out Cry:* Studies in Production Form at the University of Wisconsin–Madison," in *The Tennessee Williams Review* 3, no. 2 (Spring–Fall 1982): 9–16.

38.   See also Paul Stauffacher, "Designing Tennessee Williams' *Out Cry*" in *The Tennessee Williams Review* 3, no. 2 (Spring–Fall 1982): 17–20.

39.   Peggy W. Prenshaw describes *Out Cry* as a sequel to *The Glass Menagerie.* See "The Paradoxical Southern World of Tennessee Williams," in *Tennessee Williams: A Tribute* (5–29).

40.   Albert E. Kalson, "Tennessee Williams at the Delta Brilliant," in *Tennessee Williams: A Tribute,* 774–94.

The Three Halves of
Tennessee Williams's World

JORDAN Y. MILLER

This was sometime a paradox, but now the time gives it proof.

Hamlet, III, i

In the "rational" world of reality, division into halves produces two equal portions, and into thirds, three. But as one looks at the world of certain of the major plays of Tennessee Williams, these distinctions can become blurred and imprecise. In the manner of an Escher drawing where one figure melds into another, up and down are indistinguishable, and the laws of geometry are violated, two "halves" can become one, but still opposed to another "half" of equal value. There seem to be three, then two, a world that splits and reunites its parts, separately and simultaneously—but that is the way with paradoxes.

Camino Real, that paradoxically successful failure, provides the most graphic delineation of this unique pattern. Other plays preceding and following it display the same general quality, but none do it more clearly. It is the time that gives it proof.

When it first appeared in 1953 *Camino Real* profoundly mystified its limited audiences and, except for the rare reviewer who found its stimulating challenge worth serious consideration, suffered dismissal as a baffling, unco-ordinated and possibly pretentious display of theatrical confusion. Expensively difficult to produce in its demands on the stage technician, diffuse in emphasis and overly theatrical, and in these days of rocketing costs demanding a large cast of divergent skills, the play has seldom been revived and never with uniform critical acceptance or consistent audience support. And yet, *Camino Real* continues to appear in a wide variety of anthologies, and it

Reprinted with permission from *Studies in the Literary Imagination* 21, no. 2 (Fall 1988): 83–95.

receives increasing critical attention as one of Williams's best works, if not philosophically profound, at least the most articulate in its presentation of the playwright's view of the intensely depressing qualities of human existence. Conversely, it conveys Williams's ultimately optimistic resolution of the human condition, no matter how sordidly self-destructive it may seem. For underneath, though not always in the true classic sense, in all of his important plays Tennessee Williams is a writer of tragedy, and the ultimate tragic catastrophe must, by its very nature, end on the positive note of human dignity. Williams may not have asserted, as did Eugene O'Neill, that his concern lay in the consideration of the relationship of man to God, but the performance of his characters within these paradoxical three halves of their universe, from which God so often seems totally absent, more than once approaches the denouement of tragedy. In experiencing Williams's plays, one may vigorously deny that life is so limited within the mutually unattractive alternatives that he creates, but it is difficult to argue with the resulting conclusions.

All who have arrived along the Camino Real find themselves, we must assume, as unable to explain how they got there as is Kilroy. This is the "Royal Way," but also the "Way of Life" (Williams explicitly directed that the pronunciation be "reel" as in English, rather than the Spanish "ray-al," in order to suggest the sense of "reality"), into which one is inextricably born, and it holds within its length the full extent of what the world has to offer. The further paradox of the play is, of course, that all who appear along the Camino are, in fact, long dead. It is, then, a place of life-in-death, a purgatory if you will, but this does not prevent its also being a view of life, for Williams, like Sartre, frequently sees hell in other people, and the differences between the punishments of life and those supposedly encountered after death are not always clearly distinguishable.

The sixteen blocks that make up the Camino Real are stretched between two worlds that are the creations of the human beings inhabiting them. They owe nothing to nature, to the quirks of fate or the inexplicable acts of disinterested gods. The choices of the two worlds, the first two halves of Williams's vision of existence, are strictly limited. On the one side are the attractions of the Siete Mares, a luxury hotel catering to those of substantial means. It fits well into the nature of this tropic land, offering an apparently safe and comfortable haven from the unpleasanter aspects of the oppressive heat and the lurking dangers of the dusty square outside. In short, it offers the best of life's pleasures and a relaxing indolence. It is a place of cool shadows, of gorgeous white cockatoos amidst exotic plants. But the Siete Mares is also underlain with corruption and evil. Dominated by the threatening and sinister Gutman, in turn under control of the unseen and equally sinister generalissimo, the Sieta Mares soon reveals that it is a place of mysteriously appearing unclad female figures, of lush, overripe sensuality, of decay and degradation. Here abides the ultimate sensualist, Casanova, hopelessly pursuing the decayed beauty of Marguerite Gauthier, who must now permanently wear the white camelia of the lateness of her life. She herself, far beyond the age of youthful attractiveness, must, in turn, seek to buy her sexual affections from vile young men. It is the refuge of the Mulligans, whose millions can no longer serve to buy their happiness nor their escape from the hideous fate of the streetcleaners' carts. It is the "good" half of the world, the place where dreams ought to be fulfilled, but while offering the best there is to those who can afford to patronize it, the Siete Mares carries an ever-present sense of revulsion, of deadly sickness, defeat and despair.

On the other side of the square, the other "half" of the world of the Camino Real, the contrast is stark, for this is the "worst," but only in relative terms. It is the realm of the Ritz Men Only, with its terrifying little white ships sailing the night, to which Baron de Charlus must flee from the Siete Mares as he seeks his ultimate degradation. It is the half of the world in which resides the brass-lunged gypsy, selling her magical insights and her nubile daughter, living close by the pawnshop that will take the necessities of your livelihood and your life for a pittance. The random, disconnected songs from the bum at the upstairs window are as lacking in coherent sense as the rest of the world surrounding him.

Existence on the level of the Siete Mares or the Ritz Men Only is the sole choice, and choosing to leave one for the other offers no reasonable choice at all. But there is the third "half." Fronting on it, the other two combine into becoming the world as one lives in it, and no matter where one has chosen to reside, each abuts the desolately dry square. The square is the place where the real struggles of life are fought by the inhabitants of both sides. It is hardly a neutral ground for a fair fight in these struggles. It dominates the other "halves," now a single presentation of the essential non-choices of life, and becomes the totally sterile and destructive half, the way of literal or figurative death which seems to be able to overcome the combined factions of the Ritz Men Only and the Siete Mares. It is a mad world, my masters, a mad, mad, mad, mad world. From out of nowhere comes the piping of the streetcleaners who are bent on sweeping up the human debris that litters the place and hauling it off in their carts to some offstage hell. The life-sustaining fountain has dried up. The square is the refuge of repugnant putatas who sell revolting sex and claw at you with horrible hands. It is the spot to which the dying refugee returns from over the wall, destroyed by the frightfulness of the Terra Incognita.

Even the fiesta, centered in the square, loudly celebratory, meant, as are all fiestas, to take one's mind off the surrounding problems and evils of existence, becomes the place of humiliation for the staunch Kilroy and the ridiculous Casanova, the first of whom becomes the blinking-nosed patsy, the other the many-horned and pitiful cuckold. It is the place wherein the gypsy tells her fortunes, and wherein the moon, performing as regularly as the female biological cycle named for it, miraculously, amidst the turmoil, restores the virginity of her daughter. Here the once virile Kilroy, his "manliness" offering him no means of escape, no matter how hard and how fast he runs, becomes the Chosen Hero, seduced and destroyed in the end, ultimately able to free himself, but only at the cost of life itself.

Within the length of the Camino Real there is no salvation, essentially no hope. The hope offered by the Fugitivo proves elusive; it departs without the desperate Marguerite, and Mulligan collapses in the square before his money can get him aboard. But escape through the Fugitivo is in the end equally destructive, for those who can buy their way aboard find death in the crash in Elizabeth, New Jersey. To survive is to endure the worst along the Camino Real, with the only apparent escape in the streetcleaners' carts.

"Direct" escape—forcing the issue by attempting to scale the wall, buying one's way out, defying the streetcleaners—is, then, impossible. Life, in its unsavory, unfair choices, succeeds only in entrapping, leaving a sordid death in the streetcleaners' carts as the only alternative to the suffering and degradation. Kilroy and Casanova, their respective powers nullified in the wild fiesta, reduced to helpless impotence and humiliation, seem destined to remain, thoroughly chastened, to live the marginal existence on either side of the square.

But Williams does offer something more than the futility of the head-on defiance that gets nowhere. One of the sensualists who inhabits the Siete Mares emerges to mount the wall and cross the formidable wasteland. It is Lord Byron, whose soul is that of the complete romantic, oblivious to the surrounding realities, who can find his way out of this purgatorial Way of Life and through the hell that surrounds it. He will be followed by another who can escape, the idealist and dreamer, Don Quixote, the consummate example of total removal from reality. These two remain untouched by the two sides of the life bounding the square, and can defy its deadly aridity and that of the forbidding desert surrounding it.

Finally, there is Kilroy, a third romantic who carries in boxing gloves and belt the remnants of the glories of the past. Kilroy, unlike the other two, does die, but, like the other two who, of course, are also "dead," he is able to evade the streetcleaners and to dignify his death by following them over the wall. Kilroy, the sentimental romantic, the epitome of the confidence of eternal youthful energy, has gallantly left his one true woman because the nature of his accomplishments has made him unable to give her satisfactory physical love. Ironically, his death, the direct consequence of having committed the forbidden act with the Gypsy's daughter, brings two positive results. First, it breaks the Gypsy's spell and the daughter, now returned to lisping childhood, is no longer the marketable commodity the raucous mother once peddled. Second, it reveals the soul of Kilroy in his golden heart, outsized, preventing his former life style, but clear evidence of his generous and almost child-like good natured innocence. (Its size, as big as the head of a baby, and its removal suggestive of the desecration by Trelawny of Shelley's body, are not without their ironies.) He and Esmerelda, the Gypsy's daughter, have both been "saved," and their redemptive escape from the ways of the Camino Real is complete.

Miraculously, two other things happen. Through the acts of those who do have the will and the ability to escape, the fountain once again begins to flow, and the flowers have cracked the mountains; the violets have wedged open the rocks, and the impenetrable desert seems now to have surrendered. *Camino Real* ends not in discouragement, not in pessimism, but in a sense of optimism about the force of human determination to overcome, even in actual or symbolic death, the opposite forces arrayed relentlessly against the individual. Those left behind, as seen in Casanova and Marguerite, in their failure to escape resign themselves to a permanent, perhaps even intimate, relationship in which "love" will take on a different and stronger meaning. The Gypsy must seek other means to control events; there is no longer a patsy to crown Hero of the Fiesta.

There is the suggestion of tragedy in the play, but it is difficult to assign the qualities of the tragic protagonist to Kilroy or anyone else. Kilroy emerges more pitiful than tragic, and although in his death he becomes one of the figures who can overcome the destructive forces around him, he is knocked about by the "gods" (Gutman, the generalissimo, the streetcleaners, even the Gypsy) without ever being able to recognize his fate and to bring the forces arrayed against him to bay. He is far too sentimentally romantic, without personal depth, and he does finally escape, but with all his former glories of belt, gloves, and heart left behind. Possibly more tragic are the figures of Casanova and Marguerite. They recognize at last just what they are, becoming finally aware of their separate falls into humiliation, and in tragic fashion succeed in achieving an equilibrium, a tranquility, which to all intents and purposes marks their symbolic deaths. There can be no further struggle, but no faction within the Camino Real can any longer control them as they close out their existences immune from Gutman or any other opposing power. In the end, as the violets crack the mountains, the once overwhelming antagonists have been effectively destroyed.

Camino Real is the most graphic theatrical demonstration of Tennessee Williams's divided world, but lacking character development with clearly articulated protagonist-antagonist relationship and devoid of a coherent plot line, it surrenders the dramatic effectiveness to *A Streetcar Named Desire,* Williams's most well-developed and successful tragedy. *Camino Real* is a diffuse, spectacular showpiece. *Streetcar* is a tightly conceived and gripping dramatic portrayal of the human side of this divided world, and the central figures, flawed as they are, command audience sympathy and understanding in their ultimately tragic struggle.

The two halves that parallel the Siete Mares and the Ritz Men Only are sharply revealed. The physical presence of Belle Reve is, of course, missing, but it lives on in the persona of its sole survivor, Blanche. She stands foursquare for everything that is right and decent in the world. Plantation bred in the best tradition, she would seem to personify elegance and propriety, and to win our respect as a "lady" who values the finer aspects of life which money and position command, good literature, art, music; all the elements of what "civilization" would seem to mean are in her background as she first appears so clean, white, and apparently unsullied.

But like the unhealthy hotbed atmosphere of the Siete Mares, the dream is in reality a nightmare. The "good" half of life is compounded in horror. The glories of Belle Reve have been founded on the epic fornications of its forbears. The ravages of decay have eaten away the human body and soul as they have destroyed the physical structures of the plantation itself. The "ennobling" figure of the magnificent survivor, maintaining the stance of goodness against overwhelming destructiveness, is hopelessly flawed, ill-equipped to represent the attractions of what she attempts to sell to Stella.

Thus the "good" half of the world, from which pleasure and comfort, security and love, should emerge, is as corrupt as the overgrown lushness of the Siete Mares. The other half, that second side of existence, is a cave as dark and forbidding as the Ritz Men Only. It shelters the roaring beast who throws before his mate the bleeding produce of the hunt. On its little white ship the rutting animals perform their mating ritual under symbolic, if unseen, blinking colored lights.

The choices of life in this Tennessee Williams world are as limited and as unpleasant as those along the Camino Real. Stanley's choice is the forbidding lair he shares with his mate and in which he boisterously associates with the other creatures. Blanche's choice is the "outside" world, but as despoiled as that of Stanley. Stella, caught in between, can be seen as equally doomed, no matter which choice she ultimately makes.

In *Streetcar* Williams has set up these two "halves" of his world in manner equally repulsive, offering a picture of the world that is viciously unpleasant, irrespective of direction taken. They clash openly and fatally within the wasteland as barren in its way as its counterpart, the dry, forbidding square of *Camino Real.* This middle ground, this very similar "third half," of the Vieux Carré, with its bright lights and pulsing life, produces old flower peddlers who offer wares strictly for the dead. Roaring locomotives pass by, drowning any attempt to communicate. Its buildings are old, beautiful in their antique iron balconies and winding outside staircases, but they are ill-adapted to modern living. There are flimsy curtains instead of doorways; there are delapidated shutters that cannot fully shut out the sounds and cries from without. Privacy, upstairs and down, seems non-existent.

The irony of the final battle of the antagonists from either side within this open, noisy impersonal third half wasteland lies in the fact that both the contestants are seeking the same thing; their struggle, deadly as it is, brings the two other "halves" together in a kind of united front against what is happening to each within this forbidding urban jungle. It is not a combat between good and evil, because neither can be judged in terms of literal rights and wrongs. Each is seeking a decent existence, measured in differing terms, to be sure, but equally valid. Each regards itself as the guardian of that existence, resisting the threats of the outside intruder. As we watch in fascination it is impossible to take sides, for sympathetic agreement is extended to each person involved. Who can fault the enraged Stanley, who must endure, then violently oppose, the intruder who could destroy what he has a right to maintain and enjoy? His may be the repugnant side of the world, but who, after all, is to judge him? It is *his* world, and one which Stella, with primitive lust, has willingly succumbed to, remaining always faithful and constantly in heat to satisfy her companion in the cave. Who is given the right to tear this apart? Why should not Stanley protect himself, his paramour, and his wartime buddy from the devious wiles of a conniving bitch? Stanley, for whatever he was before he dragged his mate into the cave, and as suddenly offensive as he can become, remains so far as we know completely faithful, a good provider. He demands our sympathies.

But so does Blanche, in certainty. Pitiful and desperate as she is, hopelessly sullied by her past, still gripped by her totally confused and destructive sexuality, she, in turn, can hardly be faulted for what she is trying to bring into what she sees as the depressing and deprived life of her sister. There *are* good things in the world; much has happened to raise the level of human existence since mankind came down out of the trees. There is beauty and delicacy, love and devotion, an attractive side of life that Blanche insists upon Stella's recognizing and seeking. Blanche, having been abandoned, watching death and decay compounded around her, remains a person who, to most observers, would seem to be on the "right" side, carrying her colors with pride and dignity. She, too, demands our sympathy.

In the end, for all that repels about Blanche, and for all that she represents of the more unattractive side of human behavior, her hypocrisy and her shaky veneer of respectability that cannot stand the full glare of direct light, and for all the understandable antagonisms toward her from Stanley, the catastrophe that descends upon her is the final act of tragedy. She has fully admitted what she is and has faced the reality of her situation. She makes her final stand alone against the predatory vengeful male; she fights, and loses. She finally departs with dignity, while Stanley growls and grumbles. He has fired his ultimate weapon against her and has quite literally destroyed Blanche, but at the same time he has destroyed any semblance he may have had of his own decency. Stella, forced to disbelieve the obvious, must face the realization that the animal passion by which she has measured her happiness will one day subside and the cave will be cold and forbidding within its wilderness.

In the classical tragic sense, survival is thus denied. Blanche is now lost in the haze of a disintegrating mind, as "dead" as Kilroy in the loss of his golden heart. Salvation has presented itself momentarily in Mitch, and the possibility of her redemption in life through Mitch's clumsy but sincere love has been shattered. The catastrophe has been inevitable, but there is a strange uncanny nobility in Blanche's departure. A tranquil balance has descended on the Elysian Fields.

The three halves of the world are not as well defined in the earlier *Glass Menagerie,* but it is not difficult to see the rough general outlines which Williams developed more fully later. Amanda Wingfield's Blue Mountain, like Belle Reve, is seen only in her recounting of its idyllic qualities, but it is much further back in memory. Blanche appears within a relatively short period after the collapse; the memories are immediate and vivid. Amanda's memories are through the same impressionistic haze as the scrim which hangs before the scene as Tom introduces what is to follow. Amanda's past bears small resemblance to Blanche's sordid experiences, but Amanda's pretensions of gentility and her struggles to uphold the semblances of elegance ring just as false. The fine, gentle life and the proprieties evidenced by the Sunday afternoon gentleman callers, all seventeen of them, remain a dream that cannot be verified. They are distant from reality in the same manner as Blanche's vision of Shep Huntleigh. Its surface beauties as recalled by Amanda notwithstanding, life at Blue Mountain was in its way as sterile and unproductive of meaningfulness as Belle Reve, as lushly and oppressively decadent as life in the Siete Mares. And one wonders, given the attractions of place and persons evoked in Amanda's recall, how she could in the end do not better than the telephone lineman and the depressing urban flat in which she finds herself.

While the dismal St. Louis apartment is no brutish cave, those who must live within it have little prospect of rising above its stultifying oppressiveness. It is ruled by the infuriating dominance of Amanda, which can no more be evaded than the brutish carryings-on of Stanley. It is inhabited by the physically and emotionally crippled; its imprisoned family must escape its sordid realities with endless memories of Blue Mountain, with scratchy phonograph records from a past almost as distant as Amanda's plantation days, with fragile bits of glass, and with ceaseless visits to the movies. Although not surrounded by the literal desert of the Terra Incognita, nor the sensuously sinister entrapments of the Vieux Carré, this sad little home provides a view from its fire escape entrance onto back alleys, the garishly lit Paradise Dancehall with its jazzy blues music, and Garfinkle's Delicatessen. The broader world outside offers little more than an urban desolation as arid as *Camino Real*'s dry square. It is that other "half" of this world, providing only the deadening routines of low-paying jobs and maddening indifference to the Toms who attempt to bring it some sense of beauty, even if it is verse on the back of shoe boxes. Such hope as it may provide ends up in the appearance of the false prophet gentleman caller, whose prospects of soul-saving relief are shattered like the helpless glass figure he clumsily breaks. There is no salvation. The only escape is over the wall. Amanda, impervious to the realities literally shouted at her by Tom, sees no cause to make the attempt. Laura, at first driven to the attempt by the blindness of her mother's insensitivity, is beaten back by the desert winds exactly as the desperate fugitive who collapses into the square of *Camino Real*. Only Tom, the ultra-romantic in the image of Kilroy, can do the trick in the ultra-romantic cliché of running away to sea.

The tragedy of *The Glass Menagerie* is not as fully developed as in *Streetcar*, but the makings are here. If there is a tragic protagonist, it must be Tom, whom the furies pursue as surely as they did the hapless Orestes. Tom is compelled to recount his story in a ritual of expiation which can never actually ease what he has done. To find himself, to escape the smothering destructiveness of Amanda's tyranny, Tom is forced over the wall, and he obviously cannot return. He must roam the rootless existence of the seaman, attempting to rid himself of his sin in the retelling of his story as endlessly as Coleridge's Mariner. The pitiful figure of Amanda, never to face any knowledge of who or what she is, and Laura, never able to rise above her fears to realize such potential as is there, remain behind the gauzy curtain of memory. The tragedy is muted, its denouement one of pity, but there is no terror, only sadness, as we weep for all three as Laura puts out the candle.

To varying degrees, the three-halved world remains in others of Williams's most important plays, notably in *Cat on a Hot Tin Roof, The Night of the Iguana,* and *Sweet Bird of Youth.* In *Cat* there is once more, on the Siete Mares side, a plantation, but this time it does not exist in memory but is the active participating background. The fecundity of the land and those who would inherit it is exemplified in the fact that Big Daddy has turned this piece of soil into the best in the Delta, and in the prodigious rate by which Gooper and Mae produce their offspring. Big Daddy, the successful patriarch, stands tall and lordly over all, celebrating another milestone in his latest birthday. But while the plantation does, indeed, yield prosperity and widespread admiration, it displays the problems infesting the others. As ever with Williams, the productivity, the fecundity, is almost too much. Its attractions foster internal strife as to who may lay claim to it, which claim is consistently related to the ability of the claimants to reproduce themselves. Mae and Gooper, vigorously productive, cannot abide the thought that Brick and Maggie, who in all their married years have conceived no offspring, might become the heirs. Furthermore, all that this couple of Sister Woman and Brother Man can offer for their efforts is a pack of steadily increasing yelling, obnoxious, no-necked monsters. And Big Daddy's hulking body, outwardly such a paragon of strength, is riddled with the cancer that reduces him to howling pain.

In contrast, Williams chooses not to give us a Stanley-Stella relationship of animal eroticism and colored lights as the opposite side of things, but to emphasize the sterility of sex gone awry. The physical attractions of the still youthful body of Maggie may stimulate others to turn and stare, to burn holes through her clothes with their eyes, but the manliness of Brick, the accomplished athlete, the potential of physical strength as much as Big Daddy ever held, is lost. Physically crippled, unable to perform as he should, sexually or otherwise, and emotionally distraught, Brick is haunted by the question of his past relationship with Skipper, driving Maggie to the frenzy of her determination to obliterate that memory and bring him back. The bed around which most of Maggie's assault on Brick takes place is no little white ship, and the plantation elegance of the room itself, "Victorian with a touch of the Far East," as Williams describes it, has few counterparts in the Kowalski flat. Yet what takes place within this environment is not all that far removed from the hidden violence within the sordid cubicles of the Ritz Men Only or the uninhibited mating rituals practiced in the Elysian Fields. It is a desperate struggle of the sexes with tooth-and-claw-baring attacks by Maggie the Cat, fought between half-clad combatants giving no quarter, all overhung with the vapor from the prominent and accessible liquor cabinet. The world of Brick and Maggie as we presently see it holds its own special perversities that render it as equally unattractive in its sterility as the fertile yet tainted plantation atmosphere.

The fight for control between Gooper and Brick for the affections of Big Daddy and for the plantation itself goes on amidst everything, while Big Daddy roars his disapproval on all sides. The two worlds clash, and the battleground has its familiar desolate qualities. No sandy desert is here, but its replacement lies in the continual oppressive Southern heat, debilitatingly humid, threatening, raging in a storm which shakes the foundations of the big plantation house. Above all is the constant aura of things not quite right, the persisting sense of a poison spreading everywhere, with Big Daddy's cancer only the outward manifestation of that eating away on all sides.

Is there escape? Only in the morphine for Big Daddy (who in the original version of the play screams offstage in pain in the third act but never appears, but who maintains his presence and importance onstage until the last in the produced version), only in liquor for Brick, and only in the hope of Gooper and Mae that they can inherit the land in the face of Brick and Maggie's sterility. But there is, for Maggie, the escape of the lie, which she is determined to correct. Her report of pregnancy, yet to be accomplished but enough to suggest that all may have been righted in the eyes of Big Daddy, and her determination in both versions to wean Brick from his bottle and the "click" that it brings to keep him going, thus bringing him to her body, suggest the ultimate hope. As with both Stella and Stanley, for whom, in seeking to maintain their own life, sordid as it may be, we must have sympathetic understanding if not approval, we must also have some human empathy and compassion for Brick and Maggie. Uncertain of his own sexuality, relying on the literal crutch to ease his broken leg and on the hardly less literal supporting crutch of liquor, Brick must be regarded as a man in a mortal struggle with himself, revolted by what he may have felt for Skipper, and then by thoughts of countering it with physical intimacy with his wife. Maggie must be admired for the fight she puts up, and if there is any kind of "happy" ending, even though offstage Big Daddy will die in agony, it is the final touching approach of Maggie to Brick with audience hope that her struggle will have brought Brick to his senses and returned things to a semblance of normality.

The jungle of *The Night of the Iguana* as the venue for struggle becomes the dominant "half" of Williams's world, tending to overshadow the others. The universe outside the domain of Maxine Faulk and her crumbling world of the Costa Verde hotel remains unseen but constantly present, much as that of Belle Reve or of Blue Mountain. It is the world in which London burns and which produces the grotesque pink and golden bodies of the freakish German tourist family who cheer at the news of the city's destruction. It also supplies the wildly improbable tour group sponsored by the equally improbable Blake Tours, who would employ the improbable ex-priest, Shannon. And out of that world appear the improbable poet and "softly luminous" saint-like figure of the redemptive Hannah. It is, in Shannon's words, "fantastic," and the line between the fantastic and realistic, as Shannon observes, should be distinguished, but isn't.

Fleeing that outside world, pursued as he is by the nubile Charlotte and the vengeful fury of Miss Fellowes, Shannon must throw himself into the hovel and upon the mercy of its keeper, the lusty sensual Maxine who, despite his own past fleshly sins, offends the sensibilities of Shannon by her state of undress. Here Shannon must wrestle with his evil angel, his spook, always lurking in the jungle, capable of ultimately destroying him.

Here, equally fantastically, the Costa Verde shelters the nearly helpless, semi-senile Nonno, struggling with his last great poem, and the penniless Hannah. (Once more, the reference to beds in crowded little rooms, of separation of the connubial couches, even more literally than that which separates Brick and Maggie.) The jungle's oppressive heat, its sudden rain forest storms, provide the backdrop of these surreal personal battles, climaxed by the ultimate poem which means death for Nonno, and the surrender of Shannon who must, presumably, take the place of the deceased Fred, moving, we must assume, the beds back together again and in the same room so long ago vacated by the deceased Mr. Faulk. Is there anywhere in all of this a world of the realistic? of the normal? Not in the view of Williams, who provides no opportunity for his characters to experience any world except the fantastic dream- (read nightmare-) like aspects of ideals gone terribly amiss, the terrifying dangers of the cave, the Ritz Men Only, or the overbearing suffocating jungle. But for all this, Williams does provide release for his characters, just as the lizard makes its escape before it is scheduled for being killed and devoured. The bedevilling spook may well be gone as Shannon and Maxine go off to the beach, and Hannah is no longer tied to the helpless Nonno. The incredibly old grandfather has himself been released, for his own pursuing spirit has been exorcised in the poem, and his life is no longer needed. The Baptist Female College students have been released to complete their fantastic journey. A tranquility, not of tragedy but of release from oppressive debilitating forces, has been achieved.

Sweet Bird of Youth divides the world a little less obviously, but the usual pattern is lurking around the edges. Chance Wayne enters the repellingly sensual boudoir of the decaying Princess Kosmonopolis to become victimized and entrapped in this lushly sleazy combination of Ritz Men Only and Sieta Mares. Both Chance and the Princess are escapees from the stained and equally decaying world outside, inhabited by the dishonored and mutilated Heavenly Finley and her powerful father as corrupt in his "boss" mentality as Big Daddy is in his disease ridden body. If the Princess escapes through her return to the never-never-land of what is probably an illusion of a Hollywood comeback, Chance remains to absolve his sins to receive his own mutilation and possible death at the hands of Finley's thugs. The Easter imagery of death and resurrection is not without its ironic relevancies. Each way one turns in the world of *Sweet Bird,* one is faced with the same insensitive brute power or faded, damaged beauty.

Thus do the "three halves" of the world, paradox or not, in one way or another appear and reappear within the universe of Tennessee Williams. They separate, they blend, they become fantastic, then frighteningly real, enveloping, seeking to destroy, but, amazingly enough, more often than not providing the ultimate redemption of those who live within them. This offers a picture of a thoroughly depressing universe. One may say with justice that there are other choices, for the one world we all live in does not uniformly offer the kind of negative alternatives that Williams offers his characters. It can be a wholly repellant world, one in which solutions can often seem to lie only in the extreme violence of frontal lobotomies, seductions, or perversions as vicious as the cannibalism of *Suddenly Last Summer.*

And yet, there always seems to be hope. Blanche exits with the poise of the true lady, doomed, but commanding sympathy. Maggie the Cat has made her stand and probably has won; Tom, tortured by his memories, views his past agonies with compassion; Shannon has survived, and Hannah has secured release, with futures uncertain but far from hopeless. Chance Wayne has surrendered, but sacrifices himself for his sins and awaits his fate not whimpering, but with the strong positive nature that seems to make more of a man of himself in the end than could have been anticipated in his previous lifetime. In his approach to the tragic idea, at times verging on the classic, Williams permits his characters to achieve an ultimate dignity, perhaps still badly tarnished, but nonetheless ennobling.

Memory, Dream, and Myth in the Plays of Tennessee Williams

Mary Ann Corrigan

The escapist nature of popular culture is apparent. Not so obvious is the escapism which serious modern literature depicts and countenances in the name of achieving a "timeless" perspective on reality. The belief that humanity is fettered and degraded by temporal existence has occasioned elaborate literary attempts to annihilate or transcend time. Nathan Scott goes so far as to say in *The Broken Center* that the negation of time and the quest for a timeless eternity is the principal literary effort of our period, most especially in the case of the novel (pp. 42–43). The drama of the modern period is marked by a similar time consciousness. A desire to free man from his bondage to chronology lies behind the fantasy and dream worlds created by Strindberg and the Absurdists, the journeys into the past made by Wilder and Miller, and the resuscitation of ancient myths by many modern playwrights. Tennessee Williams' writing reveals a striking preoccupation with the problem of time. Like other modern dramatists, he has juxtaposed past and present, created worlds of fantasy, and employed mythical substructures in order to suspend the irrevocable forward direction of time in his plays. Williams frequently expresses the conflict between real and ideal in temporal terms; time, often as arch-enemy, is ranged with fact, necessity, body, mortality, and locked in combat with eternity, truth, freedom, soul, immortality. Williams' dramas are marked by a thematic obsession with time and its effect on human life to such a degree that his whole career can be viewed from the perspective of his changing attitude toward time.

In his essay, "The Timeless World of the Play," which prefaces *The Rose Tattoo,* Williams writes:

> It is this continual rush of time, so violent that it appears to be screaming, that deprives our actual lives of so much dignity and meaning, and it is . . . the *arrest of time* which has taken place in a completed work of art that gives to

Reprinted with permission from *Renascence* 28; no. 3 (Spring 1976): 155–67.

certain plays their feeling of depth and significance. . . . If the world of a play did not offer us this occasion to view its characters under that special condition of a *world without time,* then indeed, the characters and occurrences of drama would become equally pointless, equally trivial, as corresponding meetings and happenings in life.

The view of art as a source of stasis in a world of flux is certainly not new, but Williams' interpretation of this familiar tenet includes a denial of the significance of the "pointless" and "trivial" events of a life in time. Total suspension of the timely, not the union of time and eternity, is the aim of his art. The act of creation itself is an escape for Williams. "I'm a compulsive writer," he admitted in an interview in *Theatre Arts,* January 1962, "because what I am doing is creating imaginary worlds into which I can retreat from the real world because I'm—I've never made any kind of adjustment to the real world." It is not surprising that the plays motivated by an aesthetic so clearly built upon an escape from time have the quest for timelessness as their structural and thematic center.

Three major periods, coinciding approximately with the last three decades, emerge in a consideration of Williams' plays from the standpoint of the time theme. *The Glass Menagerie, Camino Real,* and *Night of the Iguana* exemplify the characteristic stance toward time that Williams adopts in each period; each of these plays, moreover, employs a different technique to achieve an arrest of time.

The events of *The Glass Menagerie* are enactments of Tom Wingfield's memories; his monologues, addressed directly to the audience, frame the play's seven animated "tableaux" and mediate between past and present. In reliving the events surrounding the visit of his sister's "gentleman caller," Tom conveys to the audience the effect of the past on the present and endows the past with timeless significance.

Within the memory sequences the further past has an effect on the present; Amanda Wingfield's reminiscences about the countless gentlemen who called on her in her youth determine her expectations for her daughter. That the shy, crippled Laura is unlikely to attract hordes of admirers is irrelevant to Amanda, who charges Tom to produce a prospective beau for his sister. The outgoing Jim O'Connor succeeds in penetrating Laura's formidable defenses—until she learns he is engaged to someone else. This encounter is the last of life's disappointments that Laura intends to let touch her. She withdraws completely into her imagination and the world of her miniature glass figurines. Tom, no longer willing to bear his mother's demands and his sister's problems, leaves home in search of the adventure that his many hours at the movies have taught him to expect from life. His final comment suggests that he never finds what he is seeking: "Laura, I tried to leave you behind me, but I am more faithful than I intended to be!" His escape is incomplete.

Williams asks for non-realistic lighting in the play, in order to set off the events occurring in memory. A general dimness gives the effect of ethereality. Williams also specifies that "the light upon Laura should be distinct from the others" and resemble the light upon a madonna in a religious painting. At one point, he calls for special light upon Amanda: "the light upon her face with its aged but childish features is cruelly sharp, satirical as a Daumier print." Such lighting reflects Tom's emotional response to the other characters: his memory canonizes Laura and criticizes Amanda.

Williams' original script and all published versions of the play include directions for the use of a screen on which legends and pictures appear at various points during the drama. While the seven scenes which comprise the play exist only in memory, the images projected on the screen convey another level of memory or illusion *within* each scene. What is unique about the Wingfields is their retreat from the world of daily existence. Each of them has a fantasy world which is infinitely more real than the world of the St. Louis tenement and which Williams depicts concretely in the projected images on the screen. Thus Amanda's reveries about her girlhood are expressed in the image of her greeting gentlemen callers (Scene I). Laura's memories of Jim O'Connor as a high school hero are also present as images on the screen (Scene II). The illusory hope for a gentleman caller for Laura is conveyed by the image, "Young man at door with flowers" (Scene III), and Tom's dreams of an adventurous future by the picture of the "sailing vessel with Jolly Roger" (Scene IV).

The play also makes extensive use of music, which, in framing each scene, serves as a mediator between the present situation of the narrator and his memories of the past. There are, in addition, three distinct musical themes played at intervals during the drama: Laura's theme, "The Glass Menagerie," which is light, delicate, and poignant; the nostalgic fiddling associated with Amanda's reveries; and the "theme three" adventure music which calls Tom to his wandering future. The music in all three cases is symbolic of the illusions which dominate the three main characters.

The techniques which emphasize memory and illusion in the drama reinforce the theme of the escape from time which controls the action. The survival tactic practiced by the Wingfields is to retreat from reality into a timeless world of their own making. Amanda's reveries are so much a part of her life that she seems completely oblivious to reality when she is in the midst of one. Launched into a description of her life as a southern belle, "she addresses Tom as though he were seated in the vacant chair at the table though he remains by portieres" (Scene I). Amanda can summon up a past filled with jonquils and juleps; no matter that her memories are embellished, for she can eternally "relive" even what she has never lived. Tom, too, retreats from what is unappealing in the present. Finding his job dull and his homelife drab, he escapes into the movies. Tom suspends the forward movements of time by participating imaginatively in the ever re-enactable adventures on the screen. All that redeems his life is the specious ideal of adventure else-where. Laura seeks refuge from the painful present in her imaginative world of the glass figures. Mesmerized by the beauty of the glass, she fails to notice the passage of time. In the world of the glass menagerie, a unicorn, a creature who Jim says is "extinct in the modern world," and a symbol for Laura her-self, frolics side by side with the other "normal" horses; in the real world Laura cannot hope for such acceptance of abnormality. Laura's retreat cannot be dismissed as lightly as Amanda's nostalgia and Tom's puerile dreams. Withdrawal from the world is a matter of necessity, not choice, for her. She is too fragile to face buffeting by the bumbling Jim O'Connors of the world. Jim, as Tom remarks to the audience, "is the most realistic character in the play, being an emissary from a world of reality that we were somehow set apart from." It is the ability, possessed by all the Wingfields, to escape from time that sets them apart from the world of reality.

The picture of life presented in *The Glass Menagerie* is a disturbing one: the only defense against the relentlessness and cruelty of life in time is the ultimately unsatisfactory retreat into a world of illusion. None of the Wing-fields has the capacity to "fight back." Amanda in her reveries is an incurable romantic whose practical schemes are doomed to failure. Laura is an object of pity; she backs away from life, not because she wants to, but because nature has ill-equipped her to fight for survival. Tom literally runs away, only to learn that his dreams were illusions and that reality mocks him wherever he goes. Williams, however, celebrates the attempt to flee the present as a noble failure.

In *Christ and Apollo* William Lynch, S. J., comments on the relation between the modern drama and the philosophies of two early heretical sects. Lynch discovers Manichean implications in various social tragedies in which poor innocents are victimized by an impersonal and cruel world. The implied philosophy of *The Glass Menagerie,* which presents the matter of quotidian existence as debasing, is also Manichean. Mind or spirit, in the form of Amanda's recollections, Tom's dreams, or Laura's fantasy, imposes itself on the recalcitrant material of experience and achieves, if only for a moment, a purity and beauty normally denied to those who are earthbound and time-bound.

Most of the plays which Williams wrote during the 1940s depict the defeat of the light of spirit by the darkness of matter. His first play, *Battle of Angels,* is explicitly built on a set of dichotomies: light vs. darkness, imagina-tion vs. practicality, life vs. death—or, in terms of the plot, the young free-spirited wanderer and the woman he impregnates vs. the woman's moribund husband and the hostile townspeople. If the hero, Val Xavier, has a "fault," it is pausing to fall in love; his lovers, past and present, prevent his escape from responsibility. When Williams rewrote the play, under the title *Orpheus Descending,* he retained the Manichean structure and added a set of classical analogies. Williams' mythological allusions suggest the utter incapacity for change or progress in the human situation. Like Orpheus, Val is an innocent alien, a visitor from a better world, who is destroyed by the evil forces which pervade this world. The only way to preserve one's purity, implies Williams, is to stay free of human ties.

Williams sets up similar struggles between matter and spirit in *Summer and Smoke* and *A Streetcar Named Desire,* when he depicts the tension between John and Alma, Stanley and Blanche, Blanche's reality and Blanche's ideality. Body and soul are irreconcilable opposites; in any direct clash, body or matter necessarily wins. In these early plays Williams presents the plight of human beings struggling with their dual natures and hemmed in by their mortality. Those who submit to the conditions of mortal existence are viewed as corrupt; those who defy them in pursuit of a timeless ideal are eventually destroyed by the corrupt anyway. No compromise between pure spirit and base matter is possible in a world in which the realities of timebound existence place limitations on the spirit's capacity to be free.

Most of the plays which Williams wrote during the 1950s assert the spirit's capacity to be free in the face of heavy odds. Time is still the enemy, but those who strive to overcome it are victors, not necessarily on a literal level, but very clearly on a spiritual plane. In changing from a Manichean to a modified Pelagian stance, Williams enlarges the possibilities for heroism. At least, in the middle plays, one's choices are related, not irrelevant, to the outcome of one's life. Although Williams, unlike the Pelagians, does not deny the existence of original sin, he does extol the ability of man to rise by sheer force of willpower above the limitations his mortality imposes upon him. *Camino Real* reveals how Williams' attitude toward the plight of humanity in time alters to offer the possibility for greatness to man.

Williams suspends the rules of strict chronology and causality by adopting in *Camino Real* a structure based on association. He writes in the play's forward that his aim is to give the audience a sense of "the continually dissolving and transforming images of a dream." The body of the drama is an enactment of the dream of Don Quixote who arrives at Camino Real, a place where "the spring of humanity has gone dry." Deserted even by the faithful Sancho Panza, Don Quixote pauses to rest before going on his never-ending journey to right wrongs:

> I'll sleep and dream for a while against the wall of this town—And my dream will be a pageant, a masque in which old meanings will be remembered and possible new ones discovered, and when I wake from this sleep and this disturbing pageant of a dream, I'll choose one among its shadows to take along with me in the place of Sancho. (Prologue)

The play's sixteen scenes, called "blocks," are not discrete entities, but tend to melt into one another as phases of a dream.

"A convention of the play is existence outside of time in a place of no specific locality," writes Williams in the foreword. The setting is a plaza in a typical, but unnamed seaport. A fountain gone dry dominates the plaza, on one side of which is the luxurious Siete Mares hotel and on the other side of which is Skid Row. The inhabitants of both sides of the plaza, rich and poor, are miserable. The only means of escape from the Camino Real is through the upstage archway leading to Terra Incognita, a wasteland between the plaza and the snow-capped peaks in the distance. Characters from different eras, from history, legend, and literature, mingle with one another on the plaza; they share in common a life of torment. An aging Casanova wears cuckold's horns. Marguerite Gautier, the formerly beautiful courtesan, must pay for the attentions of young lovers. Kilroy, an all-American ex-prizefighter, is forced to don the costume of buffoon and communicate by lighting up his nose. Baron de Charlus, Proust's effete aristocrat, tries to make himself appealing to the young men on Skid Row. Lord Byron, corrupted by success and unable to write, ventures out on the Terra Incognita. Lord Mulligan, Williams' archetype of a twentieth century business tycoon, encounters the only government officials he cannot bribe, the streetcleaners of the Camino Real, who lie in wait to cart away the corpses of those who die on the plaza.

Like so many of Williams' characters—like Blanche, who takes the streetcar named Desire to the end of the line, like Chance Wayne on a cross-country drive in *Sweet Bird of Youth,* like the minister turned tour guide in *Night of the Iguana*—the characters in *Camino Real* are wanderers, rootless, displaced persons. Gutman, the hotel proprietor who introduces and comments on the play's action, says, "This is a port of entry and departure. There are no permanent guests" (Block VIII). Camino Real is a way station, albeit a most depressing one, on the journey from birth to death. Williams uses the opening lines from Dante's *Inferno* as the play's epigraph. The inferno experienced by the characters on the Camino Real is caused by the inevitable change and dissolution which accompany time's forward motion. Marguerite, the aging whore, is counseled by her friend: "Times and conditions have undergone certain changes since we were friends in Paris, and now we dismiss young lovers with skins of silk and eyes like a child's first prayer, we put them away as lightly as we put away white gloves meant only for summer, and pick up a pair of black ones, suitable for winter" (Block I). Marguerite herself tells the no longer youthful or solvent Casanova, "Time betrays us and we betray each other" (Block X). On the Camino Real the characteristic gestures of courtesans, philanderers, poets, tycoons, and prizefighters have been rendered ineffectual and ridiculous by the passage of time.

As demanded by the stage directions, the legendary characters wear modern clothes with only vestigial touches of the period costume. The combination of contemporary and historical costuming suggests that each character represents a legend or myth that is still operative in the present. The drama indicates which is the saving myth. *Camino Real* is a paean to dreamers and idealists of all ages. The only way out of the plaza is through the Terra Incognita, and the only characters to take that route are Byron, Don Quixote, and Kilroy—romantics all.

Byron is dismayed by his inability to write the kind of poetry he used to write. Recognizing that "there is a passion for declivity in this world," he proposes to go through the Terra Incognita in hopes of regaining the pure vision of his youth. His assertion that "there is a time for departure even when there's no certain place to go" expresses the energy, willpower, and blind trust which alone can save one on the Camino Real.

For Don Quixote, as well, the vision of what life should be is far more potent than the knowledge of what life is. Williams describes his character in an interview in *Saturday Review* (March 28, 1953): "Don Quixote . . . is the supreme example of the obstinate knight gallant and unashamed at being the victim of his own romantic follies" (pp. 25–26).

Kilroy is Don Quixote's logical companion for the journey through Terra Incognita. Early in the play, Kilroy resolves to escape from the Camino Real, even sells his golden gloves for money to finance the trip, but his susceptibility to the charms of the gypsy's daughter prevents him from leaving. As in Williams' earlier plays, the pleasures of the flesh corrupt. Kilroy refuses to accept the inevitable: when the streetcleaners come for him, he fights them off as long as he can. The old woman, who cradles the dead Kilroy in the manner of the pieta, says, "Humankind cannot bear very much reality." With these words, Kilroy is resurrected to join forces with Don Quixote. The two idealists, whose gestures of defiance cause the waters of the fountain on the Camino Real to flow once more, leave for the Terra Incognita. The affirmation at the end of *Camino Real* proclaims the worth of the struggle itself, even in the absence of any tangible good resulting from the struggle.

Camino Real in offering the Terra Incognita as a remedy for the pain of being human, denies the possibility of a resolution in time of the problems posed by mortality. By including the Casanova-Marguerite subplot, Williams avoids complete escapism. Even as Don Quixote and Kilroy leave to follow their dreams, Casanova and Marguerite remain on the Camino Real to find "salvation" in their mutual love. Williams' point is obvious: idealism can conquer the limitations of mortality, love can make them bearable.

Pelagianism provides the philosophic framework of *Camino Real*. According to Lynch, what characterizes the Pelagian stance in the modern drama is the exaltation in the last act of the energy and competence of man, alone and without aid (*Christ and Apollo*, pp. 77–78). Whether or not the gesture of defiance in *Camino Real* really succeeds in overcoming the limitations of the world, time, and necessity is irrelevant. The act of defiance itself is courageous, heroic, and therefore worthwhile.

A tinge of Pelagianism is also evident in *Cat on a Hot Tin Roof* and *Suddenly Last Summer,* in which Williams commends characters who rebel against their present situation, whether with good or bad results. One play of

Williams' middle period is noteworthy, both for its emphatic treatment of time as the source of man's problems and for is obvious Pelagianism. Unlike Williams' memory play and dream play, *Sweet Bird of Youth* uses a conventional technique and structure. It tells the story of a degenerate young man who returns to his Southern hometown in the company of an aging movie queen. She wants only to drown her memories of former success by resorting to liquor, drugs, and sex; he wants to improve on his memories by marrying his former sweetheart, Heavenly, whose father had prevented their marriage years ago. But Chance Wayne is even less welcome in his hometown than he used to be, for his infection of Heavenly with venereal disease has necessitated a hysterectomy. The news of Heavenly's operation shocks Chance and forces him to question the values upon which he has based his life—money and success. Although he is repeatedly warned to leave town, Chance stays to accept his guilt and atone for it at the hands of Heavenly's brother who castrates him in revenge.

Although Chance's own transgressions are the source of his degeneration, the implication throughout the play is that Chance, like all men, is a victim of time's cruel tricks. However pure one's motives, the sins of the past take their toll. As the movie star is about to abandon Chance, a clock in the room ticks perceptively louder. Chance comments: "It's slow dynamite, a gradual explosion, blasting the world we live in to burnt-out pieces. . . . Time—who could beat it, who could defeat it ever? Maybe some saints and heroes, but not Chance Wayne." Though Princess tries to talk Chance into leaving before it is too late, he refuses to run and instead meets his executioners courageously. At the end of the play, he explains his act of defiance to the audience: "I don't ask for your pity, but just for your understanding—not even that—no. Just for your recognition of me in you, and the enemy, time, in us all."

By facing the enemy squarely, Chance achieves a spiritual victory. An earlier Williams character who fell prey to a mob, Val Xavier of *Battle of Angels,* was in the process of running away. Though Val's execution took place on Good Friday, there was no Easter Sunday in the play. By emphasizing that the events of *Sweet Bird of Youth* take place on Easter, Williams suggests that Chance's action is redemptive. The slim comfort that a gesture like his provides is an improvement over the despair that the fate of the Wingfields and Blanche DuBois arouses in the audience. In Williams' Pelagian world man exercises free will, but only within the narrow sphere of deciding whether to face reality and the burden of time, as Chance does, or to run away from them for as long as possible, as Princess does. Williams does not suggest that human beings can alter their destinies in time.

Williams' dramas of the sixties and seventies, however, reveal a different approach to the human predicament. His later characters discover the significance of their existence and the possibility of control by immersing themselves in time, rather than by escaping or defying it. In *Night of the Iguana, The Milk Train Doesn't Stop Here Anymore, Kingdom of Earth,* and *Small Craft Warnings,* it is not the "loners," but those who need each other, not the defiers, but the accommodators, who are set up as ideals. And in the later plays there is no doubt that the archetypal sin-suffering-atonement-redemption pattern is *fully* realized.

Night of the Iguana makes use of the Orestes myth and the Christian myth in an effort to resolve the problem of time. The Reverend T. Lawrence Shannon, defrocked because of his moral shortcomings and his unorthodox sermons, abandons the tour group he is leading in the Mexican rain forest and mounts a hill to the Costa Verde Hotel. Shannon is being pursued, not only by the righteous lady tourists vowing revenge for his latest peccadillo, but also by an opponent he calls the "spook," the ghost of his misdeeds. Maxine Faulk, owner of the hotel, is not surprised to see Shannon, for he comes to the seaside retreat approximately every eighteen months, when his past threatens to catch up with him. Two more unexpected guests converge on the Costa Verde: Hannah Jelkes, unmarried and "pushing forty," and her grandfather, Nonno, the "oldest practicing poet." The two are indefatigable travelers, making their way through the world by the sale of Hannah's sketches and the proceeds from Nonno's informal poetry readings. All of these characters have arrived at a critical point in their lives: Shannon, realizing his latest escapades will keep him from being reinstated in the ministry, is having an emotional breakdown; Maxine has just lost her husband; Nonno is very close to death; Hannah must help her grandfather through his last crisis and go on without him. Williams gives symbolic expression to the striving of the characters for something permanent amid their ever changing lives, when, at the end of the second act, "Shannon lowers his hands from his burning forehead and stretches them out through the rain's silver sheet as if he were reaching for something outside and beyond himself. Then nothing is visible but these reaching-out hands. A pure white flash of lightning reveals Hannah and Nonno against the wall, behind Shannon."

When Maxine has the suicidal Shannon tied to a hammock, Hannah agrees to watch over him through this bout with his spook. Nonno, meanwhile, mumbles in his cubicle, trying desperately to compose his last poem. In telling the story of her battle with her own "blue devil," Hannah indicates what is wrong with Shannon's wholly introspective approach to his problems: "My work, this occupational therapy that I gave myself—painting and doing quick character sketches—made me look out of myself, not in, and gradually, at the far end of the tunnel that I was struggling out of I began to see this faint, very faint gray light—the light of the world outside me—and I kept climbing toward it" (Act III). Shannon's looking outside of himself and freeing the iguana, another creature "at the end of his rope," coincides with Nonno's completion of his poem.

The attempt to break down the barriers of time does not so obviously affect Williams' techniques in *Night of the Iguana* as it does in *The Glass Menagerie* and *Camino Real*. Nevertheless, *Night of the Iguana* resembles *Camino Real* in that the Costa Verde functions as a kind of Never-Neverland, placed on a hill overlooking, but somehow apart from the time-drenched world below. On this hill each character strives to come to terms with time and the duality of human nature, though earthbound, strives for the infinite. The play is like *The Glass Menagerie* in that memory is an important part of each character's conception of himself. So conscious of the past are these characters that one critic was able to construct a chronology, including exact dates, for the major events in their lives (Ferdinand Leon, "Time, Fantasy, and Reality in *Night of the Iguana*," *Modern Drama*, XI, May, 1968). More than the iguana is freed before the night is over, for all the characters learn to abjure the past to which they are tied.

Shannon is the focal point of the drama about the ways in which one comes to terms with time. He is caught between his earthly inclinations and his heavenly aspirations. No such conflict between the real and ideal exists in either Maxine or Hannah. Maxine, living on the real, practical plane, and Hannah existing on the ideal level of a life in art, are thus almost allegorical figures. Shannon is symbolically related to Nonno, who is engaged in the struggle that is at the root of all attempts to escape time, the final struggle against death. Nonno's progress toward release in death and Shannon's progress toward self-knowledge are related through the poem which Nonno finally creates. The poem is a prayer that "beings of a golden kind," those who desire to "arch above earth's obscene, corrupting love," can face with courage a fall from ideal to real existence. Shannon, whose indulgence of the ideal and contemplative side of his nature, has led to his crack-up, must settle down to life on a more realistic plane, which means, for the time being, staying with the very earthbound Maxine, who admits finally her need for him.

In *Night of the Iguana* the Orestes myth characterizes Shannon's plight and endows it with a wider significance. "Myths are chosen as literary symbols for two purposes," writes Meyerhoff (*Time and Literature*, p. 80), "to suggest within a secular setting a timeless perspective of looking upon 'the human situation,' and to convey a sense of continuity and identification with mankind in general." Shannon's spook is another name for the Furies, for the guilt which human beings feel over their own transgressions. Unlike Orestes, Shannon has broken no familial code of honor, but rather, a wholly personal code. The gods, in a sense, ordained Shannon's plight, as Apollo ordained Orestes', for Shannon's sins are consequences of his given human nature. If we can believe his accounts of the seductions which led to his defrocking, he struggled valiantly against strong natural instincts which eventually triumphed ("I was the goddamnedest prig in those days that even you could imagine. I said, let's kneel down together and pray and we did, we knelt

down, but all of a sudden the kneeling position turned to a reclining position
. . ."). The paradox of desiring good while pursuing evil is inherent in the
human situation and is the source of Shannon's breakdown. This paradox also
characterizes the religious myth of the Fall.

Although the classical myth of Orestes defines the basic dramatic situation of *Night of the Iguana,* the Christian myth provides the key to the resolution of the drama. More is involved in the play's Christian perspective than
the simple equation of Shannon tied in his hammock and Christ nailed to
the cross, both "atoning" for the transgressions of mankind, although this
relationship is clearly implied by Williams. The religious ritual structure of
sin-suffering-atonement-redemption works itself out, not in Shannon's
assumption of the role of Christ-figure, but in his progress toward a truly
Christian outlook on the world. Shannon has always been willing to "suffer"
and "atone"; he does it every eighteen months with a vengeance. What
makes this encounter different from all others is the new knowledge of what
must come after atonement, of what constitutes a redeemed life. Shannon
comes to this realization largely through his contact with Hannah.

While Shannon conscientiously sets himself apart from the mass of men
in his search for God, Hannah offers him a different approach to this search,
based upon her own experience: find God in ministering to the needs of others. She first suggests this solution after his "confession" of sins in the second
act, when Shannon says his touring is aimed at collecting evidence about a
God of lightning and thunder:

> I've a strong feeling you will go back to the Church with this evidence you've
> been collecting. . . . And I think you will throw away the violent, furious ser-
> mon, you'll toss it into the chancel, and talk about . . . no, maybe talk about
> . . . nothing . . . just. . . . Lead them beside still waters because you know how
> badly they need the still waters, Mr. Shannon. (Act II)

At another point in the play Hannah mocks Shannon's pretensions to a
"voluptuous crucifixion" in the hammock, but she is basically unfailingly
sympathetic toward him. Her sympathy, coupled with Shannon's own growing concern for another suffering human, Nonno ("The old man touches
something in him which is outside of his concern with himself"), gradually
leads Shannon to recognize the truth of her "message." She reiterates it near
the end of the play when she recommends belief in the "broken gates between
people so they can reach each other, even if it's just for one night only. . . . A
little understanding exchanged between them, a wanting to help each other
through nights like this." Hannah's point is that suffering for the sins and
guilt of oneself or even all humanity is fruitless unless it issues in the redemptive act of offering help and comfort to another creature. The release of the
iguana is such an act, for it is a simple gesture of mercy, free of selfish concern.

Shannon's announcement as he frees the creature that "we are going to play God here" indicates that he has learned that the only way to find God is to be God-like or Christ-like in extending help to those in need.

An author who updates myths can break down the barriers between past and present. If he stresses "the eternal return of the same," the effect of the myth may be to undermine the importance of timely existence. But myths may also be used to define basic human situations or problems confronted differently by each age and existentially by each individual. It is this latter function which the myth serves in *Night of the Iguana,* the message of which is the necessity of finding one's place in the present. The characters of the play, as Williams says (*Theatre Arts,* January, 1962), "reach the point of utter despair and still go past it with courage." Their despair results from the burdens placed on them by their mortality and by the changes which accompany the passage of time. The drama consists in their coming together, enlightening, and helping each other through this "dark night of the soul."

The characters of Williams' later plays resolve their problems, not by taking refuge in an idealized past or in imaginative leaps, but by courageously accepting present reality and assuming responsibility for the future. In *The Milk Train Doesn't Stop Here Anymore* a redoubtable aging woman faces her imminent death, admitting for the first time her dependence on someone else, and in *Kingdom of the Earth* the inadequacy of a life of illusion convinces a backwoods farmer and an old whore to compromise their dreams. *Small Craft Warnings* also communicates the importance of working with what is imperfect in the world and in human beings.

In the first stages of his career, whether he is depicting the defeat of the forces of light by the forces of darkness or exalting the energy of self-sufficient man. Williams adopts an essentially negative attitude toward time. He views the inexorable march of time as destructive of man's work and dreams. The quest in *The Glass Menagerie* and *Camino Real* is for what is untouched by time. By contrast, in Williams' later plays the forward march of time—in extending to human beings the opportunity to create anew, to change and progress—is a source of meaning. The courage to become is what the characters of Williams' later plays seek and find.

Thematic considerations are but one aspect of aesthetic evaluation. That the later plays of Williams embody a more satisfying philosophy of living is no guarantee of their dramatic worth. Indeed, Williams' earlier plays are generally considered his best. Yet there is a paradox involved in Williams' attempt in his early plays to fashion for the stage actions which are supposedly devoid of human meaning in order to prove the significance of what cannot be humanly enacted. For it is the *plaza* which comes to life on stage, and the Terra Incognita which is doomed to remain without artistic form. As Joseph Riddel points out in an article in *Modern Drama* (Spring, 1963, p. 442), "Williams asks for two contradictory things: that we endure his realistic surface—and indeed be entertained and informed by it—and that we respond more truly by extirpating the temporal and spiritually involving our-selves in a world beneath." That the theater may not be the ideal forum for the kind of philosophy which Williams' early plays promulgate is implied in this criticism by William Lynch of the intellectual bias of modern drama: "The contemporary gesture of defiance and exaltation is completely foreign to the basic ritual gestures of the simple man. The contemporary theater has been largely a place created by and for 'intellectuals,' a place of rarefied con-cepts producing unauthentic art that does not attract the ritualistic man, the common man. And one reason for this is that the innate ritual in him is more honest and profound: it is a movement of final helplessness and appeal" (*Christ and Apollo,* pp. 75–76). Final helplessness and appeal—the gesture of Reverend Shannon at the end of Act II of *Night of the Iguana*—is the first step toward finding one's place in time and history.

Just as the lack of a philosophy that comes to terms with man's tempo-rality and mortality does not necessarily make a bad play, so the embodiment of a philosophy that provides a viable rationale for living does not of itself insure success. All that can be said is that given two plays of similar dramatic merit, the one in which mortality is seen as a source of insight rather than a hindrance to vision is the one that will be more humanly satisfying. "From *Menagerie* on, time has been chasing the Williams characters," writes Gerald Weales, but it is only from *Night of the Iguana* on, that Williams' characters have confronted time to find its human significance.

Tennessee Williams: Dramatist of Frustration

John Gassner

In an addendum written in March, 1944, for the published text of *Battle of Angels,* Tennessee Williams affirmed his allegiance to the plastic medium of the theater. "I have never for a moment doubted that there are people— millions!—to say things to," he concluded. "We come to each other, gradually, but with love. It is the short reach of my arms that hinders, not the length and multiplicity of theirs. With love and with honesty, the embrace is inevitable."[1] When *The Glass Menagerie* reached Broadway one year later, on March 31, 1945, the embrace was consummated. The thirty-one-year-old southern playwright met and won his audience, and the planet's most formidable band of critics awarded him the New York Drama Critics' Circle prize for the best American play of the 1944–45 season. If in the fall of 1945 a second occasion for an embrace, his earlier-written dramatization of a D. H. Lawrence story under the title *You Touched Me,*[2] proved less ardent, it was still an encounter with a well-disposed public that patronized the play for several months. Two years later, moreover, *A Streetcar Named Desire* quickly took its place after the Broadway *première* on December 3, 1947, as the outstanding American drama of several seasons, holding its own even against so strong a rival as *Mister Roberts* and winning a second Drama Critics' Circle award as well as the Pulitzer Prize. By common consent its author is the foremost new playwright to have appeared on the American scene in a decade, and our theater capital is at present eagerly awaiting *Summer and Smoke,* concerning which reports have been glowing ever since Margo Jones produced it in Dallas in the summer of 1947.

I

All was not well when Tennessee Williams predicted an inevitable embrace between himself and the theater, and a less resolute young man might hastily

Reprinted from *College English* 10, no. 1 (October 1948): 1–7, by permission of the journal. Copyright 1948 by the National Council of Teachers of English.

have retreated from the battlefield of the stage. After having written four unsatisfactory and unproduced full-length plays by 1940, he had seemed to be riding on the crest of the wave when *Battle of Angels* was put into production by the Theatre Guild in the fall of that year. A group of his one-acters, aptly entitled *American Blues,* since their scene was the depression period, had won a small cash award from the Group Theatre in 1939. He had received a Rockefeller Foundation fellowship and had been given a scholarship to an advanced playwrights' seminar at the New School for Social Research in February, 1940, by Theresa Helburn and John Gassner. Since both instructors were associates of the Theatre Guild, they submitted their student's play to the Guild when he showed them a draft of *Battle of Angels* at the end of the semester. The play went into rehearsal under excellent auspices, with Margaret Webster as director and Miriam Hopkins as the leading lady. But the results were catastrophic when the play opened in Boston. The play concluded melodramatically with a conflagration, which the stage manager, previously warned that he was weakening the effect by his chary use of the smokepots, decided to make thoroughly realistic. An audience already outraged by examples of repressed sexuality in a southern community was virtually smoked out of the theater, and Miss Hopkins had to brush away waves of smoke from her face in order to respond to the trickle of polite applause that greeted the fall of the curtain. The reviewers were lukewarm at best, and soon Boston's Watch and Ward Society began to make itself heard. The Theatre Guild withdrew the play after the Boston tryout and sent a hasty apology to its subscribers. The author, who had lost an unusual opportunity to make his mark in the theater, became once more, as he put it, that "most common American phenomenon, the rootless wandering writer," who ekes out a living by doing odd jobs. He was ushering in a movie theater for a weekly wage of seventeen dollars when Metro-Goldwyn-Mayer took him out to Culver City along with other young hopefuls. The studio promptly forgot about him after his submission of an outline for a screenplay that contained the germ of *The Glass Menagerie,* wrote him off as just another bad penny in Hollywood's expensive slot-machine, and dismissed him at the end of his six months' term.

If his prospects seemed bleak in the early months of 1944, Tennessee Williams nevertheless had reasons for self-confidence. He had been sufficiently inured to straitened circumstances during his youth, especially while pursuing his studies at the University of Missouri, Washington University, and the University of Iowa. His education had even been interrupted by two years of depressing employment as a clerk for a shoe company. His later apprenticeship to the writing profession had included desultory work as a bellhop in a New Orleans hotel, as a typist for engineers in Jacksonville, Florida, and as a waiter and reciter of verses in a Greenwich Village night club. He also knew the direction he was taking and had, in fact, already covered some of the road, having absorbed considerable experience and poured out a good deal of it in the remarkable one-act plays later collected under the title of *27 Wagons Full of*

Cotton. He was developing a precise naturalism, compounded of compassion and sharp observation and filled with some of those unsavory details that Boston had found offensive but that Williams considered a necessary part of the truth to which he had dedicated himself. He was certain that, although he had written poetry and short stories, his métier was the theater because he found himself continually thinking in terms of sound, color, and movement and had grasped the fact that the theater was something more than written language: "The turbulent business of my nerves demanded something more animate than written language could be."[3] He was also moving toward a fusion of the most stringent realism with symbolism and poetic language wherever such writing seemed dramatically appropriate.

Above all, Williams was ready to carve out plays that would be as singular as their author. Although one may surmise that he was much affected by Chekhov and D. H. Lawrence and possibly by Faulkner, he drew too much upon his own observation to be actually imitative. Nor did he fall neatly into the category of social and polemical dramatists who dominated the theater of the 1930's, even if his experience of the depression inclined him toward the political left. His interest was primarily in individuals rather than in social conditions. His background alone would have distinguished him from urban playwrights like Odets, Arthur Miller, and Lillian Hellman, who were attuned to political analysis and regarded personal problems under the aspect of social conditioning. By comparison with his radical contemporaries, this Mississippi-born descendant of Tennessee pioneers (he was born in Columbus on March 26, 1914) was insular and had been conventionally reared and educated. His father, formerly a salesman in the delta region, was the sales manager of a shoe company in St. Louis, and his maternal grandfather was an Episcopalian clergyman. Cities appalled Williams. He disliked St. Louis, where he spent his boyhood, and he never felt acclimated to New York. His inclinations, once he felt free to wander, took him to Florida, Taos, Mexico, or the Latin Quarter of New Orleans, where he still maintains an apartment. The pattern of his behavior established itself early in his life, and it was marked by a tendency to isolate himself, to keep his individuality inviolate, and to resort to flight whenever he felt hard-pressed.

II

The one-act plays which first drew attention to Williams foreshadow his later work both thematically and stylistically. The first to be published, *Moony's Kid Don't Cry,*[4] presents a factory worker who longs to swing an ax in the Canadian woods, a carefree youth who doesn't hesitate to buy his month-old baby a ten-dollar hobbyhorse when he still owes money to the maternity hospital.

Moony, whose effort to escape is effectively scotched by his practical wife, is a prototype of the restive young heroes of *Battle of Angels* and *The Glass Menagerie*. The sturdy one-acter *27 Wagons Full of Cotton* gives a foretaste of the rowdy humor that was to prove troublesome in *Battle of Angels* and was to establish a fateful environment for the heroine of *A Streetcar Named Desire*. The pungent naturalism of Erskine Caldwell and William Faulkner is very much in evidence in this extravaganza about a cotton-gin owner who loses his wife to the man whose cotton gin he burned down in order to acquire his business. *The Purification,* a little tragedy of incest and Spanish "honor," reveals Williams' poetic power and theatrical imagination, and *The Long Goodbye* anticipates *The Glass Menagerie* with its retrospective technique.

Most noteworthy, however, are those evidences of compassion for life's waifs which transfigure crude reality in the one-acters. Pity glows with almost unbearable intensity in the red-light district atmosphere of *Hello from Bertha,* in which an ailing harlot loses her mind. Pity assumes a quiet persuasiveness in the vignette, *Lord Byron's Love Letter,* in which two women's pathetic poverty is revealed by their effort to subsist on donations from Mardi Gras tourists to whom they display a letter from Byron; and Williams is particularly affecting in his treatment of battered characters who try to retain shreds of their former respectability in a gusty world. Self-delusion, he realizes, is the last refuge of the hopelessly defeated, and he studies its manifestations in *The Portrait of a Madonna* with such clinical precision that this one-acter would be appalling if it were less beautifully written. Its desiccated heroine, who imagines herself being violated by an invisible former admirer and who plays the southern belle of her girlhood by bandying charming talk with imaginary beaux, is almost as memorable a character as Blanche Du Bois in *A Streetcar Named Desire*. Williams would like to grant these unfortunates the shelter of illusions, and it pains him to know that the world is less tender. Mrs. Hardwick-Moore of *The Lady of Larkspur Lotion* is the butt of her landlady, who jibes at the poor woman's social pretensions and at her invention of a Brazilian rubber plantation, from which her income is incomprehensibly delayed. Only a fellow-boarder, a writer nearly as impoverished as Mrs. Hardwick-Moore, is charitable enough to realize that "there are no lies but the lies that are stuffed in the mouth by the hard-knuckled hand of need" and to indulge her increasingly reckless fabrication as she locates the plantation only a short distance from the Mediterranean but near enough to the Channel for her to distinguish the cliffs of Dover on a clear morning.

It is quite apparent that Williams was nearly fully formed in these short plays as a painter of a segment of the American scene, a dramatist of desire and frustration, and a poet of the human compensatory mechanism. It is a curious fact about American playwriting that, like O'Neill, Paul Green, Odets, and Irwin Shaw, Williams should have unfolded his talent in the one-act form.

III

When the young author wrote *Battle of Angels,* the first of the full-length plays to attract a Broadway management, he was on less securely charted territory. He did not yet know his way through the maze of a plot sustained for an entire evening. He was so poorly guided in the revisions he made for the Theatre Guild that the play as produced was inferior to the script that had been accepted, and he also appears to have been fixed on D. H. Lawrence somewhat too strongly at this stage to be able to master the play's problems. *Battle of Angels* is unsatisfactory even in the revision published in 1945, which differs in several respects from the play that failed in Boston, for it lacks the Wagnerian conflagration climax, stresses the note of social protest in one scene, and employs a prologue and epilogue as makeshift devices. He had plainly tried to throw together too many of the elements he had dramatized separately in his best one-acters. He brought his vagabond hero, Val Xavier, into a decayed town, involved him with a frenzied aristocratic girl, grouped an assorted number of repressed matrons and unsympathetic townsmen around him, and made him fall in love with the frustrated wife of a storekeeper dying of cancer. He not only made the mistake of multiplying dramatic elements instead of fusing them but piled up fortuitous situations, such as the arrival of an avenging fury in the shape of a woman from whom he had escaped and the killing of the wife, Myra, by the jealous storekeeper—a murder for which Val is innocently lynched. Williams, moreover, made the mistake of offering an ill-defined cross between a provincial vagrant and a D. H. Lawrence primitive as an example of purity of spirit. A somewhat ill-digested romanticism would have vitiated the play even if its dramaturgy had been firmer.

    Battle of Angels, nevertheless, contained some of his most imaginative dialogue and memorable character-drawing. Myra is a rounded portrait, and Williams has yet to improve upon his secondary character, Vee Talbot. Vee painted the Twelve Apostles as she saw them in visions, only to have them identified as "some man around Two River County," and paints the figure of Christ, only to discover that she has drawn Val Xavier. If Williams had been able to exercise restraint, he could have made his mark in 1940 instead of having to wait five years.

    He did achieve simplification with his next work, *You Touched Me,* a comedy in which a Canadian solider liberates a girl from her musty British environment and the mummifying influence of a spinster. But here he was working with another writer's material, paying an overdue debt to D. H. Lawrence. The lack of personal observation was apparent in this competent dramatization; the play did not bear his own special signature of anguish. Even simplification had to become a highly personal achievement in Williams' case. Only when this transpired in *The Glass Menagerie* was there no longer any doubt that the theater had acquired a new dramatist.

IV

The plays that thrust Tennessee Williams into the limelight have much in common besides their clear focus and economical construction. Both *The Glass Menagerie* and *A Streetcar Named Desire* transmute the base metal of reality into theatrical and, not infrequently, verbal poetry, and both supplement the action with symbolic elements of mood and music. A major theme is southern womanhood helpless in the grip of the presently constituted world, while its old world of social position and financial security is a Paradise Lost. But differences of emphasis and style make the two dramas distinct.

The Glass Menagerie is a memory play evoked in the comments of a narrator the poet Tom, who is now in the merchant marine, and in crucial episodes from his family life. The form departs from the "fourth wall" convention of realistic dramaturgy and suggests Japanese Noh-drama, in which story consists mostly of remembered fragments of experience. If Williams had had his way with the Broadway production, *The Glass Menagerie* would have struck its public as even more unconventional, since his text calls for the use of a screen on which pictures and legends are to be projected. Disregarded by the producer-director Eddie Dowling, these stage directions nevertheless appear in the published play. They strike the writer of this article as redundant and rather precious; the young playwright was straining for effect without realizing that his simple tale, so hauntingly self-sufficient, needs no adornment.

As plainly stated by Tom, the background is a crisis in society, for the depression decade is teetering on the brink of the second World War. His tale belongs to a time "when the huge middle-class of America was matriculating in a school for the blind," when "their eyes had failed them, or they had failed their eyes, and so they were having their fingers pressed forcibly down on the fiery Braille alphabet of a dissolving economy," while in Spain there was Guernica. But his memory invokes his home life and the provocations that finally sent him to sea. In episodes softened by the patina of time and distance he recalls the painful shyness of his lovable crippled sister, Laura, and the tragicomic efforts of his mother, Amanda, to marry her off, as well as his own desperation as an underpaid shoe-company clerk. The climax comes when, nagged by the desperate mother, Tom brings Laura a "gentleman caller" who turns out to be engaged to another girl.

Without much more story than this, Williams achieved a remarkable synthesis of sympathy and objectivity by making three-dimensional characters out of Tom's family and the gangling beau, who is trying to pull himself out of the rut of a routine position and recover his self-esteem as a schoolboy success. The carping mother could have easily become a caricature, especially when she remembers herself as a southern belle instead of a woman deserted by her husband, a telephone man who "fell in love with long distances" but who probably found an incitement in his wife's pretensions. She is redeemed for humanity by her solicitude for her children, her laughable but touching effort to sell a magazine subscription over the telephone at dawn, and her admission that the unworldly Laura must get a husband if she is to escape the fate of the "little birdlike women without any nest" Amanda has known in the South. And Laura, too shy even to take a course in typewriting after the first lesson, acquits herself with sweet dignity and becoming stoicism when let down by her first and only gentleman caller; she is an unforgettable bit of Marie Laurencin painting. At the same time, however, Williams knows that pity for the halt and blind must not exclude a sense of reality, that Tom's going out into the world was a necessary and wholesome measure of self-preservation; it is one of humanity's inalienable traits and obligations to try to save itself as best it can. Although Tom will never forget Laura and the candles she blew out, he is now part of the larger world that must find a common salvation in action, "for nowadays the world is lit by lightning."

In *A Streetcar Named Desire,* too, health and disease are at odds with each other, but here the dialectical situation flares up into relentless conflict. The lines are sharply drawn in this more naturalistic drama, whose story, unlike that of *The Glass Menagerie,* is no longer revealed impressionistically through the merciful mist of memory. Nothing is circuitous in *A Streetcar,* and the dramatic action drives directly to its fateful conclusion as plebeian and patrician confront each other. Like other southern heroines of Williams, who invariably suggest Picasso's dehydrated "Demoiselles d'Avignon," Blanche Du Bois is not only a recognizable human being but an abstraction—the abstraction of decadent aristocracy as the painter's inner eye sees it. It is her final tragedy that the life she encounters in a married sister's home cannot spare her precisely when she requires the most commiseration. Her plantation lost, the teaching profession closed to her, her reputation gone, her nerves stretched to the snapping-point, Blanche has come to Stella in the French Quarter to find her married to a lusty ex-sergeant of Polish extraction. She is delivered into his untender hands when he discovers her lurid past and, although he may be momentarily touched by her fate on learning of the unhappy marriage that drove her to moral turpitude, his standards do not call for charity. With her superior airs and queasiness she has interfered with Stanley's married happiness, and she must go. Loyal to his friend, who served in the same military outfit with him, he must forewarn Mitch, who is about to propose to her, that the southern lady has been a harlot, thus destroying her last hope. Having sensed a challenge to his robust manhood from the moment he met Blanche, he must even violate her. It is his terrible health, which is of earth and will defend itself at any cost, that destroys Blanche, and sister Stella herself must send the hapless woman to a state institution if she is to protect her marriage and preserve her faith in Stanley.

As in *The Glass Menagerie* and in the one-acters, the private drama is pyramided on a social base. Blanche is the last descendant to cling to the family plantation of Belle Reve, sold acre by acre by improvident male relatives "for their epic fornications, to put it plainly," as she says. Her simple-hearted sister declassed herself easily by an earthy marriage to Stanley Kowalski and saved herself. Blanche tried to stand firm on quicksand and was declassed right into a house of ill-fame. The substructure of the story has some resemblance to *The Cherry Orchard,* whose aristocrats were also unable to adjust to reality and were crushed by it. Nevertheless, Williams subordinated his oblation to reality, his realization that Stanley and the denizens of the New Orleans slum street called Elysian Fields represent health and survival, to a poet's pity for Blanche. For him she is not only an individual whose case must be treated individually but a symbol of the many shorn lambs for whom no wind is ever tempered except by the god-head in men's hearts and the understanding of artists like Williams himself. It is surely for this reason that the author called his play a "tragedy of incomprehension" and "entered," in the words of his quotation from Hart Crane, "the broken world to trace the visionary company of love, its voice an instant in the wind (I know not whither hurled)." It is in the light of this compassion that the pulse of the play becomes a succession of musical notes and the naturalism of the writing flares into memorable lines, as when Blanche, finding herself loved by Mitch, sobs out, "Sometimes there's God so quickly."

As his plays multiply, it will be possible to measure him against dramatists whom his writing so often recalls—against Chekhov, Gorki, O'Neill, and Lorca. That such comparisons can be even remotely envisioned for an American playwright under thirty-five is in itself an indication of the magic of his pen; and it will soon be seen whether this magic works in *Summer and Smoke,* another, but more complicated, southern drama which carries a woman's soul to Tartarus. The test may prove a severe one, since the new play is episodic enough to be considered a chronicle. Further testing will also gauge the range of his faculties. Williams has himself detected a limitation in the sameness of theme and background in his work. He is turning toward new horizons with two uncompleted plays; one of them is set in Mexico, the other in Renaissance Italy. In time we shall also discover whether he overcomes noticeable inclinations toward a preciosity that could have vitiated *The Glass Menagerie* and toward a melodramatic sensationalism which appears in the rape scene of *A Streetcar Named Desire* and in the addition of wedlock with a homosexual to Blanche's tribulations. All that is beyond question at the present time is that Tennessee Williams is already a considerable artist in a medium in which there are many craftsmen but few artists.

Notes

1.   *Pharos,* spring, 1945, p. 121.
2.   In making this dramatization Tennessee Williams had collaborated with a friend, Donald Windham.
3.   *Pharos,* spring, 1945, p. 110.
4.   *The Best One-Act Plays of 1940,* ed. Margaret Mayorga (Dodd, Mead & Co., 1941).

Tennessee Williams
and the Predicament of Women

LOUISE BLACKWELL

In a dozen plays written between 1945 and 1961, Tennessee Williams chose to feature women as major characters more often than men. This choice, in view of his unusual perception, has enabled him to display his talent in a remarkable succession of plays. After 1961, as Williams' doubts and fears about his own artistic powers have grown, his faith in sexual adjustment as the key to the meaning of life has waned; none of his more recent females attain happiness through lasting sexual relationships; some are not even concerned with such happiness; all suffer from physical or emotional mutilation (or both). For them, communication with another person in itself becomes more difficult and unattainable, or their restless search for a mate goes on without hope of fulfillment. Because of this shift in theme and characterization in the later plays, they have not been included in this short study.

Early in his career, the subtlety of Williams' themes and characterizations resulted in misinterpretation on the part of critics and audiences. From *A Streetcar Named Desire* (1947) through *The Night of the Iguana* (1961), however, Williams made his themes explicit by having major characters discuss them, but his purpose continued to be lost on some viewers and readers. As late as 1961, for instance, Hodding Carter wrote in the *New York Times Magazine* that he did not recognize the "Southern womenfolk" portrayed by Williams. On the other hand, Signi Lenea Falk has called the playwright's female characters either Southern gentlewomen or Southern wenches. While it is true that many of Williams' characters speak with Southern accents, close scrutiny reveals that their problems are the old, universal ones of the human heart in its search for reality and meaning in life.

In the plays under consideration, Williams is making a commentary on Western culture by dramatizing his belief that men and women find reality and meaning in life through satisfactory sexual relationships. His drama

From *South Atlantic Bulletin* 35 (March 1970): 9–14. Copyright © 1970 by *South Atlantic Bulletin*. Reprinted by permission of the journal.

derives from the characters' recognition of certain needs within themselves and their consequent demands for the "right" mate. Frustration is the surface evidence of the predicament of his female characters, but Williams is careful to distinguish the underlying reasons for their behavior. Analysis of the various plays reveals subtle differences in the cause of their frustration, so that there is not as much similarity among the characters as is often supposed.

One approach to the study of these characters is to categorize them according to their situation at the time of the action, so long as we allow for variations within each category. Four groups thus appear:

1. *Women who have learned to be maladjusted through adjustment to abnormal family relationships and who strive to break through their bondage in order to find a mate.*

In line with modern theories of psychology, Tennessee Williams believes that the individual learns to be maladjusted through living with and adjusting to maladjusted people. Alma Winemiller in *Summer and Smoke* (1948) is in this group. She is the only child of a rigid, scholarly, and self-righteous preacher and his wife who is described as "a spoiled and selfish girl who evaded the responsibilities of later life by slipping into a state of perverse childishness. She is known as Mr. Winemiller's 'Cross.' " Of course, she is Alma's Cross, too, as is the father.

Mrs. Winemiller is not, as Professor Falk has written, simply "senile and mean." She has had a mental break with reality; and Alma has had to learn to live with this strange creature who is her mother. In this household, then, Alma has multiple roles to play. As a result of being, at once, the daughter of her father and mother, sister and parent to her mother, and social head of the household for her father, Alma has no role that she desires for herself.

In such a household there is a failure of meaningful communication so that the private needs of the daughter are never considered by the parents. The only way Alma can get out of the house for a date with John Buchanan is to grab her purse and rush out the door, leaving her father calling after her. Rash action is often the result of inadequate communication within family units, and the warning signals are present here.

Her mother's break with mature behavior presages a reversal in Alma's character. She does not, like her mother, regress to childhood and negate sexual relations, but she does abandon her previous moralistic approach to life for a profligate sex experience. Her later life is possible because she has learned from her mother how to reverse her life for more satisfying experiences.

Blanche DuBois of *A Streetcar Named Desire* (1947) also belongs in this category. She was a dutiful child, remaining with her aged parents long beyond the marrying age for most women and later staying behind to try to save the family estate, while her sister, Stella, went out to find her place in the world. Since Blanche had adjusted to an abnormal family life, she was unable, when she had the opportunity, to relate to the so-called normal world of her sister. She was, in fact, following a family pattern when she became sexually profligate after the death of her parents. In a discussion of property matters, she says that the plantation was disposed of gradually by "improvident grandfathers and father and uncles and brothers" who exchanged the land for their "epic fornications."

In an earlier play, *The Glass Menagerie* (1945), Laura Wingfield has learned to be maladjusted from her mother, Amanda. In his notes on the characters, Williams states that Amanda Wingfield is "a little woman of great but confused vitality, clinging frantically to another time and place. . . . She is not paranoiac, but her life is paranoia." Amanda's husband and son have long since deserted her, but Laura, who has been crippled since birth, has no escape open to her. She must adjust to her mother who is so unrealistic that she denies that Laura is crippled. According to the author, she has "failed to establish contact with reality, continues to live vitally in her illusions." Indeed, the only way Laura can survive is to retreat into her own delusions.

In *You Touched Me!* (1945), written in collaboration with Donald Windham, Williams depicts Emmie Rockley as having learned to distrust men and the idea of a mature sexual relationship from her spinster aunt, Matilda Rockley. This play ends happily for Emmie, but apparently life has not looked so simple to Williams since then, as he has not given us happy solutions for complicated problems.

2. *Women who have subordinated themselves to a domineering and often inferior person in an effort to attain reality and meaning through communication with another person.*

Stella Kowalski, in *A Streetcar Named Desire* (1947), is superior in background and personal endowments to her mate, but she subordinates herself to his way of life because they have a satisfying sexual relationship. When her sister Blanche cannot believe that Stella is happy with her crude husband, Stella tells her that "there are things that happen between a man and a woman in the dark—that sort of make everything else seem—unimportant." When Stella is willing to send her sister to a mental institution rather than believe that Stanley has raped Blanche we see just how far a seemingly gentle and attractive woman will go to defend her sexual partner.

In *Period of Adjustment* (1960), Dotty Bates will tolerate insult and abuse from her husband Ralph, so long as their sexual relationship is satisfying. She knows that he married her to please her wealthy father; and he frequently lets her know that she is so homely she might never have married if he hadn't come along. After a quarrel in which Ralph repeats all of the old insults, the two finally sit down to talk matters over. When their disagreements have been smoothed over, they go to bed together, this being the essential act in the vision of Tennessee Williams if Dotty is to maintain her grasp of reality and meaning in life.

Hannah Jelkes, in *The Night of the Iguana* (1961), is an example of the woman who has made the best of a relationship that is not so good as the true mating of a woman with a man. She is an unmarried artist who has travelled for years with her aged grandfather, a minor poet. In discussing her relationship to her grandfather she states:

> We make a home for each other my grandfather and I. Do you know what I mean by a home? I don't mean a regular home. I mean I don't mean what other people mean when they speak of a home, because I don't regard a home as a . . . well, as a place, a building . . . a house . . . of wood, bricks, stone. I think of a home as being a thing that two people have between them in which each can . . . well, nest—rest—live in, emotionally speaking.

When Reverend Shannon reminds her that birds build nests in relatively permanent locations "for the purpose of mating and propagating" the species, she responds that she is not a bird but a human being that needs to nest in the heart of another being. She then tells him that she has learned to believe in brief periods of understanding between two people. Never having had a mature sexual relationship, Hannah has sacrificed her life for her grandfather and she has managed to survive with fleeting and insignificant relationships.

Although she is not the major character in *Sweet Bird of Youth* (1959), Heavenly Finley is a vital character whose life is controlled by her crude and domineering father and the memory of Chance Wayne, with whom she fell in love as a young girl. Chance, after seducing Heavenly and giving her venereal disease, leaves town. He is a handsome *cad,* but because of her few intimate contacts with him, Heavenly wastes her life yearning for his return.

3. *Women who struggle to make relationships with men who are unable or unwilling to make lasting relationships.*

In four plays, *Cat on a Hot Tin Roof* (1955), *Orpheus Descending* (1957), *Suddenly Last Summer* (1958), and *Period of Adjustment* (1960), Williams created a group of women who are remarkable for their sexual demands upon men who are either homosexual or otherwise inadequate to make a lasting relationship. In *Cat on a Hot Tin Roof* Maggie and Brick, presumably, had a satisfactory sexual relationship early in their marriage. Problems began to develop, however, when Maggie decided that Brick's close friendship with Skipper indicated homosexual tendencies. After the death of Skipper, Brick was so grieved over the loss of his friend that he became disgusted with Maggie and insisted upon sleeping separately. He would gladly have terminated the marriage, but Maggie would not leave him. In an effort to assuage his feelings, Brick began drinking heavily. Maggie finally bribes her husband to go to bed with her by locking up his liquor. Undoubtedly she is one of the most determined female characters in modern drama.

Lady Torrance, in *Orpheus Descending,* is a strong and decent woman who has been a hard-working and devoted wife to her husband, Jabe, whom she married for economic security. He is some years older than she. Actually Jabe was responsible for the death of her father when she was a young woman, but

Lady does not know this until near the end of the play. Her yearning for the love of a man her own age is aroused when Val Xavier comes to town, carrying a guitar, and asks for a job in the Torrance store. Even though Jabe is dying of cancer in the family apartment up over the store, Lady arranges to sleep with Val in a small room at the back of the store.

When Val, who is a man with no lasting ties, decides to move on, he tells Lady that he will leave her a forwarding address. She replies:

> Ask me how it felt to be coupled with death up there, and I can tell you. My skin crawled when he touched me. But I endured it. I guess my heart knew that somebody must be coming to take me out of this hell! You did. You came. Now look at me! I'm alive once more!

Through her sexual relationship with Val, Lady Torrance has attained reality and meaning in life. Although Val shows some remorse when he learns that Lady is pregnant, he is unwilling to assume responsibility for a permanent mate and he resumes his transient life.

In *Suddenly Last Summer,* Mrs. Venable and Catharine clash over a dead man, Sebastian. Sebastian was Mrs. Venable's son and Catharine her niece. Throughout his life Sebastian, a would-be poet and sexual misfit, was pampered, overprotected, and dominated by his mother. Catharine was in love with Sebastian and, at the request of his mother, she willingly agreed to travel abroad with him. Later, in spite of the threats of Mrs. Venable, she insisted upon telling the truth about how Sebastian was killed and partly devoured by a group of cannibalistic boys on a tropical island. The unique thing about Catharine is that she yearned for a sexual relationship with a man, her cousin, whom she knew to be weak and strangely perverted.

George and Isabel Haverstick, in *Period of Adjustment,* met in a veterans' hospital where George suffered from "the shakes" and Isabel was his nurse. Despite the fact that George is a weak man and Isabel knows that he shakes when he has to face certain situations in life, she expects him to be the model of composure on the first night of their honeymoon. He is not. It is on the second night after their wedding, when Isabel begins to mother and pet George again, as if she were his nurse, that the audience is led to believe the marriage will be consummated.

4. *Women who have known happiness, but who have lost their mates and who try to overcome the loss.*

The Princess Kosmonopolis in *Sweet Bird of Youth* (1959) is an aging actress who has known both happiness with a lover and popularity with audiences. After losing both, she failed in a comeback effort as actress and embarked upon a search for another lover who could return her to reality. She becomes attracted to Chance Wayne, a beach boy in Palm Beach. When he does not meet her needs, she dumps him in a Gulf Coast town where he must take his chances with some citizens who know him very well because of his treatment of Heavenly Finley. The Princess will continue her search in Hollywood.

The Rose Tattoo (1951) is one of Tennessee Williams' most down-to-earth plays about the suffering of a woman who has known and lost a mate who gave her complete sexual happiness. Serafina Delle Rose, an Italian-American living on the Gulf Coast, is completely devastated upon learning that her truck-driver husband has been killed in an automobile accident. In spite of the needs of her children, she loses touch with reality, and life has no further meaning for her. After three years of isolation, Serafina is shocked back to reality when some of her neighbors tell her that her husband had been killed while smuggling dope and that, furthermore, he had had a mistress. Shortly afterwards, she finds another mate.

Maxine Faulk in *The Night of the Iguana* (1961) has just lost her husband when the play opens. She has known sexual happiness with him, and having known reality and meaning in life through her happy relationship, Mrs. Faulk is one of those women who will waste no time in trying to re-establish a satisfying sexual relationship. It is apparently accidental that the Reverend Shannon, a guide for a group of women, should stop at Mrs. Faulk's hotel at a time when she is most in need of a mate. She has known Shannon for some years and she knows him to be a weak man, leaning toward alcoholism. But in her lonely state, she will gladly provide the strength, to say nothing of the financial support, for a relationship with him.

Regardless of whether one agrees with the earlier thesis of Tennessee Williams that most people find reality and meaning in life through satisfactory sexual adjustment, one has to acknowledge that his major female characters, in the plays written through *The Night of the Iguana,* fight a continuous battle to find a mate or to keep the mate they have already found. Even though Williams has experienced despair in recent years, and many of his plays after 1961 appear to reflect his own increasing pessimism, the plays studied in this essay demonstrate his more positive view that women willingly make sacrifices in their unceasing search for a congenial and lasting mate.

Accepting Reality:
Survivors and Dreamers in Tennessee Williams

WALTER J. MESERVE

"I survived," Tennessee Williams told Tom Buckley during an interview in 1970. "The soles of my feet were cut open and pebbles sewn inside so I could not run away—I survived."[1] This was an in-joke among Williams's friends—a quotation from Mother God Damn, the owner of the largest brothel in Shanghai, in John Colton's 1926 melodrama, *The Shanghai Gesture*. It was also a serious sigh of relief from the playwright who had just survived a stay in the psychiatric ward of the Barnes Hospital in St. Louis—survived, perhaps, even the death that he dramatized with elaborate poetic vision in many of his plays. At this point in Williams's career, Buckley was writing about a playwright who had gone through a period of failure and despair and yet now appeared to be "alive and well" in Key West. His subject, Williams, was eager to prove himself once again the consummate lyrical artist of the theater. He was a survivor as well as a dreamer who, like many of the characters in his plays, had only to accept reality and live, interested in being, as he once admitted, if not a major artist, a "special" one in the minds of friends and audiences.

Many critics and commentators on the life and works of Tennessee Williams have concentrated on the people in his plays, the few repeated themes that permeate his work, his shocking exploitation of sex and violence, and the beautifully romantic and lyrical quality of his writing. People interested Williams, as they do most creative artists. Living also interested Williams. He wrote about people who were trying to live and trying to find meaning in their lives—people like Lady in *Orpheus Descending*, whose passionate cry to Val Xavier echoes the pathetic call of many Williams characters: "No, no, don't go . . . I need you!!! To live . . . to go on living" (23).[2] Like their needs, the people fall into patterns. They are recluses like Laura in *The Glass Menagerie*, or people who have watched life from a distance like Alma in *Summer and Smoke*. They are poets and dreamers like Laura's brother

This essay was written specifically for this volume and appears in print here for the first time by permission of the author.

Tom or Val Xavier. They are faded aristocrats whose Blue Mountain or Belle Reve goes by many names.

As he watches these people and follows them through their desperate searches for happiness in life or for escape from the world, Williams shows a genuine compassion for the loneliness of man. So many of his characters are losers, as current jargon would describe them. "Oh, you weak people," cries Maggie in *Cat on a Hot Tin Roof,* "you weak, beautiful people!—who give up!" (*CHTR,* 149). These are the people Williams describes in romantically idealized images. The world is too much with them. In their innocence and sweet ignorance they try to escape the only reality they know, or think they know, which is the world in which they live. Because this earth brought them misery, they must fight back and condemn it.

With a volatile mixture of loving sentiment and sexual violence Williams has described this dwelling place with an accustomed brilliance before offering his opinion of its effect on these fragile people. Val Xavier, the ineffectual savior and ironic fool in Christ, carries his myth in a memorable image. "You know," he asks Lady, "they's a kind of bird that don't have legs so it can't light on nothing but has to stay all its life on its wings in the sky?" "They sleep on the wind and . . . never light on this earth but once when they die!" "I'd like to be one of those birds," sighs Lady. "So'd I like to be one of those birds," responds Val; "they's lots of people would like to be one of those birds and never be—corrupted" (*OD,* 25). And that is Williams's condemnation of the real world—a place of corruption and desperation that man must escape or in which he must face reality and try, like Shannon crying out to Hannah in *The Night of the Iguana,* as he describes the tethered iguana, "to go on past the end of its goddam rope. Like you! Like me! Like Grampa with his last poem." But the iguana is cut loose, and the poem is finished with two couplets that betray the feelings of those beautiful people whom Williams reveals in such romanticized images.

> An intercourse not well designed
> For beings of a golden kind
> Whose native green must arch above
> The earth's obscene, corrupting love.
> (*NI,* 124)

Themes of romantic escape and its poetic imagery are as common in Williams's plays as the gargoyle figure that represents the stifling and corrupting world surrounding his characters. Although Williams clearly saw the world of his characters through very compassionate eyes, he was neither an unthinking idealist nor a lofty romantic. He was as honest and forthright as he could be in portraying the human sufferings he saw and in laying blame where he felt it belonged. There is something of the preacher in all artists. Williams, however, was an avowed survivor who should also be remembered for a stubbornly realistic view of life. Like many of the characters in his plays, he had frequent trouble accepting reality himself, but he created a variety of characters whose understanding of that concept of acceptance sustains a persistent motif throughout his work.

Nowhere is Williams's belief in the acceptance of reality for survival on this earth more forcefully and poetically expressed than in *Camino Real,* his 1953 Broadway failure. Critics and audiences had a difficult time understanding Williams's near-epic approach to his "conception of time and the world I live in," but it was the form of his work rather than the substance that may have confused them. The characters—"mostly archetypes of certain basic attitudes and qualities," he explained in his foreword—were also not new to his plays and would be seen again. The statement in *Camino Real,* however, that is particularly revealing is made by the Survivor: "When Peeto, my pony, was born—he stood on his four legs at once, and accepted the world! He was wiser than I . . ." (*CR,* 17).

In *Camino Real* Williams, as do all fine poets, deals in ambiguities and contradictions. He nonetheless followed the two great virtues that he hoped he had inherited from his father—total honesty and total truth. Because the world and its inhabitants, as he saw them, contained contradictions, he wrote of dreamers who were realists, and survivors who did not survive. When such things happen in the modern world where man must be realistic and practical, action must be taken by whatever forces are in control of society. Although Williams's view of this society is bitter and rebelliously idealistic in *Camino Real,* he is truthful to his vision of the real world. Survivors survive by definition and dreamers are harmless and ineffectual, but in Williams's view that intercourse between dreamer and survivor, which may be nonsense to the minds of unimaginative and limited people, can bring down kingdoms on earth. Diversions, therefore, must be created for the mass of mankind, and Williams brings on a modern hero, Kilroy, who goes through the suffering and indignities endured by man before becoming a dreamer and survivor himself. Like all men, Kilroy will dream and try to survive, if not as Laura (*The Glass Menagerie*), Blanche (*A Streetcar Named Desire*), and Val (*Orpheus Descending*), then as Tom (The Glass Menagerie), Stella (Streetcar) or Maggie (Cat on a Hot Tin Roof), Rose (*The Rose Tattoo*), and Chicken (*Kingdom of Earth*).

"You've got to be realistic on the Camino Real!" declares Prudence, Camille's old friend; "Yes, you've got to be practical on it!" because "a dream is nothing to live in" (*CR,* 10–11). Then the Survivor appears, desperately seeking water, is shot by a minion of a flunky despot, and recognizes a fact that had previously escaped him. "Peeto, my pony," a part of God's nature, free as the wind and oblivious to man, "he was wiser than I . . ." (*CR,* 17). When this Survivor with his newly found wisdom attracts the attention of La Madrecita—the mother-of-us-all, mythical or earthly—Gutman calls his boss. When "that old blind woman," accompanied by "the man called the

Dreamer," approaches the Survivor, tension increases further, and the authority figure voices a fear that "the forbidden word" may be spoken. And it is—by the Dreamer to the Survivor. "Hermano!" "The cry is repeated like springing fire and a loud murmur sweeps the crowd" (*CR,* 20–21). Reacting to this most "inflammatory" word—"brother"—"in any human tongue," Gutman invokes martial law while La Madrecita and the Dreamer comfort the dying Survivor. The Fiesta is announced.

William's recognition of the brotherhood of dreamers and survivors, their understanding of the need to accept reality and the danger inherent in their thoughts and actions, is basic to his beliefs that are expressed in the characters and actions of many of his plays. In *Camino Real,* a play Williams referred to as his "testament," it is a major focus. All action in the play is prefaced by the need to be "realistic" in life; yet in Block Fifteen La Madrecita reminds the audience that "humankind cannot bear very much reality." The acceptance of reality, therefore, must be tempered by the dreams of the Dreamer and the determination of the Survivor. For those many people who wallow in the reality that becomes the practical nature of day-to-day living, Williams has little interest. They are the neighbors in *The Rose Tattoo,* Dolly and Beulah and their respective husbands in *Orpheus Descending,* or Gooper and Mae with their no-neck children in *Cat on a Hot Tin Roof.* They are not part of the "human kind" for which Williams feels strong compassion. The life in which Williams exults is clearly that of the Survivor, the person who can accept the reality of the Camino Real and still dream, the modern hero who gets "stewed, screwed and tattooed on the Camino Real" (*CR,* 157) but aligns himself with another hero from the past who believes in the romantic yet real power of mountain violets.

Williams was particularly careful in selecting the archetypes that would effectively depict the progress of the Survivor on the Camino Real when it ceased to be the Royal Way. Immediately, the most idealistic of romantic dreamers, Don Quixote, is deserted by a most practical Sancho Panza, and his replacement becomes the single lasting mythical figure of World War II whose scant face, covered by a large hat near the irritating and boastful scrawl "Kilroy was here," seemed to greet every American soldier no matter where he went. The "deal" is "rugged" on the Camino Real; "desperation" permeates the atmosphere as Kilroy reacts to Jacques Casanova, Baron de Charlus, Lord Byron, Lord and Lady Mulligan and the streetcleaners, the Gypsy and Esmeralda, and Gutman, whose near-pathetic questions—"Can this be all? Is there nothing more? Is this what the glittering wheels of heaven turn for?"—directs the audience's hope for something better. Faced with possible routes of escape by the unchartered flight of the Fugitive or a gruesome death represented by the streetcleaners, Kilroy eventually walks through the archway toward the "Terra Incognita," the route that only Byron would knowingly attempt but one that awaits everyone. By this time, however, Kilroy has learned a great deal and changed his views. He has even found another "true woman." For the realist who will survive, Williams offers advice: "Don't! Pity! Your! Self!" "The wounds of the vanity," Quixote explains, "are better accepted with a tolerant smile" (*CR*, 159). Clearly, the play offers Williams's most thoughtful view of time and the world as Quixote and Kilroy go off together—survivors and dreamers, both of them, who have accepted reality as their natures demand and wisdom dictates.

Among Williams's best-known plays, *The Glass Menagerie* has its survivors. Perhaps the closest to Williams himself of any character in his plays, Tom accepts and survives even though he cannot completely escape his haunting memories. The gentleman caller, Jim O'Connor, lives in a very ordinary world where he unthinkingly accepts the traditions of work, ambition, and marriage and the materialistic dreams that his society thrusts upon him. In *A Streetcar Named Desire* Stanley Kowalski represents that strong-grained individual whose resistance to the polish of sophisticated culture suggests his acceptance of the coarse reality in which he lives. He is not unthinking, however, nor is he without sensitivity to the problems or machinations of others. His strength is simply that he knows what he wants and will survive. So it is with Stella. Knowing what she wants, she makes a decision that will allow her to believe what she wants to believe and keep that real world she enjoys with Stanley.

It should not be surprising that a number of the major characters in Williams's plays are survivors—people who know exactly what they want and through the line of action in a given play accept the reality of the situation and work toward their dreams or desires. That acceptance of reality and development of the survivor's instincts are occasionally a major focus in Williams's plays. *Cat on a Hot Tin Roof* provides an excellent illustration. Maggie's situation is not enviable, and she knows it, but she tells Brick and the audience early in act 1 that "one thing I don't have is the charm of the defeated, my hat is still in the ring, and I am determined to win!" Like other Williams heroines, Maggie is lonely—"being with someone you love can be lonelier than living entirely alone!—if the one that y'love doesn't love you . . ." She is also frustrated and angry. She feels "all the time like a cat on a hot tin roof!" but she is determined to get what she wants. She accepts the reality that this is Big Daddy's last birthday. "I'm sorry about it," she says, "but I'm facing the facts. It takes money to take care of a drinker and that's the office that I've been elected to lately" (*CHTR*, 54). She also resents the poverty of her youth. "Always had to suck up to people I couldn't stand because they had money and I was poor as Job's turkey." That is another reason that she is like a cat on a hot tin roof, but she is determined to stay on that roof as long as she has to be there. The answer to her problem is also a problem: how to have a baby by a man who cannot stand her! Unlike Brick, however, Maggie can face the real world and accept the truth about herself as well as others. Brick is all she wants in a man; poverty is also a fear that fuels her determination to survive—

with love and security. With no doubts about her strength and desire, she may even convince Brick.

Serafina Delle Rosa, the major character in *The Rose Tatto,* is another Williams survivor who satisfies her dreams by accepting the world at her doorstep. She lacks Maggie's initial strength and determination because Williams takes a considerable part of the play to dramatize Serafina's discovery and acceptance of the real world. Only then does she reveal herself to be a true survivor, but the delay is also Williams's point in writing the play. In his introductory essay to the published version of *The Rose Tattoo,* entitled "The Timeless World of a Play," Williams argues that the playwright must arrest the passage of time in such a way that man, always haunted "by a truly awful sense of impermanence," somehow senses "the diminishing influence of life's destroyer, time" during an evening in the theater. This concern for *time* as life's destroyer drifts into *The Rose Tattoo* through Serafina's abortive attempt to hold it at bay. By refusing to accept the world that continues around her after the death of her husband, Rosario, she emotionally refuses to accept the passage of time. Williams's concern for time is repeated in Serafina's high school graduation gift to her daughter, Rosa—a seventeen-jewel Bulova watch. In all her attempts, however, Serafina is unable to present her gift, and Rosa, like her mother, cherishes the timeless world of love and life to which Williams would introduce the audience. Once this interest in "life's destroyer" has been forgotten, a reality can exist that Serafina accepts, and she can reveal her inborn determination to combine her sense of survival with her dreams.

Williams's problem in *The Rose Tattoo* was to make Serafina aware of her basic need to live in and accept the real world, and he solved it with considerable skill. During the first scene in which Serafina waits for the return of Rosario, she is full of love and life, although there is a shadow of disaster cast upon the future by Serafina's dependence on another world, by her belief in witches, charms, pagan signs, and Christian symbols. Then there is the news of Rosario's death, and Serafina's defiance of the Church as she has the body cremated. Three years pass, and Serafina appears to have rejected life. "She hasn't put on clothes since my father was killed," says Rosa. "For three years she sits at the sewing machine and never puts a dress on or goes out of the house" (*RT,* 61–62). She gets in trouble with Rosa and with the customers for her sewing, and she ceases even to try to cope with the world around her. Her demeanor and her attitude toward everyone shows her rapid disintegration, and everyone tries to make her look at life and herself realistically—the Catholic priest, her neighbors, her daughter—but without positive results. Then Alvaro, a handsome young truck driver with problems, comes into her life. He also tries to explain that there is a life to be enjoyed—one they could share. True to Williams's appreciation of man, Serafina accepts the real world through her discovery of the one real thing in her that will not be denied— her passion—although she was assisted in this discovery by undeniable evidence that she had once refused to accept that Rosario had been enjoying an affair with another woman for a long time. By the end of the play she has accepted her world, essentially found another "true man" in the manner of Kilroy, and shows herself to be a determined survivor. With "two lives again in the body," Serafina shouts happily for Alvaro: "Vengo, vengo, amore!" (*RT*, 141). and the play is over. She is living again.

The Eccentricities of a Nightingale is a better play than *Summer and Smoke*. Using the same locale and many of the same characters, it is shorter, less melodramatic, and more effective in focusing the issue Williams had in mind; and it develops a more believable character for John, the male lead. It also dramatizes a more direct and romantic confrontation between John and Alma. Williams liked this second version better and considered it a substantially different play, although the problem that consumes Alma, the Nightingale who has also "suffocated in smoke from something on fire inside of her," remains essentially the same. For American audiences, however, *Summer and Smoke* has been more popular, and Alma finds herself in the same situation at the end of each play—she is a determined survivor.

Summer and Smoke is divided into two parts, a summer and a winter. Alma represents both seasons—a wintry person because she is reserved and assumes a rather cool dignity that she thinks is essential to her position in life as the daughter of a minister; a person in whom the warm passions of summer would like to sing throughout the year. Life is passing her by, however, and her awareness of this is foreshadowed by the cold shivers she gets when she traces the letters in the name of the stone angel in the fountain—Eternity. The unhappy division in her life is also dramatized by a Doppelganger that is, as John explains, "fighting for its life in the prison of a little conventional world full of walls" (*SS*, 20). Williams once called himself a "rebellious puritan," and Alma, whose name, the audience is frequently reminded, means "soul," has the same problem. The play is, of course, a retelling of the ancient conflict between the flesh and the spirit. Seemingly, Alma has always been in love with John, the son of the doctor next door who becomes a doctor himself and at first wastes his talents in a dissolute life that angers Alma. She would like to change him and share his life but disappears into her self-imposed definition of a lady, deeply hurt, when he mentions "intimate relations." "You're not a gentleman," she cries (*SS*, 80). Although she once describes herself to John as "one of those weak and divided people who slip like shadows among you solid strong ones," she knows that "we shadowy people take on a strength of our own" (*SS*, 119).

Throughout the play Alma exhibits this strength. She speaks forthrightly to John. When her father complains that she slips out of the house in the early hours of the morning and wonders what he can tell people who ask about her odd ways, she says: "Tell them I've changed and you're waiting to see in what way" (*SS*, 99). And she has changed—not in her determination to stay in the real world but in her techniques for doing so. Unfortunately, by this time in *Summer and Smoke* John has other plans, but he does take a moment to explain their past attraction: "I thought it was just a Puritanical ice that glittered like flame. But now I believe it *was* flame, mistaken for ice." Now "the tables have turned with a vengeance!" "I came here," Alma says, "to tell you that being a gentleman doesn't seem so important to me anymore, but your're telling me I've got to remain a lady" (*SS*, 120). At the end of *The Eccentricities of a Nightingale* John and Alma share a room in a "house of convenience" in what at first appears to be a night of failure but, as the scene ends, from the fireplace that resisted John's efforts to build a fire there is a glow: "The fire has miraculously revived itself, a phoenix" (*EN*, 125). Both plays end with a scene at the fountain in which Alma attaches herself to a stranger and plans an evening in the gay section of town with a salute of understanding and appreciation to the angel Eternity. Alma struggles more than Serafina to accept reality and acknowledge her determination to survive, whereas Maggie has no struggle with reality at all. Yet they are all dreamers and survivors in the real world.

The survivor in *Orpheus Descending* is Lady Torrance, at least a survivor of importance to Williams. There are others besides Dolly Hamma and Beulah Binnings, whose level of existence is reflected in the fact that the sheriff's wife cannot remember Beulah's last name. Sheriff Talbott is also a man whose acceptance of reality is only slightly less insensitive than the clods who form a background for ignorant evil in the play. Carol Cutrere knows her place, accepts the real world that surrounds it, and will survive; she wants to live. Her brother David will never have a life of his own to consider. Lady, however, is that person who thought she knew who she was and understood the world around her. As the daughter of the "Wop" who was burned up in his orchard on Moon Lake where he sold "Dago red wine an' bootleg whiskey and beer," she has had a rough life—bought at a fire sale by a son of a bitch with whom she has not had a single good dream. Until Val came along, she had accepted this life, and with the sickness of her husband, Jabe, she contrives to rebuild the confectionery in Jabe's store to compete for the after-movie trade. She has been strong to endure this long, and now she can live and survive even with the knowledge that Jabe was one of the group who burned up her father's orchard with him in it because he sold liquor to Negroes. With Jabe dying, the confectionery opening as a consequence of her labors, and her pregnancy by Val, she has apparently survived the rigors of the world around her—"I've won, I've won, Mr. Death, I'm going to bear!"—only to be shot and killed by a rampaging Jabe (*OD*, 119). She is a survivor in a world where violence is part of the life that one must accept.

Reviewing the 24 September 1974 New York performance of *Cat on a Hot Tin Roof* for *The New York Times*, Clive Barnes appeared to make a discovery: "People used to think that Tennessee Williams's plays were about sex and violence. How wrong they were—they are about love and survival."[3] A careful reading would have brought Barnes to this conclusion much sooner in his career, but the playgoer is always subject to the moods of the stage director. Traditionally, the theater has belonged to actors and actresses. When the modern director appeared on the scene in the latter part of the nineteenth century, conflicts with actors eventually stirred such controversies that plays were written to dramatize the difficulties—Maxwell Anderson's *Joan of Lorraine,* for example. In the contemporary theater the director has increased his authority and subsequent power over a production to create memorable and sometimes monstrous perversions of classical plays. For the playwright whose insignificance in the history of theater has been only momentarily challenged, the director has become a considerable force in his or her creativity. For Tennessee Williams, who advertised his insecurity in numerous essays, a director like Elia Kazan was a major influence in the production of a play. The best illustration is the final act of *Cat on a Hot Tin Roof,* which Williams rewrote to include Big Daddy at Kazan's suggestion. As with many modern playwrights, the director has served an admirable need and a function that has sometimes gone unnoticed.[4] On other occasions directors who control the presentation of a playwright's work are also free to impose their own vision of that work. Given modern society's fascination with sex and violence—as in popular television, for example—it is logical that New York play directors would emphasize what would sell, although Williams always defended his use of sex and violence as simply a truthful part of the seamy world he dramatized.

Love and compassion are trademarks of Williams's work for the theater— the love that enraptures or escapes the beautiful people he portrays and the compassion he feels for them. Such love, however, involves a certain recognition of the world and an acceptance of the conditions reality offers. Everyone, of course, should have the freedom to search for love and to dream. Some, like Laura and Blanche, may deny the real world around them and escape into a land of make-believe. Or they may combine their dreams with a determination to survive in the real world that they have accepted. Hannah in *The Night of the Iguana* has endured a life of serene and loving acceptance, and she will survive. Shannon in the same play recognizes his need "to operate on the realistic level," which, presumably, at the end of the play, he does. In *The Milk Train Doesn't Stop Here Anymore* Chris explains to Mrs. Goforth what he has learned about an "acceptance" of "how to live and die." It is an acceptance of the real world that she can then acknowledge in her decision to "go forth alone." If his characters are not all survivors—and few are in the early scenes of Williams's plays—Williams is interested in their progress toward that state of being where acceptance is wisdom. Among his later plays his emphasis on survival is most prominent in *Kingdom of Earth* (the published version of *The Seven Descents of Myrtle*), where a realistic Myrtle knows how to survive even as she ends the play on the roof of the house with Chicken.

"When Peeto my pony was born," says the Survivor, "he stood on his four legs at once and accepted the world! He was wiser than I" (*CR,* 17). Man cannot do this at birth, but man can learn—and become wise. This Williams believed, and he saw that wisdom as a path to survival.

Notes

1. Tom Buckley, "Interview with Tennessee Williams," *Atlantic,* November 1970, 98.
2. Quotations from Williams's plays are cited in the text with the abbreviations listed here. Page numbers in the text refer to the following versions:

> *OD: Orpheus Descending* (New York: New Directions, 1958).
> *CHTR: Cat on a Hot Tin Roof* (New York: New Directions, 1955).
> *NI: The Night of the Iguana* (New York: New Directions, 1961).
> *CR: Camino Real* (New York: New Directions, 1953).
> *RT: The Rose Tattoo* (New York: New Directions, 1951).
> *SS: Summer and Smoke* (New York: New Directions, 1948).
> *EN: The Eccentricities of a Nightingale* (New York: New Directions, 1976).

3. Clive Barnes, "Williams' Eccentricities," *New York Times,* Sunday, 24 September 1974, sec. 2, p. 25.
4. See, however, Brenda Murphy's *Tennessee Williams and Elia Kazan: A Collaboration in the Theatre* (Cambridge: Cambridge Univ. Press, 1992).

Tennessee Williams' Gallery of Feminine Characters

Durant da Ponte

At the beginning of what is certainly one of Tennessee Williams' best and most successful plays—*The Glass Menagerie*—the narrator (whose name is Tom and who is clearly a thinly disguised replica of the author himself) says: "The play is memory."

In this statement, I think, can be found an important clue to one of Mr. Williams' most persistent themes and concerns—his recollections of his lost youth and particularly of the women who in various shapes and forms played such a crucial part in his development both as a sensitive adult and as a literary artist. It is probably safe to suggest that next to O'Neill and Thomas Wolfe our most autobiographical writer is Tennessee Williams. And it is hardly an exaggeration to say that frequently he is autobiographical with a vengeance.

In order that there may be no doubts concerning the autobiographical source of much of the material he has woven into his plays, Mr. Williams has stated in the preface to the printed version of *Cat on a Hot Tin Roof:* "it is a pity that so much of all creative work is so closely related to the personality of the one who does it . . . that each of us weaves about him from birth to death, a web of monstrous complexity, spun forth . . . from the spidermouth of his own singular perceptions."

That Tennessee Williams' perceptions are singularly "singular" goes almost without saying. In spite of his worldwide fame, he is not—and never has been—everyone's dish of tea. In Knoxville, for instance, productions of his plays are met with a chilly uneasiness on some respectable sides. Williams descends from one of Knoxville's oldest and most distinguished families, and until fairly recently his father and a favorite aunt (both now dead) lived in Knoxville. These people and their friends, however, suffered rather acute embarrassment at what seemed to them the invasion of privacy attendant

This essay was read at the University of Maryland by Dr. da Ponte the day before his death. The original editors decided to publish it without notes. Reprinted with permission from *Tennessee Studies in Literature* 10: 7–26. Copyright © 1965 by the University of Tennessee Press.

upon the writer's use of local material in some of his plays and stories. They found, further, his whole attitude toward them and their way of life distasteful, and they put little stock in such statements as the following:

> I write out of love for the South. But I can't expect Southerners to realize that my writing about them is an expression of love. It is out of regret for a South that no longer exists that I write of the forces that have destroyed it.

But complaints have also been heard outside the South and outside his family. In Spain, some of his works have elicited strenuous protest, one influential critic saying of the characters in *The Rose Tattoo:* "To us who are Latin such beings appear exaggerated, somewhat unhinged and eccentric men and women of the kind who in the United States provide work for those innumerable psychiatrists who flourish over there."

An even bitterer attack came from South America, where in the summer of 1961 a theatrical troupe called the New York Repertory Company presented *Suddenly, Last Summer* and *Sweet Bird of Youth.* Critics in Buenos Aires and Montevideo were not particularly impressed. But in Rio de Janerio a critical explosion occurred. A writer in the paper *Diario de Noticias* had this to say:

> People bearing vices can be presented [on the stage] provided they suffer from them. Their suffering may redeem them and arouse our understanding if not sympathy. The morbid world of Tennessee Williams has nothing of this. With him aberration is presented complacently, with all the author's tenderness, as if it were the best thing in the world. It is sad to think that Williams represents a country which is Western and "Christian," whose style of life they want to convince us should be defended against the Communist threat. Positively this rotted world does not seem worthy of defending and, on the contrary, needs to be reformed or extinguished so that something may survive to preserve man's intrinsic dignity.

Some serious American critics echo this antipathy—Edmund Fuller and John W. Aldridge, for example. Aldridge, in *Search of Heresy* (1956), called Williams' plays "antiquated"—"antiquated in the sense that they are concocted out of the scrap-basket materials of the naturalistic theatre of the thirties and are merely the Broadway analogue of the sex-crime-and-violence films which the lower orders of the same public twitch and shudder at in the theaters across the street."

Here, of course, we come upon a fundamental issue in the philosophy of aesthetics. "What Is Art?" Tolstoi asked, which is very much like asking "What is truth?" No one seems to know. Or at least there does not seem to be any general agreement. Art is certainly not life. The artist selects and combines and thus *controls* the reality with which he deals. This is something a mirror cannot do—nor can a camera. The only control here involves what you focus on. What the literary artist focuses his attention on, what raw materials he combines, tell us something about what we can call his "world view" or his view of reality. If he has a well-defined, preconceived philosophy, he will doubtless see to it that nothing is included in his work which will upset that philosophy, disturb that attitude. If, for instance, he is a determinist or an existentialist, he will hardly provide us with happy pictures of romantic love.

In other words, everything a man has been or done has some bearing on the kind of person he is, and the kind of person he is has a good deal of bearing on the kind of books he writes. But it is too easy to slip into the biographical fallacy. It does not so much matter why a writer writes the way he does as whether what he tells us has any relevance to truth and reality in some important sense—not necessarily in a sense which we approve of or are necessarily acquainted with personally. Art exists to show us what the human creature is capable of achieving—to what heights he can soar or to what depths he can sink, or to what limits he can persevere or endure. It is this spectacle which engages our attention, which (if you will) moves our soul, so that we view the spectacle with exaltation or pity or fear or dismay or even in some cases horror.

In our own day William Faulkner has been the most persistent inhabitant of "the soul's dark cottage, battered and decayed." He has not been alone. Besides Tennessee Williams, there are Truman Capote, Carson McCullers, James Joyce and others who occupy ill-lit corners. "Step outdoors, boys, and see who's around," invited Edmund Fuller, and many a reader will enunciate a resounding "Amen" to this sentiment.

A critic typically hostile of this school is Robert Ruark. Writing some years ago in his widely syndicated newspaper column, Mr. Ruark spoke out "In Defense of the South."

I am not in the slightest concerned with the moral implications of . . . the much-disputed "Baby Doll" and similar works by Master Tennessee Williams. I do not denounce the slack-lipped immorality of all the Erskine Caldwell accounts of low life in the South. You can have William Faulkner if you can read him, which I can't.

The sermon for today is that one of these days when I get to be a big boy I am going to write a book about the South which is not littered with clay-eaters, lint-headed mill hands, idiots, rotting itinerant preachers, juvenile delinquents, morons, slatterns, cripples, freaks and other characters who don't wash, live off sardines and soft drinks, hang around bus stations and breed within the family. . . .

It is possible to grow up in the South without a full chorus of nymphomaniacs, drunkards, Negro-lynchers, randy preachers, camp meetings, hookworm albinos, dirty hermits, old women and idiot relatives to form your early impressions. But the literary output of the last 25 years wouldn't have it so.

Is there any justice in such charges? Yes and no. They are correct in calling attention to what might be termed the school of Southern decadence. But they are probably wrong in denying the validity of this school's worldview, for after all it is neither unique nor new. The dislocation of personality, the struggle with suppressed desires (some of them sometimes abnormal), the inability to adjust to the circumstances of a seemingly hostile environment—these have been staple commodities in literature since the time of the ancient Greeks. Modern Southern writers have no monopoly on the grotesque, the bizarre, the violent, the horrible, the diseased or the tragic. And so, in my opinion (and I am not alone in holding to it) critics like Mr. Fuller and Mr. Ruark are pretty largely in error when they condemn writers like Tennessee Williams for not being writers like Booth Tarkington.

The two basic bones of contention, it seems to me, in the quarrel over the validity of the worldview of the so-called Southern decadents are, first, the characters who inhabit this world and, second, the attitude of their creators toward these figments of singular imaginations. The characters will occupy us at some length later; so let us examine briefly now the author's attitude toward them. And let us narrow the focus of our examination to the works of Tennessee Williams.

The main charge which has been leveled against him is that he is evasive or ambiguous. He does not tell us how he wants us to feel about this or that of his fictional creations. Indeed, it is often impossible to tell precisely how he himself feels about them. The validity of this charge Mr. Williams freely admits. In a journal he kept during a particularly depressed period in 1942, he wrote: "Oh, God—there is too much to hurt, you can't think of it all— You have to evade and evade. You have to skip rope lightly!"

And this has been a characteristic of his dramatic artistry ever since— a characteristic which the critic Walter Kerr duly noted in his review of *Cat on a Hot Tin Roof,* wherein he spoke of an "evasiveness" on the playwright's part in dealing with certain questions of character. Mr. Williams was sufficiently concerned over this charge that he elected to reply to it in what has come to be considered a classic apologia made by an author to his critics. In a little essay entitled "About 'Evasions' " he stated:

> This is not the first time that I've been suspected of dodging issues in my treatment of play characters. Critics complained, sometimes, of ambiguities in "Streetcar". . . . The truth about human character in a play, as in life, varies with the variance of experience and view-point of those that view it. No two members of an audience ever leave a theatre, after viewing a play that deals with any degree of complexity in character, with identical interpretations of the characters dealt with. This is as it should be. . . . I still feel that I deal unsparingly with what I feel is the truth of character, I would never evade it for the sake of evasion. . . . But ambiguity is sometimes deliberate and for artistically defensible reasons.

If, he continues, his audience wishes to be told exactly what to believe about each character in a play, then he is not their playwright.

> Frankly, [he concludes] I don't want people to leave the Morosco Theatre knowing everything about all the characters they have witnessed that night in violent interplay, I don't want them to be quite certain what will happen to these characters. . . . I give them clues, but not certainties. Every moment of human existence is alive with uncertainty. You may call it ambiguity, you may even call it evasion. I want them to leave the Morosco as they do leave it each night, feeling that they have met with a vividly allusive, as well as disturbingly elusive, fragment of human experience, one that not only points at truth but at the mysteries of it, much as they will leave this world when they leave it, still wondering somewhat about what happened to them, and for what reason or purpose.

As recently as two years ago, in an interview published in *Theatre Arts,* Mr. Williams, in praising a play by the British dramatist Harold Pinter, stated unequivocally: "To me the play was about the thing that I've always pushed in my writing—that I've always felt was needed to be said over and over—that human relations are terrifyingly ambiguous. If you write a character that isn't ambiguous you are writing a false character, not a true one."

Not the least ambiguous of Mr. Williams' characters, it goes without saying, are his women—an incredibly varied portrait gallery of female types which he has succeeded in investing with one common quality—an ability to fascinate. We may not like them all or find them uniformly admirable. But I do not believe that we can fail to find them interesting. Even the minor characters (like Mae in *Cat on a Hot Tin Roof* or Carol Cutrere, the wayward young aristocrat in *Orpheus Descending*) possess an arresting quality, a vivid theatricality that lifts them immediately upon their appearance on stage out of the area of the familiarly real into the realm of the most intense art (or even, if you wish, artifice).

It is in his ability to create striking feminine portraits, however, that Mr. Williams truly excels. This is no mean distinction. Consider in the history of fiction and the stage how rarely vital, rounded female figures appear. Some of Shakespeare's heroines, Becky Sharpe, Emma Bovary, Anna Karenina, possibly Molly Bloom, perhaps Hedda Gabler,—there are not many who tower above their sisters to achieve the rarefied air of absolute greatness. Edmund Fuller accounts for this circumstance on the grounds that women have traditionally been accorded a subservient and secondary role in society, and even in a more enlightened age like our own certain doubts and ambiguities exist concerning just what is or should be their rightful position.

In Tennessee Williams' case, the picture is further complicated by the fact that many of his women have been created in and are forced to operate within a particular framework—namely, the American South, both as it is and as it once was. There thus tends to be established a stereotype—let us call it the faded Southern belle—but it is a stereotype with a difference. There have been, of course, Southern belles in literature before—faded and even jaded. But there have not been many like Amanda and Laura Wingfield, Alma Winemiller, or Blanche DuBois. It is with these that a study of Tennessee Williams' women must logically begin.

Mr. Williams once described himself as "an old-fashioned romanticist," a bit of self-characterization that would doubtless come as something of a surprise to such old-fashioned romanticists as Thomas Nelson Page and James Lane Allen. And yet, analysis of his plays does actually reveal a certain romantic outlook, if by romantic we mean yearning backwards in time to a world where ideals of gentility and gentleness were cherished and defended. This notion is further buttressed by a statement the playwright made in an interview several years ago. "I'm a compulsive writer," Mr. Williams explained, "because what I am doing is creating imaginary worlds into which I can retreat from the real world because . . . I've never made any kind of adjustment to the real world."

Here quite clearly is a major clue to an understanding both of the playwright and his characters. Many of the personages he has created would seem to be projections of his own disoriented personality, frightened, timid, groping, highly sensitive, somewhat neurotic dreamers who, like their creator, are unable to adjust to the harsh realities of a world of crass materialism and brute strength. Or, if they have been forced to make an adjustment, this adjustment usually hardens and distorts them, as in the case of Amanda in *The Glass Menagerie*. For certainly in many ways Amanda *has* come to terms with the real world (although in many other ways she has not). The tenement apartment overlooking the slum alley in St. Louis where she lives is very real indeed, as is the moon that comes up over Garfinkel's Delicatessen. Against this grim world with its struggle for existence (Laura's futile attempts to learn typing, Tom's $65-a-month job in the shoe company, Amanda's magazine subscriptions) is juxtaposed a remembered world of romance—Blue Mountain, where as a girl Amanda received seventeen gentlemen callers on one memorable Sunday afternoon and where conversation dwelt on things of importance—"Never anything coarse or common or vulgar."

If we did not laugh at Amanda, I suspect we should cry, for there is a certain pathetic heroism in her efforts to provide for her children—her daughter, especially. A measure of her refusal to face actuality appears in her attitude toward Laura—the cotton wads she makes her stuff into her blouse ("gay deceivers" she calls them); her shrill denial that Laura is crippled: "Don't say crippled! You know that I never allow that word to be used!" Amanda is a curious combination of exaggerated gentility on one hand and exasperating practicality on the other. "You be the lady this time and I'll be the darky," she tells Laura at the dinner table. "Resume your seat, little sister— I want you to stay fresh and pretty—for gentlemen callers." And to Tom:

"... chew—chew! Eat food leisurely, son, and really enjoy it ... chew your food and give your salivary glands a chance to function!" At times cranky and cantankerous, at times wistful and tender, at times gallant and heroic—Amanda is one of Tennessee Williams' most impressive creations.

In a recent interview the playwright called her "an exact portrait of my mother." This, oddly enough, Mrs. Williams denies. In her reminiscences of her son, *Remember Me to Tom,* she writes:

> I think it is high time the ghost of Amanda was laid. I am *not* Amanda. I'm sure if Tom stops to think, he realizes I am not. The only resemblance I have to Amanda is that we both like jonquils. . . .
>
> I never woke Tom up with that sugary chant, "Rise and shine, rise and shine." Nor did I matchmake for Rose, who was quite able to find her own young men and, incidentally, I don't think marriage necessarily the culmination of a woman's life, for some of the happiest women I know have never been married. Nor did my husband walk out on me.

To the student of Tennessee Williams who is reasonably well acquainted with the family background, the only possible reaction to his mother's statement is: "The lady doth protest too much, methinks." All of which is neither here nor there. Amanda remains—a marvelously rich character, varied, diverse, painfully real, touching, and altogether memorable.

Laura, the sister-daughter of *The Glass Menagerie,* is another matter. In her portrait the colors are subdued, the strokes delicate. There is a fragile, haunting beauty and pathos about her. She is all gossamer and lace, but there is no phony sentimentality in her creation. She is treated gently, but she is treated honestly. Her brother Tom says: "Laura is very different from other girls. . . . She lives in a world of her own—a world of little glass ornaments. . . . She plays old phonograph records and—that's about all." She has one supreme moment in the play when, at the hands of her only gentleman caller, she learns something about life—that unicorns and blue roses are different and thus freaks in the real world and that to survive one must be "normal"—that is, pretty much like everybody else. What becomes of Laura, whose withdrawal from life has been a painful one, we never know. Tom abandons his family, just as his father before him had done. But he cannot forget. His final speech is almost unbearably poignant. "Oh, Laura, Laura, I tried to leave you behind me, but I am more faithful than I intended to be! I reach for a cigarette, I cross the street, I run into the movies or a bar, I buy a drink. I speak to the nearest stranger—anything that can blow your candles out!—for nowadays the world is lit by lightning! Blow out your candles, Laura—and so goodbye. . . ."

It is pretty generally agreed that the character of Laura in *The Glass Menagerie* is modeled upon the playwright's sister Rose. We do know what eventually became of her. Edwina Williams in *Remember Me to Tom* narrates the sad story. Rose, it seems, became mentally disturbed and withdrew almost completely from reality. Doctors advised the performance of a brain operation known as a pre-frontal lobotomy. This operation was not a success, and Rose had to be placed in an asylum, where she still is a patient. Both the playwright and his mother felt somehow responsible for Rose's tragedy, the suggestion being that the brain surgery may have aggravated her condition. "I think Tom always felt as though he had failed Rose," Mrs. Williams writes, "that had he been on hand when the big decision was made, he might have been able to stop the lobotomy. . . . Tom's sense of loss and loneliness . . . must have been devastating, although he never talked much about it. I think his was a grief beyond words, as he saw his beautiful, imaginative sister whom he had always idolized, partially destroyed. Fragile, lovely Rose, to Tom must seem a broken creature, to use one of his similes, like a soft moth that flew too near the flame and suffered severe crippling."

The whole unfortunate business seems to have preyed upon Mr. Williams' mind rather severely, for he transferred it in part to *Suddenly, Last Summer.* The details in the play are somewhat lurid, but the climax is the same as that in real life: a beautiful young girl undergoes a pre-frontal lobotomy. In the play the operation is performed against her will as a sort of vengeance by the neurotic mother of the hero (who has been eaten alive by Spanish urchins before the action of the drama begins). It is to blot out this picture and thus force the girl to stop telling this story that the mother orders the operation performed. Except for this detail of the brain surgery, the dramatic character bears no resemblance to the dramatist's sister. Katherine Holly is one of Mr. Williams' most normal and (perhaps paradoxically) least interesting young heroines, and the play itself is one of his slighter efforts.

The problem of withdrawal from reality and ultimate retreat into the private world of insanity is best illustrated in the character of Blanche DuBois, the memorable and tragic heroine of *A Streetcar Named Desire.* In this portrayal we find an interesting illustration of some of Mr. Williams' major concerns (notably the faded Southern belle unable to adjust to a hostile environment) and also of his characteristic method (a calculated ambiguity in presenting his material).

The playwright makes use of an ironic name symbolism in connection with the two sisters around whom the action of the play revolves. Blanche and Stella may at one time in the past have been appropriately designated by "white" and "star," but when we see them during the course of the play, the character of Blanche has become decidedly sullied and blackened, while Stella, far from aspiring like a star, has settled for an altogether earthy existence with a man who typifies basic, crude, primitive sexuality. Stanley Kowalski turns out to be Blanche's natural enemy and ultimate nemesis. It is he who delivers the *coup de grace,* although the decline of Blanche had been a long time coming. It was "All of those deaths," she tells Stella, explaining how Belle Reve (Beautiful Dream), their plantation home in Laurel, Mississippi, slipped through her fingers and was lost. There was the matter of her early marriage to an unfortunate youth who turned out to be a homosexual and who killed himself when she learned of his condition. The search for love and security in a hostile world turned Blanche eventually into a nymphomaniac. Death and desire followed one another with shattering rapidity. Blanche answered the midnight calls of soldiers passing the plantation. Soon her name became a byword in the town. Eventually she seduced a seventeen-year-old pupil in her English class and was asked to leave Laurel.

All this was in the past. When we see her during the action of the play, she retains the aura of elegance and gentility that had been her birthright. But gradually she reveals herself as already well advanced into the shadowy world of illusion. She is under the impression that an old admirer is going to invite her on a cruise, and this mythical person's presence lurks in the background as her last refuge. To Mitch, the young man who, it develops, is almost as unable to face reality as Blanche, she remarks: "I don't want realism. . . . I'll tell you what I want. Magic! Yes, yes, magic! I try to give that to people. I misrepresent things to them. I don't tell the truth. I tell what *ought* to be truth. And if that is sinful, then let me be damned for it!"

And damned, of course, Blanche is. Mr. Williams, in his characterization, is quite clear about the kind of person she has become. Everything Stanley has uncovered about her lurid past in Laurel is true. We see her taunt Mitch, making crude sport of his innocence. When she learns that he does not understand French, she toys with him: "Voulez vous couchez avec moi ce soir? Vous ne comprenez pas? Ah, quel dommage!—I mean it's a damned good thing. . . ." Her inability to keep her hands off the young paper boy, while making for a most sensitive and touching scene, is nevertheless symptomatic. Further, she announces that she has been flirting with Stanley (and her attitude toward him is, in point of fact, curiously ambiguous). In the climactic scene, in which Stanley rapes Blanche, he recognizes the inevitability of their encounter. As he carries her inert figure to the bed, he says: "We've had this date with each other from the beginning." The result of this encounter is that Blanche's reason snaps. When we last see her, she is being led off to an asylum, now totally unable to distinguish between illusion and reality, giving herself over to the care of the doctor with a childlike simplicity and confidence and the utterance of a farewell line that has become memorable in the modern theatre: "Whoever you are—I have always depended on the kindness of strangers."

The facts here are obvious enough; but what are we to make of them? What is Mr. Williams trying to tell us? Where do his sympathies lie? Where, logically, ought ours lie? These, it seems to me, are some provocative and rather important questions posed by this admittedly greatest of all Tennessee Williams' plays. The dramatist himself (in one of his several statements of his aims as a writer) has given a partial answer. Replying to the charge that he fills his plays with "sordid characters," he stated: "I don't think Blanche DuBois was sordid. I think she was rather noble. I don't think deeply troubled people are sordid."

Certainly Blanche is "deeply troubled." Whether her behavior can be defended is another matter. At any rate, if we feel she is worth bothering with, we must attempt to understand why she acts the way she does; we must try to appreciate what has happened to her—in a general rather than in a specific sense. In so doing, we will be led to one of the themes of the play, which, briefly stated, is this: In *A Streetcar Named Desire* the dramatist is attacking those disruptive forces in modern life that have shattered traditional values and have rendered obsolete the older civilized refinements. In the face of a rising barbarism (symbolized by Stanley Kowalski), clinging to antiquated ideals, blindly groping for security in a world of chaos and flux, the gentle and basically decent Blanche can no longer find her way. She is ultimately lost and thus becomes a fit subject for a modern tragedy. Our sympathies, it seems to me, must clearly be with her rather than with her sister, who has capitulated, who has joined the enemy. The play thus becomes a sort of commentary on modern life, brilliantly elucidated through the manipulation of a psychologically sound (in the best Freudian sense) group of character symbols.

Summer and Smoke, while less interesting theatrically than *Streetcar,* is perhaps even more allegorical, having many of the characteristics of such a medieval work as the "Debate between the Body and Soul." Alma Winemiller (her first name, as she is fond of pointing out, is Spanish for soul), is another of Mr. Williams' anachronistic Southern belles, a fugitive from another world, a world of grace and charm which is sadly out of harmony with the world she finds herself in. The time, incidentally, is not the present, but 1916. In a stage direction the author describes Alma: "She seems to belong to a more elegant age, such as the Eighteenth Century in France."

Exactly how typical a Williams heroine Alma is (and why she is depicted as she is depicted) may be understood by looking at a particularly revealing piece of self-analysis contained in the *Theatre Arts* interview referred to earlier in this discussion. The author is talking about style.

> My great bête noir as a writer has been a tendency to what people call . . . to poeticize, you know, and that's why I suppose I've written so many Southern heroines. They have the tendency to gild the lily, and they speak in a rather florid style which seems to suit me because I write out of emotion, and I get carried away by the emotion.

The floridness of language can be noted in Amanda of *The Glass Menagerie* (especially when she is reminiscing about her girlhood), in Blanche of *Streetcar* (especially when she is, to use Stanley Kowalski's phrase, "putting on airs") and particularly in Alma of *Summer and Smoke.* In this play the florid language is even called attention to by the author. John, the hero, says at one point: "You have a rather fancy way of talking." Alma: "Have I?" John: "Pyrotechnical display instead of fireworks, and that sort of thing."

A minister's daughter with prim, spinsterish ways, Alma lives only for what she considers the finer things—church socials, literary teas, music, culture, ideals and ideas, community service, elegant refinements of a genteel civilization. And yet underneath this exterior, Mr. Williams would have us believe, lurks the spirit of a passionate and love-starved woman. The author observes in an early stage direction: "Her true nature is still hidden even from herself." It takes one of the most ironic (and perhaps contrived) about-faces in modern literature to bring Alma to full self-knowledge. As John, roistering young rakehell, grows progressively more spiritual, Alma, picture of maidenly decorum, grows progressively more fleshly. At the end of the play she literally throws herself at John, announcing that she is no longer as she once was. That other girl, she claims, "doesn't exist any more, she died last summer—suffocated in smoke from something on fire inside her." John, however, is no longer interested. "But I've come around to your way of thinking," he tells Alma. And she confirms this notion. "The tables have turned, yes, the tables have turned with a vengeance! You've come around to my old way of thinking and I to yours like two people exchanging a call on each other at the same time, and each one finding the other one gone out. . . ." So all is over between them, but the experience has wrecked Alma. We last see her casually picking up a young travelling salesman and going off with him to Moon Lake Casino for a tawdry assignation— presumably the first of what will become an endless succession of such casual immoralities. Alma, in effect, is Blanche DuBois at the beginning of the downhill slide to degradation. Blanche is Alma at the end of the road. It is a chilling spectacle to which Mr. Williams treats us—much more, actually, than a simple case history of incipient nymphomania—a study, rather, of the collapse of a whole system of ideals, of an entire way of life—an allegory, perhaps, of the South, its ruin and debasement, its decline and fall. In such an allegorical treatment we find a richness and suggestivity that render his dramas perpetually interesting in much the same way that Hawthorne's tales yield fuller and fuller harvests the more painstakingly and thoroughly they are gleaned.

Another of Mr. Williams' feminine types deserving of attention is the vivid, earthy, exotic, voluptuous, full-blooded Latin. We are introduced to such a character (a minor one) in the person of Rosa Gonzales in *Summer and Smoke*. Here she is an agent of evil and brings only destruction. This type, more fully developed, becomes the heroine of two plays—*Orpheus Descending* and *The Rose Tattoo*. The first of these plays (despite Mr. Williams' inordinate fondness for it) remains essentially a lurid melodrama, while Lady, its voluptuous heroine, lacks the depth and complexity of other Williams characters. Such a charge cannot be leveled at Serafina in *The Rose Tattoo*, a wild and rollicking comedy, full of life and passion and fire.

Serafina is a Sicilian, living in an Italian colony on the Gulf Coast somewhere between New Orleans and Mobile. Volatile, even tempestuous, she roars across the stage like an unleashed natural force—a tidal wave, perhaps. She can be tender and gentle; she can be deeply religious; she can be aggressively, violently possessive. She is sometimes crude and uncouth. But mainly she is overwhelmingly, vitally alive and exuberant. She can achieve a rapture approaching religious mysticism, a sexual ecstasy which is closely akin to the sort of feeling with the blood that D. H. Lawrence is noted for describing. Lawrence, Mr. Williams has acknowledged, exerted a deep influence upon him, and this influence appears in *The Rose Tattoo,* nowhere, perhaps, more strongly than in such scenes as the one wherein Serafina recalls her blissful relationship with her now dead husband.

> I'll tell you something which maybe you won't believe. . . . I knew that I had conceived on the very night of conception! . . . . That night I woke up with a burning pain on me, here, on my left breast! A pain like a needle, quick, quick, hot little stitches. I turned on the light, I uncovered my breast!—On it I saw the rose tattoo of my husband! . . . On me, on my breast, his tattoo! And when I saw it I knew that I had conceived. . . . I screamed. But when he woke up, it was gone. It only lasted a moment. But I *did* see it, and I *did* know, when I seen it, that I had conceived, that in my body another rose was growing!

No one, it must be stressed, can be more pretentious than Tennessee Williams when he attempts to give some kind of special, weighty significance to material which, on the surface, appears perfectly obvious. *The Rose Tattoo* is (as its author has claimed), a pæan of praise to the Dionysian elements of life—a celebration of the forces of rejuvenation, fertility, fecundity. To other readers, however, it resembles nothing so much as an earthy, healthy bedroom farce played among primitive peasants and overloaded arbitrary symbolism.

The aging female properly motivated can achieve an integrated personality and a reasonable amount of happiness—as Serafina does in *The Rose Tattoo.* The aging female, improperly motivated, however, becomes a force for destruction and evil. Three characters, all fading actresses in middle life, have a sufficient number of points in common to constitute a third type in Mr. Williams' gallery of feminine characters. These are Karen Stone of *The Roman Spring of Mrs. Stone* (Tennessee Williams' only novel), the Princess Kosmonopolis of *Sweet Bird of Youth,* and Flora Goforth of *The Milk Train Doesn't Stop Here Any More.* I shall make a brief mention only of the last two, who appear in plays.

Flora Goforth, Mr. Williams' most recent creation, is still in a state of growth and change. Her original appearance on Broadway early in 1963 was greeted with marked hostility from the critics, whom she impressed as being under-developed and ill-assimilated. And in spite of the fact that the part was rewritten and the entire play revised and presented anew by Barter Theatre in September, 1963, Flora remains little less than a monster, a fading former show-girl, a man-eating virago who describes herself as an "ex-swamp bitch from Georgia." She has no redeeming qualities whatever, except perhaps a sense for bawdy humor. She is intended presumably to be tragic or at least pathetic—another female wrecked by life, dangling at the end of her rope. But her plight hardly moves us.

She is a more exaggerated Alexandra del Lago, the Princess Kosmonopolis of *Sweet Bird of Youth*. This woman, a fantastic creation, at times ridiculous, at times pathetic, sometimes approaches a sort of gaudy grandeur. A shameless opportunist, she picks up young men (as she does Chance Wayne, the hero), uses them for her sexual gratification, and then casts them aside when they have fulfilled their function. She insists that she is "not a phony," and for a brief moment we are almost tempted to believe her. She is, of course, a monster—a fact which she herself readily acknowledges. She insists on her own way, and her lover Chance (vigorous and potent though he is) is no match for her. Before she will give him the money he demands, she exacts tribute.

> When monster meets monster [she tells him], one monster has to give way, AND IT WILL NEVER BE ME. . . . I've been accused of having a death wish but I think it's life that I wish for, terribly, shamelessly, on any terms whatsoever.
>
> When I say now, the answer must not be later. I have only one way to forget these things I don't want to remember and that's through the act of lovemaking. That's the only dependable distraction so when I say now, because I need that distraction, it has to be now, not later.

Possessed of an India-rubber resilience and a colossal monomania, the Princess sweeps all before her and surges on to further questionable triumphs. She abandons Chance to his shocking fate.

> You've just been using me [she tells him]. Using me. When I needed you downstairs you shouted, "Get her a wheel chair!" Well, I didn't need a wheel chair, I came up alone, as always. I climbed back alone up the beanstalk to the ogre's country where I live, now, alone.

And so she goes—solitary, indestructible, with a certain flair, her spurious regality a sort of tarnished magnificence, the tattered banner of her misspent life streaming.

The play as a whole is a distasteful one; the characters lack anything like warmth and humanity. Mr. Williams has moved a long way from the tenderness and the fragility of *The Glass Menagerie*. Obsessed with violence, he explains in the preface to the printed version of *Sweet Bird of Youth*:

> . . . If there is any truth in the Aristotelian idea that violence is purged by its poetic representation on a stage, then it may be that my cycle of violent plays have had a moral justification after all. I know that I have felt it. I have always felt a release from the sense of meaninglessness and death when a work of tragic intention has seemed to me to have achieved that intention, even if only approximately, nearly.

Purgation by external projection is one thing—and perhaps an important thing. But of itself, being only temporary, it is clearly not enough. Something more is needed—some sort of philosophical understanding or reconciliation. Only when this is achieved can one be said to have reached that serenity of acceptance which is the aim of all art, especially true tragedy. Which brings us to *Night of the Iguana.*

In the *Theatre Arts* interview already referred to, the following dialogue occurs:

> INTERVIEWER: Some time ago you said you were hoping someday to write one play that would encompass everything that you've been trying to say. Is *Iguana* the play?
>
> WILLIAMS: I was trying to work on it in *Iguana,* yes, at least a kind of summation of what I've derived finally from these mixed feelings and attitudes.
>
> INTERVIEWER: You might say, then, that from your point of view *Iguana* is the most important of your plays.
>
> WILLIAMS: For my own personal selfish satisfaction at least. I hope it will reach other people too, but, God knows, not everybody has the same life, or problems that I have and maybe it won't communicate to them. I can only hope that it does.

The theme of the play, Mr. Williams says, "is how to live beyond despair and still live." This is a noble theme, of course, and worthy of a noble treatment. Whether or not it gets such a treatment is debatable.

The play is set in the summer of 1940 in an out-of-the-way village on the west coast of Mexico. The action occurs on the veranda of a hotel owned and operated by an American widow, Maxine Faulk, a rather hard, coarse and loud but good-hearted extrovert in her middle forties. To this place comes a bus-load of teachers from a Baptist female college in Blowing Rock, Texas, who are on a sight-seeing tour led by the ex-reverend Lawrence Shannon, a neurotic black-Irish young man of thirty-five. Shannon has been forced to give up his position in a Virginia Episcopal church because, as he puts it, he committed fornication and heresy in the same week. Only two of the school teachers come on stage; the remainder of the group stay down below the hotel in the village. Of the two who appear, one is an underage girl who has been seduced by Shannon; the other has reported the incident by telephone to the tour headquarters and gotten Shannon fired from his job as guide. Shannon is on the verge of a mental breakdown, but is presumably saved from this fate by the widow (who persuades him by play's end to remain with her) and especially by Hannah Jelkes, a prim New England spinster pushing forty, whose philosophy of understanding and acceptance forms whatever "message" the play intends to convey.

Hannah is one of Tennessee Williams' most attractive heroines, and a fitting one with which to conclude this study of Mr. Williams' women characters. Like Shannon, Hannah is at the end of her rope. But she has qualities which he lacks—insight, tolerance, clarity of vision, hope, resourcefulness, perseverance, and a sensible working philosophy of personal adjustment which enables her to triumph over the adversities of life and ultimately to prevail. These two lost creatures sustain each other through the dark night of the Iguana as elemental forces threaten to overwhelm them. At the end, they have attained a certain serenity and reconciliation (almost approaching a state of beatitude). What becomes of Hannah, Mr. Williams with typical ambiguity fails to make clear. But I think there is no doubt that she will be saved.

Everything points to this theory—notably the symbolism of the iguana. The giant lizard has been caught by Mexican boys and is tied under the hotel. There it is to be fattened and ultimately butchered and eaten. Hannah prevails upon Shannon to cut it loose, "So that," in his words, "one of God's creatures could run home safe and free." With the liberation of this reptile, which is described during its captivity as being at the end of its rope, it becomes clear that both Shannon and Hannah are liberated, too—but not necessarily to find solace with each other. Mr. Williams is no "happy-Hollywood-ending" romantic.

There is a strong temptation in reading *Night of the Iguana* to see Hannah Jelkes as spokesman or apologist for Tennessee Williams himself. Explaining how she conquered the "blue devil" that used to haunt her, she says:

HANNAH: I showed that I could—endure him and I made him respect my endurance.

SHANNON: How?

HANNAH: Just by, by just—enduring. Endurance is something that spooks and blue devils respect, and they respect all the tricks that panicky people use to outlast and outwit their panic.

SHANNON: Like poppy-seed tea?

HANNAH: Poppy-seed tea or rum-cocos or just a few deep breaths, anything, everything, that we take to give them the slip, and so keep on going.

SHANNON: To where?

HANNAH: To somewhere like this, perhaps: this veranda over the rain forest and the still-water beach, after long, difficult travels, and I don't mean just travels about the world, the earth's surface. I mean subterranean travels, the, the— journeys that the spooked and bedeviled people are forced to take through the *unlighted* sides of their natures. . . .

Describing to Shannon the two closest things she has had to a love experience (both are rather grotesque and comical), she arrives at this piece of philosophy: "Nothing human disgusts me unless it's unkind, violent!" But human beings, Shannon counters, can sometimes be driven to revolting and disgusting behavior, and he describes a particularly loathsome sight he once witnessed in the tropics. Hannah is temporarily affected but she is made of stern stuff. She ignores the grisly tale Shannon has told and turns her attention to the sad plight of the captive iguana, which Shannon at this point sets free. The play ends with another bit of symbolism. Hannah's ninety-seven-year-old grandfather (a minor poet) completes his magnum opus and then dies. Thus do all the principals come to some sort of resolution, some degree of fulfillment.

Night of the Iguana marks an interesting departure in Tennessee Williams' work. Despite its excesses, some of them shocking, it is Mr. Williams' most hopeful and optimistic play in some time. *Iguana* is Williams at his best, Williams as it were, in a new and hopeful role. If in *The Milk Train* he is marking time, it may be possible that his next play will reveal this new dimension given added emphasis.

What precisely will be the nature of this new dimension, no one, of course, can say. It may very well be along lines laid out in his so-called comedy, *Period of Adjustment*—a wise, tremendously tolerant and rather surprisingly knowledgeable play (for a bachelor, that is) about wedding-night traumas. Although this drama is less impressive than his more serious ones, it is notable for the interesting consistency of its heroine when she is placed alongside the major female portraits.

Isabel Haverstick is, if not a sister, at least a first cousin of Blanche DuBois and Alma Winemiller—although lacking the frenetic, neurotic qualities of these less fortunate ladies. The kinship is apparent immediately upon our noting how she talks. Like Blanche and Alma she is given to using the genteel circumlocution. And as in the case of Alma, another character in the play recognizes this proclivity:

Isabel: (to her host): "Mr. Bates, your animal is standing by the door as if it wants out. Shall I let it out for you?. . . . Such a sweet animal! What is this animal's name?"

To which George, Isabel's husband, says: "The animal is a dog." Isabel: "I know it's a dog." George: "Then why don't you call it a dog!"

This dialogue gives us a clue to Isabel's character. She can no more call a dog a dog than she can call a spade a spade. A constitutional over-gentility is an indispensable part of her character, for, after all, she is a product of a Baptist college, where her philosophy professor has urged her to consider three paramount questions: "Where do we *come* from? *Why? And where, oh where, are we going!*" Her host, whom she and her husband are visiting after their traumatic wedding night in the "Old Man River" Motel, instinctively recognizes her exaggerated gentility. He refers to her throughout the play as "little lady."

Isabel, however—despite all her tendencies toward an overrefined and "Southern" gentility—is not an incipient Blanche DuBois or Alma Wine-miller. She is much too wholesome and normal. She is, in other words, not a tragic—or even potentially tragic, heroine. She will adjust just as certainly as Blanche and Alma will not. And, although it is regrettable to have to say so, her very tendency toward normality militates wholly against our considering her a major theatrical creation of Tennessee Williams. Attractive as she undoubtedly is, she is nevertheless no match for her more neurotic and star-crossed sisters. Paradoxical as it may seem, these lost, abandoned and thoroughly bereft creatures stand out in the hierarchy of Williams' characters with such luminosity that they totally eclipse the normal, well-adjusted ladies (few indeed though they may be) to whom we would like to look for solutions to the problems of this enigmatic playwright's obsessive concern with human (or feminine) frailty.

The Search for Hope in the Plays of Tennessee Williams

Delma Eugene Presley

Tennessee Williams' entrance into the Roman Catholic Church in January, 1969 should be regarded not necessarily as an eccentric action, but as a logical if not decisive step in the playwright's progression toward religion. Throughout his career as a dramatist, Williams has exhibited in his plays an awareness of religious questions. However, his theological dimension has gone unnoticed by most critics who, for reasons mysterious, concentrate upon appearances of sexuality and violence to the exclusion of authentic theological and philosophical concerns. Beginning with *The Glass Menagerie* (1945) and ending with *The Milk Train Doesn't Stop Here Anymore* (1964), Williams' hero travels the difficult road from despair to hope—from the shadows of tragedy to the light of the comic vision. This journey becomes a kind of pilgrimage, especially in plays after *Camino Real* (1953), characterized by the hero's repetition of familiar affirmations. This aspect of the later works of Williams has great significance in view of the obvious decline in his reputation among critics of theatre. It may very well be that the quality of his later works suffers from debilitating effects of his emerging hope. The great and unfortunate irony of the hero's ultimate redemption is that his religious-sounding ideology reduces his stature.

I

As early as *The Glass Menagerie* and as late as *The Milk Train Doesn't Stop Here Anymore*, Williams' hero encounters three problems of a philosophical or theological nature—isolation, the absence of God, and the reality of death.[1] Tom Wingfield and Blanche Du Bois, central characters in the early plays, *The Glass Menagerie* and *A Streetcar Named Desire*, are caught in situations

Reprinted with permission from *Mississippi Quarterly* 25 (Winter 1971–72): 31–44.

which prevent any semblance of community. There may be the potential of community in the Wingfield home, but it is never realized. Tom understands but refuses to heed the advice of Amanda, his mother: "In these trying times we live in, all that we have to cling to is each other" (scene iv). His escape from responsibility is but another in a long series which began, of course, with the father's desertion. Blanche Du Bois of *Streetcar* knows what she needs when she arrives at her sister's apartment in New Orleans. She tells Stella: "I want to be *near* you, got to be *with* somebody, I *can't* be alone!" (scene i). Blanche is doomed from the start not simply because she will be overwhelmed by the bestial Stanley. Blanche, let us remember, is pathetically torn from within by conflicting emotions: her compassion is defeated by her selfishness; her need for understanding is undermined by her debauchery. Human community is not possible in *Streetcar* precisely because the people who ought to participate in that community are either unwilling or incapable.

Williams' early works suggest that, beyond human weaknesses, a cause of isolation is the inability of the flesh to coexist harmoniously with the spirit. Tom Wingfield, an avid reader of the instinct-affirming writings of D. H. Lawrence, is rebuked by a religious-sounding Amanda who would have him concentrate on life's "nobler qualities." This thematic clash again comes to the surface in a bit of clever dialogue in the eighth scene of *Streetcar*. Blanche has been spending hours in the Kowalskis' only bathroom—a circumstance which aggravates her already lacerated relationship with Stanley. After one of his impatient remarks, she replies with a paraphrase of Jesus' words in Luke 21:19: "Possess your soul in patience." Stanley immediately counters with: "It's not my soul, it's my kidneys I'm worried about." In the larger context of the drama, these words indicate that Stanley's mind is open not to the beckoning of the spirit but only to the desires and needs of the flesh. *Summer and Smoke,* written shortly after *Streetcar,* appears to have been conceived with this theme of the flesh versus the spirit as a problem to be solved. Pathos is the only emotion evoked in this experimental allegory which ends with the sad affirmation that the flesh (summer) cannot merge with the spirit (smoke). The central characters, John (the doctor of bodily ills) and Alma (Spanish for soul), are not saved from their isolation but pathetically confirmed in it.

The second major theological issue in the plays of Williams is the absence of God or a savior. The Wingfields, Amanda in particular, wish for a messiah in the form of a "gentleman caller." Indeed, *The Glass Menagerie* structurally is held together by the anticipation and arrival of Jim O'Connor. He is, as Tom points out in the opening monologue, "that long delayed but always expected something that we live for." Once Jim comes and leaves, the play's action is complete. Amanda's hopes for deliverance are fruitless since Jim has made previous commitments to the American technological dream, and, of course, a "girl named Betty." In *Streetcar,* Blanche Du Bois keeps hoping up until the end that her messiah, Shep Hundleigh (probably imaginary), will appear out of nowhere and rescue her from Stanley and his crude world. The airplane "Fugitivo" is the messianic symbol in *Camino Real.* It is either death at the hands of the street-cleaners or escape via airplane for the traveler of the road of reality. As Marguerite, the tubercular woman of pleasure, says in Block Nine: the "Fugitivo" is her only "way to escape from this abominable place!" Because of a technicality, Marguerite is unable to board this agency of salvation. Her destiny, like that of the hero Kilroy, is death in a strange land devoid of love and compassion. Probably the most obvious reference to the absence of God in a guilt-infested world comes in *Sweet Bird of Youth.* Few critics have noted the significant lines of the heckler who shouts in the second act to the crowds surrounding a politician, Boss Finley, called "a messiah from the hills":

> I don't believe it. I believe that the silence of God, the absolute speechlessness of Him is a long, long and awful thing that the whole world is lost because of. I think it's yet to be broken to any man, living or yet lived on earth—no exceptions.

The awareness of death is a third important theme in Williams' major plays. It is in the presence of death that his hero encounters questions about the nature and destiny of his life. Ultimate questions are faced particularly in *Camino Real* (1953), and in several more recent plays: *Cat on a Hot Tin Roof* (1955), *Suddenly Last Summer* (1958), *The Night of the Iguana* (1962), and *The Milk Train Doesn't Stop Here Anymore* (1964). The most serious exploration of human destiny is the memorable heart-to-heart talk between Brick and Big Daddy in the second act of *Cat on a Hot Tin Roof.* Big Daddy traces his son's alcoholism and ennui to the mystery surrounding his friendship with Skipper. Maggie, Brick's wife, had hinted earlier that Skipper harbored homosexual feelings toward her husband. Brick is stung by his father's words and counters with the "truth" that Big Daddy will not have future birthdays since his illness is not, as Big Mamma and Gooper say, a "spastic colon," but something more terrible: incurable cancer. There is no advice, no optimistic outlook, for Big Daddy. His last words are "CHRIST DAMN—ALL—LYING— SONS OF—LYING BITCHES! . . . Lying, dying, liars!" *Cat on a Hot Tin Roof,* therefore, is a play about different kinds of death in the modern world. Life cannot continue on Brick's side of the family. We know that Brick already has willed a spiritual death; he has "that cool air of detachment that people have who have given up the struggle." Life will continue for Gooper and Mae and their offspring. But, as Big Daddy and Brick indicate in the second act, the kind of existence embodied by these people is mendacious. Death is the final truth of this play.

II

If one grants the existence of these theological and philosophical aspects of Williams' works—isolation, God's absence, and death—one ought to notice as well solutions to these problems whenever they are proposed by the dramatist. When the major plays are considered as a unit, it becomes clear that few solutions are proposed prior to *Camino Real*. In this particular play, Williams shows evidence of a search for a solution; the most obvious clue is that *Camino Real*'s style is so unlike that of his previous efforts. Here the author develops an elaborate allegory in an unusual sequence of "Blocks." Technique, as Professor Mark Schorer pointed out in his famous essay on the subject, is an important indication of subject matter: "The final lesson of the modern novel is that technique is not the secondary thing it seemed to Wells, some external machination, a mechanical affair, but a deep and primary operation; not only that technique *contains* intellectual and moral implications, but that it *discovers* them."[2] The appearance of Williams' allegorical plays, *Camino Real* and later *Suddenly Last Summer,* indicate the playwright's attempt to discover a new subject matter, one containing hopeful affirmations about life's potential.

The "way of reality" and "royal road," two meanings of *Camino Real,* have many similarities to Dante's road through *The Inferno*. The play's epigraph comes from Canto I of *The Inferno:* "In the middle of the journey of our life, I came to myself in a dark wood where the straight way was lost." This particular play, like Dante's allegory of life as hell, is but part of a journey to redemption for the hero. The travelers of the Camino are universal men—the eternal optimist, Don Quixote; the great lover, Casanova; Lord Byron, the Romantic in quest of an ideal; Marguerite, a sentimental courtesan past her prime; and Kilroy, the American Everyman who attempts to hold fast to independence, sincerity, and courage. Kilroy travels the very real road of life which leads to an arid fountain in the middle of the square. He discovers that Don Quixote's map was right: "The spring of humanity has gone dry in this place." Despite the idealism of Kilroy, despite his efforts to defeat the smug and cruel enemies of sensitivity and brotherhood, he is ultimately defeated. After his death at the hands of the "street cleaners," he is taken to a medical institution where interns dissect him. They discover that his heart was made of gold which cannot be destroyed by even the most corrosive forces of modernity. In the sixteenth and last block, a resurrected Kilroy is seen carrying his gold heart under his arm. He joins Don Quixote who is prepared to venture forth again in search of the ideal. After they become partners, Quixote affirms: "The violets in the mountains have broken the rocks!" Water then rushes into the once-dry fountain. The implication is that the Camino has been redeemed through the courage of Kilroy who is now, like Christ, an eternal force.

The new hopefulness of *Camino Real,* surely Williams' turning point, does not come cheaply. The price he pays for his new theme becomes evident when one considers the thematic and structural consequences. *Camino Real* has several weaknesses which are prophetic of his recent efforts. One major problem is his too simple reduction of complex literary figures such as Don Quixote and Lord Byron. Another limitation arises from Kilroy's sudden apotheosis after his death; this is pure *deus ex machina.* Williams' literary self-consciousness leads to chaos: All at once the viewer is thrust into an incongruous symbolical environment of Dante, Cervantes, T. S. Eliot, Lord Byron, Spanish folk lore, and Christian reminiscences. Too much weight rests upon sentiment; the clearest example of this is found in the closing lines: "The violets in the mountains have broken the rocks!" The "comic" resolution of the play comes through the author's fiat and not through a dramatically believable solution. Thus Williams, by using sentiment in such a way, pronounces the play complete even if the reader or viewer mentally protests.

Suddenly Last Summer, produced five years after *Camino Real,* has a similar lack of credibility. The allegorical meaning of the play is explained by the heroine, Catharine Holly; it has to do with the consequences of possessing a daemonic vision of God and man. Professor Paul J. Hurley understands the play properly when he writes: "What his drama proclaims is that recognition of evil, if carried to the point of a consuming obsession, may be the worst form of evil. . . . A daemonic vision of human nature may irredeemably corrupt the one who possesses the vision."[3] The point of this "morality play" is made clear by Catharine. She explains that her homosexual cousin Sebastian, a would-be poet, did what all modern men have a tendency to do: He tried to "spell God's name with the wrong alphabet blocks." Since the question of God is an important one in the drama (Sebastian sacrifices himself to his "vision" of a cannibalistic God), one would expect Williams to pursue the question. Instead of dealing further with this important point, however, the playwright turns his attention to the interrelationship of mankind. Humanity, according to Catharine, may be as desperate as passengers aboard a ship which has struck an iceberg at sea. Everyone is sinking, but that is "no reason for everyone drowning hating everyone drowning." Totally disregarding man's idolatrous nature—his making into God an image of himself— Catharine touchingly affirms a positive life of community in which people accept each other even though they all share the common fate of death. If a major problem of *Suddenly Last Summer* is God's relationship to human experience, then we must conclude that the question is unanswered by the playwright. This play is similar to *Camino Real* in its vagueness about solutions which, although literally present in the drama, do not in any sense relate to the problems which they should solve. Yes, *Suddenly Last Summer* has a sense of completeness as a "morality play," but the drama nevertheless fails to come to grips with the central issue it has raised.

The two most recent plays in this discussion, as some critics have acknowledged, are explicitly theological. Once again the basis problems of the characters are isolation, the question of God, and death. In *The Night of the Iguana,* Shannon's main problem is "the oldest one in the world—the need to believe in something or someone." Hannah's emphasis upon belief is intended as a solution to Shannon's state of disbelief. Earlier he tells her that "Western theologies, the whole mythology of them, are based on the concept of God as a senile delinquent. . . . I will not and cannot continue to conduct services in praise and worship of this . . . angry, petulant old man" (Act II). While Hannah correctly senses that Shannon has a problem of belief, she is nevertheless incapable of providing an answer to this specific question. The logic of her speeches is that Shannon's problem concerning God may be resolved if he simply reaches out for other people. The clearest illustration of her logic is found in the second half of the passage quoted earlier. Here it is in full:

SHANNON: What is my problem, Miss Jelkes?

HANNAH: The oldest one in the world—the need to believe in something or in someone—almost anyone—almost anything . . . something.

SHANNON: Your voice sounds hopeless about it.

HANNAH: No, I'm not hopeless about it. In fact, I've discovered something to believe in.

SHANNON: Something like . . . God?

HANNAH: No.

SHANNON: What?

HANNAH: Broken gates between people so they can reach each other, even if it's just for one night only.

. . .

A little understanding exchanged between them, a wanting to help each other through nights like this. (Act III)

Later in this act Hannah explains that, while she is "unsure" about God, she is beginning to feel that God may be seen in the faces of suffering humanity.

Hannah's point is that the problem of belief will more or less take care of itself if Shannon will try to live in community with someone. But Shannon's problem is not isolation but belief or lack of it. Hannah insists that he deal with the question of disbelief with the answer for human isolation—community. The logic is reminiscent of that used by Catharine in *Suddenly Last Summer;* she raises the question about Sebastian's daemonic vision of God and then answers it with a simplistic statement about the importance of caring for other people.

Williams manages to solve the fundamental problem of death in *Iguana* while Hannah and Shannon are engaged in their discussion; the character involved in this solution, however, is neither the hero nor the heroine, but the heroine's father, Nonno. Everyone in the play knows that he is at death's door. His concern throughout the play is to complete his final poem—one which explores a way of looking at death. The concluding lines of the poem reveal that Nonno's solution to death is "Courage."

> O Courage could you not as well
> Select a second place to dwell,
> Not only in that golden tree
> But in the frightened heart of me?

Nonno's struggle to complete the poem parallels Shannon's efforts to understand and justify his existence in view of his conception of God. Nonno's climactic poem lends an air of calm reserve to this scene in which Shannon attempts to find something worthy of his belief. Nonno is the only character who finds a satisfactory answer to his basic question. But the play is not about Nonno. The main character, Shannon, ignores the question which first was most important and commits himself to a life of "community" with Maxine— a person who throughout the play is revealed as incapable of either understanding or empathy. Shannon's question of belief is left unanswered. One might argue that Hannah substitutes the human face for the divine image, in the tradition of Romantic thinkers, and thus redefines the question on belief. If Williams' point is that suffering humanity has replaced God, then he does not make it clear. Shannon's vigorous statements about God as a "senile delinquent" are not refuted by ignoring them.

The point about the illogical resolution of *The Night of the Iguana* can be made about *The Milk Train Doesn't Stop Here Anymore*. The chief difference is that the basic problem of the latter play is death. Furthermore, the ideology of Christopher is more nearly Christian than oriental, whereas Hannah's point of view is an uneven combination of oriental, stoic, and Christian sentiment. Christopher's mission apparently is to prepare Mrs. Goforth for death. (She is about to "go forth.") The epigraph from Yeats's "Sailing to Byzantium," in the context of the drama, implies that Mrs. Goforth is about to sail into eternity. Yet it is not clear whether Williams proposes that the solution to her problem of death is some kind of eternal life. If Christopher is a "bearer of Christ," this would seem logical. Yet the hero's mission has patently selfish origins. He visits Mrs. Goforth, just as he has visited other dying ladies, not primarily because he has a special message for her, but because this activity saves *him* from a sense of "unreality" and "lostness." An uncritical reading of the play might lead one, as it has led countless reviewers, to claim that the drama is about a "Christ figure" who comes to prepare a dying aristocrat for eternal life. But Williams has not done this in *The Milk Train Doesn't Stop Here Anymore*. Mrs. Goforth's death is merely a vehicle for the realization of a vagrant poet's unusual need for psychological comfort.

The play's meaning is further confused by the epigraph from W. B. Yeats's famous poem, "Sailing to Byzantium":

> Consume my heart away; sick with desire
> And fastened to a dying animal
> It knows not what it is; and gather me
> Into the artifice of eternity.

The poem does not suggest the same kind of eternal life represented by the image of Christ. Rather, it is Yeats's special interpretation of art in opposition to nature. The poem suggests the rejection of the natural for the unnatural "form as Grecian goldsmiths make. . . ." If Williams uses Christopher Flanders (the name connotes both Christ and death) to suggest that Mrs. Goforth has entered eternity when the drama closes, as several critics maintain, then the playwright has probably misunderstood the meaning of "Sailing to Byzantium." The basic problem of the drama, death, is left unsolved; unsolved, even though the touching communion scene at the end suggests that something has been resolved.

In the recent plays of hopefulness beyond despair, Tennessee Williams commits several errors—the greatest of which is his misleading suggestion that the dramas have been resolved. The closest either play (*Iguana* and *Milk Train*) comes to resolution is in the singular instance of Nonno's discovery of "courage" in the face of death. But it is Nonno's solution and not Shannon's. The greatest problem of the play—Shannon's struggle for belief—is ignored in the drama's resolution.

III

Since Williams' turning point is *Camino Real,* it is important to notice that at the very moment he is developing a moral point of view, he is also experimenting with a dramatic structure foreign to his genius as a writer of realistic dramas. The characters of *Camino Real* are stripped of their authenticity even though their allegorical trappings are rich in symbolic value. Williams' conception of allegory is flawed by its escape from the real. Successful allegory is symbolic in method, but the goal is usually realistic. The unreality of his major allegories, *Camino Real* and *Suddenly Last Summer,* is a clear indication that Williams has substituted sentimentality for authenticity. The only conclusion to be drawn from this development is that, despite the playwright's desperate and commendable efforts to the contrary, there are no believable solutions for the terrifying problems of his very complex characters.

That Williams is concerned with important theological issues cannot be denied. Human isolation, the absence of God, and the reality of death are fundamental concerns of Christian theology. Williams obviously recognizes this or he would not consistently use Christian-sounding language and themes in most of his recent works. Yet he has not grasped the fundamental logic inherent in the theological issues. He has not found a way to deal effectively with the problems experienced by his characters, even though he employs dramatic techniques such as false resolutions to suggest otherwise.

The great virtue of the early plays of Williams is that they are believable and concern real people. The early hero's dignity is that, despite social and psychological pressures, he does not ultimately ignore the facts of his life. Blanche's despair is a legitimate and credible response to the nature of her existence. Tom's acute sense of the disgusting aspects of life makes him what few of the latter heroes are—truthful. In this context, we can say that frustration and anxiety are far more commendable, more real, than the religious-sounding clichés of the hero in the later plays.

Despite the fact that Williams' hero ultimately achieves a limited kind of community, his problems—isolation, God's absence, and death—are not resolved in a convincing manner. Williams' difficulty is shared by many modern writers who would project theological themes. T. S. Eliot's plays tend to confirm the difficulty of Williams' task. Perhaps the only meaningful action for the hero in isolation would be to wait. But Williams, more often than not, is a writer whose plays are in the realistic traditions of Chekhov and Ibsen, not in the more somber traditions of the "theatre of the absurd" or the "literature of silence." Some argue that Williams' greatest attribute is his ability to produce conventional, realistic drama. Indeed he succeeds most of all when he describes loneliness, frustration, and the unavoidable anxiety of human experience. But in his later works he attempts more than description. He proposes sentimental, religious-sounding solutions which contribute to dramatic distortion and thematic irrelevance. Some might contend that this situation validates the conclusion of the "death of God" theologian, Gabriel Vahanian: "Christian thought . . . no longer is relevant to the situation of our post-Christian age and its cultural postulates." I would like to argue, however, that Williams' failure is not primarily due to his use or misuse of a system of theology. Rather, the major difficulty is his apparent inability to resolve in a logical manner the problems of his characters. Tennessee Williams' recent entry into the Church perhaps indicates that he is doing with his life what he has been trying to do for his characters. Somehow it is easier to be a religious playwright than a writer of religious plays. And T. S. Eliot has taught us by example the importance of knowing where one leaves off and the other begins.

Notes

1.   Eight plays by Tennessee Williams are of particular importance in this study. References within the text of this paper are always to the following editions: *The Glass Menagerie* (New York, 1945), *A Streetcar Named Desire* (New York, 1947), *Summer and Smoke* (New York, 1948), *Camino Real* (Norfolk, Conn., 1953), *Cat on a Hot Tin Roof* (New York, 1955), *Suddenly Last Summer* (New York, 1958), *The Night of the Iguana* (New York, 1962), and *The Milk Train Doesn't Stop Here Anymore* (New York, 1964).

2.   Mark Schorer, "Technique as Discovery" in *The Modern Critical Spectrum,* ed. Gerald J. and Nancy M. Goldberg (Englewood Cliffs, N.J., 1965), p. 74.

3.   Paul J. Hurley, "*Suddenly Last Summer* as 'Morality Play,' " *Modern Drama,* 9 (February 1966), 393.

Late Tennessee Williams

Ruby Cohn

Sex, South, and violence brought Tennessee Williams to a Broadway which then allowed him no deviations. From *A Streetcar Named Desire* (1947) set in New Orleans to *Sweet Bird of Youth* (1959) set in Florida, Williams usually wrote true to type. Even though *The Night of the Iguana* (1961) garnered his fourth (and final) New York Drama Critics Circle Award, Williams was edged out for the Pulitzer Prize, a more responsive barometer to current climate. *Night* started his descent from popularity, as his Lord Byron had prophesied in *Camino Real* (1953): "There is a passion for declivity in this world!" New York reviewers are imbued with this passion, but even a serious critic in a serious journal took Williams's declivity as axiomatic: "What is the significance of the large body of work which Williams has contributed to our national literature, and why has his effectiveness as a playwright suffered *a marked decline* in the last two decades?"[1] (my emphasis). The correct critical question seems to me: "Has Williams's effectiveness as a playwright suffered a recent decline?"

Williams is an untrustworthy chronicler of his creations, since he cannot resist puns, jokes, or good stories. He has often summarized the 1960s as his "Stoned Age." Stoned or sober, however, he continued each morning to fill demanding blank pages which grew into plays, stories, and even novels. In the 1960s Williams began to stray from the triad that endeared him to Broadway. Although many of his characters continue to be Southerners, his settings are not necessarily in the South. Although sex continues to be frankly discussed and dramatized, it often goes unconsummated. Violence is muted or even absent; the explosive scenes of his earlier plays simmer down to an atmosphere of resignation. Never one to rest on his laurels—or magnolia— Williams during the 1960s and 1970s moves into new territories, fashions new kinds of characters, experiments with new forms. Despite unfavorable reviews and imperceptive criticism, Williams continues to work—"Work!!— the loveliest of all four-letter words. . . ."[2] Several projects were under way when he died on February 25, 1983. Opposing most viewpoints in print,

Reprinted with permission from *Modern Drama* 27, no. 3 (September 1984): 336–44.

I think that three major Williams plays date from the last decade of his life; perhaps he sometimes worked simultaneously on *The Two-Character Play, Vieux Carré,* and *Clothes for a Summer Hotel,* which were produced in that order.

The final version of *The Two-Character Play* was published in 1976, and two earlier versions were published in 1969 and 1973. Other, unpublished revisions may exist among Williams's scattered papers, but the three printed versions show a movement toward economy of language within an increasingly ambiguous and inclusive context.

From the first, *The Two-Character Play* is cast in the old baroque form of a play within the play—Williams's only venture in that form. The play within Williams's play is called "The Two-Character Play,"[3] and it contains major elements of Williams's drama when he was Broadway's golden boy. It is set in a small town in the American South. Its two characters, brother and sister, Felice and Clare Devoto, are perhaps incestuous lovers. Violence accounts for the deaths of the siblings' parents; their father, having been threatened by their mother with commitment to an insane asylum, has shot first her and then himself. The siblings are not only orphaned, but also destitute because suicide voids collection of life insurance. And the siblings are not only destitute, but also ostracized by the townspeople, like such earlier Williams characters as Blanche Dubois, Chance Wayne, Val Xavier. In this play within the play, with its family resemblance to earlier Williams plays, brother and sister are so introverted and fearful that they do not dare to leave their Victorian home, which is bordered by sunflowers as high as the house. During the course of the play within the play, the two characters dramatize their isolation as a fugitive kind—to use an old Williams phrase—or as unnatural creatures—to use the phrase of this play. Fantasy is their heritage—in the form of iridescent soap bubbles—and fantasy may be their fate—if they can impose an ending on this play written by Felice. At the same time, violence is their heritage, and violence may be their fate, for their father's revolver is within their grasp.

Violence, fantasy, sex, South mark the Williams landscape, and "The Two-Character Play" is typical Williams also in that autobiography is transmuted to fiction. Like Williams, who has often been criticized for drawing his plays from his life, Felice Devoto draws upon *his* life to write his "Two-Character Play." It is as though Williams has synopsized critical clichés about his plays and recast them in the form of a short play. Moreover, in each successive version, the plot of the inner play grows more compact. In the 1969 publication there are so many interruptions and actors' demands for "Line" that the story can hardly be followed. The 1973 version is cleaner and clearer, yet it is marred by excessive symbolism. By 1976 "The Two-Character Play" has a simpler story line, but it remains an incomplete item in the repertoire of a pair of siblings who manage a theater company on tour, and it is an unmistakable Williams item, although his name is never mentioned.

The name of the fictional playwright—Felice Devoto—is not so ironic as it may seem. The playwright-actor-stage manager never looks happy on stage—Felice—and yet his compulsive dedication to theater can be construed as a kind of happiness. His sister Clare's lucidity is evident in a comparable dedication—their vow. Although the play within the play is a baroque form, it is to Pirandello that Williams specifically refers in the first printing of the play. A confused Clare asks whether they are going to perform Pirandello, since a papier-mâché giant is on stage, recalling the Italian playwright's last and incomplete play, *The Mountain Giants*.[4] By the second printed version, the name of Pirandello has vanished from the text, but the gigantic statue remains. To this visual residue of Pirandello, Williams adds a reminiscence of Beckett. Clare's first extended speech is delivered in fragments:

> I forget—*unalterable circumstance,* but—Remember the time that destitute old—painter—invited us to tea on the—Viale—something—somewhere and when we arrived—the concierge said, suspiciously, "Oh, him, huh, five flights up, not worth it!"—Five flights up, not worth it!—No, not exactly worth it, the old, old painter was seated in *rigor mortis* before a totally blank canvas, teakettle boiled dry on the—burner—under a skylight—that sort of light through a dirty winter skylight is—unalterable—circumstance. . . .

Age, death, artist, blank canvas, empty kettle, minimal light, and unalterable circumstance are encapsulated Beckett. This speech disappears from Williams's final version, where Beckett is recalled in a very simple line of Clare's: "There's nothing to be done."

Affected by Pirandello and Beckett, Williams embedded his typical Williams play in an absurdist frame, so that real and role overlap increasingly. Unlike the inner play, the frame play is set in a theater in an unspecified country, on a cold evening as opposed to the sunny afternoon of the inner play. Again there are two characters, brother and sister, Felice and Clare, actors in a repertory company on tour. When the frame play opens, Felice comes on stage in an astrological shirt; he is penning—to be precise, penciling—a monologue opposing fear to its near homonym fire. Clare interrupts him, unsteady from sleep or drugs. Expecting a press conference, she is surprised and disappointed to find only her actor/playwright/brother. She recognizes the partial set for "The Two-Character Play," and she sulks because that is not on their program. Felice then shows her a cablegram from the rest of their company. Declaring that the two are insane, the company has left for home. The abandoned siblings have no choice but to play "The Two-Character Play," if they are to play at all. Clare is still reluctant because Felice has refused the cuts she wanted, but when she hears mocking laughter from the audience, her old trouper spirit is aroused, and they begin "The Two-Character Play."

Occasionally, they improvise, or call for a line, or interrupt the text to comment on their actual situation. Clare cuts the performance off when the audience leaves the theater. Both actors, bone-weary, decide to check into the nearest hotel. They take time to ponder the fact that "The Two-Character Play" always stops instead of ending, and Felice explains, like a critic of the theater of the absurd: "It's possible for a play to have no ending in the usual sense of an ending, in order to make a point about nothing really ending." When Felice leaves the stage for a moment, Clare ruminates that she knew "The Two-Character Play" would be her brother's last work. She briefly recalls their glorious moments of touring, and Felice returns to announce that they are locked into this foreign theater. They are "confined"—the word they hesitated to use in the play within the play. Shivering but fearless, they return to "The Two-Character Play." They run swiftly through key scenes, but a new action starts when Clare points the revolver at Felice. We cannot tell (as earlier, at less climactic moments) whether they are in or out of "The Two-Character Play" as she drops the gun, unable to shoot. It is the turn of Felice, but he too fails to shoot. He drops the revolver, and each of them raises hands toward the other. "As they slowly embrace, there is total dark in which The Curtain Falls." An embrace is, of course, a traditional ending, but *their* embrace is a way of facing a slow death—the unalterable circumstance of absurdist drama.

As early as *Streetcar* Blanche says to Mitch: "And sometimes—there's God—so quickly." But the remark is not developed, and not until *Suddenly Last Summer* (1957) does Williams blend his own extremist characters into a metaphysical quest—in the same decade that Adamov, Beckett, and Ionesco were creating the theater of the absurd. Williams evidently read or saw them late, and Beckett alone seems to have moved him. It is Beckett's bleak hue that shades the endgame atmosphere of Williams's frame play. It is Beckett's grim, funny gamesmanship that Williams shares in *The Two-Character Play,* titled *Out Cry* in its second published version. In a fragmented world where none of the old rules hold, both playwrights convey that all we can do is act roles which will screen for a time our existential loneliness. So all of us are locked into theater—for the minimal warmth of dialogue. And the play we play is decided by the language we speak on the set where we are thrust—in Williams's case, lyrical English in a changing South. With a new self-consciousness about his art in a wider context, Williams worked for a decade at what may be his masterpiece, the 1976 *Two-Character Play.*

While putting the finishing touches to *The Two-Character Play,* Williams began a very different unappreciated play, *Vieux Carré.* First glance shows that not only the *carré* is *vieux.* Like *Streetcar, Vieux Carré* is set in the old French Quarter of New Orleans—722 Toulouse Street, to be specific. As in *Glass Menagerie,* one of the characters is a writer through whose memory the play's action is filtered. Like *The Two-Character Play, Vieux Carré* is the product of drastic revision, but rather than discontinuous tinkering through a decade, this revision expands a one-acter written nearly forty years earlier—the 1939 *Lady of Larkspur Lotion.*

The early title is a mocking reference to a forty-year-old whore who uses Larkspur Lotion, "a common treatment for body vermin." In a boardinghouse on the Vieux Carré, the "Lady" inspires contrasting attitudes in the other two characters—the scorn of the hard-nosed landlady Mrs. Wire, and the compassion of the nameless Writer, who introduces himself as Mr. Chekhov. In *Vieux Carré,* Williams retains the place and time of the main action—the Vieux Carré in 1938–1939, when one could buy "[m]eals for a quarter in the Quarter." He develops the money-hungry landlady, rejuvenates the Writer, and totally transforms the Lady into a young fashion designer of good education with "some—blood thing" draining her life away. To these characters, Williams adds a stripshow barker who is the fashion designer's lover, a tubercular homosexual painter, two starving ladies of good family, an old black maid, and a clarinet player. In spite of the relatively large cast, the landlady realizes: "There's so much loneliness in this house that you can hear it."

Besides loneliness, *Vieux Carré* dramatizes crises in the lives of this group of people. The rapacious landlady dementedly confuses the young Writer with her long-lost son, and the two old ladies exist on pickings from garbage cans. The tubercular painter is carried to the state hospital to die, and the fashion designer learns that her death is near, whereupon her lover deserts her. The Writer leaves, joining the clarinet player, who has never been admitted to the boardinghouse on the Vieux Carré. The boardinghouse tenants were given life through the Writer's memory, but the play closes: "They go when you go. . . . This house is empty now."

When the house is full, we witness the disintegration of its inhabitants. Less insistently than Tom of *Glass Menagerie* (1944), this Writer also introduces us to his neighbors and then slips into his own play as an involved character. In 1944 the narrator/character technique was relatively new, filtered through Thornton Wilder's 1938 Stage Manager and Williams's course with Erwin Piscator in 1940. By 1977–1978, when Williams wrote *Vieux Carré,* the technique was as well-worn as some of the typical Williams characters, but it is therefore right for a play set in New Orleans of 1938–1939—racist, sexist, and unselfconscious in its seediness.

In the 1939 *Lady of Larkspur Lotion,* the Writer facetiously gave his name as Mr. Chekhov, but it was not until the late 1960s (in *Confessional*) that Williams was attracted to the Russian dramatist's forte—the group protagonist. The attraction returns in *Vieux Carré,* and although Williams falls short of Chekhov's mastery, he nevertheless weaves lives skillfully into a temporary pattern dissolved by the Writer's departure. Like *The Seagull,* too, *Vieux Carré* ascribes to artists privileged threads in this pattern. Early in the play, the old painter and the young Writer make love. Painter, Writer, and fashion designer are all attracted to the frank sensuality of the stripshow barker, who tells a horrible and violent story. By play's end, death will claim the old painter and the young fashion designer in the Vieux Carré, but into the unknown West go the young Writer and the clarinet player, whose name is Sky. Against an old Williams background, the playwright newly dramatizes the fate of art. Though some artists may die on Vieux Carré, art lives on in other places and other media. (Williams's opening stage direction informs us that 722 Toulouse Street is now an art gallery.)

In sharp contrast, the setting for Williams's last major play is threatened by fire which destroyed an actual insane asylum in 1947. It is one of several reasons that Williams subtitles *Clothes for a Summer Hotel* "a ghost play." The main reason is that Williams dramatizes historical characters who are dead— ghosts. Williams himself cites "chronological licenses" as the ground of ghostliness. This is the first time that he not only bases a full-length play on actual people, but houses them in an imaginative structure where they can at once live through and look back on their lives: "The extent to which the characters should betray an awareness of their apparitional state will be determined more precisely in the course of a production." But the play's dialogue precludes the experiential innocence of *Vieux Carré*.

The Two-Character Play is the only example of a Williams play printed in three successive versions. *Vieux Carré* is the only example of a Williams expansion undertaken forty years after the original writing impetus. In contrast, only one version of *Clothes for a Summer Hotel* is presently in print, evidently a revision of the 1980 Broadway text, which was in turn a revision of a first draft completed by 1977, when Williams was interviewed by television personality Dick Cavett.

The basic set of the Williams two-act play is a mock-up façade of Highland (mental) Hospital on windy Sunset Hill, North Carolina. Despite "chronological licenses," the beginning and end of *Clothes* are centered on Scott Fitzgerald's visit to his wife, Zelda, in her hilltop asylum. Scott has been summoned from Hollywood by Zelda's doctor because of a marked improvement in her condition. Boarding a plane at once, Scott is dressed in summer clothes inadequate for the windy North Carolina hill. As husband and wife peep at each other before meeting, they are appalled at what they see: the once handsome Scott is gray and bloated; the once lovely Zelda is fat and bedraggled. A millionaire friend, Gerald Murphy, joins the celebrated writer, speaking partly in the grim present and partly in their bright past, and introducing the subject of Scott's repression of Zelda's writing. When husband and wife meet, wind howling, Williams plays the present against the past. Zelda refuses to accept Scott's proffered wedding ring to replace the one she threw away. After describing the present caustically, she lashes out at Scott: *"What was important to you was to absorb and devour!"* She voices her fear of fire, retreats into ballet dancing, then hallucinates about the parties of the past. Scott can obtain no information from Zelda's doctor, who thinks he is drunk. Zelda tries to address the audience directly, but the wind engulfs her words, and Zelda follows the Intern into the asylum.

The scene changes to 1926, with Scott so absorbed in his writing that he pays scant attention to Zelda. They quarrel about Scott's prettiness and Zelda's ambition: "What about *my* work?" Left to be merely "a dreamy young Southern lady," Zelda openly takes a French lover, Edouard. A handsome, efficient, and traditional French lover, Edouard (played by the same actor as the Intern) is dismayed by the imprudence and intensity of Zelda's passion. He disappoints her when he admits that he has grown old, "weighted down with honors." He is horrified when she tells him at a Murphy Riviera party that she swallowed a bottle of sleeping pills when he left her. Scott, interrupted at work by news of the death of Joseph Conrad, spoils the Murphy party by insulting Mrs. Patrick Campbell, hovering jealously over Zelda, and being goaded by Hemingway to violence. The stage action zigzags between Scott's impatience with Zelda's doctors and Hemingway's disruptive presence at the 1926 party. Hemingway refuses to admit his attraction to the feminine loveliness of Scott; Hemingway knows that he will betray his friends, especially Scott, when he comes to write *A Moveable Feast*. Scott mulls over the loneliness of all three writers in Williams's play—Hemingway, Fitzgerald, and Zelda.

The last scene returns to Zelda in Highland Hospital. The Intern/Edouard urges her to say goodbye to her husband, who shivers in his summer clothes. Zelda speaks a long monologue about her unsatisfied creativity, her romantic fantasies, her fearlessness at the prospect of death. She begs Scott to scatter her ashes if she should die (as Williams requested for his own ashes). She returns briefly to the reality of the windy hill, and Scott snaps at her: "The mistake of our ever having met!—The monumental error of the effort to channel our lives together in an institution called marriage." Zelda taunts Scott, and the Intern/Edouard character tries to soothe her. As she enters the iron gates of the asylum, Zelda flings a last defiant challenge at the husband who has drained her life for his art: "*I can't be your book anymore! Write yourself a new book!*" Scott again pleads with her to accept the replacement wedding ring that he offered at the play's beginning. She disappears behind the iron gates, the wind howls, and Scott faces the audience in silence.

It is uncertain whether *Clothes for a Summer Hotel* was inspired by Williams's reading of Zelda Fitzgerald's 1932 novel, *Save Me the Waltz,* or Hemingway's 1964 *A Moveable Feast,* or Nancy Milford's 1970 biography, *Zelda,* or some quite different association. It *is* certain that Williams depended on these works for his material—especially the Milford biography. Broadway reviewers sneered at this literary background—"Almost everything of interest and value in the play is contained in one of those books, and is better in its original form," wrote John Simon.[5] The original forms, however, are not theater, and Williams created theater, marking theme and characters as distinctively his own.

As in many other Williams plays, the protagonist of *Clothes* is a suffering Southern lady, but this lady is named Zelda Fitzgerald, who died in a fire in her insane asylum. Williams makes ominous use of his setting—its black gates, its howling winds, and intermittent lights resembling flames. He manipulates time to reflect Zelda's hallucinations. He portrays all three writers sympathetically, although they were ruthless to one another.

Williams incorporates Hemingway's pathetic Fitzgerald from *A Moveable Feast,* but his Scott is both loving and repressive, a generous man but a selfish artist. Williams adheres closely to Zelda's life as painstakingly researched by Milford, but he creates a more dramatic portrait of a gifted woman who rebels against the behavior code of a Southern lady. Zelda actually charged that there was a homosexual attraction between her husband and Hemingway, which Williams exploits to dramatize the betrayal of their friendship.[6] Perhaps Williams's most subtle invention was to blend Zelda's French lover into an Intern in the asylum—a living reminder of her failed rebellion and an emotional outlet for her fantasies. In this late play, Williams deftly creates extreme but sympathetic characters who are ghosts of our culture.

In theme *Clothes* asks with other late Williams plays: what is the price of artistic creation? The answer is human betrayal. Hemingway betrays friendship, Zelda betrays marriage, and Scott betrays his own humane impulses. Not only is marriage a "monumental error," but so also are friendship and other durable relations—among artists. Obsession with creation drives some artists to drink, some to drugs, and others to insanity.

All three late Williams plays probe the cost of creation. In *The Two-Character Play,* brother and sister are abandoned, but they support each other in continued play within a meaningless cosmos. Art survives beyond *Vieux Carré,* even if its artists die. And *Clothes for a Summer Hotel* resurrects three celebrated American writers as ghosts who can look back on lives misspent for art, without which there would be no art. The famous novelists are not triumphant; they rarely justify themselves; they are little more than instruments to fill demanding blank pages. Having fulfilled the same demand from his adolescence on, Williams dramatized it in these three strikingly dissimilar late works for which he garnered no prizes and little praise. But like the play within the play of *The Two-Character Play,* Williams's artistry has no ending.

Notes

1. W. Kenneth Holditch, "Surviving with Grace: Tennessee Williams Today," *The Southern Review* (Summer 1979), NS 15, 753–754.

2. *Memoirs* (Garden City, N.Y., 1975), p. 241. Zelda also says these words to Scott in *Clothes for a Summer Hotel* (New York, 1981), p. 24.

3. Since inner play and entire play are both called The Two-Character Play, I use quotation marks for the former, italics for the latter.

4.   In the Foreword to Marta Abba's translation of *The Mountain Giants* (New York, 1959), George Freedley writes: "It has been suggested that Tennessee Williams . . . might well be the dramatist to complete [the unfinished *Mountain Giants*] from the notes left by Piran-dello." I do not know who suggested this improbable collaboration. *The Mountain Giants* shares with *The Two-Character Play* a touring theater company and a play within the play.

5.   "Damsels Inducing Distress," *New York,* 7 April 1980, p. 82.

6.   Williams's memory of Hemingway's fiction is faulty. The story that Hemingway summarizes under the title "Sea Change" must have another title (which I do not know). "Sea Change" is about a woman sea-changing to lesbianism.

Death As Metaphor

NANCY M. TISCHLER

Tennessee Williams died 26 February 1983. The *New York Times* told the world about the event the following day: "He was found dead about 10:45 A.M. in his suite in the Hotel Elysee on East 54th Street." The article went on to note that

> Mr. Williams's secretary, John Uecker, who shared the playwright's two-room hotel suite, said that at about 11 PM Thursday he heard a noise from Mr. Williams's room, but did not investigate. Yesterday morning at approximately 10:45 he entered the room and found him lying next to his bed.[1]

In a rented room in a hotel in a city that was only occasionally friendly, this famous man had died alone. He must have enjoyed the irony of being in a hotel that echoed the Elysian Fields where Blanche's streetcar stopped after she had transferred from the streetcar named Desire; he too found that it stopped at the cemetery. In her case as in his, the Elysian Fields proved only a temporary home.

The mystery of the death was grotesquely developed further when the *Times* reported that

> Tennessee Williams choked to death on a plastic cap of the type used on bottles of nasal spray or eye solution. . . . an autopsy yesterday found the bottle cap blocking the larynx. . . . An empty bottle of wine and several types of medication were found in Mr. Williams's room.[2]

In a great variety of ways, the death of Tennessee Williams was of a piece with his artistic creations. He would have enjoyed the grotesque and lugubrious qualities, the symbolism, and the themes as typical Williams theater.

He always had a symbolic imagination. He thought it significant that he was born on Good Friday, and often set his plays in a background that echoed the structure of Christ's Passion. He saw the significance that his middle

This essay was written specifically for this volume and appears in print here for the first time by permission of the author.

name was *Lanier,* as if he were destined to be a Southern poet in the tradition of his namesake and ancestor, Sidney Lanier. He took the name *Tennessee* ostensibly to remind himself of his frontier forbearers who fought off savage Indians and who managed to survive these hostile attacks, a parallel—he insisted—to the lifestyle of a young writer in modern America. If he could have made so many symbolic connections with his undistinguished birth, he would have treasured the rich lode of imagery in his death.

Take, for example, the physical nature of the death—the symbolism of the stopped larynx, the lyric voice hushed forever. The violent end was a Williams signature. From his first published story, which appeared in a 1928 edition of *Weird Tales,* the tale of Nitrocis's drowning all of her dinner guests, Williams sent his people to the madhouse, had them raped, castrated, incinerated, torn apart by dogs, and eaten by adolescents. He defended this literary use of violence as both classical in origin and true to his experience of life. In "A Writer's Quest for Parnassus," he says that

> . . . writers, when they are not writing, must find some outer violence that is equivalent, or nearly, to the inner one they are used to. They find it difficult to remain long in one place, for writing books and taking voyages are corresponding gestures."[3]

One of his more grotesque images that testified to the violence of his lifestyle was the newly hatched sea turtles of the Encantadas, the Galápagos Islands. They dashed madly toward the sea while great birds of death hovered over them attacking their soft underbellies, eating their flesh. Sebastian Venable, in *Suddenly Last Summer* (scene 1), equated this vision in the "Enchanted" Islands with God (20).[4]

Death was Williams's expectation. Life was a perennial surprise. In his *Memoirs,*[5] he speaks of an experience in his teens when he suddenly became alarmed by "the recognition that my existence and my fate could dissolve as lightly as a cinder dropped in a great fall of snow" (22). This hysteria apparently lasted for much of his life. An early poem, entitled "The Siege," which appeared in *In the Winter of Cities,* describes this abnormal fear of mortality in particularly lurid terms:

> I build a tottering pillar of my blood
> to walk it upright on the tilting street.
> The stuff is liquid, it would flow downhill
> so very quickly if the hill were steep.[6]

The poem goes on to note that he is a "reckless voyager" whose springs can be dried up by a single touch of the sun.

Williams had not anticipated being a survivor; he must, in fact, have been surprised to find himself an old man. His stories of aging and loneliness started quite early. He lamented the flight of the sweet bird of youth well before most people would have considered that it had taken wing. His great admiration for the heroic old wrecks of the theater must have made him increasingly proud of his own survival. Although *Memoirs* is full of his intimations of mortality, he had pulled through so many life-threatening experiences that he must have begun to wonder if, finally, he was going to outlive his nonagenarian grandfather.

Age may have surprised him, but loneliness never did. His solitary end was a fitting culmination of a life haunted by images of loneliness. His favorite theme was the absolute isolation of the human being. He saw himself as a rootless and solitary wanderer. *The Glass Menagerie* chronicles the poet's essential cutting loose from family ties. He says in *Memoirs* that, in leaving home, he found himself. Yet it was obvious that he carried with him a terrible guilt and a need for family long after his exit.

Even those Williams characters who travel with others are doomed to travel alone. We are all sentenced, he says, in plays from *Battle of Angels* to *Small Craft Warnings,* to solitary confinement in our own skins. The characters in *The Night of the Iguana* live in isolated cells, rapping on walls, crying out, and reaching out for human companionship. In "Person to Person," Williams explains this in even more personal terms: "Personal lyricism," he says, "is the outcry of prisoner to prisoner from the cell in solitary where each is confined for the duration of his life."[7] Most of his plays represent the loneliness of people together and the tragicomic need to touch one another.

In his plays, such gestures of communication tend to be violent or embarrassing, rarely satisfying. One-night stands, a sense of using and being used, a nasty aftertaste—these are characteristic of his heroes' efforts to communicate. In his essay "A Writer's Quest for Parnassus," Williams says, "Life achieves its highest value and significance in those rare moments—they are scarcely longer than that—when two lives are confluent, when the walls of isolation momentarily collapse between two persons. . . ."[8]

Both homosexual and heterosexual encounters bring transient relief and enduring pain. In *Memoirs,* Williams speaks at length of his own insatiable search for companions and of his subsequent disgust with himself and with them. He cries out that he wants his goodness back, and then brags of his satyriasis. Only with his sister Rose, with whom he says he had a pure relationship (though he acknowledges his constant use of the incest theme in his work), and with his grandfather, whom he loved for his imperturbable aristocracy, and with Frank Merlo, his secretary and traveling companion for more than a decade, did he seem to find any sort of contentment. This restless search rings through all of his plays. One of the loveliest statements of this need for home and family is in *Night of the Iguana* when Shannon sneers at Hannah's love for her grandfather. The human is not like a bird, she says. The human can build a nest in the heart of another. ". . . I'm not a bird, Mr. Shannon, I'm a human being and when a member of that fantastic species builds a nest in the heart of another, the question of permanence isn't the first or even the last thing that's considered. . . ." As she notes, "home" is "a thing that two people have between them in which each can . . . well, nest-rest-live in . . ." (*NI,* 111).

At times in his writing, Williams expressed the restless quest for love in gently romantic imagery. Later he used repellant naturalism to portray it as nasty sexual groping. But the central point remains unchanged. Humans are essentially alone and miserable about this solitude. Much of sexuality masks the need to communicate. Lust is as much spiritual hunger as physical in Williams. As Blanche puts it, "Sometimes there's God so quickly" (*SND,* 116). Although the early stories used D. H. Lawrence and the rainbow of the flesh, Williams's people are never long content with the rose of the flesh, the singing of nightingales, or the flashing colored lights. Their search tends to lead them farther because their hunger is deeper. They want an impossible love.

The archetypal misfit was the poet, the standard Williams hero, the sensitive wanderer without family. His talent makes him an alien among normal folk. He cannot hold a job in a shoe factory or in a mercantile store. Valentine Xavier was a family name that Williams used for his first important vagabond poet in *Battle of Angels.* Tom Wingfield of *The Glass Menagerie* shared many memories with Thomas Lanier Williams, alias Tennessee— a poet trapped briefly in a middle-class nightmare.

In his short story "The Poet," Williams spoke of the nonconformist writer as a kind of Pied Piper, despised by the community but loved by the children and by the pure in heart. Williams had found his own voice by leaving home and rejecting the ties to his family. New York was one of the many cities that "swept by him like dead leaves, leaves that were brightly colored but torn away from the branches" (*GM,* 115). He stayed in each city restlessly while always preparing to move on. Apparently this grew even more pronounced near the end of his life. He had apartments or homes in Key West, New Orleans, and elsewhere, but he was like one of those birds he mentions in *Battle of Angels* (act 1, scene 2), which have no feet and which never land so long as they live. They spend their lives on the wing.

The discreet but unhelpful secretary in the next room was one of many companions Williams had hired after Frank Merlo's death. Each would stay with him briefly, but Williams was reluctant to make long-term commitments.

In fact, the writer often noted his need for struggle and solitude. The success of *The Glass Menagerie* worried him as a young man. In "On a Streetcar Named Success," he said of his early years that he lived "a life of clawing and scratching along a sheer surface and holding on tight with raw fingers to every inch of rock higher than the one caught hold of before, but it was a good life because it was the sort of life for which the human organism is created."[9] He thought that he needed to struggle in order to find a reason for work. And he loved to say that *work* was his favorite four-letter word.

His heroes were Don Quixote, the eternal quester for truth, and Don Juan, the eternal quester for love. Like the eternally panting youth on Keats's Grecian urn, he sought the ecstatic moment, not the weariness of satiation.

The spiritual loneliness made him a spokesman for lonely people. The hunger and the pain helped him speak knowingly of pain. He was never able to write completely satisfying comedy. Though he had a remarkable comic talent, he always laced his laughter with anguish. Yet his tragedy was rarely so black that he could not stop for a startled laugh. His own term for this Janus-faced vision was "slapstick tragedy." Ambivalence was essential to his art.

He had been afraid at one time that psychotherapy might kill his art, which rested so solidly on his suffering. The bountiful creativity that he knew in his early years, the glorious craftsmanship in his mature years—these were the treasures he cherished.

The great anguish he expressed in his final years was over his diminished creativity. During and after his "stoned age," he could not work as he had in earlier years. His hysteria over this loss led him deeper into drink and drugs—to help him create, to help him rest. In some ways, the drugs had killed the essential Tennessee Williams long before 1983. By 1960, he had noted the fickle crowds and critics turning from him and had begun his valiant fight to halt the slide of his theatrical career. Those final years were spent writhing among the ashes of his grandeur, thrashing about like an impotent old phoenix.

Isolation, as Blanche and Alma tell us, leads to desperate measures. One becomes nervous, gasps for breath, laughs hysterically, can neither sleep nor relax. Alma loves those pills that relax her, making her feel like a water lily on a Chinese lagoon. The Princess combines the drugs with drink, hires a gigolo keeper, and tries to forget that she has passed her time of greatness, that her beauty is gone and her talent is spent.

Such lost grandeur would appear to be the stuff of tragedy, but not when it mingles with pratfalls. The puritanical Alma puts on the plumed hat of the cavalier, rolls her eyes, and picks up a traveling salesman. The aggressively ladylike Blanche flirts roguishly with the newspaper boy. The leering satyr, the goat-footed reminder of our ridiculous sexual nature, keeps the spirituality from carrying us off into classical tragedy. Contrapuntal to Blanche's dream of purity (her constant bathing and her lofty speech) is Stanley's sneering voice, announcing that he needs the bathroom. He is worried, he explains, not about his soul, but about his kidneys (*SND*, 124). Brick proclaims his pure and ethereal love of the dead Skipper, but Big Daddy notes that his story is "half-ass" (*CHTR*, 126). This inevitable duality of human nature results in Williams's slapstick tragedy, the comic counterbalance to our pretentious grandeur. No French philosopher was needed to convince Tennessee Williams that we all live in an absurd world. His existentialism was indigenous to the American South.

This is not to say that Williams was entirely identified with any of his characters. Like any good creative artist, he imagined with greater force where he had personal experience. The experience of loneliness can make images of loneliness far more powerful. A lack of physical beauty and the love of it in others can help one sympathize with the pain that accompanies the loss of beauty. The creative imagination weaves its most intricate and compelling images out of strands of actual experience. He once said, "I can't expose a human weakness on the stage unless I know it through having it myself" (*SBY,* xii).

Williams acknowledged in his *Memoirs* and elsewhere that he used names and places and people from his own life. He admitted sharing the pain of Tom, the weakness of Blanche, the hysteria of Alma, the agony of the Princess, the fears of Flora Goforth, the drinking problem of Brick. Each of them embodies something of Williams himself. But none of them is Williams.

Even with his loneliness and satyriasis and alcoholism and addictions, Williams found a harbor for his small craft. Unlike most of his characters, he respected his own talent and disciplined himself to continual work. Work gave order to his days, meaning to his life. He insisted that his real anguish came when an actress parodied the role of Amanda or a scriptwriter cheapened a play in translating it into a film. He was distressed when audiences rejected his later plays, and desperately regretted the decline of his talent and the alienation of his audience. This marked the end of his productive life— a kind of spiritual death for him. Through his final tortured decade, he kept insisting he was on the brink of an "important" new work. He had hoped it would be *Out Cry.* More and more, his plays became self-parodies, sometimes too short or too obscene or too obscure for production. Critics found them embarrassing reminders of the once-great playwright. One critic compared these scribblings at the end to the pitiful final works of Picasso.

But even this decline and fall was both metaphor and literal fact. Williams's characters have vestiges of greatness at the center of their pain. They have known wealth or beauty or love, and now they must live on courageously without it. Flora Goforth, the aging heroine of *The Milk Train Doesn't Stop Here Anymore,* careened about the stage, dictating her memoirs at the same time her creator was typing out his. The angel of death was waiting for them both. Decadence—the rotting mansion, the crumbling giant—was the favorite theme of this Southerner. He knew all along that art and life imitate one another, and he frequently presented a public persona for the entertainment of those who sought to know the artist. The eloquently self-revelatory commentaries that introduced his plays, the interviews and public appearances, and finally the autobiography are all testimony to his creation of "Tennessee," the tormented artist, who at last took to the stage and acted out a role in his own play—and forgot the lines.

It was not just dying in a northern city, in a hotel room, alone, choked by an absurd bottlecap, that seemed to confirm Williams's creation of his own final drama. Even the funeral was the makings of a Williams drama.

He had made it clear in his plays, in his *Memoirs,* and in his will that he wanted to be buried at sea. He asked that he be "sewn up in a clean white sack and dropped overboard, twelve hours north of Havana, so that my bones may rest not too far from those of Hart Crane."[10] Hart Crane had committed suicide by leaping overboard shortly after his ship left Havana. Feeling a romantic kinship with Crane's Dionysian nature, his homosexuality, his tormented alcoholism, his love of beauty, his frenzied life, Williams asked that he be united with him in death. In "Preface to My Poems," he explains that Crane's slender book of poems was his only library for many years, and that he loved these poems for their "organic purity and sheer breath-taking power."[11]

One is reminded of Blanche's romantic dream of dying at sea from having eaten an unwashed grape. She, like her creator, saw burial at sea as the ultimate baptism, the final cleansing. Shannon saw the sea as the elemental life force, Mother Nature herself, earth's womb and tomb. Williams himself loved to live by the water and spoke often of his delight in swimming. Earth was for him the element of putrification, water the element of purification.

In contrast to this lifelong dream is the actuality of Williams's burial:

Peter Hoffman, a young New York filmmaker, wrote in detail of the event for *New York* magazine. The memorial service for Williams's New York friends was held at the Frank E. Campbell Funeral Chapel on Madison Avenue. Hoffman chronicles the comic confusion about Williams's religious preference. He had been an Episcopalian by birth, a Catholic by conversion, and a pagan by lifestyle. The coffin was Jewish Orthodox, suitable to his aesthetic taste; the religious service was Roman Catholic, performed by an Episcopalian priest; and at the last minute, a friend placed a Russian Orthodox cross around his neck. The priest performing the ceremony was the Reverend Sidney Lanier, a cousin also named for Williams's distinguished ancestor.

The St. Louis portion of the service was performed by the pastor of Our Lady of Lourdes Catholic Church, Dr. Wilkerson, who apparently had known both Williams and his work sufficiently well to comment on the combination of love and pain that bore the marks of the Christian experience. His tribute was moving:

"The tragedy of Tennessee," he said, "seems to be the revelatory sword of suffering that pierced his heart . . . more therapeutic to others than to himself. He would seem to have remained all his life among the walking wounded." He went on to say that Williams had little trouble following the admonition of the gospel to "hate his life in this world." Two years earlier, Williams had said, "Toward the end of an American writer's life, it's just dreadful."[12] After the requiem mass was the burial in Calvary Cemetery (a fitting place for a man born on Good Friday)—near the grave of his mother. There the crowd gathered in the rain to watch the last remains of Thomas Lanier Williams being placed next to the woman he had spent his life trying to escape, in a city he had always hated. In this final ironic gesture Amanda drew Tom back to her at last.

This whole sequence of events was orchestrated by Williams's younger brother Dakin, an attorney whose conflicts with his famous brother had frequently surfaced in the press. Three months earlier, when Dakin had gone to Key West to see Tennessee about his unauthorized biography, Williams had refused to see him. Tennessee had noted at the time that three people were writing biographies of him, none of whom knew him. One of them, he commented sardonically, was his brother Dakin. The despised biography was to be called *My Brother's Keeper.* Williams had laughingly commented, "I always thought I was his." (The book was finally revised and published as a joint work with Shepherd Mead, entitled *Tennessee Williams: An Intimate Biography.*)

Williams's family was always central to his life and his drama—his confused love for his mother, his reluctant love for his father, his grateful love for his grandparents, his jealous love for his brother, and his blind love for his sister Rose. Over and over he expresses in *Memoirs* his concern for Rose's comfort. His anger at his brother, Dakin, he explains as sibling rivalry; his first sight of Dakin was at his mother's bare breast. His fury at his brother for installing him in a sanatorium is overshadowed only by his outrage that the sanatorium itself was in St. Louis. The incarceration does appear to have saved his life, but it did little to enrich their relationship. Nor did Dakin's temporary success in converting Tom to Catholicism confirm him in orthodoxy. Almost as soon as he left the hospital, he disavowed the church. (Dakin's alternative impression of these years is chronicled in detail and with restraint in his recent book mentioned earlier.)

Thus it is in character that he cut his brother off with $25,000 in his will and left the rest to Rose. He had no kind words for Dakin's children, either; in fact, he rarely had kind words about any children. The tone is usually that of Maggie the Cat commenting on Brother Man's brood of "no-neck monsters." For Williams, the children he sought to endow with his considerable hoard of worldly goods—after the death of Rose, naturally—were the spiritual children of the Poet. He left the residue of his estate (the *New York Times* says $10 million[13]) to young creative artists in a trust at the University of the South at Sewanee—the college that his grandfather had attended, which had awarded Tennessee Williams an honorary doctorate of letters in 1978. As phrased in his will, this Walter E. Dakin Memorial Fund was to be used "for the purposes of encouraging creative writing and creative writers in need of financial assistance to pursue their vocations whose work is progressive, original and preferably of an experimental nature."[14]

This portion of his will resulted in some comic quarrels. In his final years, Williams was lionized by universities all over the country. He was the proud recipient of two honorary doctorates. (He did laugh at one award, wherein he was pronounced "Florida's most outstanding playwright"; he said he preferred to see himself as "Duncan Street's most promising playwright.") His papers were gathered in an impressive scholarly collection at the Humanities Research Center at the University of Texas at Austin. He left the remainder of his papers to Harvard University and asked that the creative writing department of Harvard help Sewanee administer the trust in a joint venture.[15] Harvard, unfortunately, has no creative writing department, but the university officials hurriedly agreed to find a suitable way to carry out the intent of his will.

Meanwhile, Dakin, understandably dissatisfied with the terms therein, contested the will.[16] According to press releases, he settled out of court a year later for $100,000.

It is sadly ironic that this author who spoke so disparagingly of materialism and the sweet smell of success should have died a multimillionaire, that the final news stories should have been those covering a contested will. Big Daddy was right about mendacity.

But his greatest delight would undoubtedly have been in the fact that his voice was not really stopped by that obscene plastic bottlecap. Revivals of his plays continue all over the world. Blanche and Alma and Big Daddy continue to resonate long after this lonely old man has choked and thrashed and died. He became past tense, but they live on in the present.

Tennessee Williams often spoke of the hunger he felt for communication and the enormous satisfaction in reaching out with words spoken by his characters across the footlights to audiences who shared his hunger and his loneliness. He said of Amanda, at the end of *The Glass Menagerie,* that when the scrim dropped and we could no longer hear her nagging words, her silliness was gone and she had dignity and tragic beauty. Death has the same impact as the final scrim. The tormented writer is finally at rest, regardless of where his poor bones have been deposited, and the lyric voice lives on. That is the triumph of Tennessee Williams. As he said in "The Timeless World of the Play," "Snatching the eternal out of the desperately fleeting is the great magic trick of human existence."[17] By his own definition, he proved to be a magician.

Notes

1.   "Williams Choked on a Bottle Cap," *New York Times,* 27 February 1983, sec. A1, p. 39.

2.   Ibid.

3. Tennessee Williams, *Where I Live: Selected Essays,* ed. Christine R. Day and Bob Woods (New York: New Directions, 1978), 19.

4. Quotations from Williams's plays are cited in the text with the abbreviations listed here. When lines are sufficiently identified by the context, no abbreviation is listed. Page numbers in parentheses refer to the following versions:

SLS: *Suddenly Last Summer* (New York: New Directions, 19).

NI: *Night of the Iguana,* in *Three by Tennessee* (New York: Signet, 1976).

SND: *A Streetcar Named Desire* (New York: New Directions, 1980).

GM: *The Glass Menagerie* (New York: New Directions, 1970).

CHTR: *Cat on a Hot Tin Roof* (New York: New Directions, 1975).

SBY: *Sweet Bird of Youth* (New York: Signet, 1962).

5. Tennessee Williams, *Memoirs* (Garden City, N.Y.: Doubleday, 1975), 22.
6. Tennessee Williams, *In the Winter of Cities* (New York: New Directions, 1956), 20.
7. Williams, *Where I Live,* 76.
8. Ibid., 37.
9. Ibid., 16.
10. Williams, *Memoirs,* 117.
11. Williams, *Where I Live,* 6.
12. Jerome F. Wilkerson, "Homily at the Funeral of Thomas Lanier (Tennessee) Williams, St. Louis Cathedral, 5 March 1983," *Tennessee Williams Review* 4, no. 1 (1983): 73–81.
13. "University Elated by $10 Million Williams Bequest," *New York Times* 13 March 1983, sec. 1, p. 34.
14. "Sewanee, How I Love You," *Tennessee Williams Literary Journal* 2, no. 1 (Winter 1990–91): 67–70.
15. Lindsay Groson, "Harvard to Direct Williams Bequest," *New York Times* 22 March 1983, sec. 1, p. 13.
16. Tennessee Williams, "Last Will and Testament: Document dated 11 September 1980, with codicil dated December 1982," in *Tennessee Williams Review* 4, no. 1 (1983): 82–90.
17. Williams, *Where I Live,* 52.

Index

◆

The Volume Editor

Robert A. Martin is professor of American Literature at Michigan State University. He is the editor of *The Theater Essays of Arthur Miller, Arthur Miller: New Perspectives,* and *The Writer's Craft.* His essays on F. Scott Fitzgerald, Ernest Hemingway, William Faulkner, Edith Wharton, Sylvia Plath, Joseph Heller, Kurt Vonnegut, William Gaddis, Willa Cather, Sherwood Anderson, and Martha Gellhorn have appeared in numerous leading collections and journals. He is also the co-editor of *Rewriting the Good Fight: Critical Essays on the Literature of the Spanish Civil War.* Before joining the faculty at Michigan State University, he taught for a number of years at the University of Michigan, Ann Arbor.

The General Editor

Dr. James Nagel, J. O. Eidson Distinguished Professor of American Literature at the University of Georgia, founded the scholarly journal *Studies in American Fiction* and edited it for 20 years. He is the general editor of the Critical Essays on American Literature series published by G. K. Hall Macmillan, a program that now contains over 130 volumes. He was one of the founders of the American Literature Association and serves as its executive coordinator. He is also a past president of the Ernest Hemingway Society. Among his 17 books are *Stephen Crane and Literary Impressionism, Critical Essays on* The Sun Also Rises, *Ernest Hemingway: The Writer in Context, Ernest Hemingway: The Oak Park Legacy,* and *Hemingway in Love and War,* which was selected by the *New York Times* as one of the outstanding books of 1989 and which has been made into a major motion picture. Dr. Nagel has published over 50 articles in scholarly journals and has lectured on American literature in 15 countries. His current project is a book on the contemporary short-story cycle.